# Metaverse Technologies, Security and Applications for Healthcare

**Scrivener Publishing**
100 Cummings Center, Suite 541J
Beverly, MA 01915-6106

*Publishers at Scrivener*
Martin Scrivener (martin@scrivenerpublishing.com)
Phillip Carmical (pcarmical@scrivenerpublishing.com)

# Metaverse Technologies, Security and Applications for Healthcare

Edited by

**Ajay Kumar Vyas**

*Information & Communication Technology Department, Adani University, Ahmedabad, India*

**Harleen Kaur**

*School of Engineering Sciences and Technology, Jamia Hamdard University, New Delhi, India*

**Sourabh Sharma**

*School of Engineering, Avantika University*

and

**Bhavya Alankar**

*Department of Computer Science and Engineering, Jamia Hamdard University, New Delhi, India*

Scrivener Publishing

WILEY

This edition first published 2025 by John Wiley & Sons, Inc., 111 River Street, Hoboken, NJ 07030, USA and Scrivener Publishing LLC, 100 Cummings Center, Suite 541J, Beverly, MA 01915, USA

For more information about Scrivener publications please visit www.scrivenerpublishing.com.



**Wiley Global Headquarters**
111 River Street, Hoboken, NJ 07030, USA

For details of our global editorial offices, customer services, and more information about Wiley products visit us at www.wiley.com.



***Library of Congress Cataloging-in-Publication Data***

ISBN 978-1-394-30524-7

Front cover images courtesy of Adobe Firefly
Cover design by Russell Richardson

Set in size of 11pt and Minion Pro by Manila Typesetting Company, Makati, Philippines

Printed in the USA

10 9 8 7 6 5 4 3 2 1

# Contents

# Preface

This book provides insights into information security concerns, preventive measures, and their impact on healthcare applications in the Metaverse. The Metaverse is an expanded virtual world that merges physical and digital spaces, allowing users to interact within augmented environments, meet virtually, and engage in immersive activities that simulate real-world experiences. The Metaverse holds tremendous potential for healthcare, enhancing personalized care and accessibility. While much attention has been given to its impact on entertainment and gaming, public health experts increasingly recognize its transformative potential in the healthcare industry. This book explores the role of the Metaverse in healthcare and highlights why digital information security is a major concern.

The global COVID-19 pandemic underscored the importance of digital interactions, as movement restrictions accelerated the adoption of virtual solutions for healthcare delivery. However, this shift has also amplified concerns about information security, particularly regarding patient data and healthcare transactions. This book is structured into three parts: Part I covers Metaverse technology, Part II focuses on Metaverse security, and Part III examines its applications. Across 20 comprehensive chapters, the book explores various aspects of the Metaverse in healthcare.

Chapter 1 introduces the Metaverse and its potential applications in healthcare, outlining the technological foundations, including developments in augmented reality (AR) and virtual reality (VR). It discusses threats and challenges such as data privacy and security while exploring opportunities like enhanced telemedicine, remote surgery, and patient rehabilitation. The chapter also considers future trends and the Metaverse's potential to transform patient care, medical training, and education.

Chapter 2 examines how the Metaverse is revolutionizing healthcare across different medical fields. It highlights the evolution of virtual healthcare interactions, increased accessibility, and the role of VR simulations in medical training. Telemedicine in the Metaverse is making healthcare more immersive, particularly benefiting rural and underserved areas.

The chapter also addresses challenges such as legal and ethical concerns surrounding Metaverse adoption in healthcare.

Chapter 3 explores Metaverse technologies that enhance medical facilities, including online therapy, medical education, training, and research. It discusses emerging tools like AI doctor chatbots, digital wellness avatars, and medical simulations, along with ethical concerns surrounding data privacy, patient consent, and equitable access. The chapter emphasizes the importance of governance and ethical regulations to build trust in Metaverse-based healthcare solutions.

Chapter 4 investigates how Metaverse technology can improve clinical administration and patient management. It provides a detailed overview of various healthcare applications, explores the challenges of implementation, and suggests future directions in this rapidly evolving field.

Chapter 5 discusses the foundational technologies of the Metaverse—VR, AR, AI, and the Internet of Things (IoT)—and how they merge to create immersive healthcare environments. It examines applications such as remote consultations, surgical training, and rehabilitation while addressing challenges like accessibility and data security.

Chapter 6 analyzes the advantages, limitations, and transformative effects of Metaverse technologies on healthcare. It explores the integration of 5G, AI, and machine learning (ML) in healthcare, emphasizing the benefits of real-time data transmission and low-latency communication for applications like continuous patient monitoring and remote surgery. The chapter also considers ethical and security concerns associated with these advancements.

Chapter 7 examines how the Metaverse is redefining patient experiences in virtual healthcare environments. It traces the evolution of healthcare in virtual spaces, highlights key developments, and addresses challenges such as technological barriers, ethical considerations, and inclusivity in Metaverse-based healthcare services.

Chapter 8 focuses on the role of Metaverse, VR, and AR in healthcare education and training. It discusses how these technologies enhance teaching methodologies, improve training outcomes, and create advanced simulations for medical professionals. The chapter also explores the challenges of integrating Metaverse applications into educational systems.

Chapter 9 delves into the protection of genomic data in the digital Metaverse landscape. It presents a novel deep-learning approach for classifying non-TATA promoters in genome sequencing, demonstrating how AI-driven methods enhance data security and improve gene regulation research.

Chapter 10 explores data protection regulations for e-health devices. It examines the role of digital health gadgets in preventive healthcare and discusses data acquisition, analysis, and transmission, emphasizing security measures to protect patient information.

Chapter 11 investigates cybersecurity measures in healthcare, analyzing vulnerabilities, data breaches, and their impact on healthcare organizations. It reviews literature on cyberattacks and security strategies implemented between 2015 and 2020, emphasizing the importance of strengthening IT systems.

Chapter 12 discusses the implementation of Metaverse technologies in healthcare, focusing on telemedicine, medical education, and clinical research. It highlights privacy, security, and technical barriers to adoption, outlining strategies to overcome these challenges.

Chapter 13 examines the impact of Metaverse technologies on patient care and healthcare accessibility. It explores ethical concerns related to patient consent, data privacy, and regulatory frameworks necessary for ensuring trust in virtual healthcare environments.

Chapter 14 analyzes encryption techniques for securing Metaverse interactions. It highlights asymmetric encryption and key infrastructure solutions that protect user identities and transactions in digital healthcare spaces.

Chapter 15 explores the integration of AI, VR, AR, and extended reality (XR) into healthcare models. It examines applications in patient pathway simulations, facility design, and epidemiological forecasting, showcasing how the Metaverse is reshaping healthcare planning.

Chapter 16 evaluates the role of 5G in healthcare Metaverse adoption. It discusses performance benchmarks, security risks, and the potential of next-generation virtual care solutions powered by high-speed networks.

Chapter 17 explores digital twin technology in healthcare, discussing its role in real-time data analysis, predictive analytics, and clinical simulations. The chapter emphasizes its potential in revolutionizing surgery and medical education.

Chapter 18 examines how the Metaverse and digital twin applications enhance healthcare sustainability and efficiency. It highlights technologies like holographic simulation and virtual-reality integration with medical science, demonstrating their transformative impact.

Chapter 19 investigates advanced holographic display technology and its applications in medical education and research. It explores the integration of AI-based hologram generation for emergency response training, anatomy education, and drug research.

Chapter 20 discusses the role of explainable AI (XAI) in healthcare, emphasizing transparency in AI-driven medical decisions. It explores the integration of XAI with Open Data, Knowledge Graphs, and Metaverse applications, highlighting use cases in cancer detection, dynamic pruning techniques, and personalized healthcare.

By providing a comprehensive examination of Metaverse technologies in healthcare, this book aims to equip researchers, professionals, and policymakers with the knowledge to navigate the evolving digital landscape. We hope it serves as a valuable resource for those exploring the intersection of healthcare, security, and the Metaverse.

**Ajay Kumar Vyas Ph.D.**
**Harleen Kaur Ph.D.**
**Sourabh Sharma Ph.D.**
**Bhavya Alankar Ph.D.**
March 2025

# Acknowledgments

Proper acknowledgment goes beyond merely appreciating the idea; it recognizes the efforts, motivation, and dedication that made this project possible. We are deeply grateful to all the contributors, reviewers, and Martin Scrivener and his editorial team for their unwavering support and hard work throughout the development of this book.

This book is lovingly dedicated to my late father, Shri Chhagan Lal Vyas, and my mother, Smt. Shashikala Vyas, my beloved wife, Deepshikha, and my wonderful daughters, Rakshita and Prakshita. Their love and inspiration have been my guiding force.

**Ajay Kumar Vyas Ph.D.**
**Harleen Kaur Ph.D.**
**Sourabh Sharma Ph.D.**
**Bhavya Alankar Ph.D.**

# Part I
# METAVERSE TECHNOLOGY

1

# Introduction to Metaverse for Healthcare

**Amit Sharma**

*Department of Physics, University Institute of Science, Chandigarh University, Mohali, Punjab, India*

***Abstract***
The metaverse is a shared virtual environment that has the potential to transform several industries, including healthcare. This paper explores the metaverse and examines its possible uses in the healthcare sector. We discuss the technological foundation needed to enable healthcare based on the metaverse, including developments in augmented reality and virtual reality. The threats and challenges, which include data privacy, security, and the issue of the divided field, are discussed together with opportunities and possibilities such as enhanced telemedicine, remote surgery, and even patient rehabilitation. In the last section, we outline the future ideas and concerns of bringing the metaverse into healthcare and how it could potentially transform the healthcare industry in terms of patient care and medical training and education in the future.

***Keywords*:** Metaverse, augmented reality, virtual reality, VR controller, telemedicine, rehabilitations

## 1.1 Introduction of Metaverse

The metaverse is a virtually shared space where users can interact with each other in virtual reality to play, work, and learn. It is a world out of more than just science fiction [1]. Neal Stephenson initially coined the term "metaverse" in his science-fiction novel "Snow Crash" in 1992. It imagines an enormous digital world that lives together with a physical one, where people talk to each other through their digital avatars [2]. In modern parlance, the metaverse currently refers to an AR/MR/VR-enabled (augmented/mixed/virtual reality) three-dimensional shared virtual realm

*Email:* sharma.a28@gmail.com

Ajay Kumar Vyas, Harleen Kaur, Sourabh Sharma and Bhavya Alankar (eds.) Metaverse Technologies, Security and Applications for Healthcare, (3–36) © 2025 Scrivener Publishing LLC

(see Figure 1.1). Combining the physical and digital worlds to impact our lives and their real-time interaction between devices promotes users to engage actively rather than passively [3]. The metaverse enables a dynamic three-dimensional experience beyond typical screens, allowing users to navigate the world without screen-space constraints and benefit from new experiences unattainable in physical or standard digital environments. There is a developing acknowledgment among organizations about the capability of metaverse technologies and they are likewise hoping to make huge speculations about it [4].

The idea of a metaverse is currently attracting a lot of attention. Essentially, the metaverse is frequently described as an advanced iteration of the Internet. Using augmented reality (AR), virtual reality (VR), and extended reality (XR), individuals will navigate the metaverse's virtual environments much like how we currently browse websites with a mouse [5]. Large corporations have made significant investments in creating the metaverse, which is the next advancement in internet connectivity [6]. According to the findings, the metaverse is likely to transform the medical fields, educational facilities, cultural events, e-commerce, and technological advancement [7]. Meta, which has previously been referred to as Facebook, has begun to transform from being a social media platform into a leader in the metaverse. The new branding is equally consistent with the company's integration of hybrid glasses that employ wearable sensors to provide a more realistic and engrossing virtual environment [8].

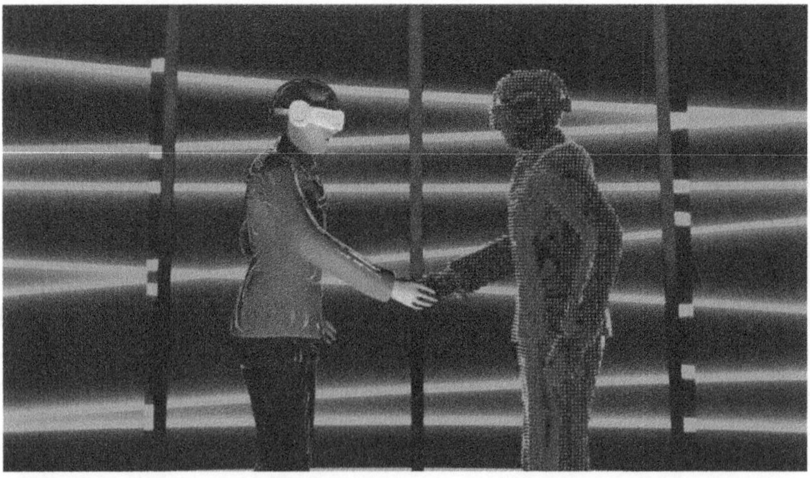

**Figure 1.1** A metaverse creates immersive digital environments for interaction and exploration [10].

This advancement is upgrading the cognitive experiences and transporting users into the feeling of being there [9].

## 1.2 Metaverse in Healthcare

The metaverse, an emergent type of digital environment, can be regarded as a promising direction for changing the healthcare sector. Building well-sized shared common spaces could solve current difficulties and ensure smooth integration, enabling user presence and behavior continuity across numerous virtual worlds [11]. This would mean that a patient's medical record could be easily transferred between hospitals, clinics, and other healthcare providers. Nevertheless, the future application of the metaverse in healthcare has its drawbacks and should be thoroughly planned. The integration of the metaverse with the real world depends on several technologies, such as augmented and virtual realities, artificial intelligence, high-speed networks, edge computation, and blockchain [12–16], on which the metaverse significantly depends. With time, the metaverse is slowly transforming the face of the health industry whereby one can seek medical assistance and even new surgical operations can be conducted virtually with better precision. Each of these innovations presents healthcare providers with a chance to repudiate the mode of delivering patient care education and practice as well as the overall healthcare sector. Some of the things that need to be solved before taking the metaverse into healthcare are identity theft and compatibility of equipment. However, using metaverse in healthcare has its pros and cons. Consequently, its development should be approached strategically and with caution to improve on these added values.

The metaverse provides opportunities for development and threats for healthcare professionals and insurance companies. They can, therefore, adapt to current trends and continuously look for possible future uses of this technology so that they will always be ahead of other companies. In this area, effective expenditures in infrastructure, the right approach to development, and a patient-centered approach will help to create a metaverse that can have a positive impact and result in better results for the healthcare system. Also, it is worth noting that the health metaverse plays another role in the opportunity to train surgical robots in the metaverse. For instance, the current concept of gamification applied in health management applications and fitness can be advanced using AR in aspects such as virtual trainers and innovative exercise modalities [17]. In addition, future acceptance and implementation of the metaverse, insurance policies, payment structures, and data governance frameworks will be critical to healthcare. The metaverse clinics in the virtual space, teleconsultation features, and the improvement of the relationship between doctors and patients mean that doctors will have a chance to interact with their patients in the future in a new and more engaging manner [18]. It is assumed that with the further development of science, the role of the metaverse in healthcare will increase, thus waiting for the creation of a system that is better, more functional, and accessible to everyone.

## 1.3 Potential Uses of Metaverse in Healthcare

It is getting quick attention for its potential to revolutionize the healthcare industry as part of the metaverse. This digital world that embraces such technologies as virtual and augmented reality is full of opportunities to enhance the level of patient care, teaching, and mentoring in the sphere of medicine and further research (see Figure 1.2).

### 1.3.1 Telemedicine and Virtual Consultations

Telemedicine is known as remote healthcare, where a patient and doctor are situated in separate locations but, with the help of technology, can interact. It has been shown that adaptive technologies give more opportunities for healthcare providers to provide remote care in an engaging form [19]. Within the virtual horizons of the metaverse, doctors and patients can

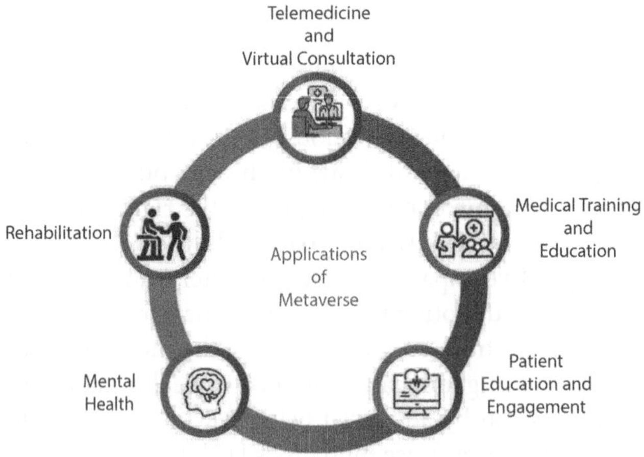


**Figure 1.2** Applications of the metaverse in healthcare.

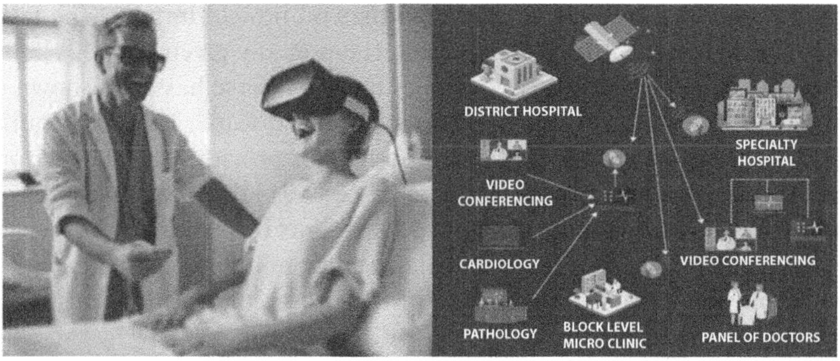


**Figure 1.3** (Left) A patient consulting with a doctor in a virtual clinic. (Right) Telemedicine case study applications [20].

interact more fluently than through normal computer-mediated communication [20]. Here, the patients can sit in a virtual waiting room, explain their complaints in a virtual consultation room, and even go through some exercises in a virtual physical therapy center (see Figure 1.3). Such better interactions will strengthen the doctor-patient relationship, improve treatment compliance, and enhance the level of care provided. The metaverse, world, or virtual game is well-made and available to people living in injectable areas or areas that are too far to access healthcare facilities. By removing the traveling component for much-needed medical attention, it is important to improve the availability of advanced types of medicine reducing health lifting options. The metaverse may also have a particularly beneficial impact on patients with mobility limitations by providing therapeutic care at home. In addition, the metaverse may contribute to absorbing excess demand from healthcare providers and facilities [21]. It will be possible to reduce the number of face-to-face sessions by outsourcing some consultations, which will allow using this time for other patients and services. This is particularly valuable during periods of high demand or limited capacity.

### 1.3.2 Medical Education and Training

The metaverse provides an exceptional opportunity for medical practitioners and learners to have practical training in a controlled environment [22]. Virtual reality allows medical students to risk patients with challenging scenarios and still master the execution of difficult situations safely and quickly [23]. As an example, future surgeons may learn how to perform techniques in a dummy and get assessed during such training.

It can, therefore, be used to direct learners on how to improve the techniques employed within the operating room at any given time [24]. The use of such active learning approaches in a metaverse has been shown to dramatically enhance student engagement and research in skills acquisition. Furthermore, using these methods entails providing a safe environment so that the students can train on those skills [25]. This is particularly useful to teachers working under the constraints of a pandemic who wish to—or have to—provide experiential education and direct patient contact, which normally would be hard to provide in a conventional classroom setting [24].

Just as in traditional lessons on anatomy, medical students can now experience anatomical dissection in a head-mounted display (Figure 1.4). These engaging lessons give students hands-on experience with the cutting edge of virtual anatomy: the virtual dissection of cadavers. In addition to this, virtual medical education simulation allows students to learn in a controlled and simulated environment where they can do patient diagnosis and treatment, perform procedures, and make decisions. Furthermore, large-scale scenario-based simulations can also be designed to enhance the ability to be critical in leadership, teamwork, and interpersonal relationships, as well as to organize tasks under time pressure. Clinical skill

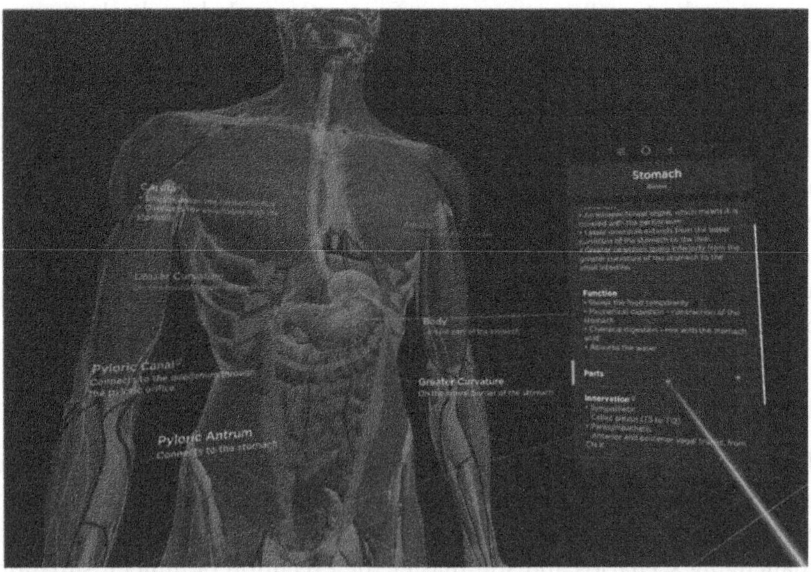


**Figure 1.4** Human anatomy dissection through computer-based simulation and 3D, VR, and AR applications [27].

development of medical students, including taking a patient's history and effective rapport with patients, can be enhanced through their participation in a virtual patient encounter [26]. Besides, the metaverse facilitates remote working, remote learning, and training in an innovative way. The system allows users everywhere in the world to communicate with experts in real time, thus creating a feeling of belonging to a community. Events such as virtual conferences and workshops allow learning and updating with the latest changes in the profession, even in difficult conditions. They can also be useful in stress management and enhancement of general health [25].

The metaverse and other virtual environments have become more useful for medical education [28]. These platforms can thus convert students into clinical settings making it easier for them to understand concepts of medicine, improve skills, and reduce errors. In addition, the metaverse addresses the shortcomings of theoretical knowledge by providing practical aspects of what is being taught in institutions which helps the medical trainees in handling real-world healthcare more sophisticatedly [23]. In the use of virtual reality, teaching practices can become more active in students' engagement in a blended learning context (see Figure 1.5). It has been suggested that active learning strategies used in these forms of play can add value to education through enrichment in the quality of interaction and learning [29]. It is expected that involving students in realistic educational situations with the help of immersive technologies will be easier than in more conventional educational settings. Thus, the engagement in the metaverse learning activities relative to patient care and virtual patient practice will develop students' practical skills as well as cognitive skills. The active learning methodologies applied within the metaverse are

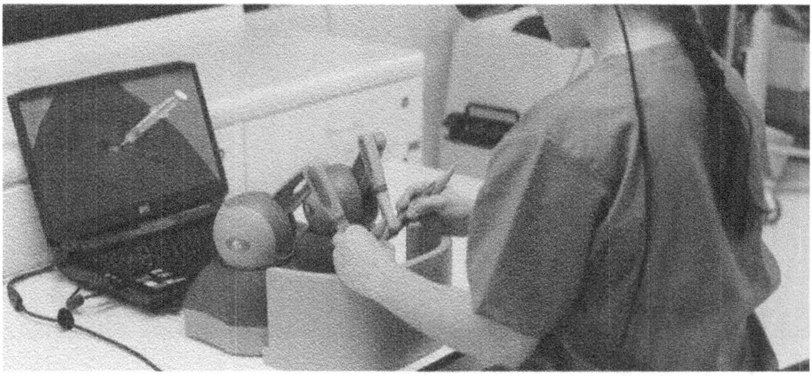

**Figure 1.5** A medical student using a virtual reality simulation to practice surgery [28].

likely to improve learning outcomes by increasing student motivation and retention and enhancing levels of engagement [23]. The potential applications of the metaverse in education and healthcare are vast and continually expanding as technology advances.

### 1.3.3 Patient Education and Engagement

Within a metaverse environment, patient education and patent engagement stand to benefit dynamically [30]. Healthcare providers can create interesting and interactive content that goes beyond information delivery, using virtual and augmented reality as immersive tools. The metaverse can also provide a virtual caregiving ecosystem for such patients. There is also the idea of providing a virtual environment, which connects individuals with patients with similar problems and allows for information and even support to be given. Moreover, the metaverse aims at enhancing public health through virtual interventions that promote comprehension regarding the management of diseases, health habits, and treatment options. Many patients will be able to find out how their primary diseases are better managed using virtual clinics and tutorials. It practically allows every stage of a simulated patient education experience to be adapted to the patient's characteristics within the spheres of the metaverse environment [31]. Targeted education is more efficient compared with the "one size fits all" approach for all patients. Patients may benefit from virtual reality images that depict specific therapeutic interventions such as surgical procedures

**Figure 1.6** Zimmer Biomet's OptiVu surgical app will let surgeons and patients visualize a procedure together [33].

related to cortical control of bimanual reach and grasp in the same user. For instance, it is possible that a patient for a certain treatment can be shown to intertwine treatments using virtual images and software (see Figure 1.6).

The metaverse also provides opportunities for patient agency. Patients use virtual tools to track their progress, set individual goals, and receive customized feedback [32]. The more informed patients are, the better their outcomes, which supports a truly consumer-driven healthcare model. Engaging, personalizing, and supporting experiences for their patients to get educated about the conditions of their bodies properly enable healthcare providers with this lifestyle change as well as optimization loop.

### 1.3.4 Mental Health

The metaverse comes with possibilities that could disrupt the way mental health services are rendered. There can be virtual therapy sections, group therapy, and mental programs conducted in the metaverse which allows people to interact and get help in an environment that feels safe. Additionally, some specific psychological conditions like anxiety and fear can be treated using the virtual reality space. Although there are no clinical studies yet to demonstrate the use of therapeutic tools in the metaverse for the treatment of psychiatric illnesses, there is an increasing trend in using virtual reality (VR), augmented reality (AR), and mixed reality (MR) for the assessment and management of mental illness [34]. With the help of the therapists, the patients can learn to cope with their fears by exposing them to fear-evoking situations in supervised conditions, therefore, improving their life quality.

VR situations have an added advantage since they are not limited to ordinary events that can be hard to recreate accurately in real life. This comes particularly handy in resolving the issue of a relatively few practitioners in psychiatry. VR scenarios can minimize the number of therapeutic appointments done face to face, as the health workers can attend the treatment from different sites [35]. Virtual environments within the metaverse could be beneficial for managing mental health disorders that have already responded positively to virtual reality interventions [36].

- **Attention Deficit Hyperactivity Disorder (ADHD):** Virtual reality (VR) technology has the potential to improve the diagnosis and treatment of ADHD in children. VR environments frequently appeal to children; hence, they may be more likely to engage or comply with what is asked of them. Virtual reality aiming at a cognitive neuropsychological approach is being developed to assist children with ADHD, showing them the strategies of efficacy and making symptoms more manageable which can make their daily self-management skills better [34].

- **Eating Disorders:** There have been positive effects of virtual reality on eating disorders. This enables healthcare providers to expose patients in a controlled virtual environment which types of foods or situations might exacerbate psychological cravings. This knowledge can then be used to help patients develop effective coping strategies [37].
- **Anxiety and Stress Disorder:** Individuals with social anxiety have shown significant improvement after participating in a VR social skills training session shown in Figure 1.7. The immersive experience allowed them to practice communication skills in a controlled environment, leading to increased self-confidence [38, 39]. Additionally, VR therapy has demonstrated effectiveness in treating phobias.
- **Autism:** Cognitive therapy using virtual reality (VR) has shown promise in helping patients with autism, and it was effective in improving life skills, concentration, cognition, and memory [38].
- **Alzheimer's Disease:** Virtual reality has shown potential in assessing navigational skills and improving cognitive

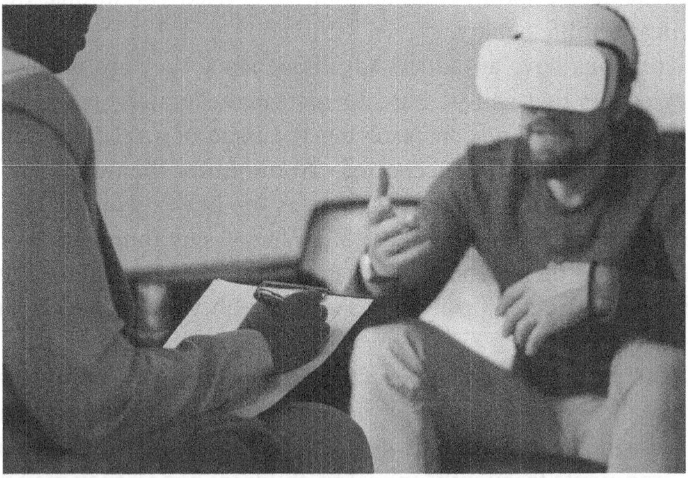

**Figure 1.7** A patient attending a virtual therapy session in the metaverse [42, 43].

function in Alzheimer's disease patients, some individuals reported experiencing negative emotions such as boredom, fear, and anxiety during VR applications [38].

- **Stress and Pain Management:** Virtual reality (VR) can be used to alleviate stress and pain by delivering immersive distractions. Studies have demonstrated that VR applications are more helpful than traditional therapy in managing conditions like depression, anxiety, fatigue, and pain. VR can also benefit chronically ill patients by mimicking situations outside the hospital, offering a change of scenery and enhancing mental well-being [38].
- **Delusions, Psychosis, and Schizophrenia:** VR cognitive therapy has been explored as a potential treatment for conditions such as persecutory delusions and paranoia in individuals experiencing psychosis, depression, and positive symptoms of schizophrenia [40, 41].

### 1.3.5 Rehabilitation

The metaverse presents a wonderful possibility for physical and cognitive rehab. Virtual reality also provides interactive exercises designed to help patients strengthen and improve their balance, coordination, etc. One example is VR-based games targeted to individuals recovering from stroke which mimic walking, reaching for objects, and grasping. Virtual reality can also be used to help with cognitive impairments such as memory loss and attention deficits. Therapists may support cognitive function and enhance the potential for independence by immersing patients in mentally stimulating activities [44].

However, rehabilitation is of great importance in healthcare as it supports the recovery process after an illness or injury [45]. It works to enhance the physical, mental, and emotional health of residents so they ultimately live more independent lives. The metaverse could be a solution to the problems raised by the COVID-19 pandemic. This, along with its ability to combat social isolation and the scarcity of conventional rehabilitation services, coincides well with the rise in demand for telerehabilitation [45]. Rehabilitation programs can use virtual environments to offer patients a safe and controlled place to practice essential skills (e.g., balance). In addition, the metaverse can help overcome both physical and mental health challenges more broadly by simulating a wide variety of real-world scenarios (see Figure 1.8).

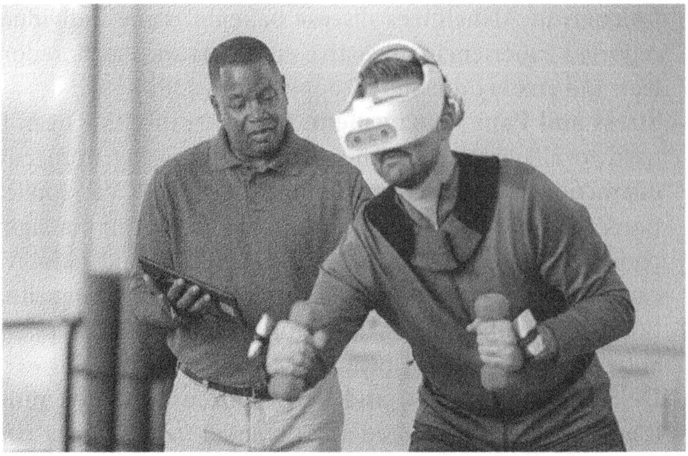

**Figure 1.8** A patient using virtual reality for physical rehabilitation [47].

Although still in relative infancy, the metaverse could bring an exponential shift regarding how we relate to and use technology. The applications also reach into rehabilitation by allowing access to therapy through remote sessions. Virtual rehabilitation programs have the great advantage of giving patients who cannot access traditional therapy sessions due to distance or lack of mobility the chance to participate. This technology increases medical accessibility to a great extent, especially among people living in remote areas. It may be thus concluded that the metaverse can bring in a 180-degree change in the healthcare industry, mainly in rehabilitation [46]. The metaverse opens up a bright perspective for healthcare, such as an improved patient experience, distant rehabilitation, and development of medical knowledge. Introducing telemedicine, wearable devices, and AI will give health professionals real-time data to set up treatment on a comfortable level and optimize results. This is a data-driven approach that could change the whole concept of healthcare delivery [46].

## 1.4 Technological Infrastructure

The technological infrastructure of the metaverse plays a pivotal role in shaping the future of healthcare. It provides the foundation for immersive virtual environments, enabling new possibilities for patient care, medical education, and research. Here are some key aspects of this infrastructure:

### 1.4.1 Technologies

1. **Augmented Reality (AR):** Augmented reality is one of the most innovative technologies with incredible properties that combine the physical world with the digital one. AR builds upon the real environment through the process of adding levels of information such as graphics on top of real-world images [48]. Its uses include giving directions in real time and visualizing the products that we have at home, among others. AR system has sophisticated tracking algorithms to place virtual objects naturally in the user's environment hence making it immersive. In the same regard, AR simultaneously integrates interactive features like buttons or menus which can be touched on the digital material within/over the real environment (see Figure 1.9). Thus, with the help of contextual awareness, AR can offer more relevant information that complies with the user's geographic location and environment. Also, it can be combined with other technologies, for example, artificial intelligence, and the Internet of Things to develop even more enhanced and unique applications. I have explained in other parts of this paper how AR can transform several business sectors and how it can improve our everyday lives as a

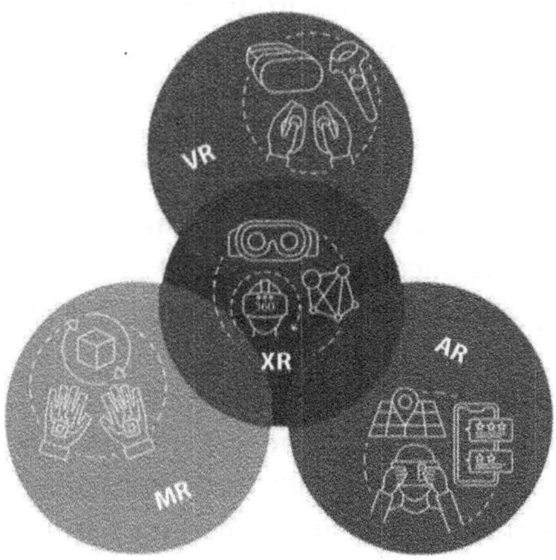


**Figure 1.9** The Venn diagram illustrates the relationship between virtual reality (VR), augmented reality (AR), mixed reality (MR), and extended reality (XR). XR encompasses all technologies that enhance the real-world experience by overlaying or immersing users in digital information. VR creates a fully immersive digital environment, AR overlays digital information onto the real world, and MR blends elements of both VR and AR [53].

result of improving our perception of reality while offering information and experiences at the same time [48].

2. **Virtual Reality (VR):** A virtual reality system can be described as a complete sensory environment that introduces the subjects to virtual reality while excluding every aspect of the real world. While models in the virtual environment are depicted in high complexity, the system does not take into account the real context. Current technologies such as VR allow users to walk through the virtual space, touch objects, as well as maneuver around [49] (see Figure 1.9). Usually, VR headsets are employed, though having a room that has a couple of large screens for inputs is also a method that can be used for creating the VR atmosphere. The following are characterized by head-mounted displays that have tiny screens that are placed directly before the eyes and can hand out high-definition content with a broad field of vision. The typically used input tracking is then complemented by stereoscopic 3D effects in order to provide an experience in VR. This means that the display is divided between the user's eyes in order to provide the user with depth perception. In particular, haptic technology can produce non-visual and non-auditory sensory and force feedback for the users. Through the sensory input, users have the chance to affect the generated VR environment but are not able to control it completely. Unlike VR, augmented reality (AR) brings additional elements to the real world by adding or superimposing new objects [50]. Users observe the actual scenery straight or via an intermediary such as a camera, while software-enhanced components such as pictures, tunes, or videos are introduced on this scenery. AR does not design a completely different experience, rather it gives an enhancement to the existing experience.
3. **Mixed Reality (MR):** A mixed reality (MR) environment integrates some aspects of the real environment with aspects of virtual environments into the same scene. In MR, both real and virtual objects are rendered such that they can be viewed in the same instance. The integration can be reached in some different ways. For example, augmented elements may be projected onto the physical environment through optical or video-see-through displays; real-world content can be placed into the virtual environment using video input,

or haptic objects with active markers that are tracked can be added into the virtual scene. MR is a combination of AR and VR making it exist in the physical world as well as the digital world [51]. Sensing and imagining technology enables users to deal with real and virtual objects and environments with the help of a mixed-reality environment (see Figure 1.9). This is because it enables a user to be fully aware of the physical world around him/her at the same time as being in a virtual world, all this without having to take the headset off. For instance, in MR, one is allowed to play a video game on a console then pick a physical water bottle and use it to communicate with an avatar in the virtual world. And so, the set can rewrite the rules of work and leisure. As the overlapping of physical and digital environments in MR, the real and virtual objects can be interactively created in real time for patients and training purposes. Before performing surgery, MR enables surgeons to have an array of perspectives on the complexity of anatomical structure to work on which enhances efficiency and efficacy. Special simulations help medical students get the practical look which is helpful for these people to increase their knowledge and improve skills in practice. Also, MR allows working in a team; professionals from other countries can consult and even participate in the treatment process without being there bodily. In light of these advancements in MR technology, the future of healthcare will even be revolutionized to a larger extent through increased efficiency, accuracy, and clientele access.

4. **Extended Reality (XR):** XR is the general term for AR, VR, and MR all-encompassing technologies together as a single form of immersive experience (see Figure 1.9). Supported by a range of hardware and software, XR extends from the improved video to the truly multi-dimensional interactions [52]. Alongside the improvement of the high-quality XR, consumers and enterprises are using it for activities such as playing games, learning classes, virtual training, and designing the product. XR streaming over the cloud through the 5G is increasing the opportunity for users to immerse in the XR experience at any location. For healthcare training, XR has made a positive impact in changing the experience by, decreasing the number of medical mistakes, improving the competencies of the trainers, decreasing the costs of

training, and giving the learners a real-life XR experience. When compared to the conventional training methodologies, the delivery of learning systems can thus enhance the quality of learning thereby reducing costs for training and subsequently increasing the levels of patient satisfaction that arise from better healthcare provision by more competent personnel.

### 1.4.2 Wearable and Hardware

As the metaverse concept moves from speculative fiction to practical reality, its impact on various sectors is becoming increasingly evident. Healthcare, in particular, stands to benefit immensely from the advanced hardware designed for the metaverse. By integrating virtual reality (VR), augmented reality (AR), and high-performance computing with medical applications, the metaverse is poised to transform patient care, medical training, and clinical research. This article explores the hardware essential for the metaverse and its pivotal role in advancing healthcare.

**1. Virtual Reality (VR) Headsets**

VR headsets are essential tools for creating immersive healthcare environments, benefiting both patients and medical professionals l (see Figure 1.10).

- **Oculus Quest 2:** This fully wireless headset with a resolution of 1832 × 1920 pixels per eye and a field of view of 90° is applied in healthcare for virtual therapy sessions and mental health treatments. Patient-centered application and utility are also possible through the portable and user-friendly technology of the device [54].
- **HTC Vive Pro:** As a VR headset, HTC VIVE Pro has a high-resolution display of 1440 × 1600 per eye and accurate tracking that is used in enhanced simulations and realistic human anatomy exercises for surgery among others. Its surgical tracking system is highly robust to capture intricate maneuvers that improve the core surgeries and trains [55].
- **Valve Index:** To be precise, the valve index has a high refresh rate of up to 144 Hz and a very wide field of view of up to 130° and is used in training its personnel. Such capabilities enable effective and elaborated medical training with features such as interactive operations, operations of simulated surgery, and many others [56].

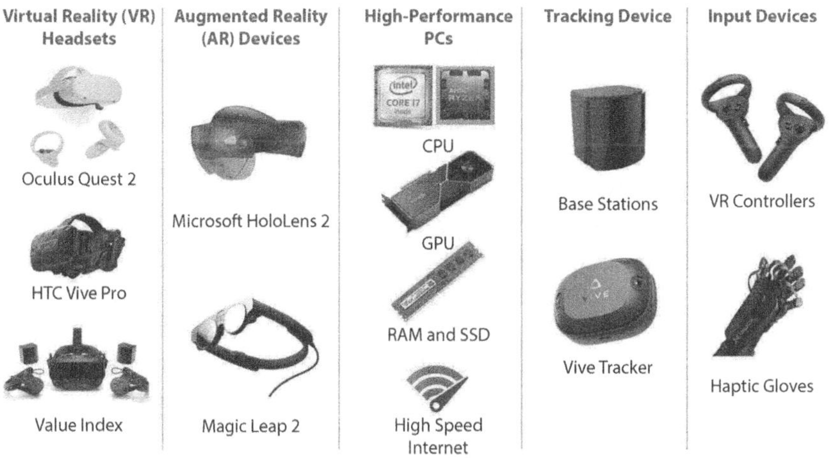


**Figure 1.10** Wearable devices and hardware used for the metaverse.

**2. Augmented Reality (AR) Devices**

Augmented reality devices offer unique applications by overlaying digital information onto the real world, proving invaluable in medical contexts:

- **Microsoft HoloLens 2:** This is another headset that gets surgeons closer to an actual view of the objects, details about the anatomy of a patient and live data during an operation l (see Figure 1.10). This device has a resolution of 2048 × 1080 pixels per eye and also hand tracking, which allows doing complex surgeries with higher accuracy as the important information is overlaid onto the surgeon's field of vision [57].
- **Magic Leap 2:** This is the second generation of augmented reality technology and is more advanced than its preceding model; its quality pictures and wide field of view make the technology useful in medical applications such as visualization and planning (see Figure 1.10). It may be used by surgeons to study detailed models of the anatomy of the patient before the operation is carried out, and this will lead to a very efficient and effective surgery in that the surgeons will be in a position to accomplish the surgeries in the best way [58].

**3. High-Performance PCs**

High-performance PCs are the backbone of the metaverse, providing the computational power needed for sophisticated medical applications:

- **CPU:** The use of complicated medical simulations and analysis of big data requires the existence of powerful multi-core processors like Intel Core i7 or AMD Ryzen 7 [59]. These processors enable real-time image processing involving high-resolution images and training that involves interactivity.
- **GPU:** Hardware, such as graphic cards NVIDIA RTX 3080 or AMD Radeon RX 6800, helps to develop real-life 3D models and simulations. These cards allow complex visualizations that are essential for educational purposes and, to a certain extent, the prognosis of patients' conditions [60].
- **RAM and Storage:** To get a better experience while playing VR simulations or to reduce the time of data processing, it is recommended to have at least 16 GB of RAM and to increase the amount of storage with an SSD of at least 1 TB.
- **Connectivity:** To take advantage of metaverse applications, and to optimize data transfer, it will require enough USB ports and a good internet connection.

**4. Tracking Devices**

Tracking devices enhance the accuracy and effectiveness of medical simulations and procedures:

- **Base Stations:** For instance, HTC VIVE base stations that employ laser technology to track the position of VR headsets and controllers are essential when it comes to accurate surgical models and advanced training simulations [61].
- **Additional Trackers:** VIVE trackers are some of the usable devices that help in tracking the location of instruments and patients during simulations hence making the training more real and effective [62].

**5. Input Devices**

Input devices facilitate interaction within VR and AR environments, playing a significant role in healthcare applications:

- **VR Controllers:** Devices such as Oculus Touch or Valve Index controllers help people to interact with the virtual environment, for example, in such applications as surgery simulation or patient exercises [63].

- **Haptic Gloves:** Another kind of device that is widely used in medical practice is HaptX Gloves which gives a kind of a sense of touch and allows to make manipulations with the objects that are located in the virtual environment. This is especially important for training purposes since realistic haptic feedback improves learning and subsequent procedure enactment [63].

**6. Network Infrastructure**

Network infrastructure supports the connectivity required for real-time data sharing and collaborative medical efforts:

- **High-Speed Internet:** High-speed fiber-broadband technologies are crucial in handling large quantities of information within a short span and with high efficiency for telemedicine, remote consultations, and integrated research.
- **Routers and Modems:** Advancement in routers and modems makes communication and data transfer fast and constant, essential for a healthcare setting.

**7. Comfort and Ergonomics**

In the healthcare sector, comfort and usability are critical:

- **Headset Padding and Straps:** APEs need to be easy and comfortable to wear for an extended period in medical training and on patients because of the need for lightweight comfortable padding and straps on the headset.
- **Ergonomic Design:** The devices for training should be ergonomic so that the doctors can use them without discomfort especially when the training is going to take a considerable amount of time or the procedure is going to be quite tiresome.

**8. Audio Equipment**

Audio equipment enhances communication and immersion:

- **Integrated Headphones:** Some of the VR headsets incorporate headset headphones that offer spatial sound which contributes to the realism of the simulations as well as interaction during telemedicine.

- **External Headsets:** Noise-cancelling headphones give increased concentration as well as blocked-out disturbances, which are perfect for training when interacting with patients.

**9. Power Supply and Battery Life**
Power management is crucial for maintaining operational efficiency:

- **Battery Life:** Sufficient battery capacity for wireless devices is important so that it will not run out of battery during training or patient treatment.
- **Charging Solutions:** New charging points and any other charging-related features make it possible to always find an available device that is charged and ready to use.

## 1.5 Benefits and Opportunities

The healthcare industry is undergoing a transformative period, driven by technological advancements, demographic shifts, and a growing emphasis on preventive care. This evolution presents a myriad of benefits and opportunities for individuals, organizations, and societies worldwide.

### 1.5.1 Improved Accessibility

Indeed, the metaverse is advantageous in dismantling geographical limitations hence making healthcare services reachable to the patients and professionals.

1. **Specialized Care:** Patients can get specialized healthcare services from an expert who may be in the other corner of the world without having to change his or her place of residence. This can be particularly beneficial where the diagnostics are rare or complicated in some way.
2. **Virtual Rehabilitation:** It might be effective in offering the opportunity to practice rehabilitation therapy because the metaverse can offer unique experiences by allowing the patient to practice exercises as guided by the therapist in a virtual world. It is especially useful for those with stroke or head injury as a result of an accident or violence [46].
3. **Mental Health Support:** It can be seen that the metaverse is a safe environment where a person who needs therapy can

find it. Teletherapy and telesupport groups enhance therapy adherence to reduce self-stigmatization and enhance access to treatment [64].

4. **Remote Collaboration:** It can help healthcare professionals connect with peers from around the globe in the true sense of the term and also exchange information and ideas in real time and possibly materials. This can enhance the treatment and also can help a lot in the analysis [65].
5. **Continuous Education:** The metaverse can foster a range of knowledge-acquisition activities such as conferences, workshops, and training sessions conducted in a virtual environment that is accessible from offices and helps them to update new advancements in the field of their interest [24].
6. **Simulation Training:** The metaverse allows healthcare professionals to practice their skills in a safe and controlled environment using realistic simulations of medical procedures. This can also enhance patients' safety and decrease medical mistakes [24].

### 1.5.2 Enhanced Patient Experience

By developing realistic and engaging experiences, the metaverse can create real-life, meaningful-use experiences to positively impact patient experience and one-on-one interactions while increasing overall health literacy.

1. **Tailored Treatment Plans:** This is particularly beneficial for healthcare professionals since they may build individual treatment in the metaverse by sharing patient information and preferences. Computer-generated models can be employed to show patients the treatments or procedures that may be taken and also the outcome.
2. **Virtual Reality Therapy:** Virtual reality comprises virtual reality and it can be applied in a plurality of therapeutic uses including pain management, stress, and mental health uses. In other words, the metaverse can assist with managing conditions by making environments therapeutic or exciting [66].
3. **Gamified Health Education:** There is an opportunity to use some elements of the game in the teaching-learning processes on offer in healthcare education. In this way, patients are encouraged to engage in virtual challenge activities, get

virtual and tangible motivational rewards, as well as monitor their progress [67].

4. **Virtual Support Groups:** In the metaverse, the patients could conveniently meet other people who went through similar experiences as them in a safe environment. In addition to the above advantages, virtual support groups also lower feelings of loneliness and offer emotional support.
5. **Interactive Patient Education:** Through virtual reality and augmented reality, healthcare providers can develop more appealing and easily memorable materials for patients' education. For example, clients can see the effects of different diseases or learn about human anatomy in three dimensions [23].
6. **Remote Consultations:** By enabling online consultations, many patients can benefit from teleconsultations where consultations can be done through metaverse decreasing the likelihood of traveling. It is argued that virtual waiting rooms and consultation rooms are less stressful for the patient as compared to a physical waiting room [68].

### 1.5.3 Cost Reduction

The use of metaverse for training, consultations, and patient management will therefore lead to notable expense decreases.

1. **Reduced Travel Costs:** The implementation of conventional training typically implies travel costs for trainers and trainees alike. In this way, the metaverse can avoid these costs through such aspects as employing virtual training sessions or workshops [18].
2. **Scalability:** Blended learning is more efficient in terms of the number of participants that it can reach as well as the cost per trainee. This is the most advantageous to large organizations and healthcare institutions.
3. **Simulation-Based Learning:** The metaverse can make the pieces of training realistic and tangible; this means that there will be a limited need for physical trainers and training equipment and equipment that are costly to acquire and maintain [23].

4. **Global Collaboration:** Enhancing the research capacity, training, and practice of professionals and institutions for global affiliation [69].

## 1.6 Challenges and Risks

With all the opportunities that the metaverse brings to the healthcare sector, one must not deny the obstacles that may come along the way of metaverse creation and implementation. It is important to remember that as outlined in a recent study [70], the metaverse is still a paradigm shift in technology advancement and international relations to provide the illusion of integration with the real world.

The first one is environmental preservation which cautions about the amount of energy that may be used to facilitate the functioning of the metaverse. Most of the new digital assets creation, ongoing maintenance, cloud-based data storage, and real-time online services and experiences depend heavily on energy [70]. With an additional feature of energy efficiency in the recent 5G technology, it is believed that the overall energy consumption will be higher than in the previous generations. What needs to be pointed out is the fact that while carbon offsetting reduces emissions, it does not do anything about the decrease in species of wildlife.

The metaverse has the potential of being libidinal, and if not taken through the responsible approach, then it may create havoc on well-being. Much attention should be paid to the elaboration of all possible outcomes and the creation of measures of protection against adverse effects. The following are the metaverse's obstacles:

### 1.6.1 Hardware

The metaverse relies heavily on VR, AR, and MR technology. For the time being, the metaverse cannot be widely adopted because the majority of these devices are not inexpensive, lightweight, or portable. Having high-quality and high-performance models that can accomplish the correct retina display and pixel density for a realistic virtual immersion is extremely difficult, aside from hardware availability [71, 72].

### 1.6.2 Ethical Concerns

One of the primary ethical concerns surrounding the metaverse in healthcare is the potential for privacy breaches. In a virtual environment, sensitive patient data, such as medical records and personal information, could be vulnerable to cyberattacks or unauthorized access. Additionally, there are concerns about the use of artificial intelligence and algorithms in the metaverse, which could lead to biases or discrimination in healthcare decision-making. Another ethical issue is the potential for exploitation of vulnerable populations. The metaverse could be used to target individuals with chronic illnesses or disabilities for deceptive or predatory practices. It is essential to establish safeguards to protect vulnerable patients and ensure their well-being in this new digital space [73].

### 1.6.3 Privacy and Data Security

Many businesses gather and handle user data in order to make money off of the massive volumes of personal data [74]. Periodically, these multinational corporations (MNCs) encounter data breaches. Thus, user privacy and physical as well as psychological security must come first when creating the metaverse, especially in the healthcare industry. The metaverse logs users' behavior in addition to email addresses and passwords. Significant security concerns are inevitable in the metaverse due to the large number of individuals and devices that are connected. This health metaverse's underlying technology stack emphasizes even more the dangers and difficulties of keeping a secure system in place. The doctor-patient relationship's integrity is in jeopardy due to these hazards. Investigating methods to stop these problems in the future is crucial [75].

### 1.6.4 Identity Hacking

It is not always clear whether an online friend will be as interesting in person as they are on social media. Similar difficulties occur in the metaverse, where people interact using avatars. Establishing your identity in the metaverse can be difficult because bots can quickly mimic your style, data, demeanor, and even your complete persona. To ensure authenticity, several validation techniques will be required, such as recognition of faces, eye scans, and voice recognition [72]. In the metaverse, virtual clones of humans may be built, mirroring both their activities and personality characteristics. The creation of such "copies" could be used for a variety of criminal purposes, including distributing false information, intentional misidentification, identity theft, and body swapping. XR could be used as a platform to portray persons participating in immoral activities, ultimately harming their social reputation.

### 1.6.5 Addiction and Mental Health

The metaverse represents an opportunity to escape the real world since the users can interact with avatars and attend events in the digital environment. However, one should be cautious with immersive effects because they may have negative connotations in actual life. Swelling, cardiovascular issues, and even mental challenges such as sadness and anxiety are reported to be a result of overreliance in the metaverse [72]. This is because some of the activities in the metaverse are actual, and with real-world stimuli, the ability to make the right decisions may be impaired thus leading to undesirable behaviors. Consistent with the previous findings, it was reported that various kinds of mental health problems such as physical and non-physical complaints, feelings of sadness, paranoid ideology, and severe mental illness are all positively associated with the overuse of digital technology. Social isolation, suicidal tendencies and feelings, mental health disorders, deterioration of physical health, and problems such as hazardous behaviors might affect highly engaged metaverse users due to advancing technology [74].

### 1.6.6 Regulatory and Legal Issues

In many areas, regulation has not been able to keep up with the rate of evolution of the metaverse. Such absence of consultation leads to confusion among healthcare professionals, patients, and policymakers. Policies that encompass every aspect of the use of metaverse in healthcare, including data privacy conduct of patients and healthcare professionals, and patient safety, among others, are crucial when it comes to the ethical use of metaverse in the healthcare sector [72].

### 1.6.7 Currency and Digital Payment

For the metaverse to enhance the delivery of care and other services that are provided in the healthcare sector, it should be adopted using standards that make it accessible to all users such as patients, caretakers, medical practitioners, and other personnel. When addressing potential factors, the proposed technology must be easy to use, not expensive, and integrable to existing healthcare systems [72]. The issue of digital disparity also needs to be solved as far as introducing metaverse-based services in healthcare and this connection, underserved communities require attention.

### 1.6.8 Technical Challenges

Healthcare needs a technology landscape able to facilitate the metaverse, and this framework has to be extensive and ever-changing. Problems associated with the network such as latency, compatibility of equipment, and integration of various networks for conveying information to the end user need to be addressed for a smooth and efficient user interface.

## 1.7 Metaverse's Prospects for the Future in Healthcare

As technology advances, we should expect the metaverse to assume a more significant role in healthcare in the future.

### 1.7.1 Predictions for the Future

- **Personalized Healthcare Experiences:** One of the metaverse's possibilities is to provide individualized experiences in the sphere of healthcare that meet the patient's needs and preferences. It is considered to apply such as virtual reality simulations, in persons' treatment strategies, education, and support settings.
- **Advanced Medical Training:** In the metaverse, the training could end up being more authentic and engaging for healthcare professionals. This could in turn see a rise in the level of skills, decreased number of mistakes, and thus increased safety of the patients.
- **Drug Discovery and Development:** The authors also pointed out how the metaverse could catalyze drug discovery by allowing researchers to virtually test new compounds and molecules.
- **Remote Patient Monitoring:** It is also possible that much more complex RPM systems will be created that will allow physicians and other caregivers to track a patient's condition, including his/her symptoms and other vital signs, in real time by using the metaverse.
- **Telehealth and Virtual Care:** The metaverse may complement the telehealth and virtual care models by providing more appealing and engaging interactions for both performers and receivers in the overall medical and healthcare domains.

### 1.7.2 Potential Technological Advancements

Several technological advancements could further impact the metaverse's role in healthcare:

- **Artificial Intelligence:** AI might also help in creating life-like personas of the characters that can better understand patient's needs and requirements and offer them better support and guidance.
- **Haptic Technology:** This working of haptic could give the users a feel of the physical touch in the virtual world improving the realistic medical simulations and training.
- **Brain-Computer Interfaces (BCI):** BCIs could enable users to control the interaction with the metaverse with their mind, which could be more natural.
- **5G and Beyond:** There will be a need for better and faster connectivity for the internet as this will form a backbone for the aspect of high-end graphics and real-time interaction for the metaverse.

### 1.7.3 Long-Term Implications

The long-term implications of the metaverse in healthcare are significant. It could lead to the following:

- **Improved Health Outcomes:** The metaverse has the potential to increase the levels of individualized care, enhanced training for the healthcare staff, and extended telemonitoring, which positively affect patient's overall well-being.
- **Increased Access to Care:** The metaverse could easily bridge the gaps in healthcare by offering specialized care to patients in question in areas that are either underserved or even in other geographic regions.
- **Reduced Healthcare Costs:** In terms of costs, the metaverse can cause a decrease in such healthcare costs due to the elaboration of different processes, their minimization by using such an approach, and cutting such factors as physical facilities' requirements.
- **New Business Models:** The metaverse may open new ventures associated with healthcare industry technology firms and other interested parties.

The presented metaverse can be beneficial for healthcare; however, the given approach will also have some drawbacks. Especially, some questions could be asked regarding the ethical considerations and challenges of the metaverse [76]. We can make use of its potential and construct an eco-friendly healthcare system that is simpler, more efficient, and accessible by addressing future issues related to this technology.

## 1.8 Conclusion

The metaverse is capable of revolutionizing the healthcare industry by bringing advanced solutions to age-old challenges. The metaverse presents a range of possibilities for enhancing patient care, medical education, and research including; virtual surgery practice, telemedicine, mental health management, patient engagement, and education. However, it has to be noted that with the emergence of this technology, proper measures should be taken so that the freedom of innovation does not overshadow the responsibility that it carries.

Hence, as the metaverse progresses, further issues such as the patient's privacy or data protection and accessibility must be discussed. More effort and research along with the participation of technologists, doctors, and policymakers are needed to establish the rules and regulations for safe and ethical application of metaverse technology for the treatment of patients. Together, we can harness the potential of the metaverse to develop an accessible, effective, and more importantly, fair system of healthcare for all.

## References

1. Cheng, S., *Metaverse. Metaverse: Concept, Content and Context*, pp. 1–23, Springer Nature Switzerland, Cham, 2023.
2. Stephenson, N., *Snow crash*, Penguin, United Kingdom, 1994.
3. Zainab, H.E., *et al.*, Virtual dimension-a primer to metaverse. *IT Prof.*, 24, 6, 27–33, 2022.
4. Yawised, K., Apasrawirote, D., Boonparn, C., From traditional business shifted towards transformation: The emerging business opportunities and challenges in 'Metaverse' era. *Incbaa*, 162, 175, 2022.
5. Dudley, J., *et al.*, Inclusive Immersion: a review of efforts to improve accessibility in virtual reality, augmented reality and the metaverse. *Virtual Reality*, 27, 4, 2989–3020, 2023.
6. Zalan, T. and Barbesino, P., Making the metaverse real. *Digital Bus.*, 3, 2, 100059, 2023.

7. Yaqoob, I., *et al.*, Metaverse applications in smart cities: Enabling technologies, opportunities, challenges, and future directions. *Internet Things*, 23, 100884, 2023.
8. Riva, G. and Wiederhold, B.K., What the metaverse is (really) and why we need to know about it. *Cyberpsychol. Behav. Social Networking*, 25, 6, 355–359, 2022.
9. Lee, L.-H., *et al.*, All one needs to know about metaverse: A complete survey on technological singularity, virtual ecosystem, and research agenda, arXiv preprint arXiv:2110.05352, 2021.
10. Duge, C., Metaverse: The Revolution of the Sports World, 2022.
11. Stephens, M., The IEEE global initiative on ethics of extended reality (XT) report, 2022.
12. Lee, L.H., Braud, T., Zhou, P., Wang, L., Xu, D., Lin, Z., Kumar, A., Bermejo, C., Hui, P., All one needs to know about metaverse: A complete survey on technological singularity, virtual ecosystem, and research agenda. *J. Latex Class Files*, 14, 1–66, 2021.
13. Huynh-The, T., Pham, Q.V., Pham, X.Q., Nguyen, T.T., Han, Z., Kim, D.S., Artificial intelligence for the metaverse: A survey. *Eng. Appl. Artif. Intell.*, 117, 1055815, 2023.
14. Gadekallu, T.R., Wang, W., Yenduri, G., Ranaweera, P., Pham, Q.V., da Costa, D.B., Liyanage, M., Blockchain for the metaverse: A review. *Future Gener. Comput. Syst.*, 143, 401–4195, 2023.
15. Nalbant, K.G. and Uyanık, S., Computer vision in the metaverse. *J. Metaverse*, 1, 1, 9–12, 2021.
16. Thomason, J., Metahealth-how will the metaverse change health care? *J. Metaverse*, 1, 1, 13–16, 2021.
17. Lewis, K.O., Popov, V., Fatima, S.S., From static web to metaverse: reinventing medical education in the post-pandemic era. *Ann. Med.*, 56, 1, 2305694, 2024.
18. Chengoden, R., Victor, N., Huynh-The, T., Yenduri, G., Jhaveri, R.H., Alazab, M., Bhattacharya, S., Hegde, P., Maddikunta, P.K.R., Gadekallu, T.R., Metaverse for healthcare: a survey on potential applications, challenges and future directions. *IEEE Access*, 11, 12765–12795, 2023.
19. Ameen, I., Metaverse in Healthcare—New Era is Coming True, Healthcare Business Club, 2022.
20. Strengthening India's Healthcare System With Telemedicine, 2022, Available: https://social-innovation.hitachi/en-in/knowledge-hub/techverse/healthcare-with-telemedicine/.
21. Bansal, G., Rajgopal, K., Chamola, V., Xiong, Z., Niyato, D., Healthcare in metaverse: A survey on current metaverse applications in healthcare. *IEEE Access*, 10, 119914–119946, 2022.
22. Kye, B., Han, N., Kim, E., Park, Y., Jo, S., Educational applications of metaverse: Possibilities and limitations. *J. Educ. Eval. Health Prof.*, *18*, 32, 2020.

23. Zhang, X., Chen, Y., Hu, L., Wang, Y., The metaverse in education: Definition, framework, features, potential applications, challenges, and future research topics. *Front. Psychol.*, *13*, 1016300, 2022.
24. Cook, A., Erwin, P.J., Triola, M.M., Computerized Virtual Patients in Health Professions Education: A Systematic Review and Meta-Analysis. *Acad. Med.*, *85*, 1589–1602, 2019.
25. Al-Elq, A.H., Simulation-based medical teaching and learning. *J. Fam. Commun. Med.*, *17*, 35–40, 2010.
26. Thomason, J., MetaHealth—How will the Metaverse Change Health Care? *J. Metaverse*, *1*, 13–16, 2021.
27. Medical Augmented Intelligence (MAI) Is a Pioneer in the Field of Medical VR Innovations Creating the Google Maps of the Human Body, Available online: www.mai.ai/bodymap/.
28. Bhugaonkar, K., Bhugaonkar, R., Masne, N., The Trend of Metaverse and Augmented & Virtual Reality Extending to the Healthcare System. *Cureus*, *12*, e29071, 2022.
29. Chen, Y., Lin, W., Zheng, Y., Xue, T., Chen, C., Chen, G., Application of Active Learning Strategies in Metaverse to Improve Student Engagement: An Immersive Blended Pedagogy Bridging Patient Care and Scientific Inquiry in Pandemic. *SSRN Electron. J.*, Available at 4098179, 2022. https://ssrn.com/abstract=4098179
30. Suh, I., McKinney, T., Siu, K.-C., Current perspective of metaverse application in medical education, research and patient care. *Virtual Worlds*, 2, 2, 115–128, MDPI, 2023.
31. Ahuja, A.S., Polascik, B.W., Doddapaneni, D., Byrnes, E.S., Sridhar, J., The digital metaverse: Applications in artificial intelligence, medical education, and integrative health. *Intgr. Med. Res.*, 12, 1, 100917, 2023.
32. Girijakumari Sreekantan Nair, S. and Chandrasekaran, B., MetaHealth: unlocking metaverse technologies in digital healthcare. *Expert Rev. Med. Devices*, 21, 727–739, 2024.
33. Z. Biomet, OptivuTM Mixed Reality, Accessed: May 14, 2022. [Online]. Available: https://www.zimmerbiomet.com/en/products-and-solutions/zb-edge/optivu.html.
34. Goharinejad, S., Goharinejad, S., Hajesmaeel-Gohari, S., *et al.*, The usefulness of virtual, augmented, and mixed reality technologies in the diagnosis and treatment of attention deficit hyperactivity disorder in children: an overview of relevant studies. *BMC Psychiatry*, 22, 4, 2022.
35. Freeman, D., Reeve, S., Robinson, A., *et al.*, Virtual reality in the assessment, understanding, and treatment of mental health disorders. *Psychol. Med.*, 47, 2393–400, 2017.
36. Sönmez, D. and Hocaoglu, C., Metaverse and Psychiatry: A Review. *Psikiyatr. Güncel Yaklaşımlar*, 16, 2, 225–238, 2024.

37. De Carvalho, M.R., Dias, T.R.S., Duchesne, M., Nardi, A.E., Appolinario, J.C., Virtual reality as a promising strategy in the assessment and treatment of bulimia nervosa and binge eating disorder: a systematic review. *Behav. Sci.*, 7, 3, 43, 2017.
38. Kim, S. and Kim, E., The use of virtual reality in psychiatry: a review. *J. Korean Acad. Child Adolesc. Psychiatry*, 31, 26–32, 2020.
39. Park, M.J., Kim, D.J., Lee, U., *et al.*, A literature overview of virtual reality (VR) in treatment of psychiatric disorders: recent advances and limitations. *Front. Psychiatry*, 10, 505, 2019.
40. Freeman, D., Bradley, J., Antley, A., *et al.*, Virtual reality in the treatment of persecutory delusions: randomised controlled experimental study testing how to reduce delusional conviction. *Br. J. Psychiatry*, 209, 62–7, 2016.
41. Torous, J., Bucci, S., Bell, I.H., *et al.*, The growing field of digital psychiatry: current evidence and the future of apps, social media, chatbots, and virtual reality. *World Psychiatry*, 20, 318–35, 2021.
42. Cho, K.-H., Park, J.-B., Kang, A., Metaverse for Exercise Rehabilitation: Possibilities and Limitations. *Int. J. Environ. Res. Public Health*, 20, 8, 5483, 2023.
43. https://www.alcimed.com/wp-content/uploads/2023/04/virtual-reality-mental-health.jpg.
44. Vivekitha, V., Caroline Vinnetia, S., Sri Roshini, R., A Metaverse-based approach to rehabilitation healthcare, in: *Metaverse Applications for Intelligent Healthcare*, pp. 182–202, IGI Global, New York, 2024.
45. Wade, D. T, A general theory of rehabilitation: Rehabilitation catalyses and assists adaption to illness, *Clin. Rehabil.*, 38, 4, 429–442, 2024.
46. Reilly, C.A., Greeley, A.B., Jevsevar, D.S., Gitajn, I.L., Virtual reality-based physical therapy for patients with lower extremity injuries: Feasibility and acceptability. *OTA Int.*, 4, 2, e132, 2021.
47. https://www.realsystem.com/wp-content/uploads/2022/11/vr-physical-upper-body-physical-therapy-1.webp
48. Azuma, R., Baillot, Y., Behringer, R., Feiner, S., Julier, S., MacIntyre, B., Recent advances in augmented reality. *IEEE Comput. Graphics Appl.*, 21, 6, 34–47, 2001.
49. Skarbez, R., Smith, M., Whitton, M.C., Revisiting Milgram and Kishino's reality-virtuality continuum. *Front. Virtual Reality*, 2, 647997, 2021.
50. Milgram, P. and Colquhoun, H., A taxonomy of real and virtual world display integration, in: *Mixed reality: Merging real and virtual worlds*, vol. 1, no. 1999, pp. 1–26, 1999.
51. Tripathi, U., Chamola, V., Jolfaei, A., Chintanpalli, A., Advancing remote healthcare using humanoid and affective systems. *IEEE Sens. J.*, 22, 18, 17606–17614, 2021.
52. Stanney, K.M., Nye, H., Haddad, S., Hale, K.S., Padron, C.K., Cohn, J.V., Extended reality (XR) environments, in: *Handbook of human factors and ergonomics*, pp. 782–815, 2021.

53. https://media.licdn.com/dms/image/D4D12AQFySu42D7PWCw/article-cover_image-shrink_600_2000/0/1692959419843?e=2147483647&v=beta&t=xsaoQH-n9Nbu-UEyHEY2hNIR9FoV5l-RHRnmAe5yQMg
54. https://www.meta.com/quest/products/quest-2/?srsltid=AfmBOoqCol-jCraH6zUhRoS7lW58KbBF2SBp6li9DgJcX4-dtYuzh3h4F
55. Le Chénéchal, M. and Chatel-Goldman, J., HTC Vive Pro time performance benchmark for scientific research, in: *Icat-Egve 2018*, 2018.
56. Angelov, V., Petkov, E., Shipkovenski, G., Kalushkov, T., Modern virtual reality headsets, in: *2020 International congress on human-computer interaction, optimization and robotic applications (HORA)*, IEEE, pp. 1–5, 2020.
57. Palumbo, A., Microsoft HoloLens 2 in medical and healthcare context: state of the art and future prospects. *Sensors*, 22, 20, 7709, 2022.
58. Metz, R., Magic leap: a startup is betting more than half a billion dollars that it will dazzle you with its new approach to creating 3-D imagery. *MIT Technol. Rev.*, 118, 2, 28–34, 2015.
59. Oi, H., Evaluation of ryzen 5 and core i7 processors with spec cpu 2017, in: *2019 IEEE International Systems Conference (SysCon)*, IEEE, pp. 1–6, 2019.
60. Subramon, M., Kramer, D., Paul, I., AMD Ryzen™ 7040 series: technology overview, in: *2023 IEEE Hot Chips 35 Symposium (HCS)*, IEEE Computer Society, pp. 1–27, 2023.
61. Flueratoru, L., Lohan, E.S., Nurmi, J., Niculescu, D., HTC Vive as a ground-truth system for anchor-based indoor localization, in: *2020 12th International Congress on Ultra Modern Telecommunications and Control Systems and Workshops (ICUMT)*, IEEE, pp. 214–221, 2020.
62. Caserman, P., Garcia-Agundez, A., Konrad, R., Göbel, S., Steinmetz, R., Real-time body tracking in virtual reality using a Vive tracker. *Virtual Reality*, 23, 155–168, 2019.
63. Whitlock, M., Harnner, E., Brubaker, J.R., Kane, S., Szafir, D.A., Interacting with distant objects in augmented reality, in: *2018 IEEE Conference on Virtual Reality (VR) and 3D User Interfaces*, IEEE, pp. 41–48, 2018.
64. Usmani, S.S., Sharath, M., Mehendale, M., Future of mental health in the metaverse. *Gen. Psychiatry*, 35, 4, 100825, 2022.
65. Popescu, G.H., Ciurlău, C.F., Stan, C.I., Băcănoiu, C., Tănase, A., Virtual workplaces in the metaverse: immersive remote collaboration tools, behavioral predictive analytics, and extended reality technologies. *Psychosociological Issues Hum. Resour. Manage.*, 10, 1, 21–34, 2022.
66. Emmelkamp, P.MG. and Meyerbröker, K., Virtual reality therapy in mental health. *Annu. Rev. Clin. Psychol.*, 17, 1, 495–519, 2021.
67. Sridhar, S., Saraswathi, S., Shri Bharathi, S.V., Devipriya, A., Gamification applications based on metaverse for healthcare industry, in: *Metaverse Technologies in Healthcare*, pp. 233–244, 2024.
68. Tan, T.F., Li, Y., Lim, J.S., Gunasekeran, D.V., Teo, Z.L., Ng, W.Y., Ting, D.S., Metaverse and virtual health care in ophthalmology: Opportunities and challenges. *Asia-Pac. J. Ophthalmol.*, 11, 3, 237–246, 2022.

69. Yang, D., Zhou, J., Chen, R., Song, Y., Song, Z., Zhang, X., Wang, Q., *et al.*, Expert consensus on the metaverse in medicine. *Clin. eHealth*, 5, 1–95, 2022.
70. Stephens, M., Metaverse and its governance. The IEEE Global Initiative on Ethics of Extended Reality (XR), 2022.
71. Kaur, R., Challenges Faced by the Metaverse in Becoming a Reality, 2022.
72. Zikas, P., Papagiannakis, G., Lydatakis, N., Kateros, S., Ntoa, S., Adami, I., Stephanidis, C., Immersive visual scripting based on VR software design patterns for experiential training. *Visual Comput.*, 36, 10, 1965–1977, 2020.
73. Vanitha, C.N. and Sathyamoorthy, M., Awareness of legal and ethical issues in healthcare: A metaverse perspective, in: *Metaverse Technologies in Healthcare*, pp. 245–261, Academic Press, Cambridge, Massachusetts, 2024.
74. Chen, D. and Zhang, R., Exploring research trends of emerging technologies in health metaverse: A bibliometric analysis, Available at SSRN 3998068, 2022.
75. Zhao, R., Zhang, Y., Zhu, Y., Lan, R., Hua, Z., Metaverse: Security and privacy concerns. *J. Metaverse*, 3, 2, 93–99, 2023.
76. Ball, M., *The metaverse: and how it will revolutionize everything*, Liveright Publishing, New York, US, 2022.

2

# Metaverse and Virtual Healthcare: Opportunities and Challenges

**Diksha Dani[1], Gaurav Agrawal[2*] and Abha Kiran Rajpoot[2]**

*[1]Department of Computer Engineering, Mukesh Patel School of Technology, Management and Engineering, SVKM's NMIMS, Mumbai, Maharashtra, India*
*[2]School of Computer Science & Engineering, Galgotias University, Greater Noida, Uttar Pradesh, India*

## *Abstract*
A virtual world made up of mixed reality, augmented reality, and virtual reality is produced by the metaverse. The COVID-19 pandemic which shocked the global society necessitated the need for a virtual healthcare domain to provide rehabilitative services to the greater population safely and efficiently. As digital technology continues to evolve at an unprecedented rate, every aspect of our society is rapidly embracing the virtual realm, eventually blurring the boundaries between the tangible and the digital domains and giving way to the emergence of the metaverse. It is too simplistic to consider the recent advances and conservative actions that can deliver reliable and directive medical care, as the demand on healthcare systems grows. This chapter looks at the various ways in which the metaverse is revolutionizing healthcare in different medical fields. The first part outlines the shifting landscape of healthcare interviews, as the metaverse enables constant virtual intelligence, promoting accessibility and simplifying healthcare delivery. By allowing healthcare professionals to practice challenging techniques in a risk-free setting, virtual reality simulations can enhance skill levels and confidence. Telemedicine is moving toward increasing immersion where patients are provided with virtual consultations and options for treatment in the metaverse. This can make a difference in improving the efficiency and effectiveness of healthcare, particularly in rural or underserved areas. A case study approach can be used to prove the success accomplished of the introduction of virtual programs for wellness with increased patient adherence and operational efficiency that is advanced for healthcare

**Corresponding author*: gauravagrawal1982@gmail.com

Ajay Kumar Vyas, Harleen Kaur, Sourabh Sharma and Bhavya Alankar (eds.) Metaverse Technologies, Security and Applications for Healthcare, (37–56) © 2025 Scrivener Publishing LLC

providers. The social implications tied to the metaverse are staggering in terms of how we will communicate, relate, and form connections.

Social intelligence within virtual environments became more immersive, allowing individuals to socialize, attend events, and participate in shared activities as if they were physically present. Nevertheless, this development poses ethical concerns related to safety, security, and the potential for digital addiction, and must address these complex social issues appropriately.

The subsequent segment explores the various applications of virtual reality technology as well as challenges in the area. The technical, legal, and ethical issues surrounding the adoption of metaverse technology must be addressed.

***Keywords*:** Metaverse, virtual reality, healthcare, augmented reality, digital medicine

## 2.1 Introduction

"Health is wealth" is the saying that we have heard while growing up. Healthcare refers to the wide range of services provided by various trained professionals in the medical sector to prevent, treat, or manage nursing, and allied health professionals to manage, cure, and prevent diseases as well as enhance both physical and emotional well-being collectively referred to as healthcare agencies that provide scientific services, produce medicinal drugs or medical systems, provide health insurance, or otherwise assist patients get hold of healthcare are blanketed in the healthcare region.

Advances in technology, changing demographics, and changing patient needs are causing an unparalleled transition in the global healthcare business. Several significant factors are expected to influence how healthcare is delivered in the future by 2024.

After the recent global COVID-19 pandemic, healthcare systems across the globe are adopting new technology to tackle persistent issues like lower costs, better contactless patient access, lack of infrastructure, and a lack of qualified personnel.

With a market valuation of US$12.31 trillion in 2023, the global hospital services market is projected to increase at a compound annual growth rate (CAGR) of 6.05% from 2024 to 2033, or roughly US$22.57 trillion [1].

Before going into how the details of the metaverse impact healthcare, the concept of the metaverse needs to be understood. The digital and physical worlds are combined in the metaverse, an augmented reality that facilitates more immersive interactions between users and digital things. It is believed that it is the next big change in the internet. The main characteristics of the

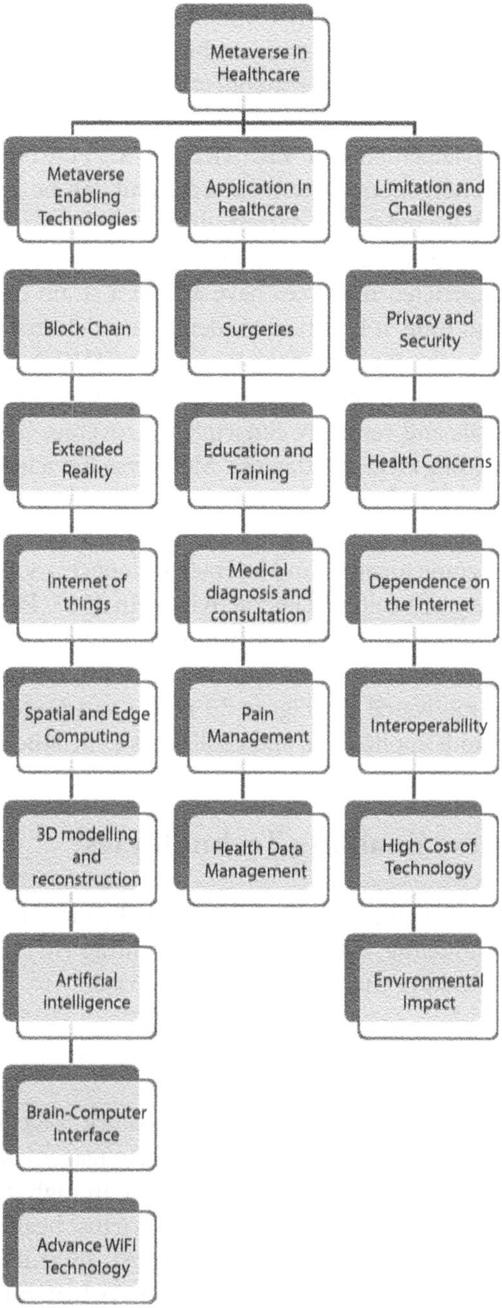


**Figure 2.1** Metaverse in healthcare.

metaverse are the 3D virtual environments in which humans can experience life in ways that are not conceivable in the real world. It is not an interconnected space, but rather a collection of distinct worlds. It is not an interconnected space but instead consists of many individual worlds. Technological advancements in VR, AR, 5G, AI, and blockchain are all catalysts to the emergence of the metaverse and can be seen as a part of Web 3.0, in which we move to a decentralized web [2].

Chronic disease, growing prices, aging populations, an insufficient health workforce, and restricted resources have all put a strain on the healthcare system throughout time. It is critical to identify models that shift healthcare from the hospital to the comfort of the home. The COVID-19 pandemic also prompted inventors and health workers to explore ways to care for patients outside of hospitals and remotely. Smartphone coverage is expanding, and more people are using wearable devices. Metaverse has a lot of potential for the healthcare sector by facilitating real experiences for medical professionals and patients alike. In metaverse patients, physicians, researchers, and practitioners can come together and interact, influence, coordinate, and participate in a variety of health-related activities. In 2017, Pfizer developed a virtual reality game called Hemocraft within Minecraft, targeting children with hemophilia to emphasize the importance of adhering to their treatment plan and staying motivated [3]. Figure 2.1 shows various technologies used in metaverse, various application, and challenges in healthcare domain.

## 2.2 Metaverse Enabling Technologies

Extended reality, 5G, big data, artificial intelligence, edge computing, blockchain, 3D modeling, and the Internet of Things (IoT) are just some of the technologies used in the medical metadatabase.

### 2.2.1 Extended Reality

The use of augmented reality (AR) and virtual reality (VR) in extended reality (XR) technologies improves patient care and engagement, revolutionizing the healthcare industry. XR technologies are in high demand because of the post-pandemic boom in the adoption of virtual healthcare caused by the breaking of physical limits through design, AI, and XR expertise. Users of virtual reality technology can interact with virtual surroundings and objects utilizing real-world movements and interactions. It offers consumers an immersive experience in which they can interact with digitally generated and interconnected virtual components. Currently, virtual reality is most commonly used in video games, providing consumers with a mature platform for immersive gameplay experiences. Augmented reality technology blends virtual objects seamlessly into the real world, providing users with information that enhances their real-world experience. To build a distinctive perceptual world, where digital and physical components can coexist and interact in real time, we find that mixed reality (MR) is the merger of both augmented reality and virtual reality. MR technology is an advancement of augmented reality by making it possible for virtual elements to be manipulated in real-time users can interact with them by, for example, rotating them to see from different angles based on their actions in the real world.

### 2.2.2 Blockchain

The digital ledger, known as blockchain technology, is distinguished by its cryptographic interconnectivity and immutability. Every item in the chain, called a block, has a timestamp indicating when it was accessed or modified in addition to a cryptographic hash that describes the block before it. Because each node in the decentralized peer-to-peer network has a copy of the blockchain, it is extremely resistant to fraud. This is where its security comes from. Because of blockchain's adaptability and capacity to work well with other cutting-edge technologies, it has been integrated into a wide range of industries. Users interact with one another, perform transactions, socialize, and explore virtual surroundings among other activities in immersive virtual spaces within the metaverse. Blockchain technology is at the core because it provides decentralization and makes decentralized features like cryptocurrency trading, digital asset ownership, and NFT monetization possible. Without the integration of blockchain technology, the metaverse will be fragmented because it will not be decentralized and thus vulnerable to centralized data storage [4]. Blockchain technology renders the metaverse accessible by ensuring digital ownership, promoting interoperability, protecting identities, and empowering content creators.

### 2.2.3 Internet of Things

The Internet of Things (IoT) refers to a network of real-world devices such as cars, appliances, and other machines that interact with software, sensors, and network connections to enable data storage and sharing [5]. In healthcare, XR technology can add value to the pillars of well-being by transforming the learning journey through immersive environments where users can gain digital skills and health literacy, reaching populations currently underserved. Regaining trust in the system could be a priority among skeptical or uncertain groups tracking patient's reactions, discovering their individual needs, and providing detailed information could build up trust in the whole system. To recourse to automated screen updating for life-support signals, alerts of fever or mycotic infections can dramatically increase the chances of proper and fast treatment. IoT increases reach in underserved areas by delivering treatment through telemedicine services, remote monitoring, and virtualized consultations. XR can deliver treatment far beyond a physical presence—for example, overcoming the limitations of cybersickness [6].

### 2.2.4 Spatial and Edge Computing

Spatial computing refers to the blending of data by computers from a real physical environment. It is a set of applications such that machines can capture, process, and interact with three-dimensional data in a naturalistic way while being more aware of their 3D surroundings. It may be as simple as flipping on the lights in a room, or it could involve 3D cameras to mimic how a plant operates. Concepts from spatial computing are essential to autonomous applications such as self-driving automobiles, warehouse automation, and supply chain automation.

Virtual reality (VR) headsets that imitate the real environment and mixed reality devices that superimpose data on real-world views are the usual means by which users interact with spatial computing. Camera sensors, digital twins, ambient computing, augmented reality (AR), virtual reality (VR), artificial intelligence (AI), and physical controls are some of the components that make up spatial computing.

Data processing near sensors, actuators, Internet of Things (IoT) objects, and people is made possible via edge computing. In actuality, edge computing equipment may be found on the customer's property or at the boundary of the access network's communication service provider's network [7].

Delivering a virtual world involves a lot of computational power since the display must be adjusted to match the movements of the characters, objects, and surrounding environment while being tracked. The metaverse benefits from edge computing because it reduces bandwidth requirements, minimizes network latency, and stores vast volumes of data locally. Latency is experienced as a lag in virtual worlds, and it decreases with increasing computer capability. Additionally, edge computing lowers bandwidth consumption by executing computations locally as opposed to remotely. It works in tandem with cloud systems when network connections are available. Additionally, edge computing local storage enhances metaverse performance by keeping relevant content closer to users, like that of intelligent mapping systems, which store and retrieve data that has been locally and recently used [8].

### 2.2.5 3D Modeling and Reconstruction

The 3D display involves computer modeling of objects, scenes, and lines using specialized software. These models are dotted, setting the framework for interactive participatory meetings. By accurately resembling the form and appearance of actual items, 3D reconstruction brings the metaverse to life. A three-dimensional framework and prototype of a particular process or product can be created using technologies such as 3D modeling.

The 3D display is important in the metaverse for a few reasons. It allows architects to practically design and test their intentions—promoting faster comprehension and collaboration. Moreover, 3D rings go further into the capability of speaking—displaying or accounting for entertainment/engagement/training/indexation than fashion. Lastly, it ensures that real-world scenarios are worthwhile both in the form of increased large-scale irrigation and consumer participation within the metaverse [9]. Patients can see their medical aid goods in 3D and can choose the right equipment. By utilizing 3D modeling tools provided by the metaverse, doctors can have a better understanding of patient's illnesses. This would let physicians know significantly more and treat them with the amount of precision that they serve. Also, the 3D modeling feature of the metaverse is used by medical researchers to construct artificial organs and analyze their health effects [36].

### 2.2.6 Brain-Computer Interface

BCI lets a person move from thinking about an action to performing this action on a device such as a computer or prosthesis. The interaction between the chip and neurons is closer to the brain's neurons and this makes the signal more clear for the interpretation of the activity of the neurons required [10].

This assumes the shape of digital avatars and functions as the primary suppliers of multimodal data, emphasizing the need for human-centric design. Because they can communicate directly with the brain, technologies like brain-computer interfaces (BCIs) have the potential to significantly enhance the metaverse experience. They enable thought-speed, intuitive human-machine communication. The app user experience includes status monitoring, avatar control, virtual interaction, and speech recognition. Neural pathways are used to generate new metaverse information [11].

### 2.2.7 Artificial Intelligence

Artificial intelligence (AI) is a branch of computer science that is dedicated to analyzing natural language cues to produce actions that resemble those of a human. AI systems demonstrate thinking, autonomy, and self-learning through preprogrammed commands. AI is consistent with several fundamental characteristics within the metaverse. First and foremost, the goal of AI research is to create machines that can comprehend natural language—a necessary skill for communicating inside the metaverse. Second, AI makes it possible to handle data more quickly and effectively by using machine learning to evaluate and absorb the massive amounts of data produced in the metaverse. AI is already being used by users in daily life through programs like machine learning–powered personalized recommendations. The goal of current AI research is to improve user relevance through a better understanding of both the physical world and human behavior.

Through the use of data created from digital actions in virtual spaces and the acceleration of development processes, artificial intelligence (AI) holds great promise for improving the metaverse. While different businesses are creating their metaverse platforms, the ultimate goal is to create a global platform that is open to everyone, without limitations, and artificial intelligence (AI) can be a key component in making this vision a reality [12, 13].

### 2.2.8 Advanced Wi-Fi Technology

The metaverse requires advanced wireless technology, which is faster, and has less latency. 5G improves digital experiences and commercial applications with rates over 20 Gbps and lower latency, which helps businesses and industries including smart cities and smart healthcare. These developments will have a big influence on the metaverse because they offer the high bandwidth and low latency needed for immersive technologies like AR, VR, and IoT, which makes it easier to create rich media content.

5G and higher Wi-Fi technology allow the metaverse in the healthcare industry to offer doctors and patients top-notch immersive experiences that will improve complicated procedures, mental health, and virtual well-being. By guaranteeing that real-time activities correspond with the surgeon's instructions, 5G's ultralow latency lowers the hazards associated with remote surgeries.

The healthcare industry's metaverse requires 5G and higher Wi-Fi technology to provide doctors and patients with top-notch immersive experiences that will improve complicated procedures, mental health, and virtual well-being. By guaranteeing that real-time activities correspond with the surgeon's instructions, 5G's ultralow latency lowers the hazards associated with remote surgeries [36].

## 2.3 Application in Healthcare

The patient experience, medical education, research, and other facets of the healthcare industry could all be significantly altered and amplified by the metaverse. Here are some examples of how the metaverse is being applied to medicine, as shown in Figure 2.2.

### 2.3.1 Metaverse in Surgeries

Surgeons can meticulously prepare for potential complications by creating precise 3D reconstructions of the patient's anatomy derived from CT scans and MRI image data.

Remote robot-assisted surgery shows promise as a viable and secure option. Transmitting live surgical maneuvers remotely has the potential to provide access to surgical expertise in distant areas for challenging or

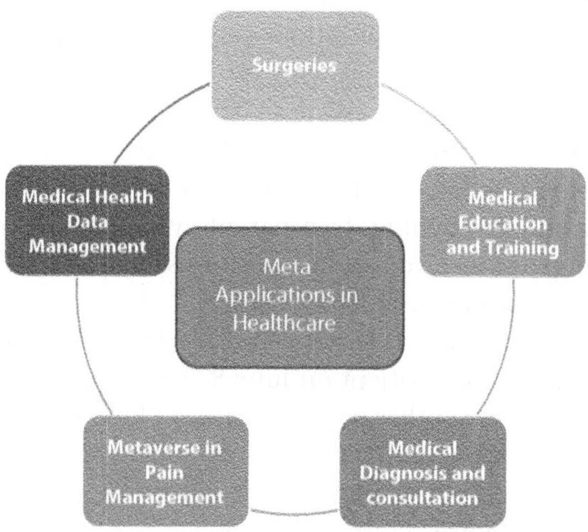


**Figure 2.2** Application of metaverse in healthcare.

uncommon procedures, thereby enhancing surgical training globally. The haptic glove technology allows users to sense the feel of touch in the virtual world [14]. This was demonstrated by [15] where the authors conducted robot-assisted laparoscopic cholecystectomy was performed on a 68-year-old female patient with a history of abdominal pain and cholelithiasis. The surgical team is in New York and the patient is in Strasbourg. A high-speed fixed-line Internet connection (ATM service) facilitates communication between two locations.

Virtual and augmented reality technologies have been noted for their significant contributions to surgical procedures and the training of surgeons. The metaverse holds vast potential benefits for both surgical and cosmetic dermatology, given that the skin, being an accessible organ, is exceptionally well-suited for visualization aided by augmented and virtual reality technologies.

In 2023, the global market size for surgical operations within the metaverse reached a valuation of US$6.28 billion. It is predicted to hit about US$73.37 billion by 2032, with a total CAGR of 31% in the 2017–2022 period and a growth rate of 40% within the forecast period between 2023 and 2032 [16]. Based on these points of the present, we may conclude that surgery planning with haptic assistance can encompass exhaustive parameters of both the surgical procedure and the outstanding results. The use of haptic communication technology lets the operators feel kinesthetic and vibrotactile feedback immediately; they make the process straightforward without compromising precision [17].

Metaverse can be overseen by surgeons and allow them to perform surgical support via the use of applications such as augmented reality, virtual reality, or mixed reality. Many growing healthcare organizations and hospitals use these technologies to create a virtual model of the patient's body.

The latest and actual use of augmented reality (AR) in live neurosurgeries at the Johns Hopkins Hospital is revolutionizing the field of medical science. Using an eye-opening, transparent eye apparatus mounted on a headset, the surgeons received cleansing visions of a patient's internal anatomy using CT scans, a form of X-ray vision.

This technology facilitated the successful fusion of three vertebrae to alleviate back pain in one patient on June 8, 2020, and the extraction of a malignant tumor from another patient's spine on June 10. Both patients are reported to be recovering well. AR holds immense promise in enhancing surgical precision and improving patient outcomes, as demonstrated by these groundbreaking procedures [18].

Another scenario of application of metaverse in surgery is image-guided neurosurgery, allowing real-time projection of images highlighting specific areas onto the patient's head, skull, or brain surface and found to be accurate and reliable [19].

Experts can help patients recuperate from surgery by providing physiotherapy, stress and anxiety reduction, and sleep aids using the metaverse technology.

### 2.3.2 Education and Training

The goal of the metaverse in medicine is to improve training effectiveness and training efficacy. It talks about the difficulties faced by cloud professionals who cannot always be there to provide professional lectures, scientific instruction, or diagnosis and treatment.

Explaining that through such manipulations of the object, it is possible to help healthcare workers become even more proficient and safe, without compromising the lives of patients. For example, the contracted business relationship management comprehensive system includes a holographic simulated learning course to teach the pupils about smoking as one of the factors leading to lung carcinoma. By so doing, through the use of this persuasive technique, the students were able to learn an elaborate way about the damage caused to the alveoli by smoking and its connection to lung cancer. With this technology, pupils can also be taught different medical procedures. For instance, creating an effective learning environment can help respiratory specialists acquire skills for performing operations such as endoscopic surgery with magnetic navigation in a shorter period [34, 35]. In the study in which the laparoscopic colorectal skills directly performed on a human cadaver model and those with an augmented reality simulator were compared to evaluate, the instructors and students explored higher scores on the augmented reality simulator rather than the cadaver [20]. Education also becomes significantly different and less limited because of the metaverse: flexibility, immersion, and the possibility to interact.

Learners can attend class anytime, anywhere, use advanced avatars, and create social and personalized learning sessions. In contrast to a traditional setting, where intellectuals are restricted, the metaverse empowers rich, multisensory support, empowering learners and enhancing collaboration and productivity. Virtual learning landscapes and smart assets improve comprehension and encourage active learning. Furthermore, the research in the metaverse focuses on student achievement, benefiting from comprehensive testing of information rather than relying solely on test scores [21]. More broadly, metaverse remeasures instruction to build students' higher-order thinking and adapt to future challenges. They are capable of doing so.

### 2.3.3 Medical Diagnosis and Consultation

Telemedicine has seen widespread adoption during the COVID-19 pandemic, but its capabilities could be further amplified with the integration of the metaverse. Within this digital realm, patients could interact with their doctors in immersive three-dimensional virtual waiting rooms, elevating telemedicine sessions to a more advanced and comprehensive level.

Such is the case with the ability to rigidly apply the metaverse to medical diagnosis, as this has the real potential of turning healthcare procedures into something utterly different. Some of the technologies such as virtual reality (VR) and augmented reality (AR) make it possible for medical experts to conduct extensive examinations and analysis through fully simulated virtual settings. Patients may also be able to get diagnoses through remote care; additionally, it means that people can get doctors and medical equipment wherever they are. Besides, the metaverse provides opportunities for joint diagnostics meaning that medical teams can discuss, share, and arrive at the correct decision collectively. Considering all the factors, it could be deduced that the integration of metaverse into medical diagnosis would enhance the delivery of medical care and its precision [22, 23].

### 2.3.4 Metaverse in Pain Management

There are so many studies that have focused on how this technology can help not only adults but also children who suffer from acute or chronic pain. The incorporation of virtual reality in the management of pain translates to several strategies that are used in the process. Some of these methods consist of mindfulness exercises which serve to help clients tune into the present, meditation with breathing exercises to calm the patient's nerves, and CBT methods that are used to encourage the patient to think positively. Moreover, interventions focus on controlling mood which reduces stress, anxiety, and depression which are some of the outcomes of pain. In addition, external stimuli in the form of cues help to distract the brain's focus from pain and take advantage of the notion stating that the less mental capacity is dedicated to the process of feeling pain the lighter the subjective experience of this sensation.

Through the strategic application of these techniques within virtual environments, individuals undergoing pain management can experience enhanced relief and improved coping mechanisms. Studies have shown that virtual reality has the potential to lessen pain and enhance the efficacy of other pain-relieving methods like hypnosis, physical therapy, or cognitive behavioral therapy [24, 25].

### 2.3.5 Medical Health Data Management

Utilizing the metaverse to supervise wellness information has changed the way that healing records are positioned away, gotten to, and expanded. People's comprehension and engagement with their wellness statistics can be upgraded by being able to securely get to their restorative statistics in immersive, intuitive groups through virtual environments. Furthermore, restorative professionals may utilize the metaverse to form lively reenactments that would empower preparing and instructing in actual-world virtual conditions for restorative professionals. In expansion, the metaverse gives a stage for statistics sharing and investigation among scholastics and training around the sector.

## 2.4 Limitations and Challenges

There exist several constraints, including hands-on training for surgeons using cadavers and the absence of a truly immersive experience. However, the emergence of more affordable virtual reality enhancements and holographic projections, which do not inducc discomfort, has the potential to challenge traditional in-person meetings significantly [26].

### 2.4.1 Privacy and Security

Large volumes of personal data are required to be collected and shared in the metaverse, which may be used maliciously or to abuse users. In a metaverse setting, for instance, who will have access to patient data and how would it be used? The technology is used to track the online behavior of users, potentially leading to even mor1e invasive and intensive tracking practices. Companies will be able to see users' physical reactions as they link to wearable and haptic devices that identify emotions and physical reactions, which violates a person's right to privacy and poses a potential security risk.

Another issue is maintaining accuracy, currency, and adherence to established medical standards within metaverse material, which is critical for preventing the spread of disinformation. Precision is essential in medicine, and any mistakes in simulations or scenarios could lead to inadequate training and represent a risk to patient safety.

### 2.4.2 Health Concerns

Due to telemedicine services and remote patient monitoring, the modern digital revolution in healthcare systems has resulted in the loss of personal communication and touch between doctors and patients. Without having to speak with patients in person, doctors remotely recommend therapies based on their descriptions or digital health information. The metaverse, on the other hand, can close this gap by providing patients and healthcare professionals with an immersive virtual environment that improves effective and efficient interaction alternatives. Because current digital treatment modes do not allow for in-person contact, many patients lose the special link that can be developed. Patients may feel alone as a result of this digital approach, which could hinder their chances of recovery [37].

Experts are also becoming more concerned about how the metaverse is affecting mental health as data suggest that excessive use of digital technology is associated with several mental health problems. A peer-reviewed paper in Psychology Today claims that diseases like depression, psychoticism, and paranoid ideation have been linked to extended usage of digital gadgets. Several indicators have been linked to digital addiction, such as spending hours on digital devices, thinking about using them all the time, getting cravings to use them, losing interest in social activities that you used to enjoy, and participating in risky behaviors like using devices while cooking or crossing the street. Using virtual reality gadgets excessively might cause unpleasant side effects like headaches, vertigo, and eye strain. Moreover, prolonged sitting and inactivity can be detrimental to one's physical well-being. These symptoms highlight the need for management techniques and awareness to address the possible negative effects of metaverse usage on mental health [27, 28].

### 2.4.3 Dependence on the Internet

Additional limits include computer computational skills and the availability of internet bandwidth for streaming photos, which is especially important in rural areas with restricted access. To use virtual and augmented reality, it is required that both students' and educators' digital devices like smartphones and laptops with appropriate processing power and internet connectivity. Furthermore, immersive experiences demand costly technology, such as visors or spectacles for virtual and augmented reality. To meet the needs of economically weaker sections, technical support, and equipment must be provided so that they can take benefit from the technology.

### 2.4.4 Interoperability

The success of metaverse systems depends on interoperability, which makes sure that services and virtual worlds are fluidly connected rather than isolated. Businesses may find it difficult to create services that function across several metaverse platforms without interoperability, and users may find it difficult to switch between different platforms. A global network of interconnected systems is created by an interoperable metaverse service, which means that developers must follow a set of public and private rules and regulations.

XR industry analysts predict that the metaverse is about to undergo a sea change similar to what happened to HTML on the internet. Similar to using a web browser, this "HTML moment" would allow users to access XR internet services through a variety of metaverse platforms [29].

### 2.4.5 High Cost of Technology

The healthcare industry will require advanced technology to fully reap the benefits of the metaverse. Infrastructure for technology needs to be updated, especially in economies that are still expanding. Virtual reality (VR) and robotic surgeries are two examples of how healthcare technology is developing quickly and how it is used in different medical services. To improve accuracy and efficiency, augmented reality (AR) and virtual reality (VR) are especially used in medical education and intricate surgical operations. The functionality of medical equipment and gadgets is enhanced by these developments.

The emergence of metaverse-focused startups has accelerated the global development of cutting-edge AR- and VR-based surgical environment enhancement technologies. However, in order to use the metaverse in healthcare effectively, precise patient condition monitoring will require high-tech wearables like gloves, eyewear, and sensors. Wearables have many advantages, but their expensive price prevents them from being widely used and forces users to buy new gear as technology advances. This would necessitate significant infrastructural spending. It is expensive to have anything from a constant 5G internet connection to wearable technology and other high-tech devices. This technology is only available to those who can afford it. Furthermore, these gadgets will continuously advance and modernize. It will be necessary to purchase new equipment in order to utilize the additional capabilities [30–32].

### 2.4.6 Environmental Impact

A large amount of processing power is needed for the metaverse, which could harm the environment. It is crucial to create more environmentally friendly methods of powering the metaverse and reducing its influence on the environment.

Another thing to consider is the waste that comes with the hardware that users need to access the metaverse, much as the current surge in trash from smartphones proved to be an issue. Waste originating from devices must be avoided by the XR hardware sector.

It seems that more and more gadgets are making their appearance on the XR market, but what happens to older gadgets? Enterprise end users need to make sure that their hardware investments are future-proof to maintain return on investment and take sustainability into account [33].

## 2.5 Conclusion

As demonstrated by its uses in surgery, medical education and training, diagnosis and consultation, pain management, and health data management, the healthcare industry stands to gain much from the integration of the metaverse. The metaverse creates new opportunities for patient care, medical education, and research advancement by facilitating detailed planning, remote surgery, and immersive therapeutic experiences for patients.

Apart from its immense potential, the metaverse presents some challenges and shortcomings. These include concerns about privacy and security, the need for accuracy and adherence to medical standards, potential negative effects on health, and dependence on internet connectivity and technological infrastructure. Addressing these concerns will be crucial to maximizing the benefits of the metaverse in healthcare while reducing risks and ensuring equitable access for all, irrespective of location or socio-economic level.

In conclusion, despite the metaverse's immense potential to revolutionize healthcare delivery, effective management of its complexities and realizing its full potential to improve global health outcomes would require collaboration across stakeholders.

## References

1. Hospital Services Market, 2023, https://www.precedenceresearch.com/hospital-services-market.
2. Hackl, C., Lueth, D., Di Bartolo, T., *Navigating the metaverse: a guide to limitless possibilities in a Web 3.0 world*, John Wiley & Sons, Hoboken, New Jersey, U.S., 2022.
3. Metaverse Technology in Healthcare Industry, 2022, https://thinkml.ai/metaverse-technology-in-healthcare-industry.
4. Metaverse and Blockchain, 2022, https://rejolut.com/blog/metaverse-and-blockchain/.
5. Asif, R. and Hassan, S.R., Exploring the Confluence of IoT and Metaverse: Future Opportunities and Challenges. *IoT*, 4, 3, 412–429, 2022, https://doi.org/10.3390/iot4030018.
6. Li, K., *et al.*, When Internet of Things Meets Metaverse: Convergence of Physical and Cyber Worlds. *IEEE Internet Things J.*, 10, 5, 4148–4173, 2023, doi: 10.1109/JIOT.2022.3232845.
7. Xu, M. and Niyato, D., Edge Computing Technologies for Metaverse, in: *Metaverse Communication and Computing Networks*, Hoang, D.T., Nguyen, D.N., Nguyen, C.T., Hossain, E., Niyato, D. (Eds.), 2023, https://doi.org/10.1002/9781394160013.ch8.
8. Wolber, A., How edge computing will support the metaverse, 2022, https://www.techrepublic.com/article/edge-computing-supports-metaverse/.
9. Gossa, K., The Power of 3D Modeling in Shaping the Future of the Metaverse, 2022, https://www.advertflair.com/post/why-3d-modeling-is-essential-for-the-future-of-the-metaverse.
10. Becher, B., Brain Computer Interfaces (BCI) Explained, 2023, https://builtin.com/hardware/brain-computer-interface-bci.
11. Zhu, H.Y., Hieu, N.Q., Hoang, D.T., Nguyen, D.N., Lin, C.-T., A Human-Centric Metaverse Enabled by Brain-Computer Interface: A Survey. *IEEE Commun. Surv. Tutorials*, 26, 3, 2120–2145, thirdquarter 2024, doi: 10.1109/COMST.2024.3387124.
12. Huynh-The, T., Pham, Q.V., Pham, X.Q., Nguyen, T.T., Han, Z., Kim, D.S., Artificial intelligence for the metaverse: A survey. *Eng. Appl. Artif. Intell.*, 117, 105581, 2023.
13. Howell, J., The Role of Artificial Intelligence (AI) in the Metaverse, 2023, https://101blockchains.com/artificial-intelligence-and-metaverse/.
14. Hassan, Z., Real-World Use Cases Of Haptic Gloves For Virtual Reality Training, 2023, https://elearningindustry.com/real-world-use-cases-of-haptic-gloves-for-virtual-reality-training.
15. Marescaux, J., Leroy, J., Rubino, F., Smith, M., Vix, M., Simone, M., Mutter, D., Transcontinental robot-assisted remote telesurgery: feasibility and potential applications. *Ann. Surg.*, 235, 4, 487–92, 2002, doi: 10.1097/00000658-200204000-00005. PMID: 11923603; PMCID: PMC1422462.

16. Precedence research, 2023, https://www.precedenceresearch.com/metaverse-in-surgical-operations-market.
17. Bonmarin, M., Läuchli, S., Navarini, A., Augmented and Virtual Reality in Dermatology—Where Do We Stand and What Comes Next? *Dermato*, 2, 1, 1–7, 2022.
18. Augmented Reality Guides Surgeries for Johns Hopkins Patients, 2021, https://www.hopkinsmedicine.org/news/articles/2021/04/augmented-reality-guides-surgeries-for-johns-hopkins-patients.
19. Tabrizi, L.B. and Mahvash, M., Augmented reality-guided neurosurgery: accuracy and intraoperative application of an image projection technique. *J. Neurosurg.*, 123, 206–211, 2015, doi: 10.3171/2014.9.JNS141001.
20. Leblanc, F., Champagne, B.J., Augestad, K.M., Neary, P.C., Senagore, A.J., Ellis, C.N., Delaney, C.P., A Comparison of Human Cadaver and Augmented Reality Simulator Models for Straight Laparoscopic Colorectal Skills Acquisition Training. *J. Am. Coll. Surg.*, 211, 2, 250–255, 2010, ISSN 1072-7515, https://doi.org/10.1016/j.jamcollsurg.04.002.2010.
21. Zhang, X., Chen, Y., Hu, L., Wang, Y., The metaverse in education: Definition, framework, features, potential applications, challenges, and future research topics. *Front. Psychol.*, 13, 1016300, 2022.
22. Wang, Y., Liu, Y., Shi, Y., Yu, Y., Yang, J., User perceptions of virtual hospital apps in China: systematic search. *JMIR Mhealth Uhealth*, 8, 8, e19487, 2020, doi: 10.2196/19487.
23. Wang, Y., Li, C., Qu, L., Cai, H., Ge, Y., Application and challenges of a metaverse in medicine. *Front. Robot. AI*, 10, 1291199, 2023, doi: 10.3389/frobt.2023.1291199.
24. Alkhaldi, N., How healthcare professionals use virtual reality for pain management, March 29, 2023, https://itrexgroup.com/blog/virtual-reality-for-pain-management/.
25. Gupta, A., Scott, K., Dukewich, M., Innovative Technology Using Virtual Reality in the Treatment of Pain: Does It Reduce Pain via Distraction, or Is There More to It? *Pain Med.*, 19, 1, 151–159, 2018, https://doi.org/10.1093/pm/pnx109.
26. Chapman, J.R., Wang, J.C., Wiechert, K., Into the Spine Metaverse: Reflections on a future Metaspine (Uni-)verse. *Global Spine J.*, 12, 4, 545–547, 2022, doi: 10.1177/21925682221085643.
27. Tharwani, K., Problems & Disadvantages Of The Metaverse, 2022, https://www.opengrowth.com/resources/problems-disadvantages-of-the-metaverse.
28. Phil, P.R.D., Will the Metaverse Impact Mental Health?, 2021, https://www.psychologytoday.com/us/blog/digital-world-real-world/202110/will-the-metaverse-impact-mental-health.
29. Swider, P., The Future of Healthcare & Patient Care in the Metaverse, 2022, https://accelerationeconomy.com/metaverse/the-future-of-healthcare-patient-care-in-the-metaverse/.

30. How will the Metaverse change the Healthcare Industry, 2022, https://sdlc-corp.com/post/how-will-the-metaverse-change-the-healthcare-industry/.
31. DelveInsight Blog, How Metaverse is Set to Transform the Healthcare Dynamics?, 2022, https://www.delveinsight. com/blog/metaverse-in-healthcare.
32. Ameen, I., Metaverse in Healthcare—New Era is Coming True, 2022, https://healthcarebusinessclub.com/articles/healthcare-provider/technology/metaverse-in-healthcare.
33. What are the Biggest Issues Facing the Metaverse?, 2023, https://www.xrtoday.com/virtual-reality/what-are-the-biggest-issues-facing-the-metaverse/.
34. Chen, C., J.W., Chen, C., Application of holographic projection technology in medical field and medical education. *Chin J. Med. Educat. Explorat.*, 19, 11, 3, 2020.
35. Zhitao Yao, W.A., Application of virtual simulation technology based on MOOCs model in clinical practice teaching of maxillofacial surgery undergraduates. *Curricul. Educat. Res.*, 10, 3, 2021.
36. Chengoden, R., *et al.*, Metaverse for Healthcare: A Survey on Potential Applications, Challenges and Future Directions. *IEEE Access*, 11, 12765–12795, 2023, doi: 10.1109/ACCESS.2023.3241628.
37. Teh, D., Is the metaverse the future of health?, 2022, [Online]. Available: https://healthmatch.io/blog/is-the-metaverse-the-future-of-health.

3

# Innovation and Accountability: An Ethical Perspective on Metaverse Healthcare

**Ajay Sudhir Bale**

*Department of ECE, New Horizon College of Engineering, Bengaluru, Karnataka, India*

### *Abstract*
This chapter focuses on metaverse technologies that guarantee to improve the medical facility via online therapy, healthcare education, medical training, research studies, and many visualization ways. These platforms provide a lot of advantages but at the same time pose a lot of ethical issues. Medical metaphysical realms, online clinical investigations, intelligent wellness avatars, AI doctor chatbots, and genes technology and scientific websites give rise to worries regarding responsibility, confidentiality, individuals' safety disputes of interest, equitable involvement, and how to make use of virtual good health findings to actual-life scenarios. Ensuring public trust in health simulation systems calls for deliberate governance, ethics-based regulations, and methods for human responsibility, notwithstanding the convenience, customization, and openness offered by the metaverse. With the growing acceptance of the metaverse, physicians need to focus on ethical considerations related to patient approval, utilization of data, procedure oversight, accessibility rules, and responsibility. This is crucial to ensure that these novel devices effectively promote medical morality and strengthen the relationship between patients and healthcare providers. There is a need for well-defined regulations, rigorous safety standards, unbiased datasets, and studies of the impact of healthcare applications in the metaverse.

***Keywords***: Metaverse, ethical, healthcare, regulations, trust

*Email*: ajaysudhirbale@gmail.com

Ajay Kumar Vyas, Harleen Kaur, Sourabh Sharma and Bhavya Alankar (eds.) Metaverse Technologies, Security and Applications for Healthcare, (57–80) © 2025 Scrivener Publishing LLC

## 3.1 Introduction

In the next generations, the digital revolution propelled by rapidly developing virtual reality (VR) and metaverse technologies is expected to significantly transform and improve healthcare. Virtual clinics, AI-assisted healthcare, genetic engineering, 3D-printed organs, and other immersive innovations offer enticing opportunities to reduce expenses, increase accessibility, deliver personalized therapy, and enhance patient outcomes [1, 2]. However, these new applications for health care in multifaceted virtual worlds also bring with them dangerous moral conundrums about patient safety, privacy of data, and the appropriate employment of artificial intelligence (AI) capabilities in situations where governance is unclear. These instances are causing complicated discussions that balance ease and rapid advancement against morality and medical ethical norms that prioritize "first no harm" [3, 4]. Researchers alert that the lack of careful protection and oversight processes that strike a balance between scientific advancement and safeguarding the public could undermine patient trust in metaverse medical care, exacerbate already-existing inequalities, and have unintended societal repercussions from clinical tools used unnaturally without or without consent [1, 5, 6].

The main worry in the ethical discussions surrounding the healthcare metaverse is that governance mechanisms, regulatory guidelines [7], and public trust calibration are moving at a slower rate than technology innovation and disruption. The primary emphasis of healthcare organizations that are drawn to the conveniences offered by AI-assisted diagnostics [8], virtual nursing care [9], robotic surgery [10], and continuous health monitoring via wearables and apps seem to have cost and clinical efficiency [11]. They consistently downplay the need for openness about data use, permission procedures for testing novel digital medicines, and accountability gaps that skew safety and effectiveness standards in the real world. Critics contend that this accelerating "ethical asymmetry," in which scientific advancements surpass moral reasoning and value-aligned oversight by an exponential amount, poses a threat to the integrity of healthcare metaverses. They see it as a place where conflicts of interest, privacy violations, unequal access, and unintentional patient harms stemming from hastily implemented, "move fast and break things" algorithms can arise. Such damages are more than hypothetical possibilities, as shown by cases of racial and gender prejudice appearing in AI-enabled clinical decision tools [1, 5, 12, 13], unlawful sharing of private therapy session data from online mental health platforms, and dangerous advice from poorly built nursery chatbots. Experts warn that in the absence of serious safeguarding measures, the healthcare metaverse runs the risk of turning into morally bankrupt "lawless territories," controlled by the same profit-before-principles mentality that has led to numerous social media and Internet platforms regularly jeopardizing user safety in the name of increased engagement and data monetization. Ethical measures are required to get ahead of comparable damages in the healthcare metaverse driven solely by returns-focused ventures, just as moral reasoning lagged to prevent damages from the unchecked rise of disinformation, emotional manipulation [14], and persuasive design on an advertising-based Internet. Because of this, some contend that the healthcare sector has to stop approaching ethics as an afterthought and adopt an "ethics-by-design" approach that incorporates permission, openness, accountability, and accessibility into metaverse experiences from the beginning. By doing this, expectations for innovation would be balanced with moral considerations for patient welfare and the preservation of the public interest [15].

Based on recent adoption case studies and policy discussions, this chapter examines the key ethical issues, gaps, and guiding principles driving the healthcare metaverse's evolution. Transparency, accountability, privacy, patient empowerment, accessibility, developer objectives, and the applicability of virtual therapies to real-world patient populations are among the fundamental concerns examined. The scope of ethical issues arising from the rapid expansion of virtual healthcare is discussed, along with governance preparedness and choices for forms of ethics by design that are seen favorably by the public. In the end, the research makes the case for the creation of an ethical framework grounded in medical ethics and moral reasoning, one that places a priority on patient rights and ethical innovation in the more complex, decentralized, and immersive healthcare metaverses that are rapidly approaching.

## 3.2 Methodology

This research employs a comprehensive methodology for reviewing the literature to succinctly outline significant perspectives, debates, and ethical challenges about the current and future use of the metaverse in healthcare. Figure 3.1 displays the situations presented in this chapter, which specifically examine scientific articles and preprints that address significant concerns, risks, and moral quandaries related to the intended and present utilization of mixed reality, VR, and augmented reality (AR) platforms in patient care, clinical investigations, healthcare training, and biological data use cases. They also prioritize risk assessments for the public sector, government, and nonprofit groups, which identify regulatory gaps, deficiencies in patient safety, and challenges in expanding immersive healthcare technology. The study is structured around market research and private sector studies that demonstrate the pace of metaverse innovation in the healthcare sector, as well as the ethical perspectives of technology businesses and medical professionals using these kinds of platforms.

The cases of possible ethical dilemmas relating to the metaverse in healthcare are presented as follows:

### 3.2.1 Medical Training Metaverse

A metaverse platform for medical education has been developed to instruct students in performing lifelike simulations of operations, diagnosing patients using VR scenarios, and participating in role-playing exercises using AI-assisted avatars portraying patients. However, concerns are raised about informed permission, patient privacy, and the morality of gathering and using virtual patient data from the metaverse for training purposes.

Medical students, residents, nurses, and other healthcare workers may benefit from medical training metaverse simulations that use virtual, augmented, and mixed-reality platforms. Virtual medical training, powered by the presence and interactivity of new extended reality (XR) technology, has many advantages, such as the ability to practice rare procedures multiple times with less risk, gather data on trainees' diagnostic abilities, and increase access to team-based crisis training through experience.

For instance, with the use of haptic gloves, goggles, and motion sensors, platforms such as Osso VR and MediVizor immerse trainees in realistic simulations of specialized surgeries, patient case assessments, procedure communication with families, device operation, and compassionate delivery of bad medical news. While the clinical student observes events from the first-person perspective, AI-powered simulated patients may exhibit symptoms and emotions. Unfortunately, several ethical concerns come up when considering medically accurate scenarios. These include protecting the privacy of patient's data, ensuring that informed consent is obtained from any actual patients whose records are used in the simulations, possible intellectual property issues with virtually recreating patented devices or surgeries, obstacles to accessibility caused by the need for expensive specialized equipment, and the overall integrity of scenario design in influencing clinical judgments. VR training poses a risk to patients if it alters real-world decision-making via the presentation of erroneous, biased, or exaggerated unpleasant experiences.

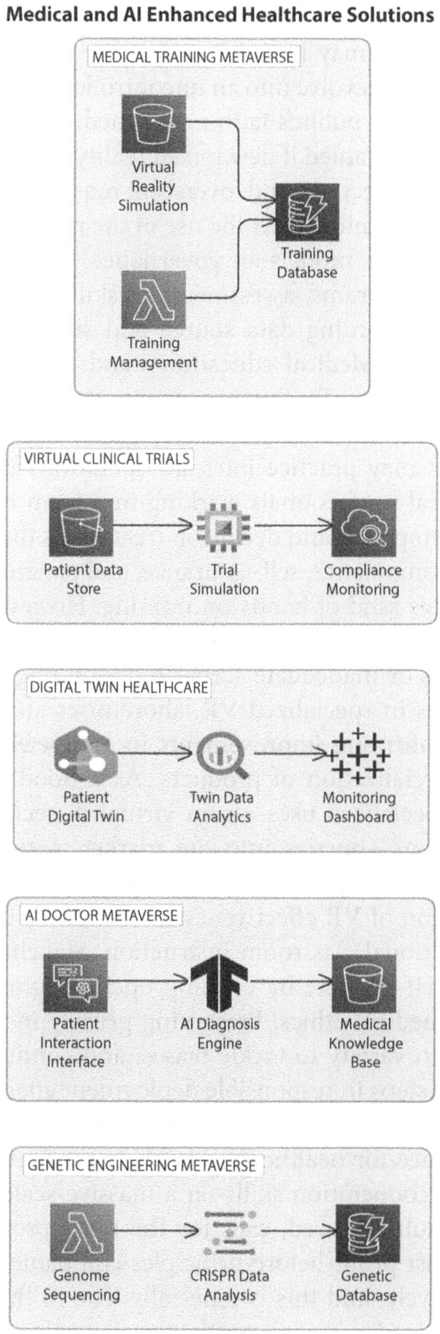


**Figure 3.1** Various cases of ethical perspective on metaverse healthcare.

There is an immediate need to address the regulatory gaps concerning the safety, effectiveness, and equality of medical education using XR. Even while clinical students may learn more quickly in the medical training metaverse, it must not devolve into an uncontrolled environment that puts profit above ethics. The public's faith in the medical industry and patient safety can only be maintained if new mixed reality training platforms meet the same rigorous, effective, and overseen requirements as traditional in-person teaching techniques. As the use of the medical metaverse grows in healthcare education, models for governance, such as ethical committees, accreditation programs, assessments of skill proficiency, and openness requirements regarding data source and simulation design, might help strike a balance. Medical education stands to benefit greatly from immersive VR platforms. Teaching using simulations has many benefits that traditional methods like lectures and textbooks just cannot match. Aspiring surgeons may practice intricate operations until they are blue in the face. Medical professionals working in a team can better evaluate potentially fatal symptoms and decide on treatments that have a chance of success. Clinical competence, self-assurance, and patient outcomes may all be improved by this kind of hands-on training. However, there are many ethical blind spots. Data abuse poses a serious threat to patient privacy. Skewed algorithms or inadequate scenario design might amplify existing biases. Investments in specialized VR laboratories are subject to disparities. Research confirming improvements in competence is also driving the rapid commercialization of products. As a flood of unproven platforms aimed at specialized uses—from virtual dissections to emergency response simulations—hurries into the market, regulations are unable to keep up. However, negative training might hurt patients if no one is watching. Validation of VR effectiveness must adhere to the same ethical standards as traditional classroom instruction. Stakeholders should take the initiative to self-regulate by creating open programs that are based on principles of medical ethics. Preserving privacy in synthetic datasets, increasing scenario variety to tackle biases, and conducting competence audits are the first steps in responsible deployment after the simulation, in addition to the required reporting of analytics for learning. There has never been a better chance for healthcare schools to cultivate leadership, critical thinking, and cooperation skills on a massive scale. The Hippocratic oath, which is results-focused, calls for the same protection of learners and patients against profit-before-principles companies trying to cash in on the VR hype cycle, and this is especially true in the medical training metaverse. Ethical leadership is essential for all participants in this ecosystem. Conscious governance enables VR-based platforms to democratize access, improve preparedness for complex care situations, meet the learning needs of underserved populations across great distances, and continuously improve the fidelity of simulations for healthcare training that is safe, ethical, and effective, regardless of physical constraints.

#### *3.2.1.1 OSSO VR*

In order to assess how well surgical trainees are prepared for a pediatric orthopedic (OP) surgery operation using VR, sliding capital female epiphysis (SCFE) pinning was used in [17]. Fourth-year medical graduates and first- and second-year OP residents who had never performed an SCFE surgery before were gathered and randomized into the SG or VR group after permission from the Institutional Review Board. Signed informed approval forms were completed by each participant. Osso VR supplied every component of the VR system [16, 17].

Every participant was given an enclosed envelope with a random assignment that placed individuals in the VR or SG groupings. A detailed method guide specifically for SCFE pins, a 6-min video showcasing the technical facets of SCFE pinning using a sawbones model, and a grading rubric were provided to all respondents. These materials mimic those that surgical trainees may easily access before surgery. The surgical procedure manual and the instructional film, which contained comprehensive directions and illustrations of the process, were given to everybody in the SG group to study for 2 hours. Before their sawbones testing, the SG participants did not get any coaching or instruction from pediatric OP specialists nor did participants get access to the VR trainer. Before receiving VR training, the randomized participants were allowed to go over the research guide and demonstration film. Following that, these participants finished quick instructions on how to use the OSSO VR system. The Osso VR system (Osso VR, Sacramento, CA) consists of two Oculus wrists and touch controllers for motion which communicate digitally into the virtual headgear, the Oculus Rift, which is worn covering the eyes. Both physical and visual information are provided via the wrist and touch controllers, which transmit forces and vibrations into the body of the user in a manner of haptic signals. For the period of the research, there were no improvements or modifications made to the VR system.

Additionally, VR users finished a specialized instruction on using the Osso VR SCFE–specific module (SCFE Focused with C-Arm Beta). Using the system's training mode and written instructions and prompts for every stage of the process, participants first completed an *in situ* pin of a SCFE in the VR setting. In this training mode, the learner receives instant feedback and their pinning accuracy is graded based on the angle and depth of the final pin position in both coronal and sagittal views. There were grades ranging from A to F, or from very good to very bad. The training area was available to the participants for up to 2 hours at a time. The VR volunteers were moved to an evaluation environment featuring real-time coaching and feedback provided by an attending pediatric OP surgeon (RT and MS) after they successfully completed three grade "A" pin positions. After participants successfully executed two more SCFE pinnings that the instructional visiting surgeon thought appropriate, VR training was concluded. The setup is shown in Figure 3.2.

The objective of [18] was to evaluate the effectiveness of OP trainees before surgery in an SCFE model utilizing three different platforms: physical simulation (PS), VR, and reading/videos. The study's 31 participants were all orthopedic trainees from the same institution: 12 senior medical students, 9 junior orthopedic residents, and 9 other trainees. The sawbones of a

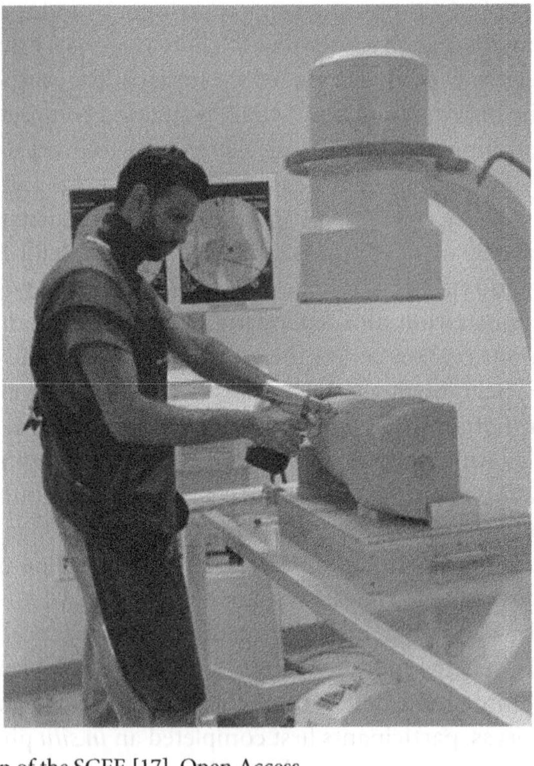

**Figure 3.2** Setup of the SCFE [17]. Open Access.

custom-made phantom limb mockup enclosing an SCFE radiopaque pediatric patient were modeled using a sawbones femur as shown in Figure 3.3.

The procedure began with loading a radiolucent table with a grade III (severe) SCFE sawbones model and then positioning a reusable phantom limb model of a left pediatric thigh for each session. In each experiment, a fresh set of bone models was used, as seen in Figure 3.3. The experimental setup used in [18] is shown in Figure 3.4. The usual read and video content was available to all groups. Participants in Group 1 were strictly prohibited from making use of any training materials or resources that were not assigned

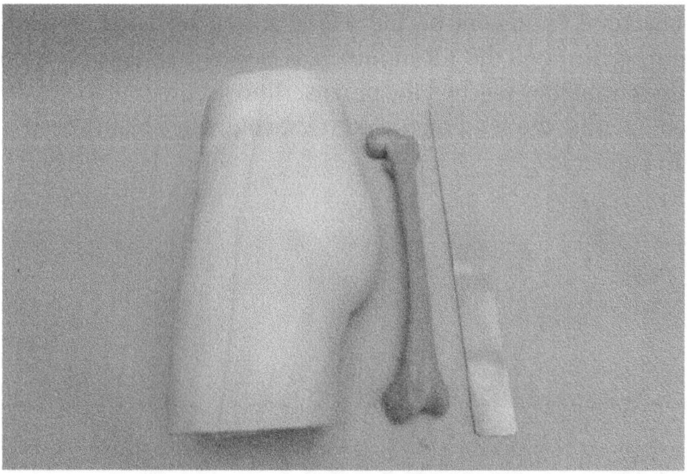

**Figure 3.3** Individualized phantom limb model [18]. Reprinted with copyright permission.

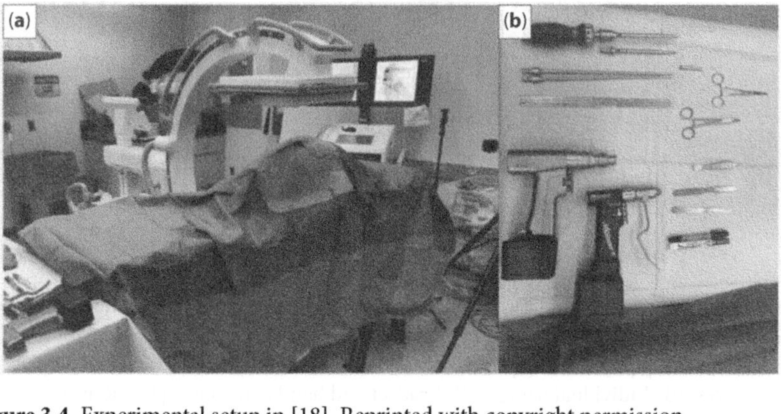


**Figure 3.4** Experimental setup in [18]. Reprinted with copyright permission.

to them. The PS class lasted for 15 min, and during that time, students practiced inserting guide pins into the SCFE sawbones model. Participants had the opportunity to address whatever inquiries they had about SCFE screw fixing, handle the actual model and instrumentation, and practice the technique throughout this time. The Osso VR system was used to instruct those enrolled in the VR group, and they were requested to finish a standardized SCFE fixation component. Using this module, users may virtually move the C-arm from an anterior to a posterior or lateral position at any point during the process. Users must not only capture photos but also decipher them by utilizing mechanical hand controls to physically move the wire that is displayed on the display. With the possible exception of vibrations, while operating a machine, hand controls did not give users any type of tactile input. In order to go through the VR module, users were instructed to complete it many times until they reached the pin insertion accuracy grade of three "A"s. While completing the VR practice courses, volunteers hadn't been timed as shown in Figure 3.5.

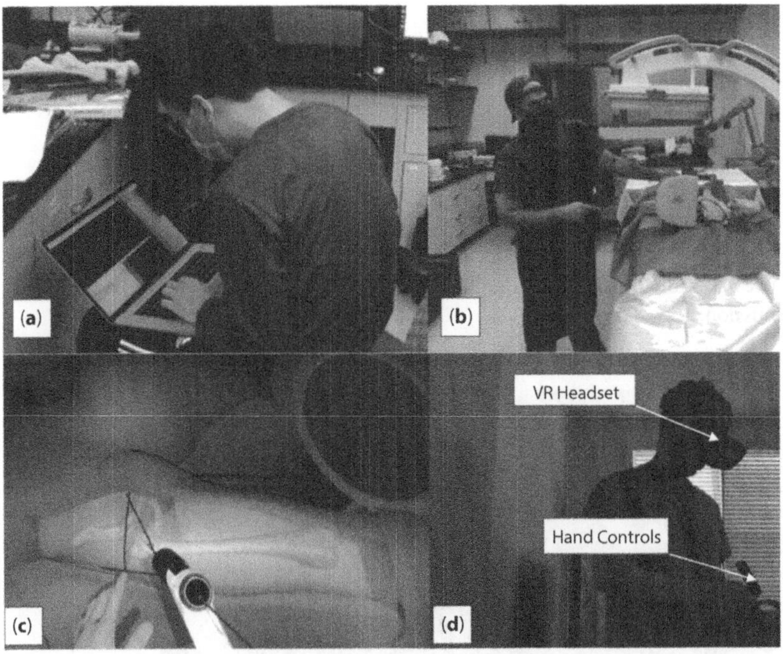


**Figure 3.5** Images depicting the randomization of subjects into three distinct groups. (a) Group 1: Reading or video content that is standardized. (b) Group 2: A model for a slid capital femoral epiphysis using physical simulation. (c) Group 3: Interactive VR Experiences. (d) Individual using a VR headset and hand controllers [18]. Reprinted with copyright permission.

At one location, researchers used a blinded, parallel, randomized design. The Osso VR training package and the Zimmer persona medial partial knee arthroplasty system's industry standardized procedure guide were examined by a senior orthopedic surgeon attending from San Francisco, CA, and Warsaw, IN, respectively in [19]. Utilizing a sawbones model, the treatment was carried out using the typical industry implantation boxes manufactured by Zimmer Biomet in Warsaw, IN. During their postgraduate year (PGY), volunteers were chosen at random to undergo training using both the fully immersive VR and TG. Three things were needed in order to be eligible: 1) being an active orthopedic surgery resident, 2) not having previous work with the Zimmer PPK implantation or its method guide, and 3) not having any prior immersive VR surgical training. Each participant was randomly assigned to either the VR or traditional group therapy (TG) groups utilizing a 2-in-1 block design. In order to provide an even split of resident years for each educational technique and to avoid incompatibility in surgery expertise, each unit corresponds to a distinct learning period (PGY 1 through 5). By not informing those who participated in their assignment until they arrived at the experiment lab, we were able to keep the allocation a secret. A sealed envelope containing the details of the resident's distribution, directions, and permission was provided to them upon arrival. The next step in their training was to be whisked away to a different area of the facility. They were moved to a separate room in the simulation lab to be tested with the blindfolded observer as soon as their training was finished. A maximum of 1 hour was given to each participant to study using their assigned technique. As much time as students needed within their allocated instruction period were allowed to examine the procedure guidelines or run the VR session again. After that, they were instructed to carry out the operation using the usual procedural trays in the field on a sawbones model. Osso VR Inc. created a VR platform that utilizes a completely immersive auditory, visual, and tactile environment. Trainees enter a virtual operating room by donning goggles and a headset (Osso VR, San Francisco, CA), as shown in Figure 3.6b. With the use of the included headphones and goggles, the user can completely isolate himself from their immediate environment, both visually and aurally. Two sensors establish limits and ensure that the learner stays inside the designated area, unimpeded by any impediments. In VR, the user's two hands serve as controllers, and the sensors follow them around as they move (Figure 3.6c). Osso VR provided all the necessary components for the VR system, which were utilized for surgical practice, and they were all returned at the end of the research.

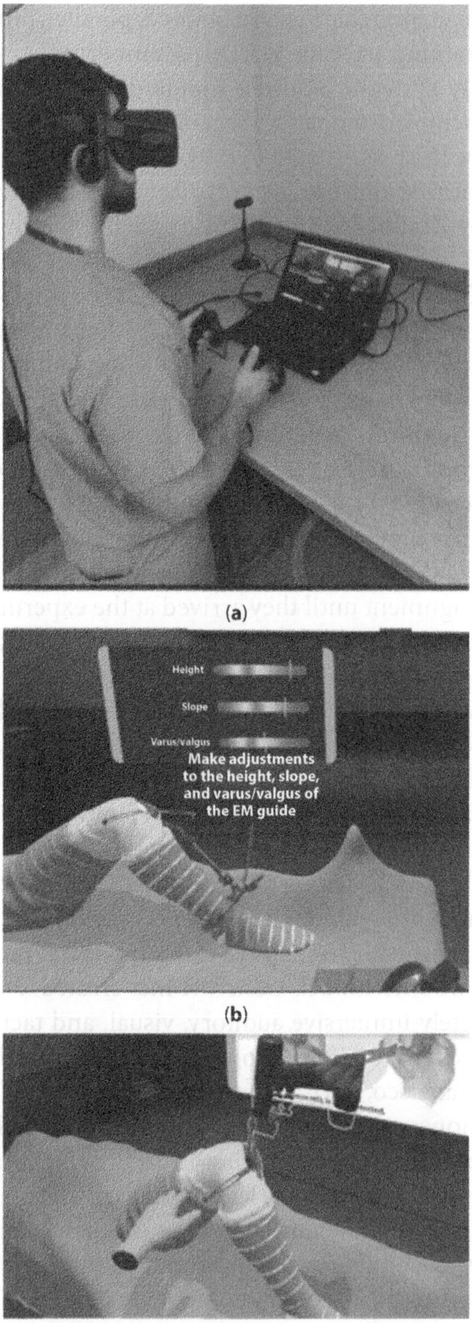


**Figure 3.6** Setup in [19]. Reprint with copyright permission.

#### *3.2.1.2 MediVizor*

In various fields of science, mediation analysis is essential for identifying indirect causal relationships. The problem is that to do a mediation analysis on small variables, one needs to look at various total effects and compare them with the direct and indirect causal effects that came from the mediation models. Conventional analytic tools, such as Excel tables, make this procedure difficult and time-consuming to do. To create MediVizor, a visualization system that allows professionals to do a visually mediating analysis of nominative variables, we collaborated extensively alongside specialists in two different scientific disciplines. Users can peruse and compare various overall impacts and their constituent direct and indirect effects thanks to the visualization design. In addition, the layout lets users see how much the direct and indirect good benefits add up to the overall effects, and how much the bad ones subtract. To assess the system and its design, the authors in [20] carried out user research with average users and two case studies with specialists in the fields of sports and communication science. The system's efficacy and generalizability are shown by the good comments from both specialists and ordinary users [20].

### 3.2.2 Virtual Clinical Trials

To expedite testing, a pharmaceutical corporation uses virtual patients rather than actual people in clinical trials for novel drugs that are conducted fully in a metaverse setting. The informed consent of virtual participants, patient safety in the absence of physical supervision, conflicts of interest in the design and analysis of the research, and the relevance of the findings to actual patients are among the major ethical issues raised by this.

Digital Twin Healthcare: The term "digital twin" refers to an electronic duplicate of a physical system or item. More and more, businesses are embracing this cutting-edge software to track and optimize their operations. The term "digital human twin" (DHT) is used to describe a model of a patient's organs, tissues, and physiological processes that are digitally replicated. Their implementation may pave the way for more tailored data-driven medicine to revolutionize patient care. Organizational management procedures and resource allocation may be enhanced by integrating DHTs with digital twins of healthcare organizations. Illness-tracking tools (DHTs) aid in tracking illness development and improving treatment strategies by simulating the intricate interplay of genetic and environmental variables across several omics. Digital hematopoietic tumor (DHT) models allow for the selection of optimal molecular treatment via simulation, and precise surgical planning with 3D modelling and AR technologies. In addition, they pave the way for the creation of novel targeted medications and individualized early diagnostic techniques. Additionally, medical education and training may be facilitated by digital twins. Medical students may learn more about the human body, practice procedures, and improve their abilities by building virtual representations of anatomy and physiology. All things considered, digital twins have tremendous promise for transforming the healthcare system via better outcomes and care for patients, lower costs, and more effective clinical study and instruction. Before digital twins can be widely used in healthcare, however, issues including the safety of data, data value, and data communication need to be resolved [21]. For this technology to be used responsibly and ethically, several ethical concerns raised by DHT need to be carefully considered. Key moral considerations about DHT in medical settings is data security and privacy: Building and using a DHT necessitate collecting a great deal of personal information, such as medical records, genetic information, and details about one's daily behaviors. Protecting sensitive information from prying eyes requires stringent data privacy and security protocols. In addition, safeguarding sensitive information from prying eyes is of the utmost importance. Protecting patients' personal information from cybercriminals requires stringent security measures, such as encryption and access controls. When it comes to protecting against dangers associated with illegal data collection, compliance with recognized security standards like ISO/IEC 27001 is crucial. Creating a DHT could need to closely monitor a person's vitals using both current and past data. Patients must completely understand the dangers and benefits of developing and using a DHT, as well as the ramifications of revealing their data, to provide their informed permission. Ensuring patient confidence requires open and honest consent procedures and a strong commitment to data protection legislation. Principles of justice and accessibility should guide the creation and implementation of the DHT. Avoiding the exacerbation of healthcare inequities requires that all people, regardless of race, financial class, or geographic location, have equitable access to this technology. There has to be an assessment of accessibility, affordability, algorithmic biases, and other moral considerations. Concerns around confidence and independence are growing in importance as DHTs gain entry to increasing amounts of private medical data and become increasingly integrated into healthcare choices. Patients need to know it their DHT is being handled with care and that they can decide how it is used, whether it is opting out or changing how much data are shared. Interacting with a dynamic DHT, which mirrors the effects of aging along with physical changes over time, may affect the individual's mental health. Mental health, self-perception, and self-esteem are all impacted by this realization. An ethical dilemma arises when considering the DHT concerning the mental aspects of aging. To aid individuals in coping with the psychological difficulties associated with aging, it is crucial to provide helpful services like counseling and psychological assistance. The development of algorithms for human DHTs is heavily dependent on data training; nevertheless, training sets that are biased or lack diversity might lead to healthcare inequities by reinforcing uneven treatment. To stop healthcare disparities from becoming worse, it is crucial to make sure algorithms are fair. The incorporation of DHTs brings up several concerns about responsibility, which are addressed in. Determining culpability becomes problematic due to the legal gap if mistakes occur, such as faulty predictions or improper diagnoses. The roles and duties of healthcare providers, IT companies, and other interested parties need to be clearly defined by legislation. Research of DHTs necessitates adherence to many governing bodies controlling AI, medical devices, data security, and healthcare. The healthcare industry, academic institutions, government agencies, and tech companies must work together to solve these problems. To fully use the DHT's promise while protecting patients' rights, privacy, and well-being, we need honest and open dialogue, strong regulatory frameworks, and constant vigilance over its ethical consequences [22].

AI Doctor Metaverse: An article published in The Wall Street Journal titled "The AI Doctor Will See You Now" presented AI systems as individuals acting as doctors. The papers in question discuss recent developments in healthcare technology that have their foundation in AI [23]. To elucidate these AI systems to the general population, these publications portray them as beyond the competence of the human doctor filling in for them. This design raises concerns: if we say an AI system can surpass humans, then we put it beyond criticism and worry; if we say that it can replace a doctor, then we humanize its technical functioning. Research in the field of science and technology studies (STS) has shown that public engagement is mediated by problems and criticism; yet, both framings avoid discussing ethical concerns altogether. People have a propensity to have very optimistic—and even godlike—expectations about AI, according to research trials [24]. This essay examines the prevalence of this narrative in English-language reports, specifically regarding AI systems as autonomous individuals capable of surpassing human doctors. Nowadays, doctors often struggle with a lack of time and resources while having access to vast quantities of patient data. At the moment of care, smart medical support predicts knowledge that is unique to each patient and their provider's requirements. The ubiquitous EHR in American healthcare now stands as a representation of the physicians' and patients' collective life experiences. Predictions based on these facts are becoming more common. Although demand forecasting models have been created, the majority of the research has concentrated on niche systems that can only predict a small range of outcomes. On the other hand, hundreds—if not thousands—of distinct models for prediction are required for the unpredictable and diverse range of situations seen in everyday medical care. Creating and releasing specialized algorithms independently is not feasible. A generic prediction model covering observed medical problems and drug usage was constructed by using massive past information in EHR. Doctor AI is part of this effort. Utilizing longitudinal time-stamped EHR data, Doctor AI was built as a temporal model utilizing recurrent neural networks (RNNs). The primary focus here in [23] is on exploring the possibility of using EHR data from the past to foretell doctor diagnoses and pharmaceutical orders.

When your doctor takes the time to learn your name and your specific medical history, you may feel valued and as if you are receiving individualized attention. However, suppose the doctor is an AI and not a human. The ability to create AI physicians that can uniquely identify each patient is within reach, thanks to the personalization algorithms that power AI systems. Do you think this enhances the doctor-patient relationship or does it make people feel uneasy and invasive? The work in [25] builds a healthcare chatbot that could tell the difference between a human and an AI-assisted bot to find out. Users were asked to contact a bot that could identify them or not twice, 10 days apart, in research that aimed to determine the risk of COVID-19. Reducing patient compliance, data suggest that AI doctors individuate. Surprisingly, most people in the human doctor condition believed they were chatting with an AI doctor. Implications for healthcare chat app design are provided by the findings.

It takes a lot of time and a lot of thought to decide in the medical industry. On top of that, it may cause doctors to miss the mark when diagnosing a patient's condition, which can result in the wrong drug being prescribed. In many instances, the symptoms and illnesses overlap, making it difficult to diagnose a specific condition since the relationship between symptoms and diseases is not always easy. Decisions in the medical industry must take many factors into account. Practitioners' perspectives may diverge as a result of this. The use of a powerful tool that considers all the aspects and produces results even in challenging scenarios will therefore aid in issue-solving.

This inspired a small but brilliant group of computer scientists and medical professionals to launch a new field of study: AI. To put it simply, AI is the subfield of computer science that studies how to program computers to do tasks normally performed by humans. A renaissance in AI research occurred at the turn of the millennium, and the technology quickly gained widespread attention and applications in many domains. Various programming languages have been created and used to implement AI challenges. The two most used languages for implementing AI issues are Lisp and Prolog. Around 1970, Alain Colmerauer in Marseilles, France, created Prolog for the first time. A declarative programming language, whose primary usage is in solving issues involving logic and reasoning [26]. A Prolog expert system (APES) that allows the domain expert to manage it (i.e., without having coding abilities) utilizing a command-line interface that supports queries and understanding base extensions using a format based on natural language was used [26]. A clear and expandable format for input is provided via the Definite Clause Grammar (DCG), an embedded grammatical definition vocabulary in the Prolog. DCG, an extension of Context-Free Grammar (CFG), is the preferred method of Prolog parsing. Among the many useful uses for Prolog and logic programming is parsing. To render it, a domain-specific language that is close enough to the input format to be maintained by the expert in the field without having Prolog or other programming abilities, the expertise is stored in text files that include Prolog assumptions with specified operators. Thus, we arrive at the central idea and objective: a system of specialists that allows domain professionals to not only query the repository of information but also establish and upkeep it with no requiring the ability to program. This makes it a nondomain-specific skilled structure, meaning that professionals in any domain, rather than programmers, could use it to build expert systems. Figure 3.7 shows the layout used in [27]. An abnormal elevation in core body temperature beyond the typical range is known as fever. A wide range of medical conditions, including infections, cancers, and many more, may induce it. There is no need to take medicine for a mild fever unless there are major underlying medical issues. Rest and fluid consumption as self-care interventions could be sufficient. High fever, on the other hand, is lethal since it is seldom associated with other major health problems or illnesses. Therefore, being familiar with the agents is crucial.

Genetic Engineering Metaverse: When it comes to promoting services and contributing to economic progress, healthcare is essential, and it is also crucial for global well-being [27]. The way patients and doctors communicate has changed due to technological developments like blockchain, AR,

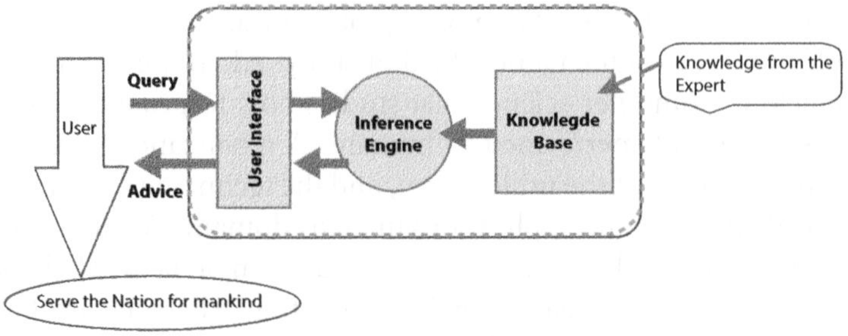


**Figure 3.7** Architecture in [26]. Reprinted with copyright permission.

and VR. Metaverse healthcare also makes use of blockchain, digital twinning, telepresence, and AI to help keep costs down and enhance results for patients. By fusing the physical and digital realms, the metaverse also provides individualized, all-encompassing healthcare. Killing millions of people every year, cancer is still one of the leading causes of mortality worldwide. Traditional cancer therapies like radiation, targeted therapy, and chemotherapy kill cancer cells, but they damage good cells as well as malignant cells and cost a pretty penny. In light of these difficulties, the demand for a computerized system that can reliably detect ACPs in

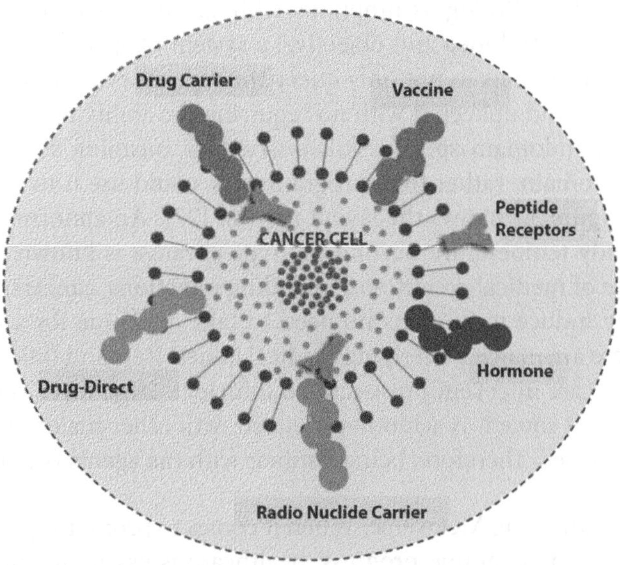


**Figure 3.8** Peptide sequencing provides a variety of possible cancer therapy alternatives that may be investigated and their efficacy assessed [27].

complicated biological sequences is increasing; this would allow for earlier diagnosis and treatment, preventing the disease from progressing. The fact that peptides have a negligible influence on everyday physiological processes has led to their widespread use in preliminary studies for a variety of indications, including for the treatment of heart disease, cancer, and hypertension. Peptide targeting is one of many cancer therapy strategies, as seen in Figure 3.8.

## 3.3 Discussion

By using cutting-edge telemedicine methods, the healthcare industry's current technological trends have effectively and efficiently embraced remote patient monitoring, guaranteeing the finest possible treatment for patients. The term "metaverse" is new and promises radical changes to many facets of existence. However, the integration of the metaverse into medicine will improve the current monitoring of patient health services by introducing new interactive aspects in a virtual world through the use of technology such as VR for operations, AR for medical training, etc. [11, 28, 29]. By linking the real and virtual worlds, the metaverse seeks to provide patients in a virtual environment with an exceptional user experience via the advancement of virtual and communications technology. The patient's bodily motions and physiological responses will be controlled and observed by the metaverse. Furthermore, when a patient interacts with different services, the metaverse may gather private data about them, including their tastes, medical statistics, biographical information, and brainwaves. Sensitive data that have been gathered are not secure in the virtual world; malevolent users may pose as other users to get access to people's personal information, or it may be disclosed to unaffiliated parties. Creating "clone clouds" and "private copies" is one potential answer to the issue of user privacy data leakage. This ensures that the user's location, actions, and objectives are kept by confounding the invader. Ensuring the privacy of behavior, communication, and senses is crucial for the current generation of metaverse-based healthcare solutions. While offering medical care, large healthcare organizations will gather sensitive data in a variety of methods, regardless of people's permission. The metaverse will be capable of offering clinicians a great virtual opportunity to treat individuals who have different health issues virtually and with the aid of multiple electronic gadgets, creating a massive quantity of digital data, through the application of unique telecommunication and virtual methods. The patients' current illnesses are communicated over the line of communication throughout the procedure, and the doctor's comments are transmitted as well via the same channel as the metaverse is a fusion of contemporary technology. Nevertheless, private patient information is included in digitally produced health information, and protecting these data from outside intrusions or hackers at various stages of the procedure is a difficult undertaking. Privacy breaches and virus incursions start with AR/VR devices. Healthcare connectivity refers to the capacity of medical professionals and other structures to exchange information about patients online with no difficulties. For example, an EHR system from a single practitioner should be able to send individual information to a different supplier's structure using present-day technology and technology, guaranteeing the accessibility and regularity of personally identifiable information. Interoperability becomes a difficult challenge as the amount of health data and new technologies in the healthcare arena rises. By combining diverse hardware and software components with mobile devices in a simulated setting, the medical sector's adoption of the metaverse promises new opportunities and problems. From collecting data to analyzing it, every metaverse-based healthcare service should interact with numerous parts to guarantee the confidentiality and integrity of highly sensitive data. To prevent serious and unanticipated repercussions during the device migration from conventional healthcare services to the virtual world, appropriate interaction protocols and data usage procedures must be put into place. Medical technology is always changing as a result of new medical advancements, bringing about digital revolutions via the integration of VR and robotic surgery in a range of medical services. The combination of AR and VR is mostly used in surgical operations and medical education to accomplish intricate surgeries with utmost accuracy. The functionality of medical equipment and gadgets will be enhanced by these hardware and software components. The rise of metaverse-oriented enterprises has led to a surge in the creation of sophisticated AR and VR solutions aimed at enhancing the surgical environment on a worldwide scale. High-tech wearables, such as glasses, gloves, detectors, and other hardware parts that can precisely detect the patients' states, are necessary to effectively transform the healthcare system that currently exists with the metaverse. Wearables are expensive, however, and as technology advances, we will also need to purchase new gear to take advantage of new features. Because the metaverse needs a high end-to-end connection to function well, the infrastructure for healthcare providers will likewise be quite expensive. First off, it is quite expensive to implement the metaverse in the healthcare industry by replacing outdated processes with wearable technology, suitable applications, and hardware to support it. The distance between an individual and a doctor is created by the current digital revolution of medical care with telemedicine services and remote patient monitoring technologies. After obtaining the relevant history of the patient and current situation, or by examining digital medical information without physically examining the patients, physicians may recommend the remote therapy technique. However, by offering feasible and effective interactive alternatives, the metaverse will provide individuals and healthcare providers with an immersive virtual environment. The majority of patients believe that they no longer have the special face-to-face chemistry that comes with the new digital style of therapy. The patient experiences loneliness while receiving care digitally, and this has an impact on the patient's pace of recovery.

## Conclusion and Future Scope

The metaverse is now an innovative company structure rather than just a piece of technology thanks to recent developments in information and communication technology (ICT). Patients and medical professionals may both gain from the healthcare industry's use of the metaverse. Using cutting-edge tools and technology may improve the services provided to patients and aid in the education of medical personnel. Legally and regulatory problems may arise as the real-world uses of the metaverse in the field of medicine keep growing with technological advances involving multiple entities like insurance, drug manufacturers, and medical professionals in offering effective patient care. The adoption of the metaverse might cause trust issues, uncertainty among different entities over proprietary rights, etc. because it lacks appropriate rules and procedures. To manage unlawful activity in the realm of VR, nevertheless, or to take appropriate action, appropriate rules must be developed within a legal structure. Since the patient's medical system consists of many components, the metaverse is particularly vulnerable to security risks. This is the health service provider's duty to ensure that user-sensitive data are secure. The deployable framework for the current metaverse platforms is strengthened by regular security fix updates. The system vulnerability will be somewhat improved by the security updates, but the fixes will become brittle due to ongoing cyber-physical assaults on the metaverse surface. Yet, endogenous safety, like the atomic distribution of keys, is a potential way to guarantee security via mechanisms that can self-evolve, self-protect, and self-immunity while taking privacy and security considerations into account when designing the system. Thus, the cyberspace of the future will be able to withstand both known and undiscovered security flaws and privacy risks.

## References

1. World Health Organization, 2023 emerging technologies and scientific innovations: a global public health perspective, 2023.
2. Beyala, L., *Digital Therapy: The New Age of Healthcare*, John Wiley & Sons, 2022.
3. Rudnicka, Z., *et al.*, Advancements in artificial intelligence-driven techniques for interventional cardiology. *Cardiol J.*, 31, 2, 2024.
4. Sagdic, K., *et al.*, Smart materials: rational design in biosystems via artificial intelligence. *Trends Biotechnol.*, 40, 8, 2022.
5. Belić, M., *et al.*, Artificial intelligence for assisting diagnostics and assessment of Parkinson's disease—A review. *Clin. Neurol. Neurosurg.*, 184, 1054425, 2019.
6. Gedefaw, L., *et al.*, Artificial intelligence-assisted diagnostic cytology and genomic testing for hematologic disorders. *Cells*, 12, 13, 1755, 2023.
7. Luo, N., *et al.*, Artificial intelligence-assisted dermatology diagnosis: from unimodal to multimodal. *Comput. Biol. Med.*, 165, 107413, 2023.
8. Tretter, M., *et al.*, Towards an Ethics for the Healthcare Metaverse. *J. Metaverse*, 3, 2, 181–189, 2023.
9. Wang, G., *et al.*, Development of metaverse for intelligent healthcare. *Nat. Mach. Intell.*, 4, 11, 922–929, 2022.
10. Thomason, J., Metahealth-how will the metaverse change health care? *J. Metaverse*, 1, 1, 13–16, 2021.
11. Lee, C.W., Application of metaverse service to healthcare industry: a strategic perspective. *Int. J. Environ. Res. Public Health*, 19, 20, 13038, 2022.
12. Bang, J. and Kim, J.-Y., Metaverse Ethics for Healthcare Using AI Technology: Challenges and Risks. *International Conference on Human-Computer Interaction*, Springer Nature Switzerland, Cham, 2023.
13. Tan, T.F., *et al.*, Metaverse and virtual health care in ophthalmology: Opportunities and challenges. *Asia-Pac. J. Ophthalmol.*, 11, 3, 237–246, 2022.
14. Wiederhold, B.K. and Riva, G., Metaverse creates new opportunities in healthcare. *Ann. Rev. Cyber. Telemed.*, 20, 3–7, 2022.
15. Bashir, A.K., *et al.*, Federated learning for the healthcare metaverse: Concepts, applications, challenges, and future directions. *IEEE Internet Things J.*, 10, 24, 2023.
16. How Osso Enterprise works, Ossovr.com, [Online]. Available: https://www.ossovr.com/osso-enterprise. [Accessed: 17-Mar-2024].
17. Cevallos, N., Zukotynski, B., Greig, D., Silva, M., Thompson, R.M., The utility of virtual reality in orthopedic surgical training. *J. Surg. Educ.*, 79, 6, 1516–1525, 2022.
18. Margalit, A., Suresh, K.V., Marrache, M., Lentz, J.M., Lee, R., Tis, J., Varghese, R., Hayashi, B., Jain, A., Laporte, D., Evaluation of a Slipped Capital Femoral Epiphysis Virtual Reality Surgical Simulation for the Orthopaedic

Trainee. *JAAOS: Global Res. Rev.*, 6, 4, e22.00028, April 2022, DOI: 10.5435/JAAOSGlobal-D-22-00028.

19. McKinney, B., Dbeis, A., Lamb, A., Frousiakis, P., Sweet, S., Virtual reality training in unicompartmental knee arthroplasty: A randomized, blinded trial. *J. Surg. Educ.*, 79, 6, 1526–1535, 2022.
20. Lan, J., Xie, X., Wu, Y., Zhou, Z., Zhang, H., Wu, Y., MediVizor: Visual Mediation Analysis of Nominal Variables. *IEEE Trans. Visual Comput. Graphics*, 30, 8, 4853–4866, 2023. doi: 10.1109/TVCG.2023.3282801.
21. Cellina, M., Cè, M., Alì, M., Irmici, G., Ibba, S., Caloro, E., Fazzini, D., Oliva, G., Papa, S., Digital Twins: The New Frontier for Personalized Medicine? *Appl. Sci.*, 13, 7940, 2023, https://doi.org/10.3390/app13137940.
22. Kamel Boulos, M.N. and Zhang, P., Digital Twins: From Personalised Medicine to Precision Public Health. *J. Pers. Med.*, 11, 745, 2021, https://doi.org/10.3390/jpm11080745.
23. Choi, E., Bahadori, M.T., Schuetz, A., Stewart, W.F., Sun, J., Doctor AI: Predicting clinical events via recurrent neural networks, in: *Proceedings of the 1st Machine Learning for Healthcare Conference*, 18–19 Aug 2016, vol. 56, pp. 301–318.
24. Bunz, M. and Braghieri, M., The AI doctor will see you now: assessing the framing of AI in news coverage. *AI Soc.*, 37, 9–22, 2022, https://doi.org/10.1007/s00146-021-01145-9.
25. Chen, J., Chen, C., Walther, J.B., Shyam Sundar, S., Do You Feel Special When an AI Doctor Remembers You? Individuation Effects of AI vs. Human Doctors on User Experience, in: *Extended Abstracts of the 2021 CHI Conference on Human Factors in Computing Systems (CHI EA '21)*, Association for Computing Machinery, New York, NY, USA, Article 299, pp. 1-7, 2021, https://doi.org/10.1145/3411763.3451735.
26. Das, S., *et al.*, AI Doctor: An intelligent approach for medical diagnosis, in: *Industry Interactive Innovations in Science, Engineering and Technology: Proceedings of the International Conference, I3SET 2016*, Springer Singapore, 2018.
27. Danish, S., Khan, A., Dang, L.M., Alonazi, M., Alanazi, S., Song, H.-K., Moon, H., Metaverse Applications in Bioinformatics: A Machine Learning Framework for the Discrimination of Anti-Cancer Peptides. *Information*, 15, 48, 2024, https://doi.org/10.3390/info15010048.
28. Chengoden, R., *et al.*, Metaverse for Healthcare: A Survey on Potential Applications, Challenges and Future Directions. *IEEE Access*, 11, 12765–12795, 2023, doi: 10.1109/ACCESS.2023.3241628.
29. Ullah, H., *et al.*, Exploring the potential of metaverse technology in healthcare: applications, challenges, and future directions. *IEEE Access*, 11, 2023.

4

# The Healthcare Metaverse: Utilizations, Obstacles, and Prospects

**Shilpa Mahajan**

*Department of Computer Science, The NorthCap University, Gurugram, Haryana, India*

***Abstract***

The new era of digitization has revolutionized the healthcare industry. This has created new ways of treating diseases with reduced costs. Among these advancements, the metaverse has recently attracted global attention as a groundbreaking digital realm with immense potential to offer a diverse variety of healthcare services to medical professionals and patients. Given the expanding demand for healthcare systems, it is vital to research cutting-edge and affordable choices that may deliver prompt and trustworthy medical treatments. This chapter investigates the usage of metaverse technology in the healthcare domain and explicates its potential to better the clinical administration of patients. It gives a detailed overview of various applications of metaverse in the healthcare industry, addressing the challenges incurred in the adaptability of healthcare applications, and suggesting future directions in this evolving field.

***Keywords***: Metaverse, augmented reality, computer-assisted therapy, robotic surgery, artificial intelligence

## Introduction

Health services have become crucial in fostering the mental, physical, and social well-being of the worldwide population. The core nature of health care is underlined by its power to reduce the harmful consequences of illness, injury, and disease while increasing well-being and longevity.

*Email*: shilpa@ncuindia.edu

Ajay Kumar Vyas, Harleen Kaur, Sourabh Sharma and Bhavya Alankar (eds.) Metaverse Technologies, Security and Applications for Healthcare, (81–100) © 2025 Scrivener Publishing LLC

Nevertheless, despite the prolonged progression of the healthcare sector, there has been a rapid and vibrant change, principally driven by the incorporation of state-of-the-art technology advancements. The healthcare industry might be greatly enhanced by the innovative technology known as the metaverse. It is an impractical digital domain that eliminates the limitations of real-world time and space and provides users with boundless opportunities to generate and encounter things that are impossible to achieve.

Research indicates that the metaverse possesses the ability to transform healthcare systems through the introduction of innovative approaches to healthcare provision. Patients and healthcare professionals can benefit from remote medical consultations and training made possible by the use of augmented reality/virtual reality (AR/VR) technology from the metaverse. Furthermore, patients are provided with health-related tools and information, enabling them to take charge of their health and make informed decisions. Throughout the pandemic, the use of telemedicine and telehealth has been crucial in providing healthcare services [1]. But there are also restrictions, obstacles, and difficulties with regard to justice in the digital healthcare system. Therefore, research on metaverse technology is essential if healthcare systems are to satisfy these needs, adjust to the pandemic, and overcome these challenges.

The metaverse's entry into the healthcare industry may be very beneficial for patients and medical professionals, but there are also significant legal and regulatory issues that must be resolved. Regarding intellectual property rights and trust issues, the absence of clear regulations and norms may lead to uncertainty among many stakeholders, such as healthcare providers, insurance companies, and pharmaceutical corporations. In order to control illicit activity in the virtual world and offer patients a secure and operative service, appropriate laws must be established within the legal framework.

This chapter gives an overview of the metaverse technology and discusses its various applications in the healthcare industry [2]. It also explores several challenges like ethical, logical, and technical issues in integrating this cutting-edge technology with healthcare. Despite these advantages, this chapter emphasizes the future scope of metaverse in health care, which is very promising.

## Metaverse

A VR simulation that surpasses standard 2D interfaces is called the metaverse. It offers an entirely realistic 3D environment with precise representations of actual locations and happenings. It takes advantage of already-existing methods to provide consumers with a fresh, realistic visual experience. The word "metaverse" refers to transcendence, and the word "universe" describes a fictitious artificial environment that is linked to the real world. This technology has gained popularity recently and has the ability to completely transform a variety of sectors, such as gaming and healthcare. The metaverse market is anticipated to grow rapidly, from US$500 million in 2020 to US$800 billion by 2024, according to industry projections. The prediction states that the AR market will reach US$855.3 billion by 2027.

Many well-known tech companies, such as Microsoft, NVIDIA, Facebook, Tencent, ByteDance, and Unity, have publicly announced their entry into the metaverse, demonstrating their significant interest in this cutting-edge field that has the potential to completely transform the digital world. Research was found in the ACM, IEEE, Science Direct, MDPI, and Springer databases. Included are identification and screening.

## Metaverse Components

Several core components shape the metaverse world. The core components are shown in Figure 4.1.

## AR/VR Technologies

These immersive technologies allow users to experience and interact with the virtual world. AR aims to enhance the experience around the user by draping digital content on top of it. AR is also used in smartphones and laptops nowadays without using additional devices like headsets. Several applications like finding stars in the sky and creating different environments can be done through AR. There are professional applications like healthcare, education, and manufacturing are using this technology to enhance user experience. Tools like HoloLens and devices like Oculus Rift and HTC VIVE provide immersive 3D experiences.

| | |
|---|---|
| •Virtual Reality (VR) and Augmented Reality (AR) Technologies | •VR Headsets<br>•AR Goggles |
| •Digital Avatars | •Personal Representation<br>•3D Virtual Environments |
| •Simulation Spaces | •Navigation: |
| •Blockchain and Cryptocurrencies | •Digital Ownership<br>•Cryptocurrencies |
| •Artificial Intelligence (AI) | •Intelligent Agents<br>•Data Analysis |
| •Networking Infrastructure | •High-Speed Internet<br>•Cloud Computing |
| •Content Creation Tools | •3D Modeling Software<br>•User-Generated Content |
| •Social Interaction Platforms | •Virtual Social Spaces<br>•Communication Tools |
| •Sensor and Haptic Technologies | •Motion Sensors<br>•Haptic Feedback |
| •Regulatory and Ethical Frameworks | •Data Privacy<br>•Ethical Guidelines |

**Figure 4.1** Metaverse components.

**Advantages of using AR/VR in Metaverse**

| |
|---|
| *It provides immersive environments where users can interact with digital content in realistic and engaging ways.* |
| *These technologies facilitate communication and collaboration within the metaverse by enabling users to interact with each other in virtual spaces.* |
| *They can tailor experiences to individual users' preferences and needs within the metaverse.* |
| *They can be used for training and simulation purposes within the metaverse, allowing users to practice skills, scenarios, or procedures in a safe and controlled virtual environment.* |

## Digital Avatars

Digital avatars in the metaverse mimic human characters in the real world [3]. They appear to be somewhat real, but we can customize avatars as per the requirements. These digital avatars are created for interaction and for customizing different applications. These applications may be customized to create full-body characters and realistic lifelike replicas.

## 3D Virtual Environments

3D virtual environments are created using computer technology. It provides a three-dimensional user experience where users can interact like creating virtual hospitals, classrooms, or social.

## Blockchain and Cryptocurrencies

Blockchain technology is essential to the metaverse. Using this technology, data can be stored anywhere in the metaverse. It also provides a secure system to connect the virtual world of the metaverse with the real world and allows the transfer of virtual assets using NFTs as shown in Figure 4.2. Digital currencies like Bitcoin and Ethereum are used for transactions within the metaverse [4]. The utilization of blockchain technology holds great potential for the storage and integration of healthcare records in the future. Blockchain technology has the potential to overcome fragmented healthcare systems, increase individual control, and optimize record storage. This makes it an attractive option, especially in the field of medicine.

- **Storage of Records**

Blockchain utilizes its decentralized structure to provide the secure storing of documents in personal blockchain wallets, resulting in several benefits like enhanced security, simplified accessibility, and the capacity to grant worldwide clinician authorization.

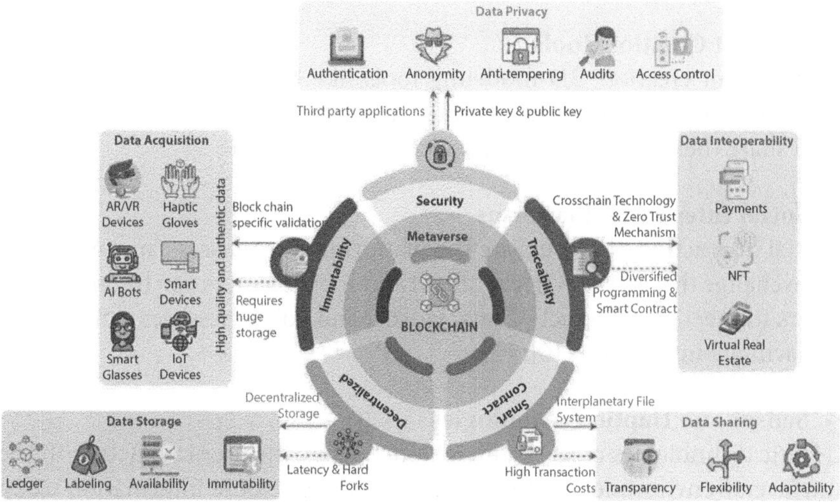


**Figure 4.2** Blockchain for the metaverse [2].

Additionally, blockchain can address the complex features of many health scenarios by encouraging collaboration between healthcare providers, which might lead to the development of a more cohesive healthcare system. The use of blockchain technology in healthcare is a significant and fascinating area of research in the metaverse, blockchain, and healthcare sectors. It has the power to transform the sector, improve patient outcomes, and get past present difficulties. In the future, tokens or NFT cryptocurrency items might be used as incentives for students to participate in events or extracurricular activities. This is one way that blockchain and gamification could be used to inspire students. There are a lot of educational activities that the metaverse may provide.

- **Artificial Intelligence (AI)**

With artificial intelligence (AI), it is possible to build a real environment in a metaverse that captures features and information from the real world and then transforms them into the virtual world. These characters and bots interact with users and provide them with real assistance and companionship. AI algorithms use vast amounts of data and perform fast computations to run the metaverse [5]. It analyzes user behavior to improve user experience, is intelligently responsive, and provides personalized content.

- **Networking Infrastructure**

High-speed internet service is required for real-time interaction and seamless operations. It uses the cloud for storing and processing large amounts of data for operations required in the metaverse.

- **Content Creation Tools**

For content creation, 3D modeling tools like Unity 3D and Blender are used for creating objects and animated characters. Users can also create and share their own content if required.

- **Social Interaction Platforms**

Social interaction platforms are the platforms where users can collaborate to exchange their ideas. Virtual offices and social lounges can be created for users to meet and interact. Chats, videos, and voice messages can be used to facilitate interactions [6].

- **Sensor and Haptic Technologies**

Haptic technologies create artificial touch when the user interacts with the metaverse environment. This technology conveys more information using vibrations instead of using voice or video media. They provide a more immersive experience by tracking the movements of users. With haptic feedback applications in the medical field, the quality of life and medical care of the patients improves. Wearable sensors can be used to gather patient statistics related to the medical field which can be later used for analyzing data using AI algorithms for detecting early-stage diseases.

- **Regulatory and Ethical Frameworks**

Millions of transactions occur in the metaverse, so it becomes necessary to follow ethics, legal framework, and trust. The user's data have to be protected and privacy is to be maintained. Proper ethical guidelines and standard procedures for content delivery are to be designed.

## Issues Faced by Healthcare Industries

The healthcare industry is encountering several issues and obstacles, including the pervasive occurrence of chronic illnesses, inadequate availability of state-of-the-art equipment in local hospitals, insufficient familiarity with advanced technologies, and limited patient understanding regarding various medical treatments, among others.

These considerable impediments have prompted health services to extend their reach to the households of citizens. The COVID-19 outbreak aggravated the situation and was the key driving force. The driving force underpins the swift shift in the healthcare industry. The industry's altering environment has driven all companies to reassess their strategy and ultimately incorporate new technologies. In this specific case, the notion of metaverse has the potential to drastically alter the existing situation. Utilizing the capabilities of these advanced technologies gives thrilling potential for discovering imaginative techniques to supply top-notch healthcare treatments and services.

The metaverse has the power to deliver genuine encounters to patients and healthcare practitioners, creating new opportunities for better healthcare results. Contemporary research reveals an increased curiosity about the Meta version and its usage in the healthcare arena. However, in spite of the abundance of research on the application of metaverse technologies in healthcare, these technologies have inherent limitations and do not fully embrace some sectors. The COVID-19 epidemic has disturbed the traditional method of monitoring well-being through physical encounters with patients, leading to the use of telemedicine as an alternate remedy [7]. Telehealth utilizes digital technology, including telephone conversations, video conferencing, email, and messaging, to deliver healthcare services remotely. The incidence of this phenomenon has dramatically increased.

In 2020, there was a substantial increase in the number of US healthcare institutions that were capable of providing telehealth services, with 95% of them being prepared for this purpose. This is a huge rise from the previous figure of 43% before the pandemic, as reported in sources. Telemedicine is the combination of technology with healthcare, including digital medicine, e-health, telehealth, and mental health as shown in Figure 4.3.

The healthcare business in the metaverse is expected to be worth US$71.97 billion by 2030, which is an impressive projection. This prediction highlights the significant capacity for expansion and creativity within the industry. Given the substantial investment that is expected shortly, there is a chance to fundamentally transform the way healthcare is provided, by improving its accessibility, cost-efficiency, and focus on the needs of patients. This chapter covers varied applications of the metaverse in the field of healthcare. This technology might be used for a variety of purposes, including enhancing medical education and training, enabling immersive clinical care, and even supporting births and surgeries [8]. These possibilities can bring about significant and profound changes. These applications not only pledge to enhance patient outcomes but also provide healthcare personnel with novel tools and skills.

The growing adoption of technology in healthcare, demonstrated by the increasing popularity of telemedicine and the impact of gaming on younger individuals, highlights a changing paradigm. VR, blockchain, and digital twins are leading the way in this technological advancement, ready to transform the healthcare industry as we now understand it.

Nevertheless, in light of the potential benefits of the metaverse, it is essential to use prudence while incorporating it into healthcare. It is

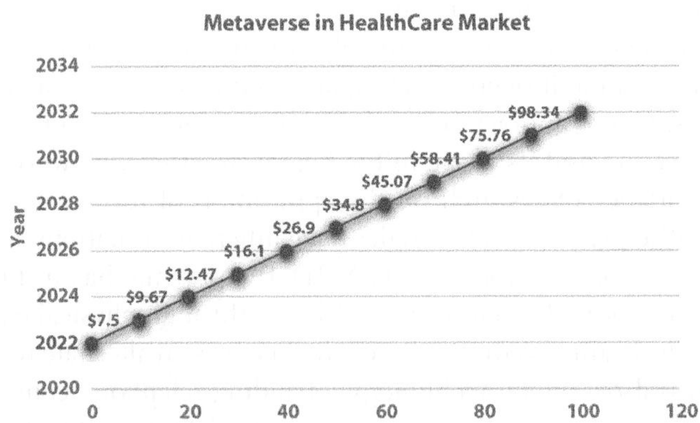


**Figure 4.3** Metaverse in the healthcare market.

imperative to thoroughly handle patient safety, data security, privacy, and ethical aspects. We need to traverse the intricate landscape of interoperability and regulatory frameworks about data ownership and distribution.

By placing patient well-being as the top priority and possessing a thorough comprehension of both the advantages and disadvantages of metaverse technologies, we can utilize them as tools to promote proactive healthcare [9]. We must perceive technology not as a source of instability, but rather as a tool that may improve the delivery of care via careful and extensive consideration. By doing this, we can protect the interests and welfare of patients while utilizing the revolutionary capacity of the metaverse to enhance healthcare results.

The metaverse improves user capabilities by integrating physical and virtual environments. It can observe physiological reactions and gather statistics of the patients, however, there are certain issues related to privacy and security of data. Novel approaches such as the "clone cloud" and "private copy" offer protection against malicious exploitation and the unauthorized disclosure of data. It is essential to prioritize privacy safeguards while creating healthcare solutions based on the metaverse, which includes factors related to senses, communication, and behavior. Additional investigation in this domain can reveal the revolutionary capabilities of the metaverse in the healthcare sector. This environment is a combination of hardware and software that includes wearable devices to collect important data about the user under examination. To successfully tackle obstacles, it is imperative to establish strong communication protocols and use efficient ways to incorporate data.

## Applications of Metaverse in Healthcare Industry

Immersive VR technology from the metaverse can improve strategy and evaluation processes through the design and testing phases [10]. This is achieved by using virtual prototypes to enable engineers and users to engage with various components more efficiently.

VR simulations are utilized for instructing orthopedic surgery trainees in the field of arthroplasty, a surgical intervention designed to reinstate joint functionality. This encompasses education and instruction for the surgical procedure known as total hip arthroplasty.

The utilization of augmented virtuality (AV) is a cutting-edge technology that offers a distinct method for immersing oneself in virtual worlds. Contrary to AR, MR integrates the characteristics of both AR. Figure 4.4 shows the AR/VR applications in healthcare sector.

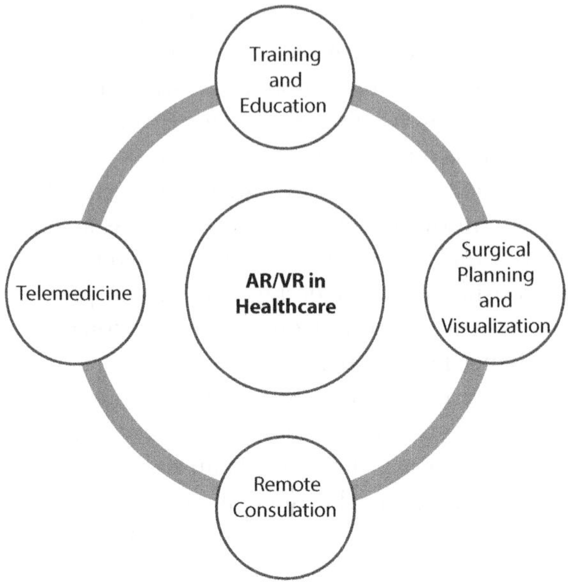


**Figure 4.4** AR/VR in metaverse.

## Limitation of AR/VR in Healthcare

| |
|---|
| *The initial investment required for implementing AR and VR technology in healthcare settings is very high.* |
| *There are still technical limitations that need to be overcome which include the cost of hardware, software development, training, and maintenance.* |
| *They need to comply with various regulations and standards to ensure patient safety and data security.* |
| *Ensuring that the data of the patients is secure is also a concern.* |
| *Training is also required to effectively use the technology in clinical practice.* |

Healthcare professionals can access immersive training simulations that replicate complex cardiovascular procedures and anatomy. The study focuses on the role of metaverse in cardiovascular medicine, while it does not include an examination of its possible implications in other fields of medicine [14]. The work proposes the combination of AI and blockchain technologies in a metaverse to deliver enhanced healthcare services. The research intends to rigorously examine how metaverse technology could boost patient enjoyment, improve medication adherence, and optimize the connection between patients and physicians by leveraging advanced digital tools and services. AR and VR technologies can visualize cardiovascular imaging data using CT scans, MRI images, and echocardiograms, in three-dimensional virtual environments.

Surgeons can use the metaverse to plan and simulate complex cardiovascular surgeries, such as heart valve replacement or coronary artery bypass grafting. Blockchain technology facilitates the tokenization of virtual assets within the metaverse, enabling fractional ownership, liquidity, and interoperability of digital assets across different virtual environments and platforms.

The surgical metaverse includes the usage of AI with surgical instruments like robots. A control tower is necessary for the processing of digital data since the use of directing methods and movement correction procedures may significantly improve accuracy [16].

This study can be used to treat patients with post-traumatic stress disorder (PTSD). In this, a treatment based on virtual therapies exposed patients to diverse virtual settings, such as a setting with a multiple theme can be demonstrated to be an efficacious method for assisting veterans in coping with trauma.

Metaverse could also assist in improving mental health. This study concludes that it is necessary to promote the benefits of metaverse on mental health and its importance in educating individuals after COVID-19 [18].

Digital twins focus on creating a detailed digital representation of physical objects and systems. This enables the creation of digital copies of real-world objects, which in turn allows for accurate predictions and optimization of their virtual counterparts. Digital twins provide proactive maintenance and surveillance of incidents, leading to enhanced operational effectiveness in the physical realm and a decreased likelihood of possible dangers.

Telemedicine is a broad word that facilitates communication between doctors and patients without being physically present. This might include methods like phone conversations, video conferences, email, and texting [19]. Telemedicine is a term that can be used interchangeably with digital medicine, e-health, and telehealth. The concept of "MED verse" is now being developed and has significant potential to bring about a revolution in medical science.

A medical system combines virtual and real-world integration with metaverse technology. The three main servers located in the cloud data center that act as the core of this system are the consultant server, the holographic distribution server, and the AI medical picture server. Through AR, medical practitioners stationed at different institutions may access a whole collection of AI medical photographs and data thanks to the integrated components. The metaverse will be utilized in the field of healthcare education to provide students with hands-on experiences in surgery and patient interactions, along with the opportunity to pick up new skills. By using a sophisticated VR simulation, the teaching process can be improved by providing medical training to improve the clinical skills of the medical students.

Metaverse is becoming more widely acknowledged as a useful resource for emergency medical education. It provides learners with an unparalleled experience that can augment the development of critical skills related to decision-making, cooperation, and resuscitation. When it comes to preparing medical personnel to handle a high volume of injured or dying patients, this technology is essential.

The cardiac patient simulator Harvey, built in 1968, is a prime example of the Gordon Institute's creative efforts in healthcare simulation. It serves as a virtual environment that accurately replicates various heart conditions. In this setup, a) a nursing student dons a VR headset. b) A simulated cardiac evaluation is being given to a virtual patient. c) The setup presents VR experiences through a variety of exhibitions to enhance cooperative learning in a group environment. d) For instance, the simulated patient's pupils' respond to light stimuli. The University of Northampton's nursing facility is advancing classroom education through these advanced simulation techniques.

The emergency management training offered by the Gordon Centre to simulate and innovate in medical sciences now incorporates platforms for AR/VR. A variety of medical conditions affecting blood pressure, pulse rate, breathing, and respiratory ailments are included in the category of pathologies.

VR simulations are a powerful and successful technology that a university in Switzerland has adopted into its medical science department to teach medical students about COVID-19 clinical diagnostics [16]. The children receive in-depth training on COVID-19, covering a wide range of essential skills. COVID-19 VR Strikes Back, a VR-based program, is used to deliver the instruction. The application, developed by ORamaVR SA, utilizes hand controllers and the Oculus Rift headgear.

Holloman is employed for the purpose of constructing three-dimensional holographic learning environments. Overall, the conducted and analogous research indicates that immersive VR improves motor movements, such as body movements, navigation, and more. This enhancement has the potential to aid in the mitigation of unconscious biases. Similarly, immersive VR enhances trainees' work performance by facilitating rapid learning through the use of Polaris, a celestial object with a specific identification. The main focus is to augment the anatomical comprehension of medical students and provide them with

**Table 4.1** Applications of metaverse in healthcare.

| Application area | Description | References |
|---|---|---|
| **Patient monitoring** | Providing virtual assistance to patients | [9, 25] |
| **Virtual physiotherapy** | Sharing patient injury details on digital twins for treatment | [8] |
| **Holographic monitoring** | Patient interaction from remote areas can be done using metaverse applications | [17, 30] |
| **Virtual biopsy** | A virtual biopsy can be possible using metaverse applications in healthcare | [29, 31] |
| **Emergency care** | Metaverse applications for emergency care and response | [6] |
| **Education and training** | Tools to facilitate clinical simulations and surgical operations and health care delivery | [6, 10–14] |
| **Dentistry** | Providing oral health care using metaverse tools | [24, 28] |
| **Gynecology** | Metaverse applications in gynecology and fetal care | [15, 18–20] |
| **Mental health** | Exploring new software for addressing mental health issues | [32–34] |
| **Physical health** | Exploring new software for addressing physical health issues | [35] |
| **Chronic Diseases** | Metaverse applications to treat chronic diseases and illnesses like cancer | [26, 27] |

instruction in vital medical procedures. Undergraduate medical and nursing students can gain a higher level of skill in the classroom with the use of HoloLens 2.

Through an immersive AR experience, the Project Polaris training program helps students better understand real-world clinical conditions, particularly when it comes to placing catheters and cannulas in the urinary tracts of both males and females. With this method, students may improve their skills, which can have a big influence on their professional paths in the future [21].

GigXR and Elsevier have collaborated to develop an advanced mixed-reality anatomy application named HoloHuman [26]. This application allows users to engage with holographic learning environments. The initiative enables both on-site and distant users to actively participate in interactive HoloHuman sessions utilizing Microsoft HoloLens headsets and mobile devices. Understanding certain anatomical features in-depth using the application's advanced 3D holographic display contributes to a deeper comprehension of human anatomy.

Practical experience in performing surgical operations has led to the development of surgical simulators in the metaverse. These simulators are a great teaching aid for aspiring surgeons and make complex surgery planning and preparation easier. Moreover, structured data produced by surgical simulators may be utilized to develop algorithms for computer-assisted therapies that depend on medical imaging [23]. A study in this field examines the shortcomings of traditional preoperative counseling techniques and finds many obstacles that impede efficient patient-surgeon communication. Table 4.1 list various applications of metaverse in healthcare.

## Challenges of Metaverse in Healthcare

Applications of metaverse in healthcare are enormous, but there are certain challenges like security, data privacy concerns of patients, cost, and maintenance in implementing metaverse solutions in healthcare [22]. The large collection and storage of patient data over the cloud and the sharing of patient data should be handled with care to prevent data breaches and unauthorized access. To prevent these flaws and to maintain integrity in virtual healthcare environments laws like HIPAA should be followed. It is crucial to maintain the balance between patient rights, ethical norms, and technological advancements to promote a secure healthcare metaverse. Figure 4.5 shows the challenges of AR/VR in healthcare.

In order to run metaverse applications and to support high-quality infrastructure, advanced hardware and uninterrupted network connectivity are required. Running metaverse solutions requires compatibility and

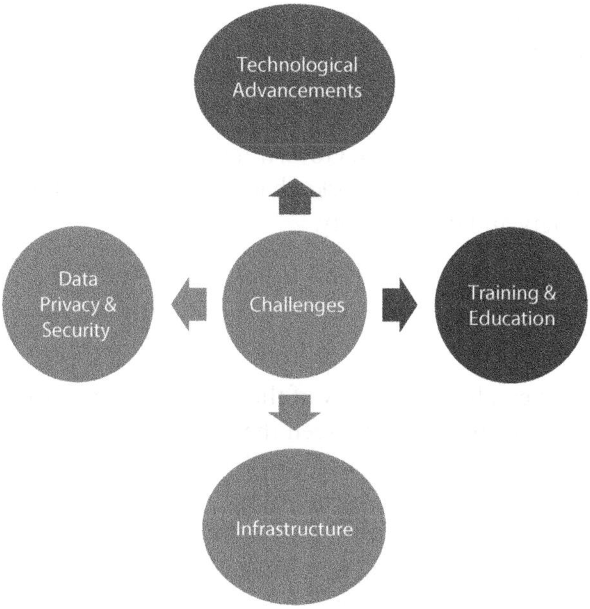


**Figure 4.5** Challenges of metaverse in healthcare.

interoperability to run on multiple platforms. This also involves high maintenance and regular updates to meet current requirements.

Ongoing research involves the amalgamation of machine learning and AI into a metaverse environment to analyze large amounts of data and more accurate result predictions. These developments result in better patient outcomes ranging from surgery, diagnostics, mental health, and rehabilitation [33].

Adequate training and education are required for professionals to familiarize themselves with new tools and advanced software and platforms. Lack of technical skills and inadequate education may result in unacceptance and change in behavior. Cost can be another measure challenge in implementing metaverse solutions in healthcare which involves infrastructure cost, maintenance, training, and other operational expenses.

## Future Directions

Looking at the current prospects of the metaverse in healthcare, it can bring a revolutionary change. Emerging technologies like AI and machine learning can further improve the accuracy and efficiency of healthcare solutions. With ongoing research and innovation, the capabilities of these machines can be enhanced which can result in more profound solutions and scope in this field.

Defining policies and regulations is crucial for the effective use of metaverse in the healthcare industry. Governments and regulatory bodies must work together to create frameworks that support innovation while ensuring patient safety and data security.

## Conclusion

This chapter gives a brief overview of the metaverse and its applications in the healthcare domain. It can be seen that the metaverse has the potential to revolutionize the healthcare industry by providing intelligent solutions for medical therapies, surgeries, and training. There are various challenges discussed in this chapter but the benefits like improved access to medical facilities and enhanced patient care make it a promising technology for future research and development.

## References

1. Jeon, H.J., Youn, H.C., Ko, S.M., Kim, T.H., Blockchain and AI Meet in the Metaverse, in: *Advances in the Convergence of Blockchain and Artificial Intelligence*, vol. *73*(10.5772), pp. 73–82, 2022.
2. Gadekallu, T.R., Wang, W., Yenduri, G., Ranaweera, P., Pham, Q.V., da Costa, D.B., Liyanage, M., Blockchain for the metaverse: A review. *Future Gener. Comput. Syst.*, *143*, 401–419, 2023.
3. Ullah, H., Manickam, S., Obaidat, M., Laghari, S.U.A., Uddin, M., Exploring the potential of metaverse technology in healthcare: Applications, challenges, and future directions. *IEEE Access*, *11*, 69686–69707, 2023.
4. Uddin, M., Manickam, S., Ullah, H., Obaidat, M., Dandoush, A., Unveiling the metaverse: Exploring emerging trends, multifaceted perspectives, and future challenges. *IEEE Access*, *11*, 87087–87103, 2023.
5. Mozumder, M.A.I., Armand, T.P.T., Imtiyaj Uddin, S.M., Athar, A., Sumon, R.I., Hussain, A., Kim, H.C., Metaverse for digital anti-aging healthcare: an overview of potential use cases based on artificial intelligence, blockchain, IoT technologies, its challenges, and future directions. *Appl. Sci.*, *13*, 8, 5127, 2023.
6. Wu, T.C. and Ho, C.T.B., A scoping review of metaverse in emergency medicine. *Australas. Emergency Care*, *26*, 1, 75–83, 2023.

7. Román-Belmonte, J.M., Rodríguez-Merchán, E.C., De la Corte-Rodríguez, H., Metaverse applied to musculoskeletal pathology: Orthoverse and Rehabverse. *Postgrad. Med.*, *135*, 5, 440–448, 2023.
8. Suh, I., McKinney, T., Siu, K.C., Current perspective of metaverse application in medical education, research and patient care. *Virtual Worlds*, 2, 2, 115–128, MDPI, 2023.
9. Skalidis, I., Muller, O., Fournier, S., CardioVerse: The cardiovascular medicine in the era of Metaverse. *Trends Cardiovasc. Med.*, *33*, 8, 471–476, 2023.
10. Pottle, J., Virtual reality and the transformation of medical education. *Future Healthcare J.*, *6*, 3, 181–185, 2019.
11. Jones, D., Hazelton, M., Evans, D.J., Pento, V., See, Z.S., Van Leugenhaege, L., Fealy, S., The road to birth: Using digital technology to visualise pregnancy anatomy, in: *Digital Anatomy: Applications of Virtual, Mixed and Augmented Reality*, pp. 325–342, Springer International Publishing, Cham, 2021.
12. Jones, D., See, Z.S., Billinghurst, M., Goodman, L., Fealy, S., Extended reality for midwifery learning: MR VR demonstration, in: *Proceedings of the 17th International Conference on Virtual-Reality Continuum and its Applications in Industry*, pp. 1–2, 2019.
13. Al-Saud, L.M., Mushtaq, F., Allsop, M.J., Culmer, P.C., Mirghani, I., Yates, E., Keeling, A., Mon-Williams, M.A., Manogue, M., Feedback and motor skill acquisition using a haptic dental simulator. *Eur. J. Dent. Educ.*, 21, 4, 240–247, 2017.
14. Almousa, O., Prates, J., Yeslam, N., Mac Gregor, D., Zhang, J., Phan, V., Nielsen, M., Smith, R., Qayumi, K., Virtual reality simulation technology for cardiopulmonary resuscitation training: An innovative hybrid system with haptic feedback. *Simul. Gaming*, 50, 1, 6–22, 2019.
15. Zikas, P., Kamarianakis, M., Kartsonaki, I., Lydatakis, N., Kateros, S., Kentros, M., Geronikolakis, E., *et al.*, Covid-19-VR strikes back: innovative medical VR training, in: *ACM SIGGRAPH 2021 Immersive Pavilion*, pp. 1–2, 2021.
16. Birrenbach, T., Zbinden, J., Papagiannakis, G., Exadaktylos, A.K., Müller, M., Hautz, W.E., Sauter, T.C., Effectiveness and utility of virtual reality simulation as an educational tool for safe performance of COVID-19 diagnostics: prospective, randomized pilot trial. *JMIR Serious Games*, 9, 4, e29586, 2021 Oct 8.
17. Hajesmaeel-Gohari, S., Sarpourian, F., Shafiei, E., Virtual reality applications to assist pregnant women: a scoping review. *BMC Pregnancy Childb.*, 21, 1–8, 2021 Dec.
18. Sridhar, A., Shiliang, Z., Woodson, R., Kwan, L., Non-pharmacological anxiety reduction with immersive virtual reality for first-trimester dilation and curettage: a pilot study. *Eur. J. Contracept. Reprod. Health Care*, 25, 6, 480–3, 2020 Nov 1.

19. Mahajan, S., Phishing uniform resource locator detection using machine learning: A step towards secure system. *Secur. Privacy*, 6, 6, e311, 2023 Nov.
20. Werner, H., Ribeiro, G., Arcoverde, V., Lopes, J., Velho, L., The use of metaverse in fetal medicine and gynecology. *Eur. J. Radiol.*, 150, 2022 May 1.
21. Dzimitrowicz, H.E. and Armstrong, A.J., Triplet Therapy: Entering the Metaverse of Metastatic Hormone-sensitive Prostate Cancer Treatment. *Eur. Urol.*, S0302–2838, 2022 Sep 13.
22. Mahajan, S. and Nanda, M., Revolutionizing Banking with Blockchain: Opportunities and Challenges Ahead, in: *Next-Generation Cybersecurity: AI, ML, and Blockchain*, pp. 287–304, 2024 May 19.
23. Scolozzi, P. and Bijlenga, P., Removal of recurrent intraorbital tumour using a system of augmented reality. *Br. J. Oral Maxillofac. Surg.*, 55, 9, 962–4, 2017 Nov 1.
24. Duman, S., Çelik Özen, D., Duman, Ş.B., Metaverse in paediatric dentistry. *Eur. Arch. Paediatr. Dent.*, 23, 4, 655–6, 2022 Aug.
25. Cho, M.G., A study on smart aging system for the elderly based on metaverse. *J. Digital Convergence*, 20, 2, 261–8, 2022.
26. Sun, M., Xie, L., Liu, Y., Li, K., Jiang, B., Lu, Y., Yang, D., The metaverse in current digital medicine. *Clin. eHealth*, 5, 52–57, 2022.
27. Bansal, Y. and Mahajan, S., Network Security Breaches: Comprehension and Its Implications, in: *Perspectives on Ethical Hacking and Penetration Testing*, pp. 239–254, IGI Global, 2023.
28. Dahiya, A., Anuradha, Mahajan, S., Gupta, S., A Review on the Role of Blockchain Technology in the Healthcare Domain, in: *Blockchain and Deep Learning for Smart Healthcare*, pp. 113–45, 2023 Dec 28.
29. McWilliam, A. and Scarfe, P., The metaverse and oncology. *Clin. Oncol.*, 35, 1, 12–4, 2023 Jan 1.
30. Tan, T.F., Li, Y., Lim, J.S., Gunasekeran, D.V., Teo, Z.L., Ng, W.Y., Ting, D.S., Metaverse and virtual health care in ophthalmology: Opportunities and challenges. *Asia-Pac. J. Ophthalmol.*, 11, 3, 237–46, 2022 May 1.
31. Mahajan, S., Blockchain in Smart Healthcare Systems: Hope or Despair?, in: *Prospects of blockchain technology for accelerating scientific advancement in healthcare*, pp. 1–20, IGI Global, 2022.
32. Almarzouqi, A., Aburayya, A., Salloum, S.A., Prediction of user's intention to use metaverse system in medical education: A hybrid SEM-ML learning approach. *IEEE Access*, 10, 43421–34, 2022 Apr 21.
33. Turbyne, C.A., Virtuality technologies in mental healthcare: The medical metaverse of tomorrow, 2022.

34. Usmani, S.S., Sharath, M., Mehendale, M., Future of mental health in the metaverse. *Gen. Psychiatr.*, 35, 4, e100825, 2022.
35. Bajaj, P., Arora, R., Khurana, M., Mahajan, S., Cloud security: the future of data storage, in: *Cyber Security and Digital Forensics: Proceedings of ICCSDF 2021*, pp. 87–98, Springer Singapore, 2022.

5

# Creating The Healthcare of Tomorrow: The Metaverse's Opportunities and Challenges

**Vedanshee Upadhyay*** **and Sourabh Sharma**

*School of Computer Science and Engineering, Avantika University, Ujjain, Madhya Pradesh, India*

***Abstract***

The healthcare industry is on the cusp of a technological revolution as the metaverse comes into being. This new concept has a range of opportunities to revamp how we deliver healthcare and people experience it through virtual reality (VR) and augmented reality (AR). The basics of metaverse in healthcare are examined in this article. We look at how these technologies that form the basis for this immersive healthcare environment, including VR, AR, artificial intelligence (AI), and the Internet of Things (IoT), are merging into one another. There are discussions about several ways that the metaverse could be used within healthcare settings such as remote consultations, medical education, surgical training, and rehabilitation treatments. Furthermore, this is also informed by the fact that the paper recognizes some of the challenges facing the incorporation of metaverse with healthcare like accessibility, data privacy, and ethical considerations. Lastly, we reflect on where this emerging sector may be heading in conclusion with an emphasis on its ability to change patient experiences and open up access to healthcare for all citizens.

***Keywords*****:** Metaverse, healthcare, virtual reality (VR), augmented reality (AR), artificial intelligence (AI), Internet of Things (IoT), medical education, ethical considerations

**Corresponding author*: vedanshee.upadhyay@avantika.edu.in

Ajay Kumar Vyas, Harleen Kaur, Sourabh Sharma and Bhavya Alankar (eds.) Metaverse Technologies, Security and Applications for Healthcare, (101–120) © 2025 Scrivener Publishing LLC

## 5.1 Introduction

To disrupt various industries, including healthcare, the metaverse is an immersive virtual world that allows users to interact with one another and digital objects. This innovative technology could revolutionize the manner in which we deliver and receive healthcare by employing state-of-the-art techniques such as virtual reality (VR), augmented reality (AR), artificial intelligence (AI), and the Internet of Things (IoT).

Metaverse has proven its disruptive potential in healthcare sectors. It is a nascent idea that defies the restrictions of a physical world making it possible for people to interact within a persistent three-dimensional place where they can do many things [1]. The metaverse offers unique possibilities for integrating advanced technologies like VR, AR, AI, and the IoT into immersive healthcare settings. This new model offers enormous potential to transform our approach to delivering and experiencing healthcare services by democratizing access, enhancing patient engagement, and refining treatment paradigms.

Remote consultations are at the center of the healthcare metaverse. Geographical and physical distances between patients and doctors can be bridged by VRs and ARs; hence, they are capable of enabling live appointments from any distance. For instance, a patient in a rural location can virtually visit a famous doctor in a distant town. It is possible for such a medical expert to examine the patient via VR technology within a detailed model of an examining room that has been rendered with exactitude [2]. In addition to that, this eliminates the problem of accessing specialized care because it does not matter where one stays and reduces time spent waiting for consultation.

Also, medical education as well as surgical training stands among such potentials that the metaverse holds. VR simulations create situations that are similar to real procedures in medicine which are incomparably hard in most cases. With lifelike anatomical representations of virtual patients, young surgeons can practice complex surgical methods under safe conditions [3]. By using this practically involved learning technique, surgical accuracy and clinical judgment can be significantly improved thus improving patient care in real-life situations. Besides that, AR can also be used to superimpose real-time patient information on the surgeon's view during surgery providing crucial information like anatomical markers as well as vital signs. Such an AR overlay may make surgeons more situationally aware of their environment potentially minimizing complications and increasing successful surgeries [4].

The metaverse's immersion capabilities may also transform rehabilitation treatments. Moreover, patients can use VR-based interventions to practice physical therapy exercises or confront phobias within a safe virtual environment. The above example from Google shows how stroke victims could regain some motor skills through video game-like interaction with VR simulacra that promotes interactivity and motivation in the rehab experience [5]. Likewise, VR exposure therapy provides a simulated and controlled setting for individuals suffering from phobias to gradually face their fears thereby leading to an effective and immersive treatment modality [6].

The healthcare metaverse is a transformative virtual space that combines digital and AR technologies, AI, and interconnected virtual platforms [7–10]. This research paper explores its various applications across medical subfields, addressing challenges and imagining future trends. The term "metaverse" has gained significant recognition in the healthcare industry, reshaping patient care, clinical research, and education [11–14]. This amalgamation forms a highly engaging, participative, and cooperative system for the healthcare fraternity and users [15–18]. This transformation not only is within the frame of data usage by doctors and healthcare institutions but also affects the patient's experience and even the traditional formal education process. Now, the healthcare metaverse is becoming a part of clinical practice when patient treatment is carried out in a new way, using innovative methods of diagnostics, treatment, and rehabilitation [19–23]. Teleconsultations and telemedicine are real-world experiences, various care providers reach out to clients across the globe. AR assists surgeons during delicate operations through the visual representation of data as well as enhancing accuracy. The metaverse is used more extensively in cases where the therapy regimes are designed depending on the patient's records. Healthcare metaverse technology implementation as applied to medical education is revamping how the future healthcare practitioner is trained and prepared. Technological teachings steadily open windows for the learners, in this case, the medical students to practice realistic clinical scenarios which, in turn, stimulate and improve their decision-making abilities as well as their procedural proficiencies. Anatomy lessons have turned into virtual dissection of canned animals adding dimension and furthering the student's knowledge in a shorter period due to the lack of access to dead bodies for dissection [24–28]. In medical research, the healthcare system offers the functionality of a collaborative environment where actual time cooperation is possible even though the researchers cooperating could be located in different geographical locations [29–34]. Due to the use of simulations and models in the metaverse, the analysis of biological structures and potential effects of drugs on them takes place in a much shorter time. Electronic medical records within the metaverse will summarize patients' data and compare and contrast multiple cases that could otherwise be unnoticeable by traditional research methods [31–33]. The use of healthcare metaverse in mental healthcare is an emerging field with massive potential. Virtual environments create exposure therapy in a safe environment that helps persons cope with phobias and anxieties. Virtual sessions involving the use of metaverse increase the availability of mental health services whereby tackles the shortage of psychologists in the world due to the increasing demand for mental health services. Despite such potential, including the integration of the healthcare metaverse in the everyday practice of medicine is not without its problems [35–42]. Extended risk is high and includes the privacy and security risks of patients' information that need better protection. This might lead to a scenario whereby the capability of giving access to enhanced healthcare services is only feasible for either the suppliers or implementers due to the costs of infrastructure. Interoperability is another major barrier; along the same vein, each mi-subspecialty has its own systems and platforms. These technologies need to be integrated into the context of the healthcare metaspace so that practitioners working in it may communicate smoothly and work together. Anything concerning the ethical part especially in certain areas such as psychological well-being requires certain measures which when implemented can avert any unwanted incidents [39–41]. Therefore, it can be said that the healthcare metaverse has a bright future. Technological developments, in particular, AI may see enhanced machinery in detection and improved treatment advice [43–49]. Privacy issues could be addressed by applying blockchain-based solutions for regulating the storing and sharing of patients' data in the metaverse [50–56]. The advance in the prototyping haptic system may expand the sense of touch within the virtual environment thus making it more appropriate for surgical practice and exercises. As time goes on, the metaverse applications can be expanded to other sectors like home healthcare that can allow the patients to be cared for from the comfort of their homes. Issues of privacies, securities, compatibility and standardization issues, and ethical ones are some of the glaring issues that have to be resolved to enable integration [38–40, 57–61]. It is under such circumstances that the healthcare metaverse waits in the wings to transform the sphere of healthcare into a patient-centered, team-based, and technologically advanced one.

The basics of the metaverse in healthcare are reviewed, but how they come together to form a realistic healthcare environment is examined here. It will examine possible applications like telemedicine consultations, medical training, surgery training, and physical therapy. Also, it will discuss the challenges that are associated with incorporating a metaverse into healthcare including access, privacy, and ethics. Finally, this developing area of research could shape future directions for patients' experience as well as equalize their accessibility to medical treatments and services.

## 5.2 Analysis: Metaverse and Healthcare

This analysis explores the potential of the metaverse, a virtual environment powered by VR, AR, AI, and IoT to transform healthcare. The focus is on four key points that demonstrate its effectiveness: expanding access to services through telemedicine, improving medical education, and redefining surgical training and treatment. Lack of space and shortage of doctors often hinder the provision of good healthcare. The metaverse may offer significant promise for creating virtual health centers. Research shows that VR sessions can be as effective as face-to-face visits in some cases [62]. Additionally, AI-supported chatbots in the virtual world can reduce the burden on primary care physicians by performing initial diagnosis and treatment recommendations [63]. A large number of books and cadavers have always been used in medical education. On the other hand, the virtual world creates a unique learning environment. Studies have shown that VR simulation is an effective tool for teaching anatomy and complex surgical procedures [64]. The immersive metaverse platform can combine VR and AR with real-time patient data to create interactive experiences for medical students and staff [18]. Surgical training combines classroom instruction with the care of real patients. Therefore, this virtual technology can provide a safer, more controlled environment for surgeons to improve their surgical procedures. This is because VR-supported simulations describe complex surgeries and allow trainees to rehearse and complete procedures before being exposed to real patients [65]. The virtual world can also enable remote collaboration between surgeons divided by geographical boundaries [66]. Physical therapy and rehabilitation often take time and vary from region to region. Metaverse opens up new possibilities for VR editing. According to some studies, VR has demonstrated its role in post-stroke treatment by improving patients' physical activity and participation [67]. Therefore, metaverse-based rehabilitation programs can be exercises that provide personalized recommendations to increase compliance and benefit.

Technologies including VR, AR, and MR allow users to have an end-to-end VR with interaction in real time between users and what they represent in the virtual environment. This unparalleled experience is partly due to techniques including front-projected holographic displays, novel human-computer interaction (HCI) solutions, including the state-of-the-art brain-computer interface (BCI), and large-scale 3D modeling [68]. However, even though these technologies are referred to as XR, it becomes necessary to distinguish these basic terms as one cannot use them synonymously [69].

AR can be defined as one of the most advanced tools that is capable of changing our vision and even behavior in the perceived environment. The ability to merge virtual objects into the physical environment is going to enrich our perception of senses and let the individual interact with the digital info in real space with rather high accuracy. Thus, AR engulfs the process of accurate and convenient 3D registration of the virtual and real objects providing a coherent integration of both real and synthetic environments. AR can provide many features such as plane detection, identification of objects, face recognition, and even movement tracking [70].

The identification of the ability to provoke the feeling of a very effective immersion as the chief VR feature corresponds well with the definition of VR as a means that relies on sophisticated hardware and software solutions to create a realistically convincing simulation of reality within the user's perceptual space [71, 72]. It provides actual images and sound, giving a complete outlook of the game that makes the experience unforgettable and changed [73].

Because of this, VR can be applied in teaching students clinical skills needed in rare situations with the use of models that simulate the situations [74]. One such example is applying VR in multiple casualty simulations to accommodate the student's practice in the triage method for efficient clinical assessment and adequate formative performance, which can be as beneficial as the simulated application [75].

Analyzing this technology, it is necessary to state that it can be helpful in the context of healthcare to provide adaptive therapeutic services. For example, a cross-sectional study [15] reveals four major research areas of VR therapy based on its application, mainly, post-traumatic stress disorder, anxiety and fear-related disorder, and pain treatment.

In the same manner, AR and MR technologies can be seen as a means of improving interaction between real and digital entities, and given that both classes proposed situated and realistic scenarios that are deemed effective for the teaching of healthcare subjects [76], both technologies could be of significant use for implementing in healthcare education across different learning contexts.

Augmented virtuality (AV) is a technology that presents a rather special means of accessing the virtual. Unlike AR which displays virtual objects within the real environment, AV real-time reconstructs real objects into virtual environments. This allows the user to have an actual bodily experience of the content to the extent they can be said to be in the digital space [77].

Mixed reality (MR) is a more complex technology that simultaneously contains traits of both AR and VR; as a consequence, MR generates a perceptual world for digital and physical objects. In the context of the current paper, an MR environment lies on top of a real environment with the incorporation of virtual elements. In other words, MR technology allows the user to view real objects together with virtual ones [77]. This creates a very strong relationship between the physical and the virtual making it possible for one to obtain a feel that is very hard to describe. Both MR visualizations and AI which include machine learning (ML) are receiving attention in the field of minimally invasive robotic surgery. Known as the surgical metaverse, this union of MR and AI is capable of making surgical procedures easier, more accurate, and more secure for the patient [78].

Artificial intelligence refers to the ability of machines to mimic human intelligence, so they can exemplify human-like cognitive skills and apply them in a similar way to how human beings do them [79]. AI can be segmented into numerous subcategories, most of which include ML, natural language processing (NLP), and computer vision (CV).

This, in turn, is useful for the metaverse as the processes can be learned through the real-life exchanges of participants and the technology, ML, through the conduct of the metaverse participants. AI improves the metaverse's capacity to exhibit human-like patterns, thereby lessening the human touch and subsequent opportunities for expansion. The metaverse also provides smooth interaction to the users through NLP technology through which the user's natural language is parsed, analyzed, and then automatically processed into providing the expected outcome. Several AI technologies like NLP, neural networks, and deep learning must all work together to improve the accuracy of speech recognition. NLP technology permits extracting natural language spoken language and converting it to a mechanical language format that is to be further processed and translated to a natural language format once again. This is an advantageous technology to the metaverse allowing users cross-regional interaction and avatars can speak using natural language.

There has been talk about launching a metaverse of medical technology and AI (MeTAI) that could address the issues of growth, assessment, regulation, and refinement of the AI-based medical practice, with virtual comparative scanning, raw data sharing, augmented regulatory science, and, most prominently, metaverse medical intervention as its constituents [80]. The concept of digital twins (DTs) is based on the dissemination of digital models of physical objects and processes [81], which makes it possible to create accurate digital representations of real physical objects [82] that enable precise expectations and enhancements of such objects' virtual versions. The use of modern AI technologies creates the prerequisites for the generation of realistic replicas of complex physical phenomena, which is very useful when designing and demonstrating extensive metaverse landscapes. Also, DTs help in the prevention and control of possible accidents and include improvements in maintenance in real-world applications. Corresponding to the real situation, the metaverse DT is the interface through which users can interact with the services of the virtual world.

DTs can be developed at the micro and macro levels, although the macroscopic level generates a replica of the whole universe [83]. This replication makes it possible to go through every possible dimension to some degree and assumes an important role in the creation of the metaverse. On the other hand, microscopic DT mimics molecular objects and gives a way to study events at the atomic level. This developmental progression shows that whether a phenomenon is simple or complex, DTs are available to match that level of complexity and are thus appropriate to use to come up with models of any given phenomena at whichever level of complexity. As human DTs appear to be a rapidly growing and potentially highly valuable area of research, it entails real data gathering from individuals and utilizing ML algorithms to deduce health information about a person in the hope of enhancing people's health and wellbeing [84]. However, the major problem is how to obtain these data, as it is hard to avoid using uncomfortable and rather high-risk health-sensing devices. Considering DT technology, one of the main research gaps that is of significant importance is the use of DT technology for specific detailed human health applications. Pulse rate, respiratory rate, oximetry, and blood pressure are significant in diagnosing physical and mental health processes like emotions, tiredness, stress, and sleep. These signals have become more important in recent times, due to the growth of virtual health and telemedicine services after the pandemic period.

The metaverse has vast connectivity for large user groups due to the ability to support linking up to the net through wireless networks. Today, many advanced technologies have emerged in recent years to attempt to enhance the effectiveness of networking systems in wireless communications. AI has been frequently integrated at different layers of the network architecture to accomplish this goal [85]. Data networking technologies including IoT, software-defined networks, and the sixth-generation (6G) Internet play a pivotal role in transmitting data across the borders of the physical and the virtual world as well as across the different sub-metaverses within a metaverse. Climbing in these advanced technologies like beyond 5G (B5G) and 6G provides immense opportunities for providing reliable, immediate, and broad connectivity for numerous metaverse devices with high mobility. The utilization of these technologies in the generation of the metaverse is beneficial as it increases the system's interconnection and availability leading to a more harmonious operation for the users [86].

The metaverse can revolutionize how people are trained by the lack of applying AR and other features of digital training in cases where people have to learn in high-stress circumstances. This way, introducing virtual elements helps to achieve the learning outcomes in less time, with more active participation of the students and efficiency in the process [87]. This could lead to a change from normal flat books to computers and robots for teaching at virtual universities. Due to the COVID-19 pandemic, flaws in the present virtual educational systems are apparent and the technologies utilized in the metaverse suggest prospects to advance educational systems. The metaverse offers the students actual physical world learning simulations without complications. The goals of healthcare education in the metaverse would be to give practical learning environments for the trainees to develop surgical and patient interaction and practice new methods and techniques. As such, it can help in medical training by improving the method of education and development of complicated clinical skills [19].

Surgical simulators have over time been developed and are associated with the metaverse. These simulators are quite helpful for the training of new surgical students and give the advantage of planning and preparation for complex operations. Besides, surgical simulators produce relevant data with a configured format, which can be utilized to develop algorithms for defining the basic protocols and procedures to be employed to execute the required treatment plans with the help of medical images. Among the studies that are located in this area [88], one of the articles describes the inefficiency of traditional forms of preoperative consultation and describes a number of factors that adversely affect the communication process between patients and surgeons. They include a lack of motivation, poor conversation skills of the physician, and language barriers. Comprehension of surgical procedures, risks, or complications can be done virtually without compromising the practical knowledge while improving the general comprehension which is a plus to the patient when explaining the issue at hand. This enables the patient to make his/her own decisions autonomously hence enhancing the patient's satisfaction.

Some other applications of surgical training include exercises designed to expose orthopedic surgery residents to arthroplasty, which is a surgery that may be aimed at providing the joint's function, for instance, total hip arthroplasty [89].

## 5.3 Discussion and Synthesis

The four themes of expanded access to care, medical and surgical care, and advances in rehabilitation paint a compelling picture of how healthy technology is. The elements here are brought together to help create a larger vision as discussed below. Telemedicine platforms can provide students with access to a wide range of scientific information and expert advice, making their education more efficient [90]. This has created a generation of doctors willing to integrate technology into their practices, able to accelerate new types of treatments that are well delivered. For example, virtual beauty treatment programs are shown, but their results depend on doctors who can refer patients through these platforms [91]. However, inconsistencies and differences remain. Despite the convenience of telemedicine, concerns remain regarding potential inconsistencies in the quality of remote diagnosis and access to technology. Similarly, the long-term effectiveness of traditional rehabilitation compared to face-to-face therapy requires further study [91]. Research is needed to address these issues to ensure the fair and effective use of these technologies. The advantage of this is that technological advances such as VR simulators have the potential to improve surgical training as they provide surgeons with a safe and controlled environment to hone their skills before working on real patients [92]. Not only did this improve safety for the patient, but it also enabled more standard training across borders. The difficulty, of course, is how to make sure that the skills one learns in a simulation environment are transferable and have an impact when it comes time to perform surgery. Particular attention is needed concerning the ethics of data privacy as well as the potential for these technologies only widen inequities in access to surgical experience [93]. The themes identified in this analysis directly link with broader research within healthcare transformation enabled by technology.

There are a number of difficulties and constraints associated with the adoption and use of the metaverse that must be resolved [94–97]. Based on the literature, the following are conclusions about the interoperability challenges. Eventually, the issues of compatibility between various platforms and technologies will arise, which will hinder the free flow of users and their assets from one metaverse to another. Privacy and Security Concerns: Due to the introduction of the metaverse, many privacy and security issues have been observed since so much personal data is created within it. Culture and privacy, unauthorized access, and security of data are some of the factors that must be taken into consideration. Content Moderation Issues: The creation of content in the metaverse by the users can create some issues associated with the moderation of the content, as proper regulation of obscene and defamatory material must be maintained for a safe and friendly environment. Digital Ownership Dilemmas: Deciding on ownership rights and how to coordinate property rights to items within the metaverse is not always clear. The problems concerning the use and protection of information, as well as authorship and ownership rights must be solved for the proper and transparent completion of transactions. Accessibility Considerations: Specifically, the metaverse must become ready for such people who have certain disabilities or belong to certain groups of society because this approach contributes to the creation of an effective and inclusive virtual environment. It is an important principle that one should allocate interfaces, contents, and interactions with different demands and peculiarities in their capabilities.

The possibilities of the metaverse for the development of new paradigms in the rules of digital communications are opening. Technology ideas like VR, AR, AI, and blockchain are some of the trends that are foreseen to shape the evolution of the metaverse. Thus, this evolution can result in a change in virtual environments and turn them into more intricate and interrelated platforms for communication, cooperation, and interactions with digital content. However, these promising opportunities are accompanied by issues of social and economic relevance as well as ethical and legal questions. The metaverse if implemented in society could bring in the availability of information and opportunities but at the same time factors such as privacy, data protection, online identity, as well as content moderation come into the picture. Governance structures are required to adapt to these issues to make sure the metaverse experience will not be dangerous or exclusionary for anyone [12, 98–103].

Emerging Trends and Innovations: It is anticipated that the metaverse is going to grow at a fast pace based on trends and new inventions in technology. Specific trends to look for are developments in virtual and AR systems, AI, and blockchain. They are the key to enhancing or creating completely new types of experience inside the metaverse, as they may revolutionize the ways of communication, working, and entertainment. Moreover, due to the integration with IoT and 5G connectivity, more possibilities of connectivity and function of the metaverse can be expected.

Potential Impact on Society and Economy: The broad application of the metaverse may change society and in particular the economy in several ways. To the same extent, it may liberate residential access to data and jobs, geographical Internet frontiers' abolishment, allowing people of different origins to exchange procedural experiences and share ideas through online platforms. They could give birth to new forms of education, healthcare, and social life. Nonetheless, there are also fears of how the metaverse might be managed to intensify already existing social ills if fairness in access to virtual environments and other technologies is not achieved. Also, the metaverse may affect traditional business sectors and industries changing the overall economy, as well as raising questions about the control and regulation of the new platform.

Ethical and Regulatory Considerations: As such, with the metaverse gradually establishing its presence in people's daily lives, there are aspects of morality and legality that have to be discussed. Some of the challenges are in the areas of privacy and cybersecurity, identity and trust, copyright and trademarks, and speech regulation. There are also negative fears in terms of the development of fake news, cyberbullying, and other related vices within the virtual environment. To deal with such challenges, the regulatory frameworks will have to change to continuously guarantee that the metaverse is safe for all users. Besides, there will be issues and questions about who will regulate the metaverse or control how the metaverse develops and if the abstract concepts of decentralization and free markets are capable of delivering on the metaverse's hyped promises.

## 5.4 Conclusion

Various applications of the metaverse will enable healthcare to be completely revolutionized, and with thematic analysis, we can see now how it may all come together. While VR consultations can make healthcare more accessible and engaging for patients, doctors-in-training are able to prepare like never before with interactive simulations of surgical diagnoses. Despite this opportunity, access to data remains a challenge along with critical issues of privacy and the requirement for common protocols that are cost-effective. It will take additional research to resolve these issues before the metaverse becomes a mainstream tool for healthcare. The importance of such analysis is to illustrate the enormous potential that exists in healthcare through a digital metaverse. New models that reshaped care delivery, education, and rehabilitation have emerged paving the way for a more patient-centric healthcare system. Additionally, the article argues that ethical considerations and data privacy concerns must be addressed first—as well as issues surrounding who has access to it—before BCIs can meaningfully make their way into mainstream healthcare.

In closing, the themes under scrutiny delineate a shifting healthcare scenario tinctured with technological evolution. Telemedicine reaches more people in need of care, and innovations in teaching and learning provide health workers with necessary skills on how to use these technologies effectively. VR is reshaping rehabilitation—an encouraging untapped horizon. The analysis ultimately unveils the interdependency of these technological evolutions teetering toward the revolutionization of healthcare service delivery systems: armadas ironed with outcome-based patient regimes.

This convergence results in an extremely sophisticated system for delivering to the users what is expected to be highly individualized and interactive experiences. Today, the importance of the metaverse is emerging in the business world, and companies are actively adapting for further evolution and improvement of the customers' experience. With the growth of the metaverse, people are likely to experience a shift in both the social and business contexts in completely new ways. The emergence of the metaverse makes it possible to build a second life presence implementing alternative digital personas that reflect the user in the virtual world.

Technological sociology can therefore be said to have become an influential force, working toward the direction of changing social dynamics as well as having a great impact on the world economy, as can be attested through this new technological paradigm. What is more important is the undeniable fact that many new professions appear in line with the constant development of the sphere of technological creation, thus defining the economic process in modern society.

Therefore, as the metaverse evolves, it is expected to expand the possibilities of the virtual and actual, as well as how people interact with technology, culture, and business on an international level.

## References

1. Yi, J., Yao, L., Li, T., Sun, Y., Development of metaverse for intelligent healthcare. *Nat. Mach. Intell.*, 4, 2, 147–152, 2022.
2. Tiwari, A., Dubey, A., Yadav, A.K., Bhansali, R., Bagaria, V., A review of Smart future of healthcare in the digital age to improve Quality of orthopaedic

patient care in metaverse called: The Healthverse!! *J. Clin. Orthop. Trauma*, 48, 102340, 102340, 2024.

3. The Health Care Metaverse Is More Than a Virtual Reality, Boston Consulting Group. bcg.com, 2023, January 19.
4. Metaverse in Healthcare Industry: Applications, Advantages, Challenges, and More, intelivita.com, 2023.
5. Alty, J.L., Daniel, K., Nilsson, M.H., Virtual reality exposure therapy for anxiety disorders: A systematic review. *J. Anxiety Disord.*, 62, 21–34, 2018.
6. Laver, K.E., Lange, B., George, S., Deutsch, J.E., Saposnik, G., Crotty, M., Virtual reality for stroke rehabilitation. *Cochrane Libr.*, 11, 11, CD008349, 2017.
7. Dwivedi, Y.K., Hughes, L., Baabdullah, A.M., Ribeiro-Navarrete, S., Giannakis, M., Al-Debei, M.M., Dennehy, D., Metri, B., Buhalis, D., Cheung, C.M.K., Conboy, K., Doyle, R., Dubey, R., Dutot, V., Felix, R., Goyal, D.P., Gustafsson, A., Hinsch, C., Jebabli, I., Wamba, S.F., Metaverse beyond the hype: Multidisciplinary perspectives on emerging challenges, opportunities, and agenda for research, practice and policy. *Int. J. Inf. Manage.*, 66, 102542, 102542, 2022.
8. Xi, N., Chen, J., Gama, F., Riar, M., Hamari, J., The challenges of entering the metaverse: An experiment on the effect of extended reality on workload. *Inf. Syst. Front.*, 25, 2, 659–680, 2023.
9. Mozumder, M.A.I., Sheeraz, M.M., Athar, A., Aich, S., Kim, H.C., Overview: Technology Roadmap of the Future Trend of Metaverse based on IoT, Blockchain, AI Technique, and Medical Domain Metaverse Activity. *International Conference on Advanced Communication Technology, ICACT*, 2022- February.
10. Yang, D., Zhou, J., Chen, R., Song, Y., Song, Z., Zhang, X., Wang, Q., Wang, K., Zhou, C., Sun, J., Zhang, L., Bai, L., Wang, Y., Wang, X., Lu, Y., Xin, H., Powell, C.A., Thüemmler, C., Chavannes, N.H., Bai, C., Expert consensus on the metaverse in medicine. *Clin. EHealth*, 5, 1–9, 2022.
11. Huynh-The, T., Pham, Q.V., Pham, X.Q., Nguyen, T.T., Han, Z., Kim, D.S., Artificial intelligence for the metaverse: A survey. *Eng. Appl. Artif. Intell.*, 117, 105581, 105581, 2023.
12. Koohang, A., Nord, J.H., Ooi, K.B., Tan, G.W.H., Al-Emran, M., Aw, E.C.X., Baabdullah, A.M., Buhalis, D., Cham, T.H., Dennis, C., Dutot, V., Dwivedi, Y.K., Hughes, L., Mogaji, E., Pandey, N., Phau, I., Raman, R., Sharma, A., Sigala, M., Wong, L.W., Shaping the Metaverse into Reality: A Holistic Multidisciplinary Understanding of Opportunities, Challenges, and Avenues for Future Investigation. *J. Comput. Inf. Syst.*, 63, 3, 735–765, 2023.
13. Petrigna, L. and Musumeci, G., The Metaverse: A New Challenge for the Healthcare System: A Scoping Review. *J. Funct. Morphol. Kinesiol.*, 7, 3, 63, 2022.
14. Usmani, S.S., Sharath, M., Mehendale, M., Future of mental health in the metaverse. *Gen. Psychiatry*, 35, 4, e100825, 2022.

15. Liu, Z., Ren, L., Xiao, C., Zhang, K., Demian, P., Virtual Reality Aided Therapy towards Health 4.0: A Two-Decade Bibliometric Analysis. *Int. J. Environ. Res. Public Health*, 19, 3, 1525, 2022.
16. Zhu, H.Y., Hieu, N.Q., Hoang, D.T., Nguyen, D.N., Lin, C.-T., A human-centric metaverse enabled by brain-computer interface: A survey. *IEEE Commun. Surv. Tutor.*, 26, 3, 2120–2145, 2024.
17. Zhou, Y., Xiao, X., Chen, G., Zhao, X., Chen, J., Self-powered sensing technologies for human Metaverse interfacing. *Joule*, 6, 7, 1381–1389, 2022.
18. Chengoden, R., Victor, N., Huynh-The, T., Yenduri, G., Jhaveri, R.H., Alazab, M., Bhattacharya, S., Hegde, P., Maddikunta, P.K.R., Gadekallu, T.R., Metaverse for Healthcare: A Survey on Potential Applications, Challenges and Future Directions. *IEEE Access*, 11, 12765–12795, 2023.
19. Román-Belmonte, J.M., Rodríguez-Merchán, E.C., de la Corte-Rodríguez, H., Metaverse applied to musculoskeletal pathology: Orthoverse and Rehabverse. *Postgrad. Med.*, 135, 5, 440–448, 2023.
20. Park, J.Y., Lee, K., Chung, D.R., Public interest in the digital transformation accelerated by the COVID-19 pandemic and perception of its future impact. *Korean J. Intern. Med.*, 37, 6, 1223–1233, 2022.
21. Bhattacharya, P., Obaidat, M.S., Savaliya, D., Sanghavi, S., Tanwar, S., Sadaun, B., Metaverse assisted Telesurgery in Healthcare 5.0: An interplay of Blockchain and Explainable AI. *Proceedings of the 2022 International Conference on Computer, Information and Telecommunication Systems, CITS 2022*, 2022.
22. Ali, S., Abdullah, Armand, T.P.T., Athar, A., Hussain, A., Ali, M., Yaseen, M., Joo, M.I., Kim, H.C., Metaverse in Healthcare Integrated with Explainable AI and Blockchain: Enabling Immersiveness, Ensuring Trust, and Providing Patient Data Security. *Sensors*, 23, 2, 565, 2023.
23. Bansal, G., Rajgopal, K., Chamola, V., Xiong, Z., Niyato, D., Healthcare in Metaverse: A Survey on Current Metaverse Applications in Healthcare. *IEEE Access*, 10, 119914–119946, 2022.
24. Li, K., Cui, Y., Li, W., Lv, T., Yuan, X., Li, S., Ni, W., Simsek, M., Dressler, F., When Internet of Things Meets Metaverse: Convergence of Physical and Cyber Worlds. *IEEE Internet Things J.*, 10, 5, 4148–4173, 2023.
25. Zhang, X., Yang, D., Yow, C.H., Huang, L., Wu, X., Huang, X., Guo, J., Zhou, S., Cai, Y., Metaverse for Cultural Heritages. *Electronics (Switzerland)*, 11, 22, 3730, 2022.
26. Musamih, A., Yaqoob, I., Salah, K., Jayaraman, R., Al-Hammadi, Y., Omar, M., Ellahham, S., Metaverse in Healthcare: Applications, Challenges, and Future Directions. *IEEE Consum. Electron. Mag.*, 12, 4, 33–46, 2023.
27. Zhou, H., Gao, J.Y., Chen, Y., The paradigm and future value of the metaverse for the intervention of cognitive decline. *Front. Public Health*, 10, 1016680, 2022.
28. Kala, N., Revolutionizing Medical Education with Metaverse. *Int. J. Sci. Res. Comput. Sci. Eng. Inf. Technol.*, 8, 4, 26–32, 2022.

29. Ahad, A., Tahir, M., Yau, K.-L.A., 5G-based smart healthcare network: Architecture, taxonomy, challenges and future research directions. *IEEE Access*, 7, 100747–100762, 2019.
30. Popescu, G.H., Virtual Patient Diagnosis and Treatment, Networked Medical Devices, and Artificial Intelligence-based Diagnostic Algorithms in the Healthcare Metaverse and Immersive 3D Worlds. *Am. J. Med. Res.*, 9, 2, 153–168, 2022.
31. Newell, M., Wearable Healthcare Monitoring Devices, 3D Medical Imaging Data, and Virtualized Care Systems in the Decentralized and Interconnected Metaverse. *Am. J. Med. Res.*, 9, 2, 137–152, 2022.
32. Perkins, J., Immersive Metaverse Experiences in Decentralized 3D Virtual Clinical Spaces: Artificial Intelligence-driven Diagnostic Algorithms, Wearable Internet of Medical Things Sensor Devices, and Healthcare Modeling and Simulation Tools. *Am. J. Med. Res.*, 9, 2, 89–104, 2022.
33. Nica, E., Virtual healthcare technologies and consultation systems, smart operating rooms, and remote sensing data fusion algorithms in the medical metaverse. *Am. J. Med. Res.*, 9, 2, 105–120, 2022.
34. Lăzăroiu, G., Immersive virtual reality technologies, 3D data modeling and simulation tools, and artificial intelligence-based diagnostic algorithms on metaverse medical platforms. *Am. J. Med. Res.*, 9, 2, 57–72, 2022.
35. Bashir, A.K., Victor, N., Bhattacharya, S., Huynh-The, T., Chengoden, R., Yenduri, G., Maddikunta, P.K.R., Pham, Q.V., Gadekallu, T.R., Liyanage, M., Federated Learning for the Healthcare Metaverse: Concepts, Applications, Challenges, and Future Directions. *IEEE Internet Things J.*, 10, 24, 21873–21891, 2023.
36. Ullah, H., Manickam, S., Obaidat, M., Laghari, S.U.A., Uddin, M., Exploring the Potential of Metaverse Technology in Healthcare: Applications, Challenges, and Future Directions. *IEEE Access*, 11, 69686–69707, 2023.
37. Mozumder, M.A.I., Armand, T.P.T., Imtiyaj Uddin, S.M., Athar, A., Sumon, R.I., Hussain, A., Kim, H.C., Metaverse for Digital Anti-Aging Healthcare: An Overview of Potential Use Cases Based on Artificial Intelligence, Blockchain, IoT Technologies, Its Challenges, and Future Directions. *Appl. Sci. (Switzerland)*, 13, 8, 5127, 2023.
38. Athar, A., Ali, S.M., Mozumder, M.A.I., Ali, S., Kim, H.C., Applications and Possible Challenges of Healthcare Metaverse. *International Conference on Advanced Communication Technology, ICACT*, 2023-February.
39. Sun, M., Xie, L., Liu, Y., Li, K., Jiang, B., Lu, Y., Yang, Y., Yu, H., Song, Y., Bai, C., Yang, D., The metaverse in current digital medicine. *Clin. eHealth*, 5, 52–57, 2022.
40. Shao, L., Tang, W.E.I., Zhang, Z., Chen, X., Medical metaverse: Technologies, applications, challenges and future. *J. Mech. Med. Biol.*, 23, 2, 2350028, 2023.
41. Yang, Y., Siau, K., Xie, W., Sun, Y., Smart Health: Intelligent Healthcare Systems in the Metaverse, Artificial Intelligence, and Data Science Era. *J. Organ. End User Comput. (JOEUC)*, 34, 1, 1–14, 2022.

42. Randazzo, G., Reitano, G., Carletti, F., Iafrate, M., Betto, G., Novara, G., Dal Moro, F., Zattoni, F., Urology: a trip into metaverse. *World J. Urol.*, 41, 10, 2647–2657, 2023.
43. Moztarzadeh, O., Jamshidi, M., Sargolzaei, S., Jamshidi, A., Baghalipour, N., Malekzadeh Moghani, M., Hauer, L., Metaverse and Healthcare: Machine Learning-Enabled Digital Twins of Cancer. *Bioengineering*, 10, 4, 455, 2023.
44. Zhang, T., Shen, J., Lai, C.F., Ji, S., Ren, Y., Multi-server assisted data sharing supporting secure deduplication for metaverse healthcare systems. *Future Gener. Comput. Syst.*, 140, 299–310, 2023.
45. Bhugaonkar, K., Bhugaonkar, R., Masne, N., The Trend of Metaverse and Augmented & Virtual Reality Extending to the Healthcare System. *Cureus*, 14, 9, e29071, 2022.
46. Wiederhold, B.K. and Riva, G., Metaverse Creates New Opportunities in Healthcare. *Annu. Rev. CyberTherapy Telemed.*, 20, 3–7, 2022.
47. Aloqaily, M., Bouachir, O., Karray, F., Ridhawi, I.A., Saddik, A.E., Integrating Digital Twin and Advanced Intelligent Technologies to Realize the Metaverse. *IEEE Consum. Electron. Mag.*, 12, 6, 47–55, 2022.
48. Cerasa, A., Gaggioli, A., Marino, F., Riva, G., Pioggia, G., The promise of the metaverse in mental health: the new era of MEDverse. *Heliyon*, 8, 11, Article e11762, 2022.
49. Wang, J., Chen, S., Liu, Y., Lau, R., Intelligent Metaverse Scene Content Construction. *IEEE Access*, 11, 76222–76241, 2023.
50. Song, Y.T. and Qin, J., Metaverse and Personal Healthcare. *Procedia Comput. Sci.*, 210, 189–197, 2022.
51. Shine, T., Thomason, J., Khan, I., Maher, M., Kurihara, K., El-Hassan, O., Blockchain in Healthcare: 2023 Predictions From Around the Globe. *Blockchain Healthcare Today*, 6, 2, 2023. doi: 10.30953/bhty.v6.245
52. Zhang, G., Dai, Y., Wu, J., Zhu, X., Lu, Y., Swarm Learning-based Secure and Fair Model Sharing for Metaverse Healthcare. *Mobile Netw. Appl.*, 28, 4, 1498–1509, 2023.
53. Moztarzadeh, O., Jamshidi, M., Sargolzaei, S., Keikhaee, F., Jamshidi, A., Shadroo, S., Hauer, L., Metaverse and Medical Diagnosis: A Blockchain-Based Digital Twinning Approach Based on MobileNetV2 Algorithm for Cervical Vertebral Maturation. *Diagnostics*, 13, 8, 1485, 2023.
54. Letafati, M. and Otoum, S., On the privacy and security for e-health services in the metaverse: An overview. *Ad Hoc Netw.*, 150, 103262, 103262, 2023.
55. Bhatia, B. and Joshi, S., Applications of Metaverse in the Healthcare Industry. *International Conference on Innovative Data Communication Technologies and Application, ICIDCA 2023 - Proceedings*, 2023.
56. Uddin, M., Manickam, S., Ullah, H., Obaidat, M., Dandoush, A., Unveiling the Metaverse: Exploring Emerging Trends, Multifaceted Perspectives, and Future Challenges. *IEEE Access*, 11, 87087–87103, 2023.
57. Rane, N.L., Achari, A., Choudhary, S.P., Mallick, S.K., Pande, C.B., Srivastava, A., Moharir, K., A decision framework for potential dam site selection using

GIS, MIF and TOPSIS in Ulhas river basin, India. *J. Clean. Prod.*, 423, 138890, 138890, 2023.
58. Rane, N.L., Achari, A., Saha, A., Poddar, I., Rane, J., Pande, C.B., Roy, R., An integrated GIS, MIF, and TOPSIS approach for appraising electric vehicle charging station suitability zones in Mumbai, India. *Sustain. Cities Soc.*, 97, 104717, 104717, 2023.
59. Gautam, V.K., Pande, C.B., Moharir, K.N., Varade, A.M., Rane, N.L., Egbueri, J.C., Alshehri, F., Prediction of Sodium Hazard of Irrigation Purpose using Artificial Neural Network Modelling. *Sustainability*, 15, 9, 7593, 2023.
60. Rane, N.L., Anand, A., Deepak, K., Evaluating the Selection Criteria of Formwork System (FS) for RCC Building Construction. *Int. J. Eng. Trends Technol.*, 71, 3, 197–205, 2023.
61. Rane, N.L., Achari, A., Hashemizadeh, A., Phalak, S., Pande, C.B., Giduturi, M., Khan, M.Y., Tolche, A.D., Tamam, N., Abbas, M., Yadav, K.K., Identification of sustainable urban settlement sites using interrelationship based multi-influencing factor technique and GIS. *Geocarto Int.*, 38, 1, 1–27, 2023.
62. Dascal, J., *et al.*, Virtual reality and medical inpatients: A systematic review of randomized, controlled trials. *Innovations Clin. Neurosci.*, 14, 1–2, 14, 2017.
63. Janeh, O. and Steinicke, F., A review of the potential of virtual walking techniques for gait rehabilitation. *Front. Hum. Neurosci.*, 15, 717291, 2021.
64. Shah, N.K., *et al.*, Comparison of virtual reality platforms to enhance medical education for procedures. *Front. Virtual Real.*, 3, 1000035, 2022.
65. Mao, R.Q., Lan, L., Kay, J., Lohre, R., Ayeni, O.R., Goel, D.P., Immersive Virtual Reality for Surgical Training: A Systematic Review. *J. Surg. Res.*, 268, 40–58, 2021.
66. Massetti, M. and Chiariello, G.A., The metaverse in medicine. *Eur. Heart J. Suppl.*, 25, Supplement_B, B104–B107, 2023.
67. A Review of Virtual Reality Applications in Post-Stroke Rehabilitation, 2020.
68. Jaynes, C., Seales, W.B., Calvert, K., Fei, Z., Griffioen, J., The Metaverse: a networked collection of inexpensive, self- configuring, immersive environments, in: *Proceedings of the workshop on Virtual environments 2003*, pp. 115–124, 2003.
69. Çöltekin, A., *et al.*, Extended reality in spatial sciences: A review of research challenges and future directions. *ISPRS Int. J. Geo-Inf.*, 9, 7, 439, 2020.
70. Musamih, A., *et al.*, Metaverse in healthcare: Applications, challenges, and future directions. *IEEE Consum. Electron. Mag.*, 12, 4, 33–46, 2022.
71. Steffen, J.H., Gaskin, J.E., Meservy, T.O., Jenkins, J.L., Wolman, I., Framework of affordances for virtual reality and augmented reality. *J. Manage. Inf. Syst.*, 36, 3, 683–729, 2019.
72. Parong, J., *et al.*, The mediating role of presence differs across types of spatial learning in immersive technologies. *Comput. Hum. Behav.*, 107, 106290, 2020.
73. Rashid, M.M., Choi, P., Kwon, K.-R., Kwon, S.-G., Lee, S.-H., Emergence of the Metaverse: How Blockchain, AI, AR/VR, and Digital Transformation Technologies will change the Future World.

74. Gout, L., Hart, A., Houze-Cerfon, C.-H., Sarin, R., Ciottone, G.R., Bounes, V., Creating a novel disaster medicine virtual reality training environment. *Prehospital Disaster Med.*, 35, 2, 225–228, 2020.
75. Price, M.F., *et al.*, Comparative study of a simulated incident with multiple victims and immersive virtual reality. *Nurse Educ. Today*, 71, 48–53, 2018.
76. Gerup, J., Soerensen, C.B., Dieckmann, P., Augmented reality and mixed reality for healthcare education beyond surgery: an integrative review. *Int. J. Med. Educ.*, 11, 1, 2020.
77. Wang, Y., *et al.*, A survey on metaverse: Fundamentals, security, and privacy. *IEEE Commun. Surv. Tutor.*, 25, 1, 319–352, 2022.
78. van Leeuwen, F.W. and van der Hage, J.A., Where Robotic Surgery Meets the Metaverse. *Cancers*, 14, 6161, 2022.
79. Russell, S.J., *Artificial intelligence a modern approach*, Pearson Education, Inc., 2010.
80. Hulsen, T., Applications of the metaverse in medicine and healthcare. *Adv. Lab. Med.*, 5, 2, 159–165, 2024.
81. Chu, N.H., Hoang, D.T., Nguyen, D.N., Phan, K.T., Dutkiewicz, E., Metaslicing: A novel resource allocation framework for metaverse, arXiv preprint arXiv:2205.11087, 2022.
82. Yaqoob, I., Salah, K., Uddin, M., Jayaraman, R., Omar, M., Imran, M., Blockchain for digital twins: Recent advances and future research challenges. *IEEE Network*, 34, 5, 290–298, 2020.
83. Lv, Z., Xie, S., Li, Y., Hossain, M.S., El Saddik, A., Building the Metaverse by Digital Twins at All Scales, State, Relation. *Virtual Reality Intell. Hardware*, 4, 6, 459–470, 2022.
84. Al-Zyoud, I., Laamarti, F., Ma, X., Tobón, D., El Saddik, A., Towards a Machine Learning-Based Digital Twin for Non-Invasive Human Bio-Signal Fusion. *Sensors*, 22, 24, 9747, 2022.
85. Chen, M., Challita, U., Saad, W., Yin, C., Debbah, M., Artificial neural networks-based machine learning for wireless networks: A tutorial. *IEEE Commun. Surv. Tutor.*, 21, 4, 3039–3071, 2019.
86. Du, H., Niyato, D., Miao, C., Kang, J., Kim, D.I., Optimal targeted advertising strategy for secure wireless edge metaverse, in: *GLOBECOM 2022-2022 IEEE Global Communications Conference*, IEEE, pp. 4346–4351, 2022.
87. Wu, T.-C. and Ho, C.-T.B., A scoping review of metaverse in emergency medicine. *Australas. Emergency Care*, 26, 1, 75–83, 2022.
88. Anwer, A., Jamil, Y., Bilal, M., Provision of surgical pre-operative patient counseling services through the Metaverse technology. *Int. J. Surg.*, 104, 106792, 2022.
89. Hooper, J., *et al.*, Virtual reality simulation facilitates resident training in total hip arthroplasty: a randomized controlled trial. *J. Arthroplasty*, 34, 10, 2278–2283, 2019.

90. Alonso, S.G., Marques, G., Barrachina, I., Garcia-Zapirain, B., Arambarri, J., Salvador, J.C., de la Torre Díez, I., Telemedicine and e-Health Research Solutions in Literature for Combatting COVID-19: A Systematic Review. *Health Technol. (Berl.)*, 11, 2, 257–266, 2021.
91. Van Der Vleuten, C.P.M., Medical education using new technologies: Facing the future. *Lancet*, 387, 1530–1532, 2016.
92. Mirelman, A., Raviv, G., Roth, I., Meir, A., Hodgins, H.S., Virtual reality in neurorehabilitation. *J. Neurol. Phys. Ther.*, 42, 4, 200–208, 2018.
93. Satava, R.M., Virtual reality surgical simulation: The art and science. *Am. J. Surg.*, 179, 3, 291–302, 2000.
94. Xu, M., *et al.*, A full dive into realizing the edge-enabled metaverse: Visions, enabling technologies, and challenges. *IEEE Commun. Surv. Tutor.*, 25, 1, 656–700, 2022.
95. Shi, F., *et al.*, A new technology perspective of the Metaverse: Its essence, framework and challenges. *Digit. Commun. Netw.*, 2023. doi: https://doi.org/10.1016/j.dcan.2023.02.017
96. Lee, L.-H., *et al.*, All one needs to know about metaverse: A complete survey on technological singularity, virtual ecosystem, and research agenda, arXiv Prepr. arXiv2110.05352, 2021.
97. Athar, A., Ali, S.M., Mozumder, M.A.I., Ali, S., Kim, H.-C., Applications and possible challenges of healthcare metaverse, in: *2023 25th International Conference on Advanced Communication Technology (ICACT)*, pp. 328–332, 2023.
98. Cho, J., tom Dieck, M.C., Jung, T., What is the metaverse? Challenges, opportunities, definition, and future research directions, in: *International XR Conference*, pp. 3–26, 2022.
99. Yaqoob, I., Salah, K., Jayaraman, R., Omar, M., Metaverse applica- tions in smart cities: Enabling technologies, opportunities, challenges, and future directions. *Internet Things*, 23, 100884, 2023.
100. Khazanchi, D., Kumar Vyas, A., Kant Hiran, K., Padmanaban, S., *Blockchain 3.0 for Sustainable Development*, De Gruyter, Berlin, Boston, 2021, https://doi.org/10.1515/9783110702507.
101. Kant Hiran, K., Khazanchi, D., Kumar Vyas, A., Padmanaban, S., *Machine Learning for Sustainable Development*, De Gruyter, Berlin, Boston, 2021, https://doi.org/10.1515/9783110702514.
102. Vyas, A.K., Balamurugan, S., Hiran, K.K., Dhiman, H.S. (Eds.), *Artificial Intelligence for Renewable Energy Systems*, John Wiley & Sons, USA, 2022.
103. Singh, S., Arya, R.K., Sahana, B.C., Vyas, A.K. (Eds.), *RF Circuits for 5G Applications: Designing with mmWave Circuitry*, John Wiley & Sons, USA, 2023.

# 6

# The Role of Metaverse, AI, and 5G in Modernizing Healthcare Platforms

**Baby Chithra R., Salna Joy and Ajay Sudhir Bale***

*Department of ECE, New Horizon College of Engineering, Bengaluru, Karnataka, India*

***Abstract***

The combination of 5G technology, the metaverse, and artificial intelligence (AI) makes a greater impact and advancement in the field of healthcare. This review paper explores and analyzes the various applications, limitations, benefits, the adverse effects of these state-of-the-art technologies and their transformation to the healthcare systems and sectors. The healthcare sectors such as continuous patient monitoring, telemedicine, and remote surgery can be improvised with the help of 5G for its rare properties like, quick in enabling real-time data transmission, low-latency communication capabilities, and high speed. Implementing any technology without testing will be risky. However, the risk factors can be minimized if the testing part can be accomplished with the help of a virtual platform like metaverse. Computer-generated interactive environments with a virtual reality interstellar help implement innovative solutions for medical training, mental health therapies, and virtual consultations. It is highly possible to play a major role in transforming the healthcare systems with AI for its cutting-edge technologies like enhancing the accuracy of diagnosis, prevailing in transforming the healthcare systems. Furthermore, this chapter includes the integration of 5G, metaverse, and AI and machine learning (AIML) will make revolutionary changes in healthcare and also discuss suggestions for future directions, ethical considerations, and better usage to afford and empathize with these technologies.

***Keywords***: 5G healthcare, metaverse healthcare, AIML, integration of 5G metaverse and AI

**Corresponding author*: ajaysudhirbale@gmail.com

Ajay Kumar Vyas, Harleen Kaur, Sourabh Sharma and Bhavya Alankar (eds.) Metaverse Technologies, Security and Applications for Healthcare, (121–146) © 2025 Scrivener Publishing LLC

# 6.1 Introduction

## 6.1.1 Metaverse

In recent days, the metaverse has been in everyone's interest and the growth of that cutting technology is very exponential and moving toward its peak now. Preparing a miniature of a model or testing a technology by building a prototype consumes more money and time. Metaverse offers a 3D environment to understand the pros and cons so that unnecessary risk factors can be avoided physically and financially unlike in the traditional trial and error methods [1, 2]. The use of metaverse in the health sector makes a tremendous change and huge transformation and takes the health sector to the next level [3, 4]. Metaverse being an integrating platform for mixed reality, digital twins, and artificial intelligence (AI) contributes more toward refining the health sector through medical technology and AI (MeTAI) [5, 6]. The MeTAI not only reduces the complications of integrating the usage of mixed technology but also provides a secure environment and gives good satisfaction to the patients [7, 8].

Metaverse is the convergence platform (as shown in Figure 6.1 inspired from [3]) to the advanced technologies like blockchain technology, virtual reality (VR), augmented reality (AR), and MR together acting as mixed

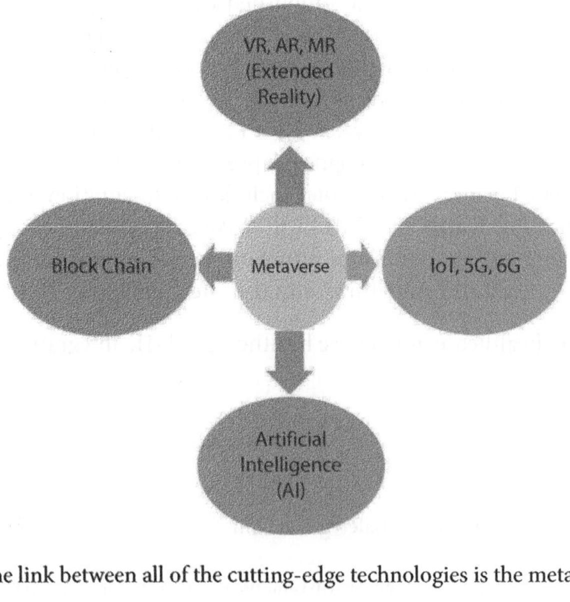


**Figure 6.1** The link between all of the cutting-edge technologies is the metaverse.

reality and also to the IoT, 5G, 6G, and AI [9, 10]. Integration of these technologies would give a tremendous transformation to the healthcare sector. The privacy of the patient's data is ensured with the help of blockchain technology [11, 12]. Various applications are shown in Table 6.1.

The predictive healthcare models can be well developed and enhanced with the help of AI. To realize the full strength of the metaverse in healthcare, a partnership has to be made among stakeholders like healthcare

**Table 6.1** Various applications of metaverse.

| Ref | Technology used | Outcome | Limitations |
|---|---|---|---|
| [1] | VR, AR, mixed reality, and digital twin tech | 1. Improved development and implementation of AI<br>2. Enhanced medical training<br>3. Advanced diagnostics and therapies | 1. Limited accessibility<br>2. High-speed internet, privacy and security, informed consent |
| [2] | Virtual collaborations like IoT, AR, VR, and digital twin platforms | 1. Wearable health monitors<br>2. Machine learning models are used for personalized treatment recommendations. | 1. No empirical validation<br>2. Lack of diversity in the literature<br>3. High implementation cost |
| [3] | Avatar-based interactions<br>Immersive simulations<br>Interoperable ecosystem | 1. Improved access to healthcare<br>2. Enhanced medical training<br>3. Transformed patient experience | 1. Very little accessibility<br>2. Early-stage technology<br>3. Privacy and security<br>4. Data regulations |
| [4] | IoT<br>6G<br>Data fusion techniques<br>Blockchain technology | 1. Enhanced security and privacy of health data<br>2. Improved effectiveness of healthcare analytics<br>3. Real-time anomaly detection | 1. 6G dependence<br>2. Scalability challenges<br>3. Data privacy concerns<br>4. Acceptance and trust-related issues |

providers, policymakers, and patients [2]. Real-time data handling capabilities of 5G- and 6G-enhanced AI environments play a pivotal role in the healthcare sector in diagnosing major diseases. A novel method for 6G-enabled IoT anomaly detection in metaverse healthcare and fitness data analytics is presented in [2]. It leverages 6G networks' ultralow latency and high bandwidth, integrating diverse data sources, blockchain technology for data integrity, and an improved isolation forest with particle swarm optimization for real-time anomaly detection [3–7, 13, 14].

### 6.1.2 AI

AI and machine learning (ML) are rapidly transforming healthcare research, predicting outcomes and categorizing observations based on human training. These models are essential for processing patient EMR data. However, ethical considerations must be taken into account during the development process, to ensure interpretability, transparency, and transparency in the end product [8, 9]. AI and precision medicine are expected to revolutionize healthcare by identifying patients with unique needs and utilizing advanced computation and inference. Translational research aims to address challenges in personalized diagnosis and prognostication using nongenomic and genomic determinants [10, 15, 16]. Immersion technology can be easier to learn and comprehend for healthcare workers with the help of user-centered design and training programs. Furthermore, concerns about privacy and corporate overreach about the monetization of personal data, similar to what happens on popular Web 2.0 platforms, might also arise. Focused research seeking to determine stakeholders' views toward these solutions and their capacity to deploy these technologies could potentially solve these potential application hurdles [11]. The metaverse, a virtual world, has the potential to improve personal healthcare services. However, challenges like data security and privacy remain. To address these, a swarm learning–based model-sharing framework is proposed. This framework integrates distributed ML and blockchain to protect patient data and ensure fairness in healthcare-AI model sharing. Simulation results show improved accuracy compared to local and central training [12–15]. The applications of AI in different domains are shown in Table 6.2.

**Table 6.2** AI in cross-domain applications.

| Ref | Technology used | Outcome | Limitations |
|---|---|---|---|
| [8] | Deep learning techniques like supervised, unsupervised learning, support vector machine (SVM)<br>Natural language processing (NLP),<br>Computer vision, and predicting modeling | Improved diagnostic accuracy<br>Tailored treatment plans based on patient's data<br>Streamlined administrative processes<br>Early identification of risk | An issue with data completeness<br>Complex technical challenges<br>Regulatory barriers |
| [9] | NLP, SVM, and structured data like demographics<br>Integration of electronic health records with ML and NLP | Enhanced data utilization<br>Improved clinical decision-making<br>Streamlined healthcare processes<br>Identification of public trends | Variability in EHR data quality and completeness<br>Challenges in standardizing data from different sources<br>High computational requirements<br>Interoperability challenges |
| [10] | NLP techniques like tokenization and word embeddings<br>Named entity recognition | Improved text classification<br>Comprehensive survey insights<br>Improved ability to monitor and analyze patient discussions | Difficulty in interpreting the result and decision-making processes |

(*Continued*)

**Table 6.2** AI in cross-domain applications. (*Continued*)

| Ref | Technology used | Outcome | Limitations |
|---|---|---|---|
| [11] | IoT, extended reality and Edge AI, blockchain, and 6G technologies | Improved connectivity and data processing<br>Immersive user experiences<br>Synchronized transmission of multiple data flows<br>Automated processes using smart contracts | Ethical and regulatory issues |
| [12] | IBM AI fairness toolkit | Experimental success<br>Clinical decision support<br>Technology integration | Differences in the clinical environments and the workflows |

### 6.1.3 5G and Beyond

The service level agreements (SLAs) in 5G healthcare systems address challenges like latency, reliability, and security. It discusses enabling technologies like network slicing, edge computing, and AI. It highlights 5G's potential for advanced healthcare applications like remote surgery and telemedicine. Fan *et al.* [16] discuss an autonomous organization of blockchain networks, exploring the potential of 5G technology in transforming digital health, leveraging big data for patient-centered care, and highlighting the need for robust infrastructure, security measures, and regulatory frameworks in healthcare [17, 18]. Impact of COVID-19: Examines how 5G can help with telemedicine and remote consultations to solve healthcare issues during the pandemic. Future issues: Describes the issues that 5G in healthcare will face in the future, such as managing the growing amount of health data and integrating it with current systems as well as guaranteeing data security. Technological Solutions: Covers methods to get over these obstacles and improve healthcare delivery, such as AI, edge computing, and sophisticated analytics. Case Studies: Offers case studies that demonstrate how 5G was successfully implemented in healthcare during the pandemic and outline possible uses in the future [19]. The key features of 5G technology, including its rapid data transfer speeds, minimal latency, and large capacity are best used in [20]. In the healthcare sector, the main pillars that will enable platforms like 5G-enabled healthcare include huge machine-type communications, ultra-reliable low-latency connectivity, and improved mobile broadband [20–22]. Applications: Covers a range

**Table 6.3** 5G applications.

| Ref | Technology used | Outcome | Limitations |
|---|---|---|---|
| [20] | 5G connectivity among the terrestrial, airborne, and space layers<br>Big data analytics and cloud computing | Enhanced healthcare services like enabling superior healthcare delivery<br>Development of patient-centric digital health ecosystems | Technical complexity in implementing multilayered 5G network architecture<br>Addressing ethical-related concerns |
| [21] | Enhanced mobile broadband (eMBB)<br>Ultra-reliable low latency communication (URLLC)<br>Massive machine type communication (mMTC) | Improved connectivity<br>Support for smart cities | High-cost infrastructure requirement<br>Poor management of interference and spectrum<br>Potential interoperability issues |
| [22] | Internet of Nano-Things (IoNT)<br>Diagnostic imaging<br>IoT and edged devices<br>Robotics | Seamless integration of 5G with other advanced technologies needs further development | Most studies have a small sample size<br>Technical constraints like patient positioning and limited operating angles |
| [23] | 5G networks<br>AI-connected smart devices<br>IoT for data collection | Remote surgery using 5G<br>Real-time health monitoring<br>Integration of AI for smarter decision | Coverage issues<br>Regulatory barrios<br>Security risks |

of 5G applications in the healthcare industry, including real-time health monitoring, remote surgery, and telemedicine. Future Prospects: The articles [20, 23] explore how 5G can transform healthcare in the future, highlighting the need for innovation, infrastructure investment, and resolving security and privacy issues [20, 23]. 5G and its cross-domain applications as discussed above are summarized in Table 6.3.

## 6.2 Application of Metaverse in Healthcare

The virtual twins of every actual CT scanner model in MeTAI can create virtual "raw" data by scanning digital patients [24–28]. Then, AI analysis can be carried out in the domains of virtual data and images. Sharing such realistically generated data, as opposed to the original data from a real computer, should be less difficult while revealing vendor-specific sensitive information. At the moment, the use of image-domain modeling and simulation techniques, such as HeartFlow31, has yielded useful diagnostic data. In the raw data domain, deep learning–based radiomics may work in concert to produce additional information. Because motion artifacts from atrial fibrillation's high and irregular heart rates can taint reconstructed pictures, coronary artery stenoses, for instance, may be better measured in the sinogram domain32. MeTAI has the potential to greatly assist in enabling deep learning–based studies on actual and realistically generated raw data, either in a single domain (data and images) or in several domains [1]. Healthcare businesses might benefit from the metaverse as a potential training tool for disaster preparedness. It provides an affordable, scalable, and instantaneous in-hospital disaster readiness training approach. The COVID-19 pandemic and other emerging virtual simulation techniques may be further incorporated into the metaverse. It is a promising addition to traditional training methods because of its low implementation cost [3, 29, 30]. The concept of digital twin computing, which combines data from real and virtual things, is the result of ongoing efforts to create sophisticated computer models of the human body and the devices that photograph it. It is required to develop vendor-specific virtual tomographic scanners, customized computational avatars with anatomical features that the scanners can resolve, and graphical tools with AI capabilities to add, remove, and alter diseases in these avatars in order to fully utilize these advancements for medical imaging. Potential pathologies can be simulated inside the patient's avatar and scanned using each type of virtual CT scanner if the patient is referred for a CT scan due to a heart condition. AI diagnostic tools and competing deep reconstruction methods can be used to realistically recreate the photos and analyze them [3]. The way that professionals and people use medical data and tools to comprehend illnesses, choose treatments, and carry out interventions will be one of MeTAI's most significant effects, for instance, a complicated surgical and therapeutic scenario in such a virtual environment. The trial-and-error approach can be used again to virtually practice processes. Surgeons can try various techniques (like plastic surgery) on avatars in MeTAI. Another example is radiotherapy. MeTAI would extend the routine optimization of treatment regimens through patient-specific computer simulations to all medical interventions [7]. The metaverse is a cutting-edge digital technology that offers realistic experiences for patients and medical personnel, and it has great potential for the healthcare industry. The integration of multiple supporting technologies guarantees that patient care is immersive, individualized, and intimate [22, 31]. Additionally, it provides intelligent and adaptive solutions, removing obstacles between healthcare practitioners and recipients. The healthcare sector has undergone significant fundamental changes since the outbreak [32, 33]. The younger generation is enthusiastic about virtual healthcare systems and related digital technologies and is becoming more active in healthcare decision-making. To guarantee maximum customer pleasure, implementing cutting-edge digital tools and services is now crucial, as it permits improved medication adherence, tracking, and monitoring of health conditions [3, 34]. The healthcare industry has been significantly impacted by this digital revolution, which has improved operational effectiveness, service accessibility, and the patient-clinician experience through cloud computing, AR, VR, and AI technology [35].

How different digital technologies are integrated into the healthcare ecosystem is illustrated in Figure 6.2. These technologies are divided into four quadrants: augmentation, simulation, external, and intimate, depending on how they are used and interact with the ecosystem. VR emphasizes the use of AR in healthcare, with a particular emphasis on how technology might support interventional and surgical treatments. It has sensors and instruments to improve medical procedures, as well as 3D organ modeling for improved visibility. Lifelogging highlights the personal monitoring and alert systems made possible by technological advancements. It has alert systems and vital sign monitoring to continuously monitor a patient's health. Mirror world illustrates how digital technology can be used to teach medicine. It includes virtual and digital labs created for training and teaching, giving medical professionals access to immersive learning environments. The virtual world is centered on simulating actual healthcare situations. It has workshops and virtual operating rooms that offer a secure setting for practice and consultation,

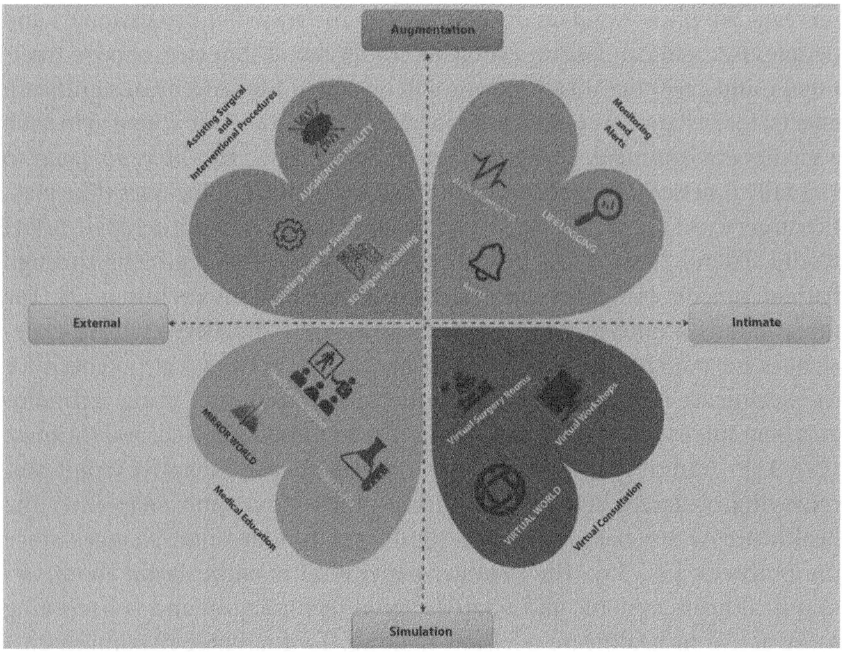


**Figure 6.2** Four axes metaverse deployments in healthcare [31]. Open access.

improving communication between medical professionals and patients. The combination of AR, lifelogging, mirror worlds, and virtual worlds results in a tailored, effective, and immersive healthcare system [34], as shown in Table 6.3.

The metaverse is improved by 5G and other technological innovations, which offer seamless and immersive prospects for medical education and training. Because current wireless networks have latency problems, performing remote surgery in the 3D environment of the metaverse is dangerous because delays can compromise patient safety. However, the time lag between a remote surgeon's input and real-time action is greatly reduced by the ultralow latency of 5G and future networks, increasing the safety and dependability of remote surgeries [22]. Technology developments leading up to 5G will greatly improve the metaverse and bring it closer to realizing its full potential. These next-generation networks offer the low latency and high bandwidth that immersive technologies like AR, VR, and IoT demand to create rich media content. As such, 5G and beyond will have a significant impact on the metaverse's ability to produce creative material more

**Table 6.4** Characteristics of four metaverse deployments [34].

| Item | Augmented reality | Life-logging | Mirror worlds | Virtual world |
|---|---|---|---|---|
| **Concept** | An interactive setting where virtual 2D or 3D elements are superimposed over actual space | Technology to record, save, and distribute information about objects and people as well as daily experiences | A virtual environment that replicates the actual world while providing more information | a digitally constructed virtual world |
| **Features** | utilizing location-based technologies to create a smart environment as well as networks | utilizing augmented technologies to record data about things and people | Making use of GPS, modeling, virtual mapping, and lifelogging technologies | Avatars that interact and represent the user's ego |
| **Value/Needs** | offers material that is immersive and blends convenience, imagination, and the actual world. | A great deal of knowledge and experience from the actual world is available at all times and may be shared with others. | increased usefulness by adding and incorporating outside data into the digital realm | offers a brand-new, virtual environment that doesn't exist in reality where different people can carry out tasks |
| **Core Technology** | Processing of unstructured data, 3D printing, and 5G networks | Internet-based platform, widely used sensor, and 5G network | Data storage, GIS systems, blockchain technology, and 3D technologies | Blockchain technology, artificial intelligence, 5G networks, and graphics |
| **Challenges** | Perplexity in the area of augmented reality when the reality is overlay<br>Character ownership in augmented reality, etc. | Infringement of property rights, including portraits, and disclosure of internal information | Dual position ban violation, etc.<br>Manipulation of the information led to unfair commerce. | issue and significant platform lock-in effect<br>Ignorance of reality and dread of chaos that might lead to moral and ethical issues |

effectively and efficiently [32]. The healthcare industry can reap substantial benefits from advancements in the metaverse. 5G and beyond technology will enable high-quality immersive experiences that will benefit both doctors and patients. These technologies' high-speed and low-latency connectivity will improve mental health treatments, virtual wellness programs, and intricate surgical procedures, among other aspects of healthcare [33]. These characteristics are summarized in Table 6.4.

Digital technologies are changing every facet of healthcare, from patient monitoring and education to diagnosis and treatment. Typical applications include

- Medical Therapeutics: This field emphasizes the use of digital platforms to deliver mental health services and therapeutic support. It includes virtual counseling and virtual physiotherapy.
- Medical Diagnosis: Showcases advancements in diagnostic visualization and accuracy with holographic imaging and virtual biopsies.
- Surgeries: Includes gesture-based support and nanobot surgery, showcasing state-of-the-art methods that improve accuracy and results in surgical operations.
- Patient Monitoring: Consists of vital monitoring and alert response systems, stressing rapid interventions and ongoing health tracking.
- Medical Education: Discusses drug development and virtual experiments to show how digital tools support medical education and research.

Applications of the metaverse in medical education are incredibly useful. They include code blue, surgical, and clinical simulation training. The metaverse efficiently promotes contacts amongst foreign colleagues for scientific education and mentorship, according to a recent study. Figure 6.3 depicts trainees from different academic institutions engaging in case discussions with global specialists in ophthalmology at 3D surgical rounds hosted by MetaMed Media. Moreover, attendees can relive these events in a way that is immersive thanks to 3D volumetric capture. As AR and VR technology has evolved, surgical training—which calls on sophisticated hand skills and interaction—has found greater success with immersive experiences [3].

In order to provide more effective, safe, and practical healthcare services in the digital sphere, the research in [35] suggests fusing blockchain

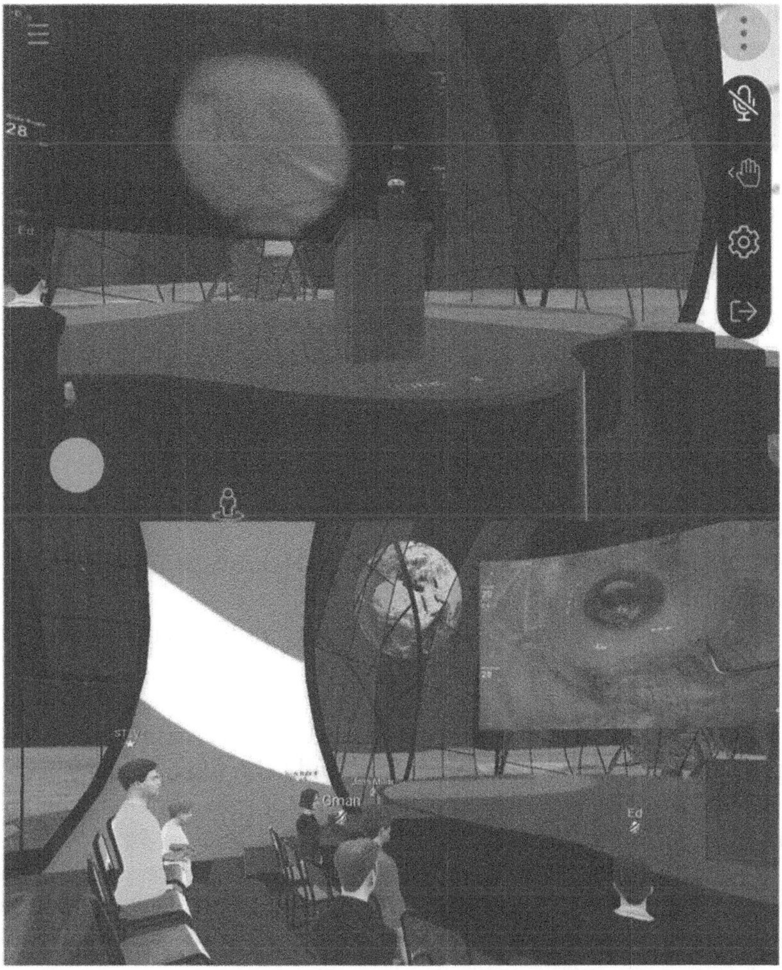


**Figure 6.3** Hosted by MetaMed media, 3D ophthalmic surgical rounds [3]. Open access.

technology with AI within the metaverse. Three settings are included in the proposed network: the metaverse, the patient's, and the doctor's environment. Blockchain technology facilitates interactions between medical professionals and patients in the metaverse setting while maintaining data confidentiality and privacy. Hazarika and Rahmati [36] discuss an environment, wherein nurses, physicians, and patients register on the blockchain and are represented by avatars. Every consultation activity is captured, sent, and kept on the blockchain, including voice, text, photos, videos, and clinical data. Then, explainable AI (XAI) models are used for these data for illness diagnosis and prognosis.

The AI algorithm for the metaverse is explained as follows:

Contributions to the framework:

a. NLP Data: Text data that may include patient notes, medical records, or any other natural language inputs.
b. Sensor Data: Data from medical sensors, such as heart rate monitors and blood pressure sensors.
c. Image Data: Medical images such as X-rays, MRIs, or CT scans.
d. Trained Model: An AI model that has been previously trained on relevant medical data.

Output:
O(XAI): The output of the XAI process, which provides insights into how the model made its predictions.

Steps involved in the diagnosis process and for the recommendation of treatments:

1. Procedure Initialization: The procedure AI_model is initialized with the input data (NLP, sensor, and image data) and the trained model.
2. Load Data: The input data (NLP data, sensor data, and image data) are loaded into a unified dataset (Data).
3. Preprocess Data: The loaded data undergoes preprocessing. This step involves cleaning and transforming the data into a format suitable for the AI model. Preprocessing can include normalization, tokenization (for NLP data), feature extraction, etc.
4. Make Prediction: The preprocessed data are fed into the trained model to make predictions. The result is stored in the variable Prediction.
5. Generate Explanations Based on Data Type:

If the Data Include Medical Images:

a. Import GradCAM: GradCAM (Gradient-weighted Class Activation Mapping) is a technique used to generate visual explanations for CNN-based models. It highlights regions in the image that are important for the prediction.
b. Heatmap Generation: The make_gradcam_heatmap function is called to generate a heatmap that shows the areas of the image that influenced the model's prediction.

Else (For Other Data Types):

a. Import LIME: LIME (Local Interpretable Model-agnostic Explanations) is a technique used to explain predictions by approximating the model locally with an interpretable model.
b. LIME Explainer Initialization: A LIME explainer is created using the trained model and data.
c. Compute LIME Values: LIME values are computed for the data, providing insights into which features influenced the prediction.

6. Display Explanations: Depending on the type of data and explanation method used, either the GradCAM heatmap or LIME values are displayed to visualize the model's decision-making process.
7. Output XAI Results: The XAI results are prepared for output. For LIME, an image plot of the LIME values is created. For GradCAM, the heatmap is displayed. These outputs provide a visual and interpretable explanation of the model's predictions.
8. End: The procedure concludes, having provided both the model's prediction and the XAI explanations.

Hazarika and Rahmati [36] guarantee the transparency and interpretability of the predictions produced by the AI model, which is essential in delicate domains such as healthcare, where comprehending the rationale behind a forecast might have equal significance to the prediction itself.

## 6.3 5G and AI Integration with Metaverse

Due to the significant expansion of commercialized fifth-generation (5G) mobile networks and the anticipated development of 6G technology by 2030, there will be a rising need for ultra-reliable low-latency communications (URLLC). This is to ensure that the overall latency is reduced to 1 to 5 ms or less, thereby replacing conventional connection methods. In addition, maintaining a delay threshold in the range of milliseconds to submilliseconds is crucial to enable various groundbreaking technologies for AR/VR uses, made possible by 5G networks. These devices include uses in industry, holographic screens, and the tactile Internet. 5G can collaborate with additional radio methods, such as Wi-Fi, due to its multi-radio accessing technology (multi-RAT) characteristics. Wi-Fi, a license-free technology, may reach speeds of up to 200 Mbps. Wi-Fi is widely recognized as the most common unlicensed wireless protocol for enabling rapid access to the internet in wireless local area networks (WLANs). It is projected to facilitate the use of 9.5 billion devices for upcoming AR/VR capabilities. Wi-Fi 6, sometimes referred to as Wi-Fi 802.11ax, outperforms previous generations by achieving a faster transmission of 9.6 Gbps. While 5G offers significant implementation versatility by accommodating a wide variety of consumers and offerings, Wi-Fi is comparably simpler to install using broadband routers and access points to supply complete network accessibility. 5G networks utilize two frequency bands: sub-6G with a memory bandwidth of 100 MHz and millimeter wave (mmWave) with a bandwidth of 400 MHz. On the other hand, Wi-Fi 6 stations use three overlapping channels with a bandwidth of 60 to 80 MHz to achieve powerful and immersive surroundings for AR/VR. In addition, 5G provides significant benefits in comparison to Wi-Fi 6. While Wi-Fi 6 is restricted to a certain bandwidth for each individual, 5G allows complete end-to-end connection by using the benefits of both mid-band and low-band frequencies. Furthermore, 5G also ensures a very low latency environment via the utilization of high-band frequencies in mmWave technology. Wi-Fi 6 is predicted to have a theoretical latency of 36 ms, whereas the targeted hypothetical latency for 5G falls between 6 and 9 ms. The delay demands for an AR/VR structure encompass a virtual remote setting with a delay that typically falls within the range of 40 ms to 300 ms. This allows for the delivery of more visually immersive content, including a greater frame rate, and high dynamic range (HDR). While 5G's enhanced mobile broadband (eMBB) is crucial for providing more bandwidth compared to 4G, it offers limited improvements in low latency while reducing bandwidth [9]. Hence, the use of ultra-wideband (UWB) wireless technology is necessary to provide a low-latency system that is optimized for high-quality audio and future AR/VR apps. This is achieved by facilitating prompt transfer with a greater throughput. An optimal antenna layout is necessary for this UWB system to effectively cover both the traditional LTE and sub-6G bands concurrently. An interface that encompasses both line-of-sight (LOS) and non-line-of-sight (NLOS) conditions is necessary for this design. Additionally, new hardware concepts are needed to meet the bandwidth demands of 6G networks. This can be achieved by utilizing radio frequency (RF) micro-electromechanical system (MEMS)–powered terahertz switches, which enable the handling of a broader spectrum range with quicker response times. Delays in the simulated world and AR/VR gadgets are caused by different factors when providing consumers with an improved perspective of their artificial world. The minimal end-to-end latency in AR/VR devices is a result of the several stages involved in sensor sampling, data processing and fusion, picture processing and coding, communication, and deciphering, and projecting each picture frame. Figure 6.4 illustrates the primary factors contributing to the incidence of motion-to-photon (MTP) delay. Hence, it is imperative to explore novel network architectures, technologies, methodologies, and devices to enhance conventional AR/VR systems by delivering a realistic and uninterrupted VR simulation with minimal end-to-end latency. It is necessary to maintain the MTP latency below 20 ms due to the high sensitivity of VR web features to low latency, which might result in user disorientation. Maintaining a low MTP latency is difficult because of the sequential nature of the VR terminal's motion capturing, logic computation, image illustration, and screen projection processes. Therefore, notwithstanding the significant progress in AR/VR technology, the main obstacle to achieving an entire immersion and improving the field of vision is the delay of MTP, which also leads to shadowing and low projection quality. To provide realistic digital expertise, head-mounted display (HMD) users must have a minimum MTP latency of less than 7 ms. Misregistration happens whenever data collected from the HMDs do not accurately align with the user's perception of the space around them and time. This problem occurs due to a discrepancy in accurately estimating the periodicity of the data collected presented on the HMD, taking into account both the orientation and position of the actuators [17]. Figure 6.4 provides a concise overview of the several sorts of errors that occur due to MTP delay in AR/VR systems. The picture outlines three significant

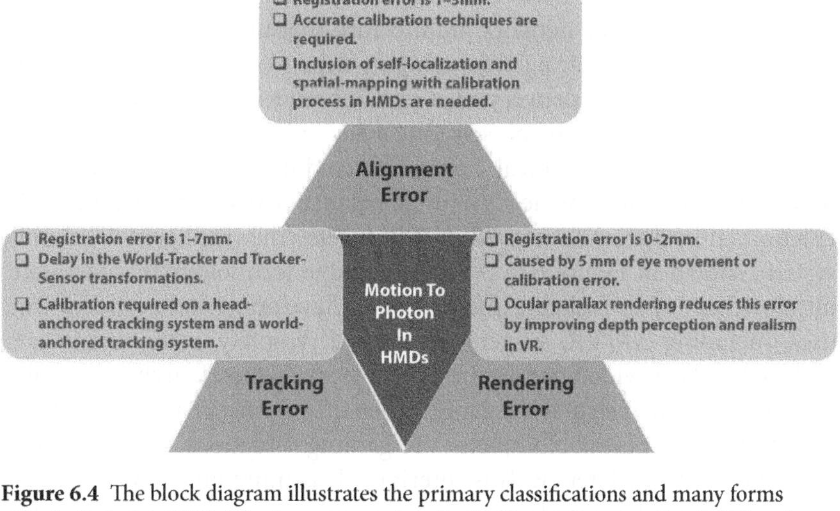


**Figure 6.4** The block diagram illustrates the primary classifications and many forms of faults linked to MTP delay in augmented reality (AR) and virtual reality (VR) head-mounted displays (HMDs) [36].

mistakes that often occur in HMDs during MTP processing. These faults include position, monitoring, and rendering problems. The figure also provides information on the amount of these errors and the techniques required to minimize them. Optical see-through (OST) virtual headgear and simulation devices are often used to convert virtual material into the physical environment. Nevertheless, delay may also have an impact on them, namely, in the circumstances of misregistration. Various methods, such as temporal warping or post-render warping, have been shown to enhance the overall quality and uniformity of delay on the monitor display and the graphic rendering processor.

The work in [36] examines current technology, along with many innovative ideas and developments in ultralow-latency telecommunications throughout the 5G and beyond period. Techniques like Wi-Fi 7 and the tactile Internet will enable new opportunities in autonomous movement, robotics, and control of factories. This will motivate vendors of communication services to enhance customer service in real-time scenarios like internet-based gaming and AR/VR uses. By utilizing wireless networks with network layout, it is possible to achieve low-latency connection. This can be accomplished by identifying the most efficient path for transmitting packets via the transmitter's Packet Data Convergence Protocol (PDCP) to the receiver's PDCP, regardless of the location of the gadget or the software (such as a data center or cloud supplier), and then returning the packets. This necessitates fulfilling all the prerequisites for an optimum exchange of messages, including the use of appropriate techniques and the establishment of an efficient network configuration. Besides, such technologies need a smart portable network architecture that utilizes mmWave-based technology to meet their need for a highly dependable and low-delay connection, enabling the delivery of a genuine and uninterrupted spatially sensitive interaction to the person. The delay in VR and AR developments is caused by many technical hurdles, including video distribution via mobile networks and the need to find a balance between gesture/head circulation and functionality in AR/VR headsets. The intelligent 5G mobile system, shown in Figure 6.5, is a cutting-edge technology that facilitates ultralow-latency and reliable interactions in developing and near-real-time uses, including AR/VR, surgery performed remotely, autonomous cars, and multi-player video games. In [37], a smart network architecture was demonstrated for a virtual VR gaming arena. The concept aimed to achieve optimum efficiency in complete VR gaming situations, ensuring both reliability and low latency. This interior VR gaming arena system needs minimal latency to provide precise synchronization of position and interactivity among a number of players. The participants were asked to use

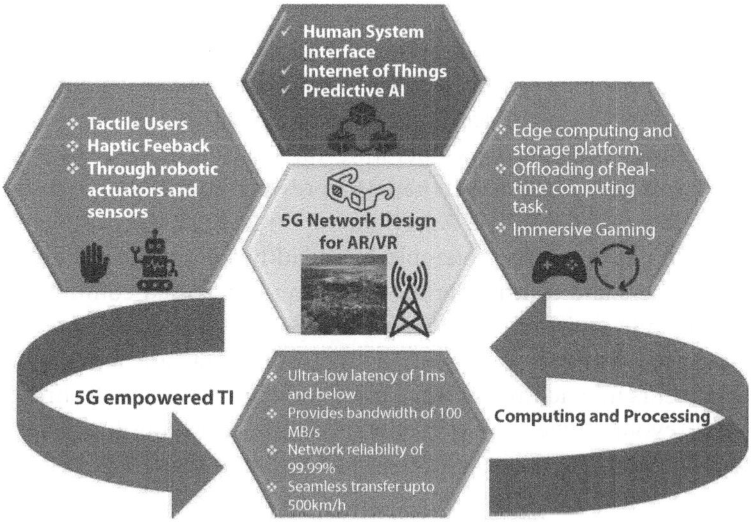


**Figure 6.5** The figure illustrates the functionalities of a network architecture that utilizes advanced technologies like computing at the edge and the tactile Internet to provide rapid connectivity with minimal delay for augmented reality (AR) and virtual reality (VR) applications in a 5G-enabled environment [36].

head-mounted displays (HMDs) that were outfitted with multiple access points (mmAP) operating in the mmWave band. These points of connectivity were linked to a distributed computation network with an operating capacity of approximately 60 GHz. The edge computing system of many edge computation servers to a temporary store device is presented in [38]. Its purpose was to transfer the participant's monitoring information and forecast postures using a prediction frame based on the HD frames collected as part of their real-time duties. This kind of network architecture configuration ensures a balance between the time it takes to communicate and processing, by making effective judgments on job outsourcing, server location, and server selection. There is an urgent requirement to develop the cellular control hierarchy for vital networks to prevent the delay that apps used by users encounter. As a result, Neutrino was developed as a cellular control layer [38] to provide a reliable way to reach mobile networks by linking the IP core to the cell sites, simultaneously assuring reduced latency. The cellular control layer ensures low latency and dependable connection to the cellular primary network by constantly refreshing the client's state with data that the user provides for retrieval from the Internet or similar carrier offerings. This allows for interaction discussions to be formed for any device. The control system employs a uniformity policy to reduce service interruption in the event of mistakes, ensuring that devices consistently obtain read-your-writes compatibility. The controls, which contributed a latency of 72.5 to 99.6 ms in session setup, might result in delays of up to 1.9 ms in accessing data. The Neutrino test configuration had two dual-socket servers operating on Ubuntu 18.04.3 with kernel 4.15.0-74-generic. Each server had 18 cores per socket and a combined memory capacity of 128 GB. Additional optimizations were implemented on Neutrino to meet the tolerable bandwidth compromise required by mobile carriers and to mitigate the problem of increased communication overhead while capitalizing on the advantages of reduced latency.

The game business has seen a significant transformation due to advancements in machine vision, AR/VR, and 3D-rendering technologies. This has revolutionized the overall experience of playing for game players (GPs). Contemporary games tend to be decentralized and powered by peer-to-peer (P2P) systems, where peer GPs participate in virtual worlds (GEs), and the data are saved on game servers (GSs). Within VR GEs, GPs engage in gameplay using VR technology that includes HMD and hand controls. This immersive experience allows GPs to fully immerse themselves in the virtual GE while playing games such as Beat Sabre, Iron Man, or Star Trek. In contrast, an AR game (e.g., Pokemon Go or Sun-seeker) takes the actual surroundings of the player and transforms them into a digital interface, adding more information to the real world. Following the relaunch of Oculus Quest and the change in name of Facebook to Meta, a significant advancement is anticipated in AR/VR graphical environments. This progress will manifest in the form of real-time 360-degree navigation, enhanced object conversations, and a fourfold improvement in tactile gadget controls. In the future, there will be a transition for extended reality (XR) engines that will allow movements of the eyes and physiological interactions (ears, hands, and facial expression) of general practitioners (GPs) to be shown and transmitted across P2P networks [39].

## 6.4 Conclusion and Future Scope

A new age of cutting-edge medical treatments and patient care is on the horizon, thanks to the convergence of 5G, AI, and the metaverse, which is going to radically alter healthcare systems [40–43]. Healthcare providers now have cutting-edge resources at their fingertips thanks to the metaverse's immersive virtual settings, which may be used for mental health therapy, virtual consultations, and medical training. More precise diagnoses, individualized treatment programs, and predictive analytics for preventative care are all made possible by AI, which plays a crucial part in this revolution. ML algorithms can sift through mountains of patient data in search of insights and trends that human doctors would miss. This might result in better illness identification and more precise treatments. Critical healthcare applications, including remote surgery and continuous patient monitoring, rely on real-time data transfer, which is made possible with the incorporation of 5G technology, which offers ultrafast, low-latency connectivity. More thorough and faster patient data gathering is made possible by the smooth functioning of IoT devices in healthcare settings, which is made possible by this high-speed connection. New opportunities for telemedicine are opening up as these technologies merge, opening the door to high-quality remote consultations and the remote execution of even complicated medical operations. The metaverse provides an ideal environment for the development of digital twins of human anatomy and medical devices, facilitating accurate modeling and preparation for surgical operations. Data privacy, security, and the ethical application of AI to healthcare decision-making are major concerns that arise with the use of these sophisticated technologies. Ensuring strong cybersecurity protections and upholding patient confidence will be of utmost importance as healthcare institutions continue to depend on these digital platforms. Furthermore, to make the most of these emerging technologies, healthcare providers would need to undergo continuous training and education. Notwithstanding these obstacles, the healthcare industry stands to gain a great deal from incorporating metaverse, AI, and 5G into its operations; this will lead to better patient outcomes, wider availability of specialist treatment, and a more streamlined, individualized, and technologically sophisticated system as a whole. Metaverse, AI, and 5G integration in healthcare have the potential to revolutionize healthcare delivery and scientific inquiry in the future. From individualized medication to worldwide collaborative care, these technologies are ripe for a revolution in healthcare. Metaverse simulations and advanced AI algorithms might analyze specific patient data and visualize results in virtual settings, enabling highly personalized treatment programs. Immersive metaverse platforms provide realistic settings devoid of danger where medical students and residents may practice intricate operations. The integration of metaverse technology with 5G's high bandwidth and low latency may pave the way for remote surgeries and expert consultations in real time, allowing for seamless worldwide cooperation among healthcare specialists. By analyzing massive databases to anticipate disease outbreaks and identify at-risk patients, AI-powered predictive healthcare has the potential to move the emphasis from treatment to prevention. Innovative mental healthcare and rehabilitation programs may also find a home in the metaverse, where they may be more easily accessible and more effectively used. Revolutionizing preventative care and early intervention might be achieved by continuous health monitoring facilitated by 5G-connected devices and AI analysis. Virtual consultations might make specialized care more accessible to underprivileged places, while drug discovery via metaverse simulations controlled by AI could speed up the process. Strong ethical standards and regulatory frameworks are going to be required to protect patient privacy and make responsible use of AI in healthcare choices as these technologies progress. Additional intriguing prospects include the development of individualized health ecosystems and the merging of healthcare systems with smart city infrastructure. Shortly, the healthcare industry may see a dramatic shift as a result of the integration of metaverse, AI, and 5G technologies. This convergence has the potential to revolutionize patient care, increase healthcare efficiency, and provide new approaches to medical education and research.

## References

1. Wang, G., Badal, A., Jia, X., Maltz, J.S., Mueller, K., Myers, K.J., Niu, C., *et al.*, Development of metaverse for intelligent healthcare. *Nat. Mach. Intell.*, 4, 11, 922–929, 2022.
2. Shah, V. and Khang, A., Metaverse-Enabling IoT Technology for a Futuristic Healthcare System, in: *Handbook of Research on AI-Based Technologies and Applications in the Era of the Metaverse*, pp. 165–173, IGI Global, 2023.
3. Li, Y., Gunasekeran, D.V., RaviChandran, N., Tan, T.F., Ong, J.C.L., Thirunavukarasu, A.J., Polascik, B.W., Habash, R., Khaderi, K., Ting, D.SW., The next generation of healthcare ecosystem in the metaverse. *Biomed. J.*, 47, 3, 100679, 2023.
4. Zhu, K.-T., Wu, Y., Yang, R., Yuan, Q., Anomaly Detection in Metaverse Healthcare and Fitness: Bigdata Analytics Using 6G-Enabled Internets of Things. *Wireless Pers. Commun.*, 1–20, 2024.
5. Välimäki, M.A., Lantta, T., Hipp, K., Varpula, J., Liu, G., Tang, Y., Chen, W., Hu, S., Li, X., Measured and perceived impacts of evidence-based leadership in nursing: A mixed-methods systematic review protocol. *BMJ Open*, 11, 10, e55356, 2021.
6. Chen, Z.S. and Ruan, J.Q., Metaverse healthcare supply chain: Conceptual framework and barrier identification. *Eng. Appl. Artif. Intell.*, 133, 108113, 2024.
7. Xi, N., Chen, J., Gama, F., Riar, M., Hamari, J., The challenges of entering the metaverse: An experiment on the effect of extended reality on workload. *Inf. Syst. Front.*, 25, 2, 659–680, 2023.

8. Rubinger, L., Gazendam, A., Ekhtiari, S., Bhandari, M., Machine learning and artificial intelligence in research and healthcare. *Injury*, 54, S69–S73, 2023.
9. Mehta, N. and Devarakonda, M.V., Machine learning, natural language programming, and electronic health records: The next step in the artificial intelligence journey? *J. Allergy Clin. Immunol.*, 141, 6, 2019–2021, 2018.
10. Lavanya, P.M. and Sasikala, E., Deep learning techniques on text classification using Natural language processing (NLP) in social healthcare network: A comprehensive survey, in: *2021 3rd international conference on signal processing and communication (ICPSC)*, IEEE, pp. 603–609, 2021.
11. Maksymyuk, T., Gazda, J., Shubyn, B., Karpin, O., Kapshii, O., Urikova, O., Amhoud, E.-M., Liyanage, M., Jo, M., Dohler, M., Metaverse of Things in 6G era: an emerging fusion of IoT, XR, edge AI and blockchain technologies, in: *IEEE International Conference on Advanced Trends in Radioelectronics, Telecommunications and Computer Engineering*, Springer Nature Switzerland, Cham, pp. 546–564, 2022.
12. Johnson, K.B., Wei, W.-Q., Weeraratne, D., Frisse, M.E., Misulis, K., Rhee, K., Zhao, J., Snowdon, J.L., Precision medicine, AI, and the future of personalized health care. *Clin. Transl. Sci.*, 14, 1, 86–93, 2021.
13. Jokanović, V., The Extraordinary Importance of 6G Network Development and 3D Holography in Future Healthcare, in: *Deep Learning in Internet of Things for Next Generation Healthcare*, pp. 224–241, Chapman and Hall/ CRC, 2024.
14. Aloqaily, M., Bouachir, O., Ridhawi, I.A., Guizani, M., Realizing the metaverse in the 6g era with ai-enabled network orchestration. *IEEE Netw.*, 37, 2, 78–85, 2023.
15. Zhang, G., Dai, Y., Wu, J., Zhu, X., Lu, Y., Swarm Learning-based Secure and Fair Model Sharing for Metaverse Healthcare. *Mobile Netw. Appl.*, 1–12, 2023.
16. Fan, H., Gao, J., Xu, Y., Fortino, G., Qi, W., Metaverse Driven Edge-Fogging-Cloud Network for Complex Human Activity Recognition Using Sensors Fusion, in: *2023 International Conference on Intelligent Metaverse Technologies & Applications (iMETA)*, IEEE, pp. 1–6, 2023.
17. Bhattacharya, P., Ralegankar, V.K., Gupta, R., Tanwar, S., Rodrigues, J.J.P.C., Quant-Meta: Quantum Key Distribution Framework for Telesurgery in Metaverse Environment. *2023 IEEE Globecom Workshops (GC Wkshps)*, Kuala Lumpur, Malaysia, pp. 1868–1873, 2023, doi: 10.1109/ GCWkshps58843.2023.10464607.
18. Román-Belmonte, J.M., Carlos Rodríguez-Merchán, E., De la Corte-Rodríguez, H., Metaverse applied to musculoskeletal pathology: Orthoverse and Rehabverse. *Postgrad. Med.*, 135, 5, 440–448, 2023.
19. Qureshi, H.N., Manalastas, M., Zaidi, S.M.A., Imran, A., Kalaa, M.O.A., Service level agreements for 5G and beyond: overview, challenges and enablers of 5G-healthcare systems. *IEEE Access*, 9, 1044–1061, 2020.

20. Franchi, A., Franchi, L., Franchi, T., Digital health, big data and connectivity: 5G and beyond for patient-centred care. *Int. J. Digit. Health*, 1, 1, 1, 2021.
21. Bansal, H., Introduction to 5g and beyond, in: *Applications of 5G and Beyond in Smart Cities*, pp. 1–26, CRC Press, 2023.
22. Moglia, A., Georgiou, K., Marinov, B., Georgiou, E., Berchiolli, R.N., Satava, R.M., Cuschieri, A., 5G in healthcare: from COVID-19 to future challenges. *IEEE J. Biomed. Health. Inf.*, 26, 8, 4187–4196, 2022.
23. Javaid, M., Haleem, A., Singh, R.P., Suman, R., 5G technology for healthcare: Features, serviceable pillars, and applications. *Intell. Pharm.*, 1, 1, 2–10, 2023.
24. Bale, A.S., Ghorpade, N., Hashim, M.F., Vaishnav, J., Almaspoor, Z., A Comprehensive Study on Metaverse and Its Impacts on Humans. *Adv. Hum. Comput. Interact.*, 2022, 3247060, 11, 2022, https://doi.org/10.1155/2022/3247060.
25. Bale, A.S., Solanki, R.S., Mouneswari, V., Sanamdikar, S., Gulati, P., Trivedi, P.U., Psychological Confidence by AI: Enhancement Quality & Future of Mobility For People With Disabilities of Neurological Impairment. *J. ReAtt. Ther. Dev. Divers.*, 6, 8s, 62–75, 2023, Retrieved from https://jrtdd.com/index.php/journal/article/view/859.
26. Bale, A.S., Joy, S., R., B.C., S., R.R., N., V., 4 Augmented reality in cross-domain applications, in: *Augmented and Virtual Reality in Social Learning: Technological Impacts and Challenges*, R. Kumar, V. Jain, A.A. Elngar, A. Al-Haraizah (Eds.), pp. 43–62, De Gruyter, Berlin, Boston, 2024, https://doi.org/10.1515/9783110981445-004.
27. Bale, A.S., Purohit, T.P., Hashim, M.F., Navale, S., Blockchain and Its Applications in Industry 4.0, in: *A Roadmap for Enabling Industry 4.0 by Artificial Intelligence*, Chatterjee, J.M., Garg, H., Thakur, R.N. (Eds.), 2022, https://doi.org/10.1002/9781119905141.ch16.
28. Kumar, S.S., Sudhir Bale, A., Matapati, P.M., N, V., Conceptual Study of Artificial Intelligence in Smart Cities with Industry 4.0. *2021 International Conference on Advance Computing and Innovative Technologies in Engineering (ICACITE)*, Greater Noida, India, pp. 575–577, 2021, doi: 10.1109/ICACITE51222.2021.9404607.
29. Bale, A.S., Biswas, A., Malik, S., Uchoi, E., Soni, S.U., Soni, A., IoT Applications in Blockchain Technology. *2023 International Conference on Computer Science and Emerging Technologies (CSET)*, Bangalore, India, pp. 1–6, 2023, doi: 10.1109/CSET58993.2023.10346695.
30. Bale, A.S., Saravana Kumar, S., Varun Yogi, S., Vura, S., Baby Chithra, R., Vinay, N., Pravesh, P., Chapter 8 - Network and security leveraging IoT and image processing: A quantum leap forward, in: *Emerging Methodologies and Applications in Modelling, System Assurances*, P. Johri, A. Anand, J. Vain, J. Singh, M.Q. (Eds.), pp. 123–141, Academic Press, 2022, ISBN 9780323902403, https://doi.org/10.1016/B978-0-323-90240-3.00008-4.

31. Chengoden, R., *et al.*, Metaverse for Healthcare: A Survey on Potential Applications, Challenges and Future Directions. *IEEE Access*, 11, 12765–12795, 2023, doi: 10.1109/ACCESS.2023.3241628.
32. Dogra, A., Jha, R.K., Jain, S., A survey on beyond 5G network with the advent of 6G: Architecture and emerging technologies. *IEEE Access*, 9, 67512–67547, 2021.
33. Sun, M., Xie, L., Liu, Y., Li, K., Jiang, B., Lu, Y., Yang, Y., Yu, H., Song, Y., Bai, C., Yang, D., The metaverse in current digital medicine. *Clin. eHealth*, 5, 52–57, Dec. 2022.
34. Lee, C.W., Application of Metaverse Service to Healthcare Industry: A Strategic Perspective. *Int. J. Environ. Res. Public Health*, 19, 20, 13038, 2022, https://doi.org/10.3390/ijerph192013038.
35. Ali, S., Abdullah, Armand, T.P.T., Athar, A., Hussain, A., Ali, M., Yaseen, M., Joo, M.I., Kim, H.C., Metaverse in Healthcare Integrated with Explainable AI and Blockchain: Enabling Immersiveness, Ensuring Trust, and Providing Patient Data Security. *Sensors*, 23, 565, 2023, https://doi.org/10.3390/s23020565.
36. Hazarika, A. and Rahmati, M., Towards an Evolved Immersive Experience: Exploring 5G- and Beyond-Enabled Ultra-Low-Latency Communications for Augmented and Virtual Reality. *Sensors*, 23, 3682, 2023, https://doi.org/10.3390/s23073682.
37. Elbamby, M.S., Perfecto, C., Bennis, M., Doppler, K., Toward Low-Latency and Ultra-Reliable Virtual Reality. *IEEE Netw.*, 32, 78–84, 2018.
38. Ahmad, M., Jafri, S.U., Ikram, A., Qasmi, W.N.A., Nawazish, M.A., Uzmi, Z.A., Qazi, Z.A., A low latency and consistent cellular control plane, in: *Proceedings of the Annual Conference of the ACM, Special Interest Group on Data Communication on the Applications, Technologies, Architectures, and Protocols for Computer Communication, Virtual Event*, 10–14 August 2020, pp. 648–661.
39. Bhattacharya, P., Verma, A., Prasad, V.K., Tanwar, S., Bhushan, B., Florea, B.C., Taralunga, D.D., Alqahtani, F., Tolba, A., Game-o-Meta: Trusted Federated Learning Scheme for P2P Gaming Metaverse beyond 5G Networks. *Sensors*, 23, 4201, 2023, https://doi.org/10.3390/s23094201.
40. Khazanchi, D., Kumar Vyas, A., Kant Hiran, K., Padmanaban, S., *Blockchain 3.0 for Sustainable Development*, De Gruyter, Berlin, Boston, 2021, https://doi.org/10.1515/9783110702507.
41. Kant Hiran, K., Khazanchi, D., Kumar Vyas, A., Padmanaban, S., *Machine Learning for Sustainable Development*, De Gruyter, Berlin, Boston, 2021, https://doi.org/10.1515/9783110702514.
42. Vyas, A.K., Balamurugan, S., Hiran, K.K., Dhiman, H.S. (Eds.), *Artificial Intelligence for Renewable Energy Systems*, John Wiley & Sons, 2022, ISBN: 9781119761693.
43. Singh, S., Arya, R.K., Sahana, B.C., Vyas, A.K. (Eds.), *RF Circuits for 5G Applications: Designing with mmWave Circuitry*, John Wiley & Sons, 2023.

7

# Metaverse Makeover: Transforming Patient Care and Wellness in Virtual Realms

**Ritesh Kumar Jain[1]*, Ajay Kumar Vyas[2], Vishnu Agarwal[3] and Paras Kothari[1]**

[1]*Department of Computer Science & Engineering, Geetanjali Institute of Technical Studies, Udaipur, Rajasthan, India*
[2]*Department of ICT, Adani University, Ahmedabad, Gujarat, India*
[3]*Department of Mechanical Engineering, Geetanjali Institute of Technical Studies, Udaipur, Rajasthan, India*

## *Abstract*

Virtual technologies have come up as a revolutionary way of giving patient care and have opened up a new era of patient satisfaction and well-being. Among these technological developments, the metaverse is a strong phenomenon that can affect healthcare delivery and user engagement at an enormous level. In this chapter, we will explore how the metaverse plays a big role in changing the medical services provided to patients residing in virtual domains from one level to another.

The metaverse, as the future platform, will likely integrate virtual reality, augmented reality, and the Internet into one space or a group of collective spaces that are virtual but shared in real time, which allows user interaction to go beyond physical barriers. In this chapter, we will track healthcare development in virtual environments from its early days until now with a focus on current achievements, especially the development of metaverse as a promising new field.

The metaverse is an inclusive and virtual metaverse in which people have the opportunity to interact with each other in real time, transcending the limits set by physical spaces. Through the adoption of a fusion of technologies such as virtual reality, augmented reality, and the Internet, the metaverse gives individuals a platform on which they can have immersive and collaborative experiences. The current paper aims to map out the evolution of healthcare in simulation settings from their beginning as some kind of historical accident to their current leading-edge status, focusing on the rise of the metaverse as a new frontier.

**Corresponding author*: ritesh.jain@gits.ac.in

Ajay Kumar Vyas, Harleen Kaur, Sourabh Sharma and Bhavya Alankar (eds.) Metaverse Technologies, Security and Applications for Healthcare, (147–172) © 2025 Scrivener Publishing LLC

A review of present research and success stories will be conducted to discuss how diverse the use of the metaverse in healthcare can be, ranging from virtual clinics and telemedicine portals to wellness initiatives. An analysis will also be made on how the metaverse helps to engage patients through the use of gamification techniques, virtual support communities, and immersive educational encounters.

Also, in this chapter, we will examine issues and problems that are connected with making the metaverse a part of the healthcare system; these are moral issues, technological restrictions, and the fact that not all people using such a platform can be reached for their needs.

We will also identify future directions and prospects for using artificial intelligence, patient-driven healthcare delivery, and interactive research collaborations supported by metaverse technology. The article mainly aims to investigate the metaverse as an agent of change in the healthcare industry. Through analysis of how virtual world technologies can redefine patient care improve health, and also to shape the entire health field, we are making our contribution in this regard.

***Keywords***: Metaverse, virtual reality, augmented reality, healthcare, patient care, telemedicine, wellness, gamification

## 7.1 Introduction

- **Background and Overview**

The paradigm of our perception and interaction with the environment has been turned around by digital technologies, which are used in many aspects of human life. Virtual reality (VR), augmented reality (AR), and the metaverse have all played a role in this transformative process. The metaverse is only known for its applications in entertainment, gaming, and social networking; healthcare applications are still to be exploited.

Metaverse, which was initially conceptualized in science fiction and is currently being built on top of technological advancements, is a shared virtual space where users can interact with each other and digital objects in real time. It is different from individual VR experiences as it creates an interconnected environment that transcends traditional boundaries. This fast-moving dynamic digital universe could well be the setting where future healthcare delivery and engagement may take place.

Given this, the current study examines the use of the metaverse to stakeholders such as patients in the area of care and health from a transformative view. This chapter will be demonstrated by analyzing the characteristics and potentials of the metaverse in healthcare scenarios and how it can revolutionize comprehensive healthcare and enhance individuals' well-being. Hence, through theoretical explorations, case studies, and future forecasts, it becomes easier for us to have a better perspective of these opportunities and issues that come with metaverse technologies for alterations in patient care and well-being in virtual worlds.

- **Definition of the Metaverse**

The term "metaverse" came from Neal Stephenson's Sci-fi novel titled "Snow Crash" released in 1992 and has evolved to a collective virtual experience that is beyond the single. In simple terms, the metaverse is a persistent, VR space that allows the user to socially engage in real time with other users and virtual objects.

This differs from the traditional VR systems where experience is mostly in the discrete category. It offers complex solutions that are based on VR, AR, and Internet components instead of a separate site. In addition, it also stimulates concurrent relations, cooperation, and interaction and similarly controls the relations among the users no matter what their geographical position and physical disabilities are.

Integrating various virtual settings that range from social networking to education and virtual markets, the metaverse resembles an extraordinary dynamic platform; people can exist, work, and play in the metaverse, eliminating the divide between the real and the virtual.

The social platform offers huge prospects in the provision of healthcare; as we can see, the metaverse can be applied as a groundbreaking instrument in the delivery of care to patients and raising health consciousness into virtual domains.

By leveraging on the powers of metaverse, healthcare providers are in a position to dispel territorial limitations hence enhancing the access to medical services while at the same time offering satisfactory experiences to patients and customers through other related applications. Thus, this paper seeks to understand this potential that is found in the metaverse in terms of healthcare and provide an analysis of what it is, what it can do, and how it will affect the delivery of patient care and wellness within virtual environments.

- **Importance of Healthcare in Virtual Realms**

Over recent times, advancements in technology have made the healthcare sector reap more benefits that come with embracing virtual worlds in addressing issues to do with patient care, promotion of health, and, in general, changing the face of traditional healthcare systems. Virtual environments are platforms that provide SCM-unbounded opportunities to mitigate the problematics of distance, widen the spectrum of medical services, and enhance patient engagement through the experience.

In VR, healthcare can limit physical location, which is one of the advantages noted. People can be treated without even leaving their homes so there are no issues or hindrances when it comes to accessing healthcare for them when they live in isolated areas that are not served by adequate healthcare facilities. Such platforms enable remote consultations, virtual diagnosis, and monitoring hence putting in the toolkit of health providers the ability to reach out to the patients wherever they may be.

In addition, the concept of innovation can become especially useful in virtual worlds when it comes to the introduction of revolutionary ideas and solutions concerning healthcare. Some possible alternatives are given by virtual clinics and hospitals, involving and stimulating interactive wellness programs and support communities. It provides healthcare professionals with VR simulations in even more realistic, improved situations that enhance both their knowledge and abilities to reason and decide in a risk-free practice setting.

In the current use of the virtual environment, the functionality of gamification and social interaction aspects also help boost patient engagement and compliance with recommended treatments. These are among the communities in which patient, chronic illness or mental health patient-to-patient support, and education are provided.

Far from merely incorporating healthcare into virtual worlds, the providers can widen care access and offer the best patient experience, instruct wellness, and achieve good health outcomes. While this paper provided more information on the role of healthcare in virtual worlds within the context of the metaverse, it also indicates how it has enormous potential to transform patient care, and wellness as a whole.

## 7.2 The Evolution of Healthcare in Virtual Environments

- **Historical Context:**

The idea and application of virtual environments in health can be traced back to the mid-1900s when early efforts toward computer-based training and education in the medical field were observed [1]. One of the first works was carried out by Ivan Sutherland in the 1960s—he was the creator of the first head-mounted display (HMD) system which contributed to the process of making virtual experiences immersive [2]. Subsequent years witnessed slow but steady advancements in the areas of computer graphics and processing, and input/output interfaces that enabled the development of advanced VR and AR systems.

The popularization of VR started in the 1980s with the innovations of companies like VPL Research which developed the first VR headsets and gloves for business and military use [3]. In healthcare, initial experiments were of medical training simulator's ministration and anatomical interactive models [4]. For example, the "Virtual Reality in Medicine" project at the University of North Carolina that began in the late 1980s was looking at surgical simulation and visualization through the use of VR technology [5].

I found that by the 1990s, many industries became interested in VR and AR technologies, which enhanced their interest and their willingness to invest in healthcare applications [6]. However, there are the following disadvantages of early VR/AR systems: high costs, technical constraints, and low availability that did not allow the widespread application of technology in healthcare. Still, pioneering programs such as the application of VR technology in the Virtual Reality Medical Center in treating cases of anxiety disorders confirmed the effectiveness of virtual environment immersion [7].

All in all, the evolution of virtual environments in the context of healthcare offers a rich story, rich with technological advancement and experience. These primary attempts opened up the doors for what the metaverse can and should be—a compelling tool that can revolutionize patient education as well as health and wellness within virtual realities.

- **Advancements in Virtual Reality (VR) and Augmented Reality (AR) Technologies:**

In recent times, there have been some remarkable signs of progress in VR and AR technologies due to the rapid developments in computing power, graphics processing, and sensor technology [8]. The evolution of VR technology from its earlier versions that had clumsy hardware and limited graphic capabilities to a more immersive and accessible system is evident [9]. The use of HMDs, motion tracking sensors, and haptic feedback devices has improved the user experience and realism of virtual environments by having smaller, cheaper, and more sophisticated designs [10].

Similarly, incredible headway has been made in AR technology by which digital information can be overlaid on the physical world in real time [11]. The introduction of AR apps on smartphones is what has driven the proliferation of mobile AR apps. This has been possible because of the many enhancements that have been made to smartphone cameras, sensors, and processing power that make them more powerful and useful [12].

The applications of AR technology are very diverse across different industries, from interactive gaming experiences to navigation aids and educational tools [13].

The evolution of VR and AR technologies in the healthcare sector has led to a paradigm shift by introducing new platforms for medical training, patient care, and wellness promotion [14]. Healthcare professionals can now practice complex procedures in VR environments through VR-based simulations which, in turn, help them improve their skills as well as confidence while reducing risks to patients [15]. AR applications have significantly improved the accuracy and outcomes of surgical procedures by providing real-time guidance and visualizations to surgeons during operations [16].

In conclusion, the ongoing progress and development of VR and AR technologies represent a significant hope for changing the way healthcare is delivered and patient experiences in VR.

- **Emergence of the Metaverse in Healthcare:**

The use of virtual environments especially in patient care and health maintenance has received a new facelift with the introduction of a metaverse in healthcare. The metaverse is quite ambiguous and has been conceived as a type of VR, which took its roots in science fiction literature; it has rapidly grown in popularity as the potential paradigm for future interactions and cooperation [17]. Thus, in healthcare, the metaverse qualifies VR, AR, and Internet technologies as transformational, interconnected digital environments [18].

While, today, the primary use of healthcare applications in the metaverse is yet to be developed, they are promising to radically transform conventional medical practice [4]. The use of the metaverse in virtual clinics and hospitals, telemedicine platforms, and wellness programs signifies that these pioneers are applying the metaverse to advance the reach of medical services and patient satisfaction [19]. These virtual environments erase geographic accessibility constraints, hence enabling remote patient care and perfectly interprofessional communication among healthcare givers across the globe.

In addition, the metaverse is the management and incubator for new patient education, recovery, and rehabilitation [20]. Using web application games and virtual care groups, tailored and improved forms of engaging and activating patients are offered [21]. Through the metaverse of the connected digital environment, the patients can be captured more actively to improve their compliance with the prescribed treatment regimens and reduce the gap and inequality in access to healthcare and overall well-being [22].

Ultimately, the emergence of the metaverse in the context of the provision of medical services becomes the transition to new approaches to interaction within healthcare that are more active, integrated, and patient-oriented. As the nature of the metaverse grows, it still brings the potential for a complete shift in patient and wellness care in the virtual space [23–29].

## 7.3 Applications of the Metaverse in Patient Care

- **Virtual Clinics and Hospitals:**

The notion of virtual clinics and hospitals embedded into the metaverse is a completely new concept of healthcare with a patient-oriented, convenient, and effective environment for successful outcomes. These healthcare facilities are like virtual wonderlands of digitized composite spaces that offer a multitude of healthcare advantages that are as rich as the array of points of care that one is bestowed with an opportunity to pursue interactively. The idea of virtual clinics/hospitals transcends the actual physical clinics since it brings improved healthcare to patients in any place with an Internet connection.

In the clinic or hospital set in a virtual environment, the patient can interact through avatars, talk to professionals, and even get treated through avatars in a way that is comfortable to him. Through the use of avatar technology, patients would be able to engage in a live conversation with their healthcare practitioners or converse about their complaints, worries, or treatment choices and options in a secure, confidential way. In these virtual environments, patients may be privileged to detailed records of their health, physical tests, and plans of treatment that will enable them to be equipped to participate in their healthcare.

Teledermatology, for instance, is one of the crucial benefits of virtual clinics and hospitals in that it can potentially lead to better access to health facilities for people in hopelessly remote areas that have extremely limited health practices. This eliminated limitations of geographical location since patients from any geographical area can easily access their healthcare providers and specialists without the need to travel physically. The e-accessibility improvements could increase the chances of early diagnosis and treatment of medical conditions, hence better overall health and eliminating health disparities.

Besides giving flexible and convenient virtual clinics and hospitals for patients and healthcare providers, they do offer telemedicine services.

Patients are allowed to book appointments, consult, and use medical services at their convenience, unrestricted by conventional office hours or waiting time. On the other hand, healthcare providers can leverage virtual platforms for administrative functions better, including streamlining their administrative tasks, making appointments, and providing personalized care to their patients. Of course, some privacy concerns arise with the emergence of virtual clinics and hospitals: patient privacy, data security, and regulatory compliance. It is upon healthcare organizations to ensure that their virtual platforms conform to the best standards, say, the Health Insurance Portability and Accountability Act (HIPAA), for safeguarding patient information and thus maintaining confidentiality. There must be proper cybersecurity to prevent data breaches or any access to medical records by unauthorized entities.

This would change the game in healthcare with virtual clinics and hospitals in the long term, providing new and more effective ways to increase access, convenience, and patient-centered care.

The following is what healthcare organizations will do: enable the creation of virtual spaces in which patients will be better informed and have better health outcomes using immersive technology in the metaverse, hence transforming the future delivery of healthcare. However, there are ethical, legal, and technical issues that must be well considered in providing secure and effective implementation of virtual health solutions.

- **Telemedicine and Remote Consultations:**

Telemedicine and remote consultations are part and parcel of healthcare in the metaverse—the new dimension bringing out revolutionary solutions to both patients and healthcare providers. Metaverse telemedicine platforms use VR, AR, and Internet technologies in the creation of immersive and secure environments for remote healthcare interactions. It is from peoples' homes that they can walk into virtual consultation rooms with no barriers of distance or travel, which normally act against access to health services. Improved accessibility is, therefore, a godsend for rural or underserved populations or those with limited mobility or chronically ill patients.

Through virtual consultation, patients and health professionals interact in real-time through communication and interaction, much the same way it happens in an in-person medical appointment. With the use of high-definition video conferencing, patients can discuss their symptoms, case history, and the various options for treatment with health professionals to obtain personalized care and advice without considering their location. Moreover, it allows metaverse telemedicine platforms to support remote physical examinations, thus allowing healthcare providers to conduct a virtual physical examination, review diagnostic tests, and monitor vital signs in real-time.

One of the most distinguishing advantages of telemedicine within the metaverse has to do with its inherent ability to extend access to specialized medical expertise. No more will a patient have to waste hours traveling long distances just for a specialist consultation or second opinion, but through virtual consultation, they can connect with healthcare providers around the world and empower themselves. This may facilitate access to a wider expertise base, possibly leading to earlier diagnosis and treatment of medical conditions and improved management of chronic diseases and complicated health issues.

Continuity of care is also maintained through telemedicine in the metaverse by providing seamless interaction and collaboration from health providers who are placed in different places and disciplines. Virtual consultation promotes smooth exchange of medical records, test results, and treatment plans, hence patients receive full and integrated care irrespective of their location. Telemedicine within an integrated bigger healthcare ecosystem enhances efficiency, reduces service duplication, promotes patient safety, and ultimately improves patient outcomes.

Apart from influencing access to care and continuity of care, telemedicine is associated with patient engagement and satisfaction in the metaverse. It is through the provision of convenient and flexible appointment options that patients will be motivated enough to have a more active role in managing their health through virtual consultations. They are appreciative that they enjoy the convenience of being able to plan their appointments at times most convenient to themselves without having to take off from work or make provisions to reach a physical clinic. This sort of advanced patient engagement may result in increased treatment adherence, higher patient satisfaction rates, and hence better health outcomes.

Nevertheless, the growing deployment of telemedicine in the metaverse results in difficulties and concerns that must be tackled. These issues are related to patient privacy and data security, regulatory compliance, reimbursement policies, and technological infrastructure. Healthcare organizations should use cybersecurity systems that are very secure to protect patient data and comply with regulations such as HIPAA. Besides, there ought to be clear-cut regulations and reimbursement models for policymakers to smoothly support the integration of telemedicine into the mainstream healthcare system.

- **Virtual Health Monitoring and Diagnostics:**

The metaverse will become an avenue for health delivery: health monitoring might as well be virtual and might as well, in effect, involve solutions such as virtual diagnostics, among others. Wearable sensor devices, together with artificial intelligence (AI) algorithms and the Internet of Things (IoT) devices, are fundamental enablers that give way to the complete transformation of tracking, analysis, and deployment of patients' health data. Such innovative technology does provide real-time and continuous monitoring of vital signs, symptoms, and health behaviors. This provides patients and their providers with actionable insights into the health status of patients, enabling timely interventions when necessary.

These may include interactive dashboards, visual representations, and even personalized health reports within the virtual world. This will result in the patients being exposed to health data that are easily interpreted. Following the trends in health metrics, setting personal health goals, and receiving instant health recommendation notifications that are according to one's health requirements and his or her own choice are extremely easy with the help of this interface for the patients. Such personal feedback allows the patient to manage his or her health on his or her own by way of choice related to lifestyle and treatment modalities.

The virtual solutions in health monitoring and diagnostics promise to change the face of health prevention dramatically by making way for early-stage preemptive interventions and pre-diagnosis of health problems. Both technologies keep track of the slightest change or deviation from normal, which is important because, through constant monitoring of all important health parameters: heart rate, arterial pressure, and glucose levels, it might be an indicative one for an arising problem. This allows for early detection—right in the smallest of blood vessels; this means that health providers can intervene very fast to stop the progression of diseases/complications, resulting in improved general health outcomes.

Virtual health monitoring and diagnostic solutions have added benefits in the management of chronic conditions. For example, patients with chronic diseases like diabetes, hypertension, or heart disease may, through the use of wearable sensors and IoT devices, monitor the progress of their symptoms daily. It processes all the data in real time, while AI-driven algorithms recognize the trends and patterns that can be signatories of changes in the patient's condition. Information derived in such a manner is used by the providers of healthcare to modify plans of treatment, optimization of medication regimens, and even interventions that may be patient-specific.

Moreover, virtual eHealth solutions for monitoring health and diagnosis also contribute to personalized medicine since they customize the interventions and treatment protocols to the characteristics of every patient. The huge set of patient data is used by the AI algorithms to mine the relationship between the indicators, genetic markers, the lifestyle of the patient, and outcomes of treatment, which further helps in carrying out better and precision-targeted healthcare interventions with maximum effectiveness and minimum side effects. This kind of personalized approach in healthcare may, therefore, translate to improved treatment compliance and a better experience for the patient, and hence patient outcomes.

## 7.4 Improving Healthcare Education and Training

- **Simulation-Based Learning:**

Simulation-based learning in the metaverse is a new, innovative way of delivering healthcare education, whereby medical practitioners receive highly immersive and practice-based training experiences very similar to what they observe in the physical world of clinical scenarios. This allows Jason's students to experience several clinical scenarios, surgical procedures, and emergency interventions via virtual simulations in a safe, controlled environment. The simulations are correct to replicate real problems of clinical practice so that the learners can gain experience, practical skills, and competencies for development.

One of the main benefits of simulation-based learning in the metaverse is that it helps in the development of several qualities, like critical thinking ability, clinical judgment, and procedural competence, in health professionals. The student might then have the opportunity to work through patient cases and scenarios that will, therefore, support the application of making sound quality clinical decisions from theoretical knowledge into practice. Simulated patient experiences enable learners to develop the ability to believe in themselves and pick up the art of dealing with complicated clinical situations skillfully and precisely. In addition, metaverse-based simulation learning gives instant performance feedback to learners.

This can help identify the areas that require improvement and, in most cases, help refine the skills almost in real time. The virtual simulations can bring in the in-built measurements like assessment tools and performance metrics to the learners, which means that it can measure the proficiency and competency gained by the learners, thus providing a clear view of their progress and achievement. This further drives a learning and improvement loop, hence cultivating the excellence culture in the performance and professional development of the healthcare provider. In addition to individual skill development, this kind of simulation-based learning would also offer cross-disciplinary collaboration and team training environments in the metaverse of humankind.

Virtual environments with healthcare professionals from a diversity of backgrounds see the conduction of simulated patient-care scenarios with focuses on improvements in communication, teamwork, coordination of care, and others. Collaborative simulation provides the learners with an opportunity to acquire an understanding of the roles and responsibilities of others, hence enabling them to effectively work within a multidisciplinary team in providing quality patient care. Apart from other benefits, simulation-based learning within the metaverse provides a means of assessing competency and proficiency among healthcare professionals. Virtual simulations can be designed through VR, such that the specific clinical skills and competencies needed could be assessed by educators in learners' performance under standardized and objective conditions.

This would help teachers identify areas they have achieved and those in need of improvement, which guides the development of intervention and learning plans to better support the development of the learner professionally. In most scenarios, the potential for very great changes in the entire field lies with simulation-based learning in the metaverse of healthcare education. Consistent with this, simulation-based learning provides learners with direct, immersive, organizational, and practical experiences geared toward instilling the development of critical thinking, clinical judgment, and procedural competence to promote interdisciplinary teamwork in team training.

Continuous development in the sophistication and complexity of virtual simulation technologies propels it to the forefront of the education of health professionals for multidimensional clinical practice, from which more patient safety and outcomes are actualized.

- **Virtual Medical Training and Skills Development:**

The metaverse offers next-generation virtual medical training and skills development programs to provide interactive and interesting learning environments for its learners using innovative immersive technologies. Such programs represent modern forms of teaching and learning, which are based on simulation and include different areas of medicine, from anatomy and physiology to surgical technology and diagnostic procedures. Within such programs, students have an opportunity to experiment and apply them in a virtual world safely and without restraints. In such laboratories, students can dissect and study anatomical structures to such an unbelievable accuracy and detail level that understanding the physiology and pathology of the human subject is greatly facilitated.

Some other medicine training courses go the extra mile and offer surgical simulations and real medical procedures by the use of virtual tools and devices to practice whatever one would be doing in a real-life kind of situation. The simulations will give learners the platform to perfect their surgical skills, like suturing, laparoscopy, and endoscopy, in a zero-risk milieu that may assist them in further improving their skills and acquiring competence under the guidance of professionals. The learners are also involved in diagnostic simulations, where they assess clinical data and make accurate decisions toward making a diagnosis from the virtual patient cases and scenarios presented to them.

The virtual medical training platform is flexible enough to adjust the modules of learning according to the needs and objectives of the learners. The learner chooses among several virtual scenarios and case studies to refine the training in the area where they feel that they would require more practice or focus or learning is specifically needed. Learners can track their progress and even receive advice and support based on their requirements, which increases the effectiveness of the learning experience through mechanisms of adaptive feedback and performance analytics.

These are integrated with elements of VR, AR, and gamification in a virtual medical training program to increase engagement, motivation, and retention among learners. The other features of the product, coupled with an interactive learning environment, make learning a joyful and effective process by attracting and not letting the learner divert from the learning process. Elements like gamified points, badges, and leaderboards are factors to motivate excellence or mastery and have the potential to engage learners to participate actively toward striving for improvement and accomplishment.

Finally, within a metaverse environment, there are virtual training and skills development programs that enable medical practitioners to be apprised of the latest developments in the medical field and to learn the acquisition of new skills. The programs make it easily accessible with the use of the most modern technologies and techniques that would assist learners in keeping abreast of the emerging trends and best practices in healthcare. In other words, these virtual medical training programs improve patient outcomes and their safety by improving the quality of care that the health provider offers to the patients.

The virtual metaverse of medical education and training programs is summarily described, in a learner-centric way, through interactive and effective modes of learning experiences for the enhancement of knowledge, skills, and competencies of the learners. These programs motivate the learners to acquire high-performance exposure to the delivery of high-quality care services to their patients. The advancement and sophistication of the technologies applied to training virtual medicine will very soon be at the helm of the changing aspect of healthcare education and professional development.

- **Continuing Education in Virtual Environments:**

The paradigm keeps shifting with further education being offered in virtual environments for professionals to engage in lifelong learning. This keeps health professionals aware of the current best practices, assisting them to gain new skills and improve their clinical expertise while at their workplace. The learning and development virtual programs would heavily utilize the latest technologies to give an interactive and immersive learning experience, thus removing for the learner the barriers created due to time and space. Flexibility is hence one of the greatest advantages of virtual continued education programs since it allows health practitioners to access educational resources and take part in learning activities from any part of the world.

They are now able to be part of virtual conferences, workshops, and seminars that save them the huge costs and time wastage that these conventional face-to-face events would be associated with. The nature of access, therefore, could be considered quite democratizing, in the least since it provides access to healthcare professionals in the various backgrounds and settings where they work their lifelong learning and professional development. Learners interact with the best faculty members and get to meet other students; they engage themselves in activities such as case-based discussions, simulations, and role-playing exercises.

All these aspects of interaction develop active learning and critical thinking. In turn, they assist learners in applying their theoretical learning to practice scenarios and accordingly develop their problem-solving ability for real-life cases. They also provide a safe and supportive ground for the learner to be able to ask questions, make clarifications, and share ideas with peers and mentors, thus promoting teamwork and the ongoing development of individuals. Online life-learning platforms integrate countless multimedia content, many interactive presentations, and countless self-assessment tools, taking into account the various learning styles and preferences of each one.

The visual dynamics, interactive simulations, and multimedia are sophisticated enough to prompt learners into intricate details of such complicated topics, thereby helping to support the learning objectives and encourage knowledge retention simultaneously. Moreover, the use of self-assessment tools will also be helpful to learners by helping them check their progress, what needs to be done, and how they can follow up on the professional development that is taking place over some time for them to take their learning journey into control and set some personal goals. Virtual and online applications to continuing education: These are applied to the continuing education of healthcare professionals to further their knowledge base and to allow opportunities for practicing clinical skills within current, dynamic aspects of the profession.

Continual learning and professional development allow healthcare professionals to provide quality care, respond to the dynamic trends in healthcare, and improve patient outcomes. The role of emerging virtual continuing education technologies will increase further with the development and innovation of future healthcare education and workforce development, at the same time, making sure that healthcare professionals are competent, confident, and compassionate throughout their working lives.

## 7.5 Challenges and Considerations

- **Ethical and Privacy Concerns:**

With the birth and development of the virtual realms in healthcare, many ethical and privacy issues appeared. The establishment of virtual healthcare platforms raises varied ethical dilemmas such as collection, storage, and sharing of sensitive patient data. The related concerns are, at the very heart, issues of consent, confidentiality, and data security, all requiring extremely careful attention if patient trust and safety are to be guarded.

The idea of informed consent within virtual health environments also takes different shades. All patients must be in a position to understand very clearly how their data within the virtual platforms shall be collected, used, and shared; hence, they will have to give clear consent to the same. Informed consent in such environments brings with it special challenges since patients may not even be in a position to understand fully what it would mean to share their health information within those digital spaces. It may, therefore, seem just that the healthcare providers develop strong mechanisms of consent and transparent communication, for the empowerment of the patients to make an informed decision regarding their data. Figure 7.1 highlights the primary challenges of the metaverse in healthcare and wellness, including data privacy, high initial costs, and trust issues.

The other ethical principle that must be maintained within the virtual healthcare environment is confidentiality. The patient has to entrust their respective sensitive medical information and the protection of their rights to privacy to the healthcare provider. All these issues are further exaggerated in a virtual world. Thus, there is a very great need for tight security to

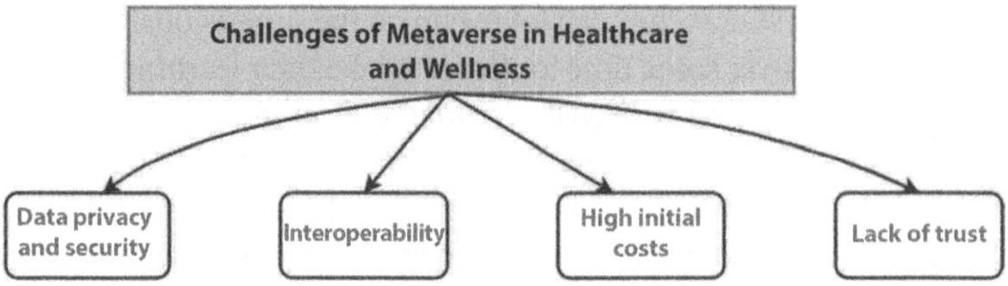


**Figure 7.1** Challenges of metaverse in healthcare and wellness.

ensure that the data of the patient is safe from unauthorized access, data breaches, and even cyberattacks. Other important tools to reduce these risks and make sure that no patient's data should be revealed are encryption, access controls, and secure authentication protocols.

This will include the application of regulatory frameworks such as the HIPAA, to which health services must adhere while working in such virtual environments. The HIPAA has put forth very stringent requirements about the protection of patients' health information, hence guaranteeing that information confidentiality, integrity, and availability are achieved. HIPAA has set rules with a very complex punch to healthcare organizations, and in case they do not want to pay for the legal consequences, they must go across these laws and strictly implement great privacy and security activities.

Finally, anonymization of patient data presents another value-added ethical challenge in virtual care environments. Indeed, the very aim of anonymization is to produce protection for the patient's privacy by removing any identifying information from its datasets, though this certainly is not perfect and can be circumvented. Even the aggregated datasets have the potential for reidentification using advanced data linkage techniques and thereby pose risks to patient privacy. Advanced anonymization techniques and methods for de-identification of data must thus be adopted by a healthcare provider to minimize reidentification and protect, therefore, patient anonymity.

As the benefits of virtual care need to be balanced and weighed against ethics, it requires ongoing transparency, dialogue, and strong governance frameworks. Health organizations should communicate with the patient in terms of how his/her data will be used, at the same time, ensuring that the development and implementation of the respective technologies of virtual healthcare are built on ethical principles. More so, these ethical predicaments form an interdisciplinary collaboration of health professionals, ethicists, policymakers, and technologists who should look into the future to establish standards of practice in virtual healthcare.

• **Technological Limitations:**

In health scenarios, virtually, any of the cases tend to present relevant technological barriers to the implementation of such technologies as VR and AR. With the big steps experienced in recent years, still, this progress can still be hampered by these limitations in different areas of VR/AR application, ranging from hardware functionalities and capabilities to user experience and integration with existing systems in healthcare.

The critical technology challenge in the way of VR/AR technology in healthcare, for the most part, includes hardware. Most of the time, VR/AR gadgets have limits in aspects such as field of view, screen resolution, and battery endurance, among others. This can be a limitation in the full immersion and the usability of this technology. These conditions could, therefore, act as detractors to overall user experience and effectiveness for VR/AR applications, more so in complex medical scenarios where pinpoint precision and absolute attention to the minutest of detail are required.

Moreover, the possibility of latency issues and the possibility of motion sickness can highly affect VR/AR interactions. This can be very important for the former in sensitive medical scenarios where the user has to perform exact movement or prolonged interaction within the virtual environments. That would reduce comfort and the engagement of the user, particularly. Stated otherwise, these two are critical to the success of VR/AR-based interventions or training programs.

However, a key challenge is making VR/AR platforms interoperate with existing health systems and data infrastructure. To meet the scalability in the virtual solutions and mass acceptability, there is a compulsion for smooth exchange and integration of data between varied VR/AR platforms and electronic health record (EHR) systems. Most often, there is a challenge to this due to a variation in protocols, standards, and data formats. As a result, achieving seamless integration and data exchange becomes challenging.

For these technical challenges, the ongoing research, innovation, and collaboration of the multidisciplinary team will be able to address them. Researchers and developers focus on hardware limitations, such as improved performance, comfort, and usability of VR/AR devices. Some of these are enhancements of the display technology, optimization for battery life, and enhancement of tracking capability to enhance the immersive experience and bring it nearer to the real world, minimizing motion sickness to the least.

Efforts are also being put in place regarding standardization and the development of protocols that will make it possible for data exchange interoperability in the virtual healthcare environment. Efforts in the area include open-source software platforms with their interoperability frameworks, allowing smooth data exchange and integration between the VR/AR application and the existing healthcare system. The initiatives encourage collaboration and standardization to help remove the interoperability obstacles that have served to impede the faster adoption of virtual health solutions.

- **Accessibility and Equity Issues:**

On the other hand, the exponential scaling of virtual health services and digital health tools comes with some big problems regarding accessibility and equity, mostly among the vulnerable and underserved groups. Modern-day healthcare disparities are further compounded by the impacts of a mix of socioeconomic status, digital literacy, and access to technology that fairly impacts healthcare delivery, hence placing this whole area on an uneven field where there is a gap in the digital divide. Differences in people's income levels are very important in influencing the way through which they will have access to services on virtual healthcare.

Low-income people, therefore, might not be able to afford such VR/AR devices or high-speed Internet connections that are required to gain access to such platforms. They may further have differences in digital literacy and educational differences, which make it more difficult because poor knowledge of technology may not help them navigate the virtual healthcare interfaces properly and be able to make the most out of the digital health tool. The progress of broadband Internet and VR/AR devices poses a lot of problems, especially in rural and remote areas.

Most importantly, communities that are often neglected have no room to experience the luxury of reliable Internet infrastructure, which enables the use of high-speed broadband and thus limits their involvement in virtual health consultations and access to most health resources available over the web. Furthermore, those living in settings with remoteness and limited resources may be left with no other option than to bear the costs affordably that are necessary for the acquisition of VR/AR devices, hence leading to an increase in disparities related to the services offered virtually for the health sector. Furthermore, some members of these disadvantaged groups and disabled people might not even access affordable healthcare because of affordability, accessibility, and usability. These virtual health services have presented new access to healthcare, although it may be that the elderly are very technologically unsavvy and thus be able to require more assistance to access these virtual health services.

On the other hand, users with disabilities are very likely to face accessibility issues in a virtual environment, such as the nonavailability of accessibility features in user interfaces or the unavailability of accommodation for assistive technologies. On the other hand, some of the major barriers related to discrepancies in the use of virtual health services are that of language and culture. Low language proficiency or cultural misunderstandings, which would otherwise lead to misunderstandings and barriers in care, could be even more menacing to the patient-healthcare provider communication in the virtual environment.

Additionally, cultural incompetence will make the virtual healthcare delivery platform widen the gap among minority populations, thence ensuring poor health outcomes. This is imperative for ensuring access and equity in the development of virtual healthcare. For example, if the virtual health solution were to be made inclusive, accessible, and culturally competent, then the solution has to think of community engagement strategies so that they can get the maximum benefit out of these opportunities. With the promotion of digital literacy and further broadband infrastructure, reducing the costs of VR/AR devices would, therefore, mean closing the gap in the digital divide for this population so that they can benefit more from the services of virtual healthcare.

Furthermore, such virtual platforms are to be devised and designed by the health professionals and the developers themselves, for the patients with diverse preferences to access and use the same in the first place. These are made possible by the inclusion of, among others, multilingual support services, services that take care of the disabled, and information that takes care of the culture-sensitive nature of the virtual health service to patients despite their cultural background or situation.

## 7.6 Future Directions and Opportunities

- **Integration of Artificial Intelligence (AI) and Machine Learning (ML):** Involving AI and machine learning to this possible advancement could even further improve the state of the virtual health metaverse. This would include AI-powered algorithms that can mine large patient data to derive actionable insights for real-time clinical decision-making. It could improve diagnostic accuracy, predict the progress of the disease by using machine learning algorithms, and maybe further lead to a very tailored treatment plan that can be suited to a single patient's profile and preferences. AI-driven virtual assistants and chatbots deliver health advice that is personalized through chatbots and handle queries by patients, as well as remote monitoring and triage in the virtual space. These are AI-based tools such as simulations and predictive modeling, which assist in healthcare scenario simulation, healthcare outcome prediction, resource optimization, and process optimization

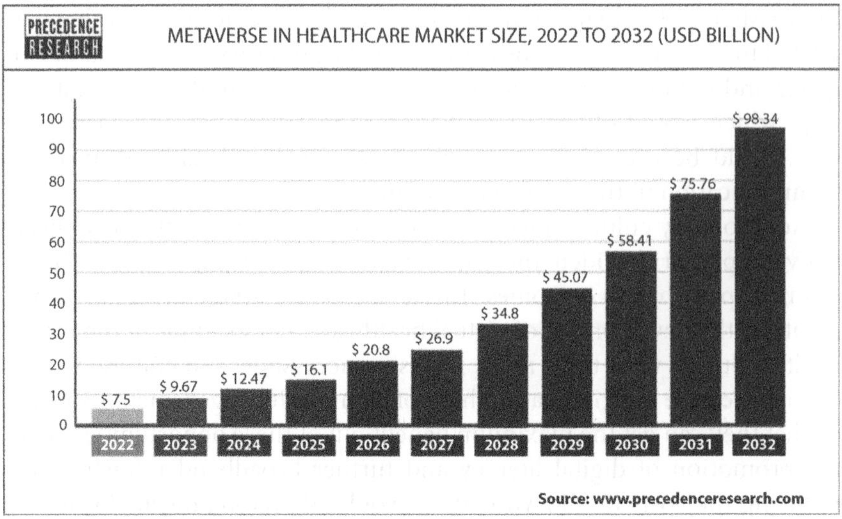


**Figure 7.2** Future of metaverse in the healthcare market. (source: https://www.precedenceresearch.com/metaverse-in-healthcare-market).

in healthcare delivery. AI and ML can further help the metaverse contribute to an increase and the addition of more value to the effectiveness, efficiency, and personalization of patients' care within the parameters of virtual platforms. Figure 7.2 presents projections for the growth of the metaverse in healthcare from 2022 to 2032, showcasing a significant market expansion.

- **Personalized Healthcare Experiences:**

One of the predicted future developments in the metaverse is the customization of health experience [30]. The virtual health platforms have potential opportunities in which the providers can tailor the interventions, treatment plans, and, at best, the entire wellness approach to fit the individual needs and objectives using the provided patient data, preferences, and insights into their behavior. Custom health dashboards, virtual coaches, and adaptive interfaces providing individualized feedback, recommendations, and support might find their base in the envisioned idea for patients to be able to strengthen the self-regulation of health and well-being [31]. It would be much more immersive and engaging than one developed with the aid of VR and AR technologies, enforcing higher levels of engagement, adherence, and satisfaction [32]. A further study established that personalized virtual environments could elicit a sense of autonomy, ownership, and empowerment in patients, hence bringing positive changes in behavior and consequently better health outcomes [33–36]. It would, therefore, mean that virtual health platforms would increase the level of patient involvement, adherence, and overall satisfaction with possible improved health outcomes and wellness as a result of the incorporation of personalization [37–39].

- **Collaborative Research and Development Efforts:**
In this respect, an innovative metaverse solution for virtual healthcare calls for a collaborative research and development environment with other bodies ranging from industries to academia. This means multidisciplinary collaboration—the coming together of ideas, expertise, and resources from healthcare providers, technologists, and researchers with policymakers, as well as stakeholders in the concerned industry. By sharing best practices, knowledge, and data, we can advance the development and implementation of virtual health technologies and standards. Open-source platforms, hackathons, and innovation challenges, among others, have been enabled to bring in quick ideation and fine-tuning of solutions in virtual health that allow iterative feedback and improvement cycles. Furthermore, academic-government-industry partnerships are playing a driving role in investment and bringing to the forefront scalability and sustainability for their innovative solutions of virtual care accessible to populations and varied sets of health settings.

## 7.7 Conclusion

- **Recap of Key Findings:**
It underlines the critical nature of research and development collaboration to realize in full the potential for transformation that the metaverse can play in enhancing patient care and well being and fostering an enabling culture of innovation, inclusion, and impact. We will consider here the transformative capacity of the metaverse in how it may change patient care and wellness in virtual environments. We reviewed some metaverse applications in healthcare: virtual clinics, telehealth, simulation-based education of health professionals for healthcare, and personalized healthcare. On top of that, we also consider the challenges and issues in the integration of such solutions within our healthcare system: ethical and privacy issues, technological inadequacy, and access-related problems.

- **Implications for the Future of Healthcare:**
However, the metaverse offers—challenges aside—an unprecedented opportunity to increase accessibility, quality, and outcomes of healthcare delivery, opportunities that both patients and providers should be aware

of to exploit the full potential of what the digital frontier in healthcare has to offer. The metaverse is a transformational and illustrative explanation of the future of health in this paper. It had the potential to bring back human experiences in healthcare using VR, AR, and AI technologies that have so far helped in breaking barriers, pushing the unbreakable until now, in the patient delivery of care, education, and research. The healthcare virtual platform democratizes access to healthcare services, personalizing the experience of the patient and stimulating innovations within the whole field of healthcare. In addition, virtual worlds in learning and training are successfully applied in medicine by effectively empowering good clinical performance, fostering interprofessional collaboration, and ensuring improved patient outcomes.

• **Call to Action for Further Exploration and Implementation:**
As the metaverse develops further, it will slowly bear very strongly upon shaping the future of how the metaverse may gradually have a very great bearing on shaping the future of how healthcare delivery occurs, the promotion of wellness, and new developments in medicine. As we embark on this journey of turning toward a metaverse-enabled healthcare ecosystem, it is more than obligatory that, together, we follow a call for more research and implementation. Addressing these challenges and barriers to the broader adoption of virtual care solutions will require intervention on the part of all these parties: from healthcare providers to policymakers, from technologists to researchers, and industry stakeholders, working together. This might include investments focusing on the conduct of research and development activities in a bid to improve accessibility, usability, and interconnectivity of the various virtual health platforms, taking the regulatory environment to one that encourages innovation but at the same time safeguards the rights and privacy of patients. Furthermore, digital inclusion programs within the metaverse would be necessary so that all, regardless of their status or location, could afford to have access to and use this metaverse.

We realize together, with our research and efforts in creating advanced implementation for virtual healthcare solutions, that the metaverse may change patient care and wellness in virtual domains, but still beyond. In essence, the metaverse represents an intrinsic change in the delivery of health and wellness promotion, opening new, unparalleled avenues for individuals and institutions to redefine the future of health.

The metaverse can thus be used to bring about innovation, collaboration, and inclusivity in developing a healthcare system that is equitable, accessible, and patient-oriented.

## References


1. Bassano, C., Caruso, G., Fiorentino, A., Virtual reality in medicine: Historical review and future perspectives. *La Clin. Ter.*, 172, 2, e192–e197, 2021.
2. Fuchs, P. and Bishop, G., Virtual reality: History and future, in: *Encyclopedia of Computer Graphics and Games*, pp. 1–12, 2020.
3. Garcia-Palacios, A., Hoffman, H., Carlin, A., Furness, T., Botella, C., Virtual reality in the treatment of spider phobia: A controlled study. *Behav. Res. Ther.*, 40, 9, 983–993, 2002.
4. Huang, Y. and Turchin, A., Augmented and virtual reality in healthcare: A focus on medical education. *J. Healthc. Inf. Manage.*, 33, 1, 11–15, 2019.
5. Pimentel, T. and Teixeira, K., Virtual reality: Past, present, and future, in: *Virtual Reality - Perspectives, Challenges, and Trends*, pp. 3–23, IntechOpen, London, United Kingdom, 2019, https://doi.org/10.5772/intechopen.84765.
6. Riva, G., Mantovani, F., Wiederhold, B., Wiederhold, M., Neuroscience of virtual reality: From virtual exposure to embodied medicine. *Cyberpsychol. Behav. Soc. Netw.*, 23, 1, 3–5, 2020.
7. Azuma, R., A survey of augmented reality. *Presence: Teleoperators Virtual Environ.*, 6, 4, 355–385, 2019.
8. Bacigalupo, R., Cudd, P., Littlewood, C., Bissell, P., Hawkeye and friends: Studying the use of a tangible user interface to support medication management in the home, in: *Proceedings of the SIGCHI Conference on Human Factors in Computing Systems*, pp. 2651–2660, 2013.
9. Bach, C., The quest for realism in virtual reality. *J. Simul.*, 15, 1, 1–10, 2021.
10. Billinghurst, M. and Dunser, A., Augmented reality in the classroom. *Computer*, 45, 7, 56–63, 2012.
11. Burdea, G. and Coiffet, P., *Virtual reality technology*, vol. 2, Springer, Cham, Switzerland, 2003.
12. Freeman, D., Reeve, S., Robinson, A., Ehlers, A., Clark, D., Spanlang, B., Slater, M., Virtual reality in the assessment, understanding, and treatment of mental health disorders. *Psychol. Med.*, 47, 14, 2393–2400, 2017.
13. Kaufmann, H. and Dünser, A., Augmented reality in education and training. *TechTrends*, 61, 2, 159–170, 2017.
14. Pratt, P., Sun, S., Sheffield, B., Simpson, M., Lubarsky, D., Ball, W., MagicLeap as a novel surgical visualization tool, in: *2018 IEEE International Conference on Systems, Man, and Cybernetics (SMC)*, IEEE, pp. 472–477, 2018.
15. Slater, M. and Sanchez-Vives, M., Enhancing our lives with immersive virtual reality. *Front. Rob. AI*, 3, 74, 2016.
16. Andersen, P., Poulsen, L., Ebbesen, M., Sørensen, A., Andersen, J., Virtual reality and the metaverse in healthcare: A narrative review. *JMIR Serious Games*, 9, 3, e28597, 2021.
17. Baschera, G., Bétrancourt, M., Zumbach, J., Augmented reality and virtual reality for patient education: A narrative review. *JMIR Serious Games*, 10, 1, e30478, 2022.

18. Ferizi, U., Keuper, M., Slodicka, L., Oecking, C., Telemedicine in the metaverse: Opportunities and challenges. *Front. Digital Health*, 4, 798532, 2022.
19. Peng, W. and Wang, X., Virtual reality and augmented reality in the metaverse for healthcare. *J. Med. Internet Res.*, 23, 12, e32800, 2021.
20. Rohr, C. and Ganz, A., Virtual and augmented reality in the metaverse: Implications for healthcare. *J. Med. Internet Res.*, 23, 7, e30034, 2021.
21. Rojas, D., Castro, L., Amaral, T., Virtual reality and the metaverse in patient care: A systematic review. *JMIR Serious Games*, 8, 4, e18272, 2020.
22. Stephenson, N., *Snow Crash*, Bantam Books, New York, USA, 1992.
23. Vyas, A.K. and Dhiman, H.S., Predication of negative dispersion for photonic crystal fiber using extreme learning machine. *J. Opt. Commun.*, 45, 2, 219–225, 000010151520210124, 2021, https://doi.org/10.1515/joc-2021-0124.
24. Vyas, A.K., Multiple rings based photonic crystal fiber for terahertz application. *Optik*, 231, 166424, 2021.
25. Vyas, A.K., Hiran, K.K., Dhiman, H., Modelling of symmetrical quadrature optical ring resonator with four different topologies and performance analysis using machine learning approach. *J. Opt. Commun.*, 44, No. s1 (2024), 000010151520200270, 2021, https://doi.org/10.1515/joc-2020-0270.
26. Vyas, A.K., Impact Analysis of the Number of Core on Hexagonal Multicore Fibre. *J. Opt. Commun.*, 489–498, 2020, https://doi.org/10.1515/joc-2019-0238.
27. Vyas, A.K., Elliptical air holes based photonic crystal fiber for narrow band gap and peak power at 1.55 micrometre wavelength. *Optik – Int. J. Light Electron Opt.*, Elsevier, 184, 28–34, May 2019.
28. Vyas, A.K., Analysis of different structure and nonlinear distortion of multicore fiber for power over fiber applications. *Optik – Int. J. Light Electron Opt.*, Elsevier, 168, 184–191, September 2018.
29. Khatri, N., Vyas, A.K., Abdul-Qawy, A.S.H., Rene, E.R., Artificial neural network based models for predicting the effluent quality of a combined upflow anaerobic sludge blanket and facultative pond: Performance evaluation and comparison of different algorithms. *Environ. Res.*, 217, 114843, 2023.
30. Cipresso, P., Giglioli, I., Raya, M.A., Riva, G., The past, present, and future of virtual and augmented reality research: A network and cluster analysis of the literature. *Front. Psychol.*, 11, 1174, 2020.
31. Pareek, A., Godiya, S., Sharma, R.K., Jain, A., AIoMT: Artificial intelligence and internet of medical things framework for healthcare in the metaverse. *J. King Saud Univ. Comput. Inf. Sci.*, 32, 11, 1373–1381, 2020.
32. Wootton, R., Liu, J., Bonnardot, L., Telemedicine in China. *Telemed. e-Health*, 18, 5, 364–369, 2012.
33. Cook, D.A., Levinson, A.J., Garside, S., Dupras, D.M., Erwin, P.J., Internet-based learning in the health professions: A meta-analysis. *JAMA*, 300, 10, 1181–1196, 2008.

34. Khazanchi, D., Kumar Vyas, A., Kant Hiran, K., Padmanaban, S., *Blockchain 3.0 for Sustainable Development*, De Gruyter, Berlin, Boston, 2021, https://doi.org/10.1515/9783110702507.
35. Kant Hiran, K., Khazanchi, D., Kumar Vyas, A., Padmanaban, S., *Machine Learning for Sustainable Development*, De Gruyter, Berlin, Boston, 2021, https://doi.org/10.1515/9783110702514.
36. Vyas, A.K., Balamurugan, S., Hiran, K.K., Dhiman, H.S. (Eds.), *Artificial Intelligence for Renewable Energy Systems*, John Wiley & Sons, Hoboken, NJ, USA, 2022, ISBN: 9781119761693.
37. Doshi, R., Hiran, K., Prakash, B., Vyas, A.K., Deep Belief Network based Image processing for Local Directional Segmentation in Brain Tumor detection. *J. Electron. Imaging*, SPIE, (SCIE), 32, 6, 062502–062502, 2023.
38. Tanna, J., Jha, S., Muruganant, M., Singh, A.K., Vyas, A.K., Kumar, S., Heat Pulse Probe-based Smart Soil Moisture Detection System. *IEEE Sens. J.*, 23, 11, 11428–11436, 2023. doi: 10.1109/JSEN.2023.3266070.
39. Patidar, Y., Jain, M., Vyas, A., Routing in Wireless Sensor Networks and Internet of Things: Systematic Analysis and Discussion, in: *AIoT and Smart Sensing Technologies for Smart Devices*, F. Al-Turjman (Ed.), IGI Global, USA, 2024.

# 8

# Metaverse in Medical Training and Education

**Avnish Bora**[1*] **and Sunil Vyas**[2]

[1]*JIET, Jodhpur, Rajasthan, India*
[2]*Aster Hospital, Dubai, UAE*

***Abstract***

The chapter explores the transforming landscape of metaverse, virtual reality (VR), and augmented reality (AR) applications specifically in the field of teaching and learning in healthcare practices. The fundamentals of these cutting-edge technologies have evolved significantly in the past decade varying from scientific fiction to training and education practices. The immersive learning experiences using healthcare services enable healthcare practitioners to engage in complex processes of anatomical structures and surgeries. As these are risk-free, they motivate learners to explore and perform surgical simulations to achieve proficiency from beginners to expert level. Hence, integrating modern technological tools and classroom experiences improves the methodological approaches of practitioners with accuracy. Furthermore, VR and AR in the metaverse provide personalized, engaging experiments for better understanding.

This chapter presents a comprehensive overview and discusses the possible impacts on teaching and learning outcomes. The claims and challenges in implementation are discussed in a seminal study. The technological progression leading to healthcare outcomes with the help of advanced simulations and augmented clinical practices is deliberated. With this work insights into the evolving landscape of healthcare education can be witnessed.

***Keywords***: Experiential learning, smart healthcare, healthcare innovation, augmented reality and virtual reality, telemedicine, simulations-based learning

**Corresponding author*: avnish.bora@jietjodhpur.ac.in

Ajay Kumar Vyas, Harleen Kaur, Sourabh Sharma and Bhavya Alankar (eds.) Metaverse Technologies, Security and Applications for Healthcare, (173–198) © 2025 Scrivener Publishing LLC

## 8.1 Introduction

Technological advancements are revolutionizing the teaching-learning landscape. The personalized, self-paced technology methods are enabling learners to shift from traditional models of education. These tools facilitate the learner with experiential, collaborative, and engaging learning. It helps in acclimatizing the subject with critical thinking. New horizons for education have been opened by the dawn of the metaverse. It creates a shared virtual space framed in conjunction with physical realism and persistent virtual space [1]. Table 8.1 gives the historical overview and development of metaverse. The restrictions of classroom ambiance are overcome by the convergent and engaging environment. The metaverse is built on multiple key technologies, including virtual reality (VR) and augmented reality (AR) primarily. The smart and secure systems are developed with artificial intelligence (AI), and blockchain. These tools help in teaching and learning practices by creating an immersive, interactive, and persistent virtual environment. It allows learners to participate in a proactive, pragmatic way. The tailored knowledge pathways, atomized evaluations, and smart learning systems are enhanced by AI, while the blockchain technique ensures secure and transparent recordkeeping of educational credentials and achievements.

**Table 8.1** Historical overview and development of metaverse.

| Particulars | Timeline | Description |
|---|---|---|
| Origins in science fiction | 1980s | Early Inspiration |
| | 1981–1984 | William Gibson created the term "cyberspace" in his brief on "Burning Chrome" and later disseminated it in his novel "Neuromancer." This concept laid the groundwork for the idea of virtual worlds interconnected through a digital network. |
| The birth of the metaverse | 1990s | 1992: Neal Stephenson came up with the term "metaverse" in his novel "Snow Crash." It is a virtual reality–based descendant of the internet, where handlers relate through avatars in a 3D space |

(*Continued*)

**Table 8.1** Historical overview and development of metaverse. (*Continued*)

| **Particulars** | **Timeline** | **Description** |
|---|---|---|
| Early virtual worlds and online communities | Late 1990s–Early 2000s | First Virtual Worlds<br>1996: *Active Worlds*, one of the first virtual worlds, was launched, allowing users to create and explore 3D environments and interact with others.<br>1999: *The Sims* by Electronic Arts introduced a simulation game where players control virtual people, foreshadowing social interaction in virtual spaces |
| Metaverse-like environment | 2003 | "Second Life" developed by Linden Lab. It allowed users to create content, own virtual property, and interact socially and economically. |
| Technological advancements and industry adoption | 2010s | VR and AR Innovations<br>Consumer-grade VR headsets were released, like the Oculus Rift. It revitalized curiosity in immersive virtual experiences. |
| Corporate investments and expansion | Late 2010s–Early 2020s | Facebook rebranded to Meta, signaling a significant shift in focus toward building the metaverse. The company invested heavily in developing VR and AR technologies and platforms like Horizon Worlds. |
| Current trends and future prospects | 2020s | Broader Applications and Integration<br>The metaverse is now being explored for various applications beyond gaming, including education, healthcare, virtual workplaces, and social platforms. Major tech companies like Microsoft, Google, and Apple are investing in metaverse-related technologies. |

The concept of the metaverse has evolved significantly over the years, starting from its origins in science fiction to its current applications in various industries. Here is a historical overview of its development [2–6]:

The unique and noteworthy advantage of the metaverse in learning is its capability to facilitate experiential learning, especially in the field of healthcare. Figure 8.1 shows the optimized outcomes for healthcare practitioners that can be obtained by the use of technology, leading to experiential and immersive learning practices.

The student's engagement in developing practical, real-world skills is challenging in traditional and theoretical frameworks. Meanwhile, the metaverse allows students toward different learning experiences. For example, it lets the practitioner rehearse the surgery in a simulated environment. It improves the understanding of the concept. However, there is a requirement to shift the learning framework from traditional to technology-enabled.

The virtual environment created by the metaverse allows educators and learners to interactively explore and collaborate which is else difficult in real-world practices. Thus, there is a significant impact in transforming education and teaching-learning methods [7]. Multiple applications of augmentation create flexibility and accessibility for student engagement. The "Internet of the future" is referred commonly to as a virtual space virtually that assimilates AR and VR in the metaverse.

However, regardless of its promising strategic and commercial claims, there is a lack of empirical evidence for assessing its educational value [8].

Moreover, metaverse technology fosters the following:

- A collaborative learning environment that transcends geographical boundaries.
- Customized learning understandings are custom-made to the requirements and preferences of specific students.
- Enhance engaging and interactive learning practices.

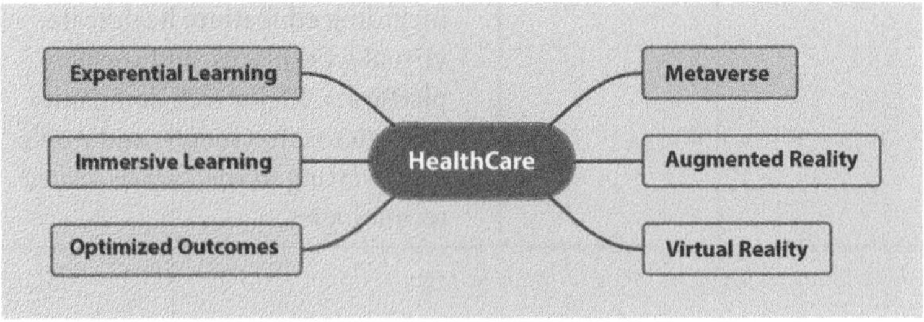


**Figure 8.1** Healthcare learning experiences.

There are multiple challenges in integrating the technology in traditional classes like bridging the digital divide and maintaining data privacy and infrastructure requirements. Furthermore, educators must be adequately trained to utilize metaverse technologies effectively, and there must be a focus on developing pedagogical approaches that leverage the unique affordances of the metaverse. Figure 8.2 shows the network of cutting-edge technologies related to the metaverse and its various components.

The metaverse's prominent building technologies are AR and VR. To establish a virtual presence in the metaverse, VR and AR technologies are integrated. The training of medical professionals with these technologies has revolutionized the traditional clinical practices. By simulating realistic environments and procedures, VR and AR provide unparalleled opportunities for hands-on practice without the intrinsic dangers related to traditional training methods.

VR-based educational tools have the potential to develop learner engagement, enable immersive knowledge understanding, and improve knowledge retention in education [9]. The importance of applying educational theories such as constructivism, experiential learning, and gamification within VR environments certainly can optimize learning outcomes [10].

The rapid advancement of VR and AR technologies offers a compelling case for their integration into medical education. VR, which makes an entirely digital atmosphere, and AR, which overlays digital data onto the real world, both serve unique and complementary roles in enhancing the educational experience. Medicinal scholars can now explore complex

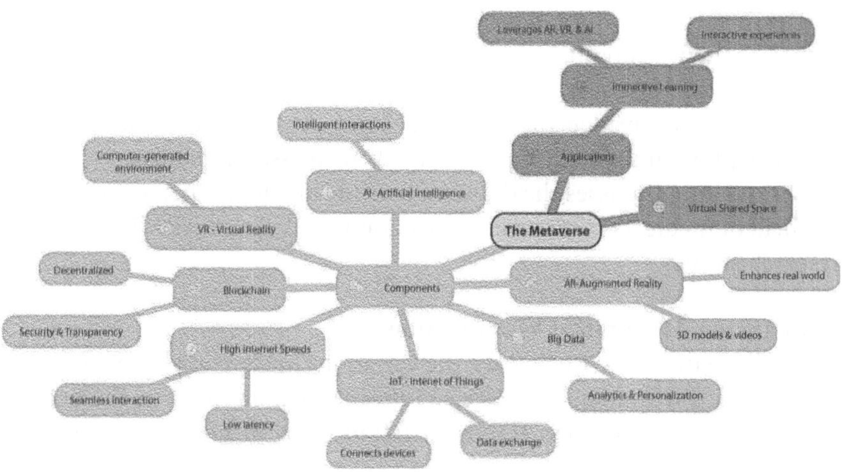


**Figure 8.2** Metaverse-enabled technology.

functional assemblies in three dimensions, exercise surgical procedures in a risk-free environment, and engage in realistic patient interactions through simulated experiences.

VR provides a dynamic, three-dimensional picture of structures that lets people interact with them. Recent developments in motion sensing, haptics, and display technologies have made VR, a great tool for practical training. The main applications of VR are in surgery and other interventional treatments. AR, on the other hand, applies virtual data and structures on top of real-world things to improve or alter it. It seems beneficial to employ AR apps to comprehend physiological processes and anatomical structures.

Revolutionary and promising technologies like AR and mixed reality have grown significantly in recent years. For educational purposes to the healthcare trainees and practitioners, AR and mixed reality technologies are gradually being integrated to learn and practice in safe, risk-free simulation-based settings.

Researchers in the field have investigated the different hardware for efficiency and learning impacts involving VR and AR applications. These encouraging results are required to be included in the curriculum [11–13].

The major advantage of these technologies is the enhanced visualization to ensure the complex anatomical structures. These result in a more immersive and intuitive understanding of the human anatomy for improved clinical decision-making. Moreover, as technological growth advances, integrating patients' medical images and data can be useful in minimally invasive surgery, upskilling the surgeries and thereby shaping the future of healthcare training.

The incorporation of simulation-based training in the curriculum increases the learning practices and enhances the skills. Embracing these technologies in teaching and learning would support the evolving healthcare market and bridge the gap by ensuring that educators and practitioners equip future medical professionals with essential skills.

This section discusses the different benefits of VR and AR techniques in the field of medical training and education with VR and AR with different research studies.

- **Enhancing Anatomical Visualization**

The skills to interact with and see the variations in the complex anatomical structure of the human body are significantly enhanced with the help of AR and VR technologies. 3D visualization helps in understanding concepts than that of 2D visualization as in conventional learning methods.

Furthermore, it improves the understanding and retention of anatomical knowledge among the learners.

- **Surgical Simulation and Skill Development**
The important application of VR in medical training is surgical simulation. It creates a surgical environment where the trainees practice without risk and get immediate feedback that hones their skills. Also, multiple scenarios can be created for a better understanding of the case.

- **Procedural Rehearsals and Error Reduction**
Intraoperative procedural guidance can be sought with AR technologies. It provides real-time specific information for surgical interventions. Displaying feedback from systems helps reduce error and improves precision through better decision-making, resulting in improved patient outcomes.

- **Remote Collaboration and Telemedicine**
VR-based training allows students to learn despite physical distancing measures. Furthermore, AR applications enable remote experts to guide on-site practitioners through complex procedures, enhancing the quality of care in underserved areas.

- **Personalized and Adaptive Learning**
The optimum outcome of individuals is maintained based on the pace of the learner's abilities. VR and AR technologies help in offering tailored assistance to understand a particular concept. Apart from the above-listed benefits, these technologies have their challenges. One of the prominent challenges is its high costs and the need for specialized equipment with maintenance. In conclusion, it can be said that the integration of VR and AR technologies in medical teaching and learning offers transformative potential, enhancing the learning experience and preparing healthcare professionals for the complexities of modern medical practice.

By embracing these techniques, the gap, between theoretical and practical aspects can be filled. The immersive, interactive, and personalized training environments, with VR and AR, create a real-time learning environment. The accessibility and affordability of these tools are likely to improve, making them essential components of medical education. These innovations will ensure that future medical professionals are well-equipped to deliver high-quality patient care in an ever-evolving healthcare landscape.

## 8.2 Virtual Reality

A VR system is an entirely immersive system that operates without any awareness of the outside world. VR generates virtual worlds using sensory input. In a VR environment, the user is submerged in and able to interact with an entirely manufactured ecosphere. This ecosphere might impersonate elements of real-life settings, genuine or imagined, but it could also transcend physical realism by constructing a universe in that the standard physical rules regulating time, space, mechanism, substantial qualities, and other parts of the natural world do not hold.

The term "virtuality continuum" [14], as in Figure 8.3, describes the variety of actual and virtual item combinations that may be shown in any particular display setting. Real environments, or those seen through a traditional video display of a real-world scene or by directly observing the scene without any electronic display, are at one end of the continuum and are made up completely of real items. Conversely, virtual settings, like those seen in a standard computer-generated simulation, consist solely of virtual items. The mixed reality setting, which combines and presents both virtual and real-world items on a single screen, is halfway between these two extremes.

Using VR technology, users may see the virtual environment, walk about, and intermingle with virtual landscapes or things. The effect is most generally created by VR headsets, which feature a head-mounted display (HMD) with a tiny screen in front of the eyes, but it may also be created by specifically designed places with several huge displays. VR headsets provide a broad vision and high-definition material. Input tracking is typically used in conjunction with a display that splits amongst the user's eyes to produce a stereoscopic three-dimensional effect and provide an immersive, realistic experience. Although haptic technology may provide additional

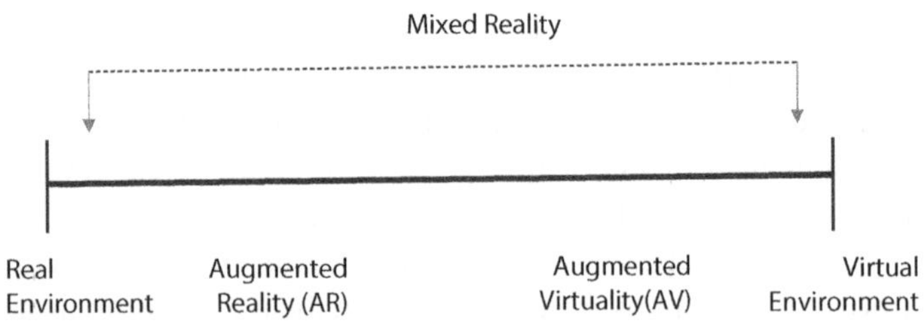


**Figure 8.3** Reality virtuality continuum.

sensory and force feedback kinds, VR normally comprises auditory and visual feedback.

Figure 8.4 shows the fundamental elements of VR technology. These elements work together to make VR very useful in the healthcare industry, where it is applied to surgical training, pain treatment, and rehabilitation. VR has the potential to provide surgeons with a risk-free practice setting by simulating complicated surgeries. Additionally, VR may be used to provide relaxing surroundings for patients undergoing unpleasant procedures, therefore lowering anxiety and suffering. The VR potential enhances the outcome of medical training and learning. It offers interactive engaged activities, as well as dynamic experiences.

At its core is the VR hardware, which immerses the user in a 3D visual and audio experience, taking them away from the real-world environment. The users' motion experiences are tracked by motion tracking sensors, and they project them into the virtual world, which enables in-the-moment interaction with the environments. The physical engagement in the virtual world is improved by haptic response devices like gloves or suits to deliver tangible sensations.

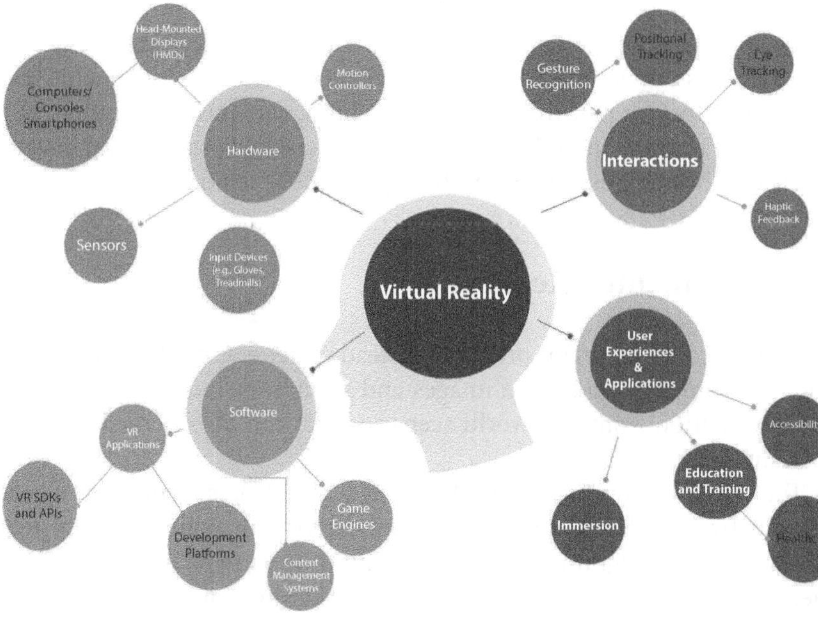


Figure 8.4 Virtual reality elements.

**Medical Applications [15–17]:**

- **Practicing Advanced Surgical Training and Complex Surgical Procedures:**
As VR gives surgeons precise feedback by mimicking real-life events, advanced surgical procedures can be practiced without endangering patients. The simulation-based teaching has produced a considerable improvement in advanced surgical training for complicated operations. This training approach lowers the learning curve and improves technical competency, making surgeons more equipped to handle obstacles in the real world.

- **Patient Education:**
The blend of VR and AR inside the metaverse has transformed surgical simulations, anatomy training, and patient education. The patient's engagement and comprehension are improved by the interactive experiences and grasp of the medical procedures. The interactive experiences enhance patient education by promoting a better grasp of medical diseases and procedures, hence improving patient engagement and comprehension.

- **Surgical Planning and Training:**
The intricacies of the human body are examined by apprentices in 3D models in conventional classroom study. However, with these technologies, students can not only examine but also experience and plan with surgical simulators for risk-free trials. These abilities are further reinforced by procedural training modules, which provide repeated practice and instant feedback—both necessary for mastering complex methods.

## 8.3 Augmented Reality

AR advances in dominant practices instead of generating the new, unlike VR. The computer-generated images and sounds are superimposed over the information from real-world scenarios that can be observed through the camera.

The virtuality continuum, as shown in Figure 8.3, is a continuum that spans between the real environment and the virtual environment as proposed by Paul Milgram and Fumio Kishino. It comprises AR and augmented virtuality (AV), where AR is closer to the real world and AV is closer to a purely virtual environment.

To discover pertinent elements, AR software processes images of the real environment captured by cameras and other sensors. Next, the AR system overlays digital content that corresponds with the user's perspective of the real ecosphere. This digital information can improve the learner's perception and engagement with their environment by incorporating anything from straightforward text labels to intricate 3D models.

**Augmentation**

AR can remove the objects apart from adding them to real situations, applicable to all senses not only to the sight. Researchers have emphasized more on amalgamation of physical and virtual images along with graphics, so far. However, AR could be extended to include sound to experience the real ecosystem with the help of headphones. It would augment synthetic, directional three-dimensional sound, while the microphones available would detect external sounds from the environment. This would give the system a chance to cover up selected real sounds from the environment by generating a masking signal that exactly canceled the incoming real sound.

Hence, AR aims at bringing together virtual information that simplifies the user's experience with the immediate surroundings including live video streams. It enhances the interaction with the real world and the prominent application of this tool is medical visualization.

The development of AR has taken four decades; the next section discusses the historical development of AR techniques.

**Historical Development:**

In the 1950s, the filmmaker Morton Heilig believed that watching a film may tempt the spectators to engage in the action on screen by absorbing all the senses, it was the time when the term AR initially appeared practically. A concept prototype Sensorama was created by Heilig that preceded digital computers, in 1955, and was first shown in "The Cinema of the Future." Ivan Sutherland created the HMD in 1962. An optical see-through HMD device for AR was developed in 1968. Myron Krueger created The Video Place, a space where people may interact with virtual things for the first time in 1975. While assisting employees in assembling wires and cables for an airplane, the AR term was used by Boeing's Tom Caudell and David Mizell. It is used and pixels were the key points. The first significant paper mentioning the prototype AR system was delivered by Seligmann. It was not until 1994 seen in Figure 8.3, as a continuum that extends from the real environment to the virtual environment. Both AV and AR are situated in the middle, with AV being more closely related to the virtual world and AR being more closely related to the real world. In 1997, Ronald Azuma described AR as an amalgamation

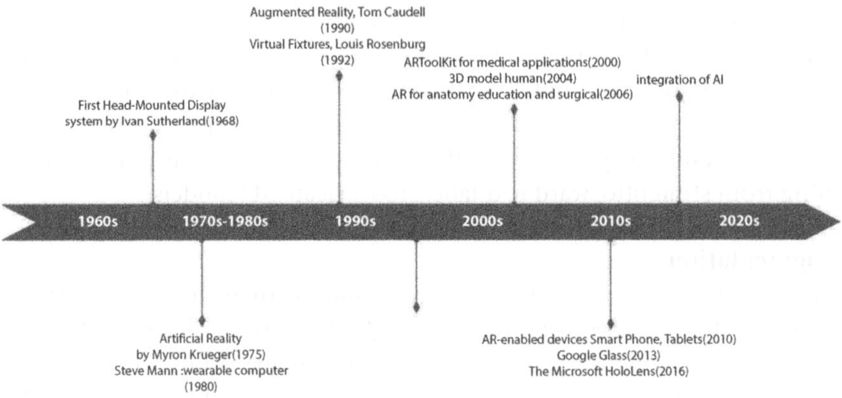


**Figure 8.5** Historical development of augmented reality.

of real and virtual worlds that are both registered in three dimensions and dynamic in real time [18]. As time goes on, an increasing number of AR applications, particularly for mobile devices, are being created. These days, a growing number of AR systems and apps are being developed thanks to new technological advancements, which might transform mobile AR [19–22]. The historical development of AR is shown in Figure 8.5.

**Medical Applications of AR:**

As AR gives more real output and understanding of the environment, the following are the medical applications that can be useful, which are discussed in this section.

### AR-Assisted Physical Examination

The AR-assisted examination reduces errors and provides better patient care, as the patient's body data are superimposed with digital data for augmentation. The real-time visual risk-free assistance improves the examination of medical practitioners and learners. The augmentation speeds up healthcare learning practices by giving learners practice in making diagnoses in different clinical settings.

### Emergency Response Training

The different critical situations leading to emergent actions can be experienced with AR-assisted emergency response training. The practitioners can develop the skills in various simulated settings. AR allows learners to diagnose injuries, engage with virtual patients, and execute surgeries under simulated emergency settings by superimposing digital scenarios over the actual environment thereby improving the decision-making abilities for better outcomes.

**Anatomy Visualization**
The dynamic and practical understanding of human anatomical structures can be explored with the use of AR. The experts and students alike may examine and work with intricate anatomical structures from any perspective, improving their conception of intricate systems and 3D associations.

**Augmented Reality Apps for Medical Students**
AR apps with important features that enhance the learning of users such as case studies, regular tests, and simulation of procedures help in the retention of theoretical concepts beyond conventional approaches. This flexible, anytime learning approach allows for self-paced, interactive learning experiences and engagement with organs and tissues.

**AR-Assisted Patient Education**
AR-assisted medical information of patients improves communication during clinical procedures. It gives the patient a holistic view of the case under treatment and educates them about the medical issues. It enhances the care and thereby course of therapy for better results.

## 8.4 The Technology

The technology that is revolutionizing multiple industries from entertainment to healthcare and education are metaverse, VR, and AR. These technologies use advanced algorithms, hardware, and software for bridging the real and virtual environments.

### 8.4.1 Augmented Reality (AR)

The key components of AR technology are discussed in the next segment. With the help of images, sounds, and other digital information, data are overlaid onto the physical world in real time to enhance AR.

**Hardware:**
**Capturing Devices**
AR devices use cameras and sensors to capture and record real-world scenes. Smartphones to AR glasses alongside cameras use sensors, GPS, gyroscopes, and accelerometers to assist in monitoring the orientation and location of the device, making it possible to precisely position digital information in the real environment.

**Processing:**
For managing the real-time processing and integrating virtual elements with augmentation, there is a need for strong processors.

**Software Development Kits:** Realistic and interactive environments are created by the different resources that are provided by software development kits (SDK). These include different operating system platforms and utilize technologies like motion tracking, environmental awareness, and light estimates.
**Computer Vision and Smart Learning:** The basis of AR is computer vision algorithms that allow the system to recognize objects, surfaces, and surroundings. These skills are strengthened by machine learning, which enables AR systems to progressively be developed more accurately and introduces flexibility with adaptability.

**Output Display Technologies:**
**Heads-up displays, or HUDs**, let users view both the augmented content and the real environment by projecting digital material onto the lenses of AR glasses. Applications for this technology range from navigation to medical education.
**Projection-Based AR:** Some AR systems combine the virtual and real worlds without the use of a screen or glasses by projecting digital material directly onto tangible surfaces using projectors.

**Tracking and Mapping:**
Concurrent localization and mapping is a vital AR technique that allows the system to track the position of the device inside the virtual environment and map it in real time. It promises that when the user moves, virtual objects are exactly attached to real-life places.

### 8.4.2 Virtual Reality (VR)

The real-life experiences are replicated by VR technology. The major components of this technology are as follows:

**Hardware:**
The hardware components include different types of displays to offer VR experiences. Among these, the HMDs are the prominent ones. The popularly used HMDs are Oculus Rift, HTC VIVE, and PlayStation VR. These have wide-angle lenses and high-resolution screens that create an engaging

experience for the user. The 3D space with the sense of depth is created by HMDs, which have a variability of refresh rates of 90 Hz or higher.

The other important component is to track the motion of the user. It uses sensors including external cameras, gyroscopes, and accelerometers. The immersed and engaged feeling of the user is created with the help of haptic feedback devices.

**Software:**
Unity and Unreal Engine are the most frequently used VR engines. It helps creators to intricate 3D environments with modeling and control. The tracking with the help of sensors can be programmed throughout space.

The animated effects give the virtual world an interactive effect. 3D modeling software is used for content creation. The sound effect is the most important aspect that is dynamically modified for an immersive experience, and it is spatially controlled as per the movement of the user.

The creative applications of AR and VR are in rapid growth. The developments in software algorithms, hardware capabilities, and creative applications, AR and VR technologies, are useful in education and training especially for medical and healthcare practitioners to improve their learning outcomes.

## 8.5 Market of AR and VR in Healthcare Practice

With the growing technology, the market of AR and VR is increasing. This section highlights the important works in the field of medical science and the significant milestones.

The prototype for an AR system was designed to assist with surgical procedures by Dr. Steven K. Feiner, Blair MacIntyre, and Doree Seligmann of Columbia University in the early 1990s. It provided real-time guidance during surgeries. The "Virtual Fixtures" system, which used AR to overlay virtual objects onto the real world was developed in 1998 by Dr. Louis Rosenberg's work at the U.S. Air Force Armstrong Lab. It provided surgeons with enhanced guidance and precision during procedures. In the 1980s, a notable pioneer was Dr. Richard Satava, who worked on developing VR surgical simulators. It allowed practitioners to do the surgical procedures in a virtual environment before the actual patients. In the next decade, multiple projects involving simulators were initiated for immersive experiences and prior practices to hone skills.

The Visible Human Project in 1994 was launched by Dr. Michael J. Ackerman, at the National Library of Medicine. It created the 3D representation of human anatomy for medical education research and uses. The data of this work have been used to understand the human body and enhance medical education and research. Some Noteworthy Applications of AR VR techniques in healthcare practices have laid the foundation for their prevalent use in various medical fields, from surgical training and planning to patient rehabilitation and pain management. Some of the applications are the following:

*AccuVein:* The AR technique helps healthcare professionals locate veins for venepuncture by projecting a map of the veins onto the skin.
*SnowWorld:* The VR system, developed by Dr. Hunter Hoffman and Dr. David Patterson, uses VR for pain management.
*Medivis's SurgicalAR:* Medivis's SurgicalAR uses AR technology to provide surgeons with enhanced visualization of the patient's anatomy during complex procedures, improving accuracy and outcomes.

The healthcare sector in the upcoming years is expected to witness a significant boom, especially in teaching and learning medical practices. The AR and VR are going to play a vital role in that. Telemedicine acceptance with technological breakthroughs also demands training programs.

The world expected a compound annual growth rate (CAGR) of 27.2% between 2022 and 2030, according to research by Grand View Research of the AR and VR market. The improvement in patient education using different procedures and use of surgical training instruments are driving this expansion. The presurgery planning and visualization of possible outcomes help practitioners and learners for better patient care. Healthcare applications for AR and VR technologies are anticipated to advance in sophistication as they develop, thus propelling market expansion.

The notable individuals who have contributed to AR and VR technology spread from academia to industry. Ivan Sutherland is referred to as the "Father of Computer Graphics," for his first HMD system. AR in the early 1990s was proposed by Tom Caudell while working at Boeing. Steve Mann, a professor at the University of Toronto, has made significant contributions to the field of wearable computing and AR. Meanwhile, in the field of VR, Jaron Lanier, from VPL Research, and Douglas Engelbart are prominent individuals known for their in immersive computing.

Table 8.2 gives a list of prominent technology developers and vendors in the AR and VR market, particularly focused on medical and healthcare technologies.

**Table 8.2** Prominent developers in the AR and VR market.

| S. no. | Product & company | Services/applications | References |
|---|---|---|---|
| 1 | Microsoft HoloLens | Microsoft's HoloLens is a foremost AR device used extensively in healthcare for surgical planning, anatomy visualization, and medical training. HoloLens provides a mixed-reality experience that integrates 3D holographic images with the physical world, letting medical professionals visualize and intermingle with patient information in novel ways. | |
| 2 | Google Glass Enterprise Edition | Google Glass, initially a consumer product, has been adapted for enterprise use, including healthcare. It is used in clinical settings for hands-free access to patient records, real-time telemedicine consultations, and surgical assistance, enhancing both efficiency and patient care. | |
| 3 | Osso VR Surgical Training Platform | Osso VR provides a VR-based platform focused on surgical training. It offers highly realistic, immersive simulations that allow surgeons to exercise and refine their skills in a controlled, risk-free environment. This platform is widely used by medical institutions and healthcare providers for training purposes. | https://www.ossovr.com/post/guide-to-using-vr-in-medical-education-programs |

(*Continued*)

**Table 8.2** Prominent developers in the AR and VR market. (*Continued*)

| S. no. | Product & company | Services/applications | References |
|---|---|---|---|
| 4 | Medtronic StealthStation™ S8 Surgical Navigation System | Medtronic is a leader in medical technology and has integrated AR into its surgical navigation systems. The StealthStation™ S8 system uses AR to assist surgeons with real-time 3D visualization during complex procedures, enhancing precision and outcomes. | |
| 5 | Magic Leap Magic Leap 2 | Magic Leap provides an advanced AR headset, Magic Leap 2, which is being increasingly adopted in healthcare for medical training, remote surgery assistance, and patient education. Its high-quality visualization and interactive capabilities make it ideal for detailed medical applications. | |
| 6 | FundamentalVR Fundamental Surgery | FundamentalVR offers a VR simulation platform designed for surgical training. It combines VR with haptic feedback, providing a realistic training environment where surgeons can practice various procedures before actual patients. | |

(*Continued*)

**Table 8.2** Prominent developers in the AR and VR market. (*Continued*)

| S. no. | Product & company | Services/applications | References |
|---|---|---|---|
| 7 | Brainlab Mixed Reality Viewer | Brainlab develops advanced medical technology systems that incorporate AR for surgical navigation and planning. Their Mixed Reality Viewer allows surgeons to interact with 3D patient data during surgery, improving precision in neurosurgery and orthopedic procedures. | https://www.brainlab.com/surgery-products/overview-platform-products/mixed-reality/ |
| 8 | SentiAR Augmented Reality Visualization Platform | SentiAR focuses on providing AR visualization for interventional procedures, particularly in cardiology. Their platform projects 3D images of the patient's structure in actuality, enabling physicians to navigate complex procedures with greater accuracy. | https://sentiar.com/ |
| 9 | EchoPixel True 3D™ | EchoPixel provides an AR platform called True 3D™, which turns medical images into interactive, holographic models. This technology is used for diagnostic purposes, surgical planning, and patient engagement, allowing physicians to explore and interact with patient-specific anatomy in three dimensions. | https://echopixeltech.com/ |

(*Continued*)

**Table 8.2** Prominent developers in the AR and VR market. (*Continued*)

| S. no. | Product & company | Services/applications | References |
|---|---|---|---|
| 10 | Augmedics vision Spine System | Augmedics developed the Xvision Spine System, an AR headset designed to give surgeons X-ray–like vision, allowing them to see the patient's anatomy through skin and tissue in real time during spinal surgery. This technology enhances accuracy and safety in complex spinal procedures. | https://augmedics.com/ |

## 8.6 Case Studies

| Institution | Technology used | Case study description |
|---|---|---|
| Imperial College London | Microsoft HoloLens (AR) | Used HoloLens to enhance surgical training by visualizing 3D anatomical structures overlaid on cadavers. |
| Stanford University School of Medicine | VR Simulations | Implemented VR in the anatomy curriculum for immersive exploration of human anatomy. |
| Mayo Clinic | Osso VR (VR) | Adopted Osso VR's platform for training orthopedic surgeons in complex procedures. |

| | | |
|---|---|---|
| Childrenâ€™s Hospital Los Angeles (CHLA) | VR Simulation | Used VR to simulate pediatric emergencies for training healthcare providers. |
| Johns Hopkins University | AR Visualization Tools | Integrated AR into neurosurgical procedures for real-time visualization during surgery. |
| University of Queensland | Touch Surgery (Mobile VR/AR App) | Used the Touch Surgery app to enhance surgical training with step-by-step simulations. |
| Case Western Reserve University | Microsoft HoloLens (AR) | Collaborated with Microsoft to use HoloLens for teaching anatomy with 3D models. |
| The Royal London Hospital | VR Simulation | Implemented VR simulations for trauma team training in managing major incidents. |

## 8.7 Future Directions

As VR and AR continue to evolve, their applications in medical training and education are poised for significant expansion. The future of these technologies is marked by several emerging trends and potential developments that promise to revolutionize how healthcare specialists are made proficient.

**Metaverse Technologies Integration:**
The idea of a completely immersive, networked digital environment called the metaverse is going to change medical education and training. Inside the metaverse, the medical practitioners and students may work jointly within shared virtual spaces, to perform remote procedures, and participate in

international educational programs. Hence, the geographical boundaries can be removed and access to medical education can be improved by enabling real-time, hands-on learning experiences throughout the globe.

**Tactile Immersion and Haptic Feedback:**
The advancements in haptic feedback technology can greatly improve the tactile realism of VR and AR simulations. It will improve effective surgical simulations and practices. It will also allow the user to feel the virtual objects and immersive retention.

**Ethical and Security Considerations:**
Patient data security and confidentiality are the critical areas to address. The ethical and security issues as VR and AR technology proliferate in the healthcare industry are crucial. It needs strong encryption techniques, safe data processing procedures, and moral standards to safeguard patients and medical personnel. Hence, it will probably be the main area of future growth.

**Opportunities for Research and Development:**
These technologies generate research and development opportunities as 3D imaging, cross-platform interoperability, and real-time data analytics are advancing. The continuous advancements in VR and AR technology will keep creating new ways in which they may be used in medical education.

**Challenges and Limitations:**
Medical teaching and learning are being transformed by VR and AR; however, there are challenges and limitations. These limitations range from infrastructure and technical issues to data privacy, security, and ethical issues. Advanced hardware devices are necessary for getting a high-resolution immersive experience. These demands may cause problems with restricted range of vision, discomfort with prolonged usage, and delay, all of which might make them less useful for medical instruction. Significant infrastructure improvements while adopting VR and AR in healthcare facilities necessitate reliable internet access and dedicated areas for VR laboratories. VR and AR systems frequently gather and process significant volumes of sensitive data, including medical and biometric data. It is very important to ensure the security and privacy of this data, especially in medical settings where patient privacy is crucial. Furthermore, it is important to carefully monitor the risk of relying too much on virtual settings in place of real-world experience as well as the accuracy of simulations. The initial expenditure required for VR and AR technologies

is high. Hence, it may hinder the general adoption of these technologies for a large number of medical institutions, especially those operating in resource-constrained environments.

## 8.8 Conclusion

In conclusion with the metaverse, comprehensive and enhanced engagement in medical practices can be experienced. As the healthcare sector is developing, it is also critical to address the practical aspects of the curriculum by incorporating AR and VR techniques. Incorporating VR and AR into the medical curriculum not only improves the learning experience but also gives aspiring medical professionals the abilities and self-assurance. The integration of VR and AR in medical education and training signifies a revolutionary advancement within the healthcare industry. These cutting-edge technologies bridge the learning gap between theory and practice through the provision of controlled environments and the simulation of real-life events. These new approaches make it easy to study complex features in a risk-free environment and offer chances for remote learning and teamwork. It allows customized educational opportunities catered to individual requirements, fostering a more profound comprehension of medical principles and practices.

Nonetheless, there are challenges in putting these technologies into practice. Apart from the expensive setup required, the validation of studies is to be practiced.

VR and AR have the power to completely transform medical education and practices. These tools will probably become more widely available as technology develops. The future of medical education will depend on how well these technologies are adopted, as they will equip medical practitioners with the knowledge and abilities needed to fulfill the changing needs of the medical industry.

## References


1. Mystakidis, S., Metaverse Learning: Innovating Education through Immersive Experiences. *J. Virtual Worlds Res.*, 15, 1, 1–12, 2022.
2. Gibson, W., *Neuromancer*, Ace Books, 1984.
3. Stephenson.pdf.
4. Castronova, E., *Synthetic Worlds: The Business and Culture of Online Games*, University of Chicago Press, 2005.

5. Au, W.J., *The Making of Second Life: Notes from the New World*, Harper Business, Harper Business, 2008.
6. Zuckerberg.pdf.
7. Kye, B., Han, N., Kim, E., Park, Y., Jo, S., Educational applications of metaverse: possibilities and limitations. *J. Educ. Eval. Health Prof.*, 18, 1–13, 2021, doi: 10.3352/JEEHP.2021.18.32.
8. Onu, P., Pradhan, A., Mbohwa, C., Potential to use metaverse for future teaching and learning. *Educ. Inf. Technol.*, 29, 7, 8893–8924, May 2024, doi: 10.1007/s10639-023-12167-9.
9. Vats, S. and Joshi, R., The Impact of Virtual Reality in Education: A Comprehensive Research Study, pp. 126–136, 2024, doi: 10.1007/978-3-031-50204-0_11.
10. Marougkas, A., Troussas, C., Krouska, A., Sgouropoulou, C., Virtual Reality in Education: A Review of Learning Theories, Approaches and Methodologies for the Last Decade. *Electronics*, 12, 13, 2832, Jun. 2023, doi: 10.3390/electronics12132832.
11. Uppot, R.N., Laguna, B., McCarthy, C.J., De Novi, G., Phelps, A., Siegel, E., Courtier, J., Implementing virtual and augmented reality tools for radiology education and training, communication, and clinical care, *Radiology*, 291, 5–10, 2019.
12. Gerup, J., Soerensen, C.B., Dieckmann, P., Augmented reality and mixed reality for healthcare education beyond surgery: an integrative review. *Int. J. Med. Educ.*, 11, 1, 2020.
13. Bohr, A. and Memarzadeh, K., The rise of artificial intelligence in healthcare applications, in: *Artificial Intelligence in Healthcare*, pp. 25–60, Acad. Press, 2020.
14. Milgram, P., Takemura, H., Utsumi, A., Kishino, F., Augmented reality: a class of displays on the reality-virtuality continuum. *Telemanipulator and Telepresence Technologies*, vol. 2351, p. 2351, 1995, [Online]. Available: http://etclab.mie.utoronto.ca/people/paul_dir/SPIE94/SPIE94.full.html.
15. Patel, V.L., Yoskowitz, N.A., Arocha, J.F., Virtual reality in medicine, in: *Biomedical Information Technology*, pp. 305–321, Acad. Press, 2009.
16. L, J., Virtual reality: The promise of the future. *Interact. Learn.*, 19, 709–715, 1992, doi: 10.20595/jjbf.19.0_3.
17. Nagemdran, M., Gurusamy, K.S., Aggarwal, R., Palanivelu, L., Davidson, B.R., Virtual reality training for surgical trainees in laparoscopic surgery. *Cochrane Database Syst. Rev.*, 21, 1, 14651858, 2009, doi: 10.1002/14651858.CD006575.pub2.
18. Carmigniani, J. and Furht, B., *Handbook of Augmented Reality*, Springer, 2011, doi: 10.1007/978-1-4614-0064-6.
19. Khazanchi, D., Kumar Vyas, A., Kant Hiran, K., Padmanaban, S., *Blockchain 3.0 for Sustainable Development*, De Gruyter, Berlin, Boston, 2021, https://doi.org/10.1515/9783110702507.

20. Kant Hiran, K., Khazanchi, D., Kumar Vyas, A., Padmanaban, S., *Machine Learning for Sustainable Development*, De Gruyter, Berlin, Boston, 2021, https://doi.org/10.1515/9783110702514.
21. Vyas, A.K., Balamurugan, S., Hiran, K.K., Dhiman, H.S. (Eds.), *Artificial Intelligence for Renewable Energy Systems*, John Wiley & Sons, 2022, ISBN: 9781119761693.
22. Khatri, N., Vyas, A.K., Abdul-Qawy, A.S.H., Rene, E.R., Artificial neural network based models for predicting the effluent quality of a combined upflow anaerobic sludge blanket and facultative pond: Performance evaluation and comparison of different algorithms. *Environ. Res.*, 217, 114843, 2023.

# Part II

# SECURITY FOR METAVERSE

9

# Securing Healthcare in the Metaverse: Advance Deep Learning Algorithms for Non-TATA Promoter Classification in Genome Sequencing

**Om Varshney[1], Yashasvi Agrawal[1], Yashasvi Kanathey[1], Yoginii Waykole[1], Om Mishra[2] and Harsh S. Dhiman[3*]**

[1]*Department of Artificial Intelligence and Machine Learning, Symbiosis Institute of Technology, Symbiosis International, Pune, Maharashtra, India*
[2]*Rajiv Gandhi National Cyber Law Centre, National Law Institute University, Bhopal, Madhya Pradesh, India*
[3]*Ernst & Young LLP, The Ruby, Dadar, Mumbai, Maharashtra, India*

## *Abstract*
As healthcare transitions into the realm of the metaverse, ensuring data security and privacy becomes paramount. This manuscript addresses the critical task of safeguarding genomic data within this digital landscape. Specifically, we focus on classifying non-TATA promoters in genome sequencing, a pivotal step in understanding gene regulation. Leveraging advanced deep learning algorithms, we propose a novel approach to accurately identify non-TATA promoters, thus aiding in comprehending gene expression patterns. Our method integrates cutting-edge techniques from deep learning and genomic analysis to enhance classification accuracy and efficiency. Through extensive experimentation and validation, we demonstrate the effectiveness of our approach in securing healthcare data within the metaverse while advancing the understanding of gene regulation mechanisms. This research contributes to the ongoing efforts in harnessing emerging technologies to revolutionize healthcare delivery in virtual environments.

***Keywords*:** Metaverse, healthcare, classifier, DNA, artificial intelligence

**Corresponding author*: hsdhiman1098@gmail.com

Ajay Kumar Vyas, Harleen Kaur, Sourabh Sharma and Bhavya Alankar (eds.) Metaverse Technologies, Security and Applications for Healthcare, (201–218) © 2025 Scrivener Publishing LLC

## 9.1 Introduction

In the field of genomics, a fundamental understanding of genetic mechanisms is paramount in unraveling the intricacies of cellular processes [1, 2] and, by extension, life itself. DNA, as a molecular blueprint for life, holds the key to the creation of proteins within organisms [3, 4].

However, DNA sequences are notoriously long, and, as such, decoding them poses a significant challenge [5, 6]. Nonetheless, scientists have identified specific regions of interest within DNA known as promoter groups. These promoter segments are of utmost importance as they play a central role in characterizing proteins [7, 8].

The focus of this project is the detection of a vital promoter group known as non-TATA promoters [9, 10]. These non-TATA promoters serve as critical initiators of the gene transcription process, playing a pivotal role in binding RNA polymerase to the gene's promoter region and ultimately triggering the transcription of the associated gene [11, 12].

Aligned with our engagement with artificial intelligence systems, we have undertaken the development of a robust discriminatory system aimed at accurately identifying the presence or absence of non-TATA promoters. Our study presents a comprehensive comparative analysis of various deep learning models, evaluating their performance in addressing this binary classification challenge.

## 9.2 Literature Review

| Title | Year | Key findings | Future scope |
|---|---|---|---|
| Recognition of Prokaryotic and Eukaryotic Promoters Using Convolutional Deep Learning Neural Networks | 2017 | The study successfully employed convolutional neural networks (CNNs) to accurately identify promoters in a variety of organisms, achieving high accuracy. The CNNProm program has the potential to be applied to newly sequenced genomes. A random substitution procedure was proposed for discovering conserved promoter elements. | Expanding the use of CNN models to additional genomes for improved accuracy. Fine-tuning and optimizing CNN models for specific genome types. Integration of CNNProm into genomic applications. |

| Title | Year | Key findings | Future scope |
|---|---|---|---|
| Predicting the Sequence Specificities of DNA- and RNA-binding proteins by Deep Learning | 2015 | Deep learning, particularly DeepBind, accurately reveals DNA- and RNA-binding protein sequence specificities from experimental data. Outperforms other methods on diverse data, even when training on *in vitro* and testing on *in vivo* data. Provides visualizations of specificities and is a fully automatic software tool. | Annotating functional consequences of genetic variants. Integrating with genomic research. Improving visualization techniques. Cross-species analysis for evolutionary insights. Real-time analysis possibilities. |
| Promoter Analysis and Prediction in the Human Genome Using Sequence-Based Deep Learning Models | 2019 | Developed a deep learning approach to predict exact transcription start site positions in long genomic sequences, reducing false positives. Achieved a low error rate of 0.02 per 1000 base pairs, outperforming other human promoter prediction programs. | Extend to other organisms. Comparative analysis for transcriptional regulation insights. Integration with functional genomics. Develop visualization tools. Explore applications in disease research. Create a user-friendly interface for research. |
| Prediction of Prokaryotic and Eukaryotic Promoters Using Convolutional Deep Learning Neural Networks | 2016 | Used CNNs to accurately identify promoters in human, *Arabidopsis, Escherichia coli,* and *Mycoplasma pneumonia.* CNNs outperformed previous methods, achieving high classification accuracy. Applied CNNs to recognize complex promoter regions in human and Arabidopsis genomes. The CNNProm program is a user-friendly deep learning tool for promoter identification, applicable to various genomes. | Expand to more organisms. Explore functional implications of predicted promoters. Compare promoters across species. Develop visualization tools. Investigate real-world applications. Promote wider adoption of the CNNProm programs. |

(*Continued*)

(*Continued*)

| Title | Year | Key findings | Future scope |
|---|---|---|---|
| PromID: Human Promoter Prediction by Deep Learning | 2018 | Identifying promoters in unique human genes is challenging. Developed a deep learning approach to predict exact transcription start site (TSS) positions. Focused on TSS location prediction, not just classification. Models achieved high precision (0.77) and MCC (0.76), outperforming existing tools. | Extend to other organisms. Explore functional implications. Compare TSS prediction across genomes. Develop visualization tools. Investigate real-world applications. Promote wider adoption of the method among research. |
| A Literature Review of WaveNet: Theory, Application, and Optimization | 2019 | WaveNet is a powerful neural network for speech processing, excelling in text-to-speech synthesis and other applications. The paper reviews WaveNet's literature, covering its foundations, applications, and potential improvements. | Explore new speech-related tasks. Investigate real-time implementation. Integrate WaveNet with virtual assistants. Develop user-friendly tools. Enhance performance through collaboration with other AI models. |
| Fundamentals of Recurrent Neural Network (RNN) and Long Short-Term Memory Network | 2020 | LSTM networks are widely discussed in the literature but often lack detailed training and unrolling formulas. This tutorial aims to explain essential RNN and LSTM fundamentals in a single document. It formally derives the RNN formulation from differential equations and introduces the RNN unrolling technique. The tutorial addresses training difficulties by transforming the standard RNN into the "Vanilla LSTM" network. It provides equations and descriptions of LSTM components for improved clarity. | Expand Understanding: Offer more pedagogical alternatives to enrich the LSTM system. Implement in Software: Provide insights and derivations for implementing the augmented LSTM model for experimentation and research. Foster Collaborative Research: Encourage further research and collaboration in LSTM development and application. |

| Title | Year | Key findings | Future scope |
|---|---|---|---|
| A Survey of Convolutional Neural Networks: Analysis, Applications, and Prospects | 2021 | CNNs are highly influential in deep learning with applications in computer vision and natural language processing. Existing reviews often lack a comprehensive perspective and recent ideas. This review covers 1D, 2D, and multidimensional convolutions, models, and applications. It offers insights into achieving state-of-the-art results and provides practical guidelines. | Explore innovative concepts and applications. Foster industry-academia collaboration. Promote real-world CNN implementations. Encourage interdisciplinary connections to advance CNN research. |
| Recent Advances in Convolutional Neural Networks | 2018 | Deep learning, especially CNNs, excels in visual recognition, speech recognition, and natural language processing. Advances in data annotation and GPU strength drive swift CNN research with state-of-the-art outcomes. The paper surveys CNN improvements in design, activation, loss, regularization, optimization, and speed. Various applications of CNNs in computer vision, speech, and language processing are discussed. | Seek further innovations. Encourage interdisciplinary collaboration. Promote real-world CNN use. Address ethical AI concerns. Enhance computation efficiency. |

## 9.3 Methodology

For this study, we have selected the following deep learning architectures deemed suitable for the task at hand:

1. Sequence processing models such as RNN, LSTM, and GRU.
2. Convolutional models.
3. Sequence processing models augmented by convolutional models.
4. Variants of WaveNet.

Within each architecture, we have developed two distinct models to facilitate an in-depth interclass and intraclass analysis. The subsequent sections provide detailed elaboration on each of the aforementioned architectures.

### 9.3.1 Preprocessing

The initial dataset was presented in the form of binary strings, which were subsequently loaded and vectorized to prepare them for input into our deep learning models.

Additionally, for our CNN-based architecture, as it required a two-dimensional input, we further applied one-hot encoding to align the data appropriately with our model's requirements.

Further insights into the methodology applied during the preprocessing phase are provided in the appendix.

### 9.3.2 Sequence Modeling

Given the inherent sequential nature of DNA strands, we have opted for standard sequence processing models to establish our baseline.

Considering the task's requirements, we have focused on LSTM and GRU models for the promoter classification. RNN models were not included due to their known limitations in processing lengthy sequences effectively [13].

For each of the sub-architectures, we implemented an embedding layer followed by two LSTM/GRU layers. Table 9.1 provides a summary of the selected hyperparameters.

### 9.3.3 Convolutional Models

While DNA sequences retain a fundamental sequential nature, their extensive length poses a significant challenge. Consequently, we have employed fully convolutional networks to address this challenge effectively [14, 15].

**Table 9.1** Model embedding units and layer configurations for LSTM and GRU architectures.

| Model | Embedding | Units |
|---|---|---|
| LSTM | 128 | 64 |
| GRU | 128 | 64 |

**Table 9.2** Layer configurations with batch normalization and dropout for convolutional model versions.

| Model | Layers | Batch normalization | Dropout |
|---|---|---|---|
| Version 0 | 3 | No | No |
| Version 1 | 3 | Yes | 20% |

Instead of representing the classification as a many-to-one sequence modeling task, we transformed it into a dimensionality reduction problem complemented by a classification head.

For this purpose, we have implemented a neural network comprising 1D convolutional and pooling layers. Within this architecture, we have developed two distinct versions. Table 9.2 presents the key specifications for each version.

### 9.3.4 Combining Sequence Modeling and Feature Extraction

Building upon the successful feature extraction approach, we naturally progressed toward a hybrid model, combining the strengths of both methodologies. To achieve this, we designed an architecture that incorporates convolutional layers for efficient feature extraction from sequences complemented by LSTM layers for effective processing.

Within this architecture, we trained one model with batch normalization and another without it. Table 9.3 presents a concise summary of our design decisions.

### 9.3.5 WaveNet

Originally introduced in 2015 by researchers at DeepMind, WaveNet emerged as a generative autoregressive model primarily intended for synthetic audio generation.

The key breakthrough in this research was the integration of dilated convolutions, a technique that enabled the training of sequences spanning thousands of steps without the need for excessively deep neural architectures.

Adapting the concept of dilated convolutions as an effective dimensionality reduction tool, we applied it to the challenge of promoter classification. Further details regarding this approach are provided in the appendix.

Once again, we trained two variations of this architecture. The first approach maintains a consistent number of feature maps and kernel

**Table 9.3** Hybrid model configurations with convolutional layers for feature extraction and LSTM/GRU layers for sequence processing.

| Model | Convolution layers | Batch normalization | LSTM/GRU layers |
|---|---|---|---|
| Version 0 | 2 | No | 1 |
| Version 1 | 2 | Yes | 1 |

**Table 9.4** WaveNet model configurations.

| Model | Kernel size | Number of features | Convolutional layers |
|---|---|---|---|
| Version 0 | 2 | 20 | 5 |
| Version 1 | Exponentially decreasing | Exponentially increasing | 5 |

dimensions, while the other implements a design featuring an increasing number of filters coupled with a decrease in kernel size.

Table 9.4 offers a comprehensive summary of our chosen parameters.

## 9.4 Experimental Setup

### 9.4.1 Data Collection

All data used in this study has been sourced from the Central European Institute of Technology through their Python package, genomic_benchmarks.

This comprehensive package encompasses various genetic datasets pertaining to both humans and animals.

**Table 9.5** Data characteristics.

| Data modality | No. of samples | Sample length |
|---|---|---|
| Training set | 27,097 | Hundreds |
| Testing set | 9034 | Hundreds |

Using the package's standard helper function, we successfully downloaded the dataset to our system. Subsequently, the data were loaded into TensorFlow through the designated data pipeline. It is important to note that the provided data had already been predivided into training and testing sets, with no additional validation split provided.

Table 9.5 offers an overview of our data distribution:

## 9.5 Evaluation Metrics

Our evaluation of the various architectures was based on the following criteria:

1. Accuracy, precision, and recall
2. Computation time
3. Number of parameters

For each category of model architecture, we conducted an initial intraclass evaluation, followed by a subsequent interclass comparison of the best models.

In many classification tasks, especially in fields like medical diagnostics, information security, or quality control, you want to minimize false negatives. This is because false negatives represent cases that are genuinely positive (in your context, non-TATA promoters) but are incorrectly classified as negative. Missing these cases can have serious consequences.

Achieving the lowest possible count of false negatives is the goal of many classification jobs, including those found in fields like medical diagnostics, information security, and quality control. This emphasis is justified by the consequences that could result from these erroneous negatives.

False negatives occur when the classifier mistakenly labels a case as positive when it is actually negative. These cases concern non-TATA promoters, which is relevant to your particular issue. This indicates that the classifier fails to identify non-TATA promoters and incorrectly labels them as negative.

Thus, recall emerges as a preferred choice among the available metrics.

## 9.6 Training Parameters

Across all our models, we utilized the following parameters:

- Optimizer: Adam
- Loss function: Binary cross-entropy
- Metrics: Accuracy, precision, and recall
- Max-Epochs: 100

The training process incorporated the following callbacks:

- Constant-exponential learning rate scheduler
- Early stopping with a minimum delta of 1
- A logging callback for streaming training information to a designated buffer
- A model checkpoint callback for monitoring model performance at each epoch and reverting to the best model at the end of the training loop.

Details regarding our constant-exponential learning rate scheduler have been provided in the appendix.

## 9.7 Results and Discussion

In the case of non-TATA promoter classification, the significance of minimizing false negatives, and thus ensuring a high recall rate, depends on the specific objectives and potential consequences of missing non-TATA promoters. Missing true instances of non-TATA promoters could lead to treatment delays, allowing the progression of pathological conditions.

### 9.7.1 LSTM

From Table 9.6 we can see that LSTM_V_1 clearly overfits the data, so among the two LSTM models, LSTM_V_0 outperforms LSTM_V_1 since it has a good recall and does not overfit.

Figure 9.1 shows learning curves of LSTM V0 with progressive improvement in accuracy along with consistent loss drop on all runs.

Figure 9.2. shows learning curves for LSTM V1 with a much smoother development of accuracy, besides sharp loss drop.

**Table 9.6** Training and testing results for LSTM models.

| **Model** | **Train accuracy** | **Train precision** | **Train recall** |
|---|---|---|---|
| LSTM_V_0 | 0.893 | 0.970 | 0.955 |
| LSTM_V_1 | 0.991 | 0.996 | 0.984 |
| Model | Test accuracy | Test precision | Test recall |
| LSTM_V_0 | 0.839 | 0.970 | 0.955 |
| LSTM_V_1 | 0.914 | 0.956 | 0.882 |

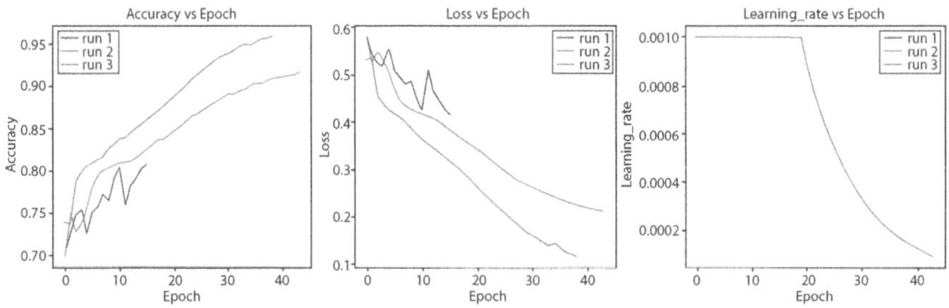


**Figure 9.1** Learning curves - LSTM V0.

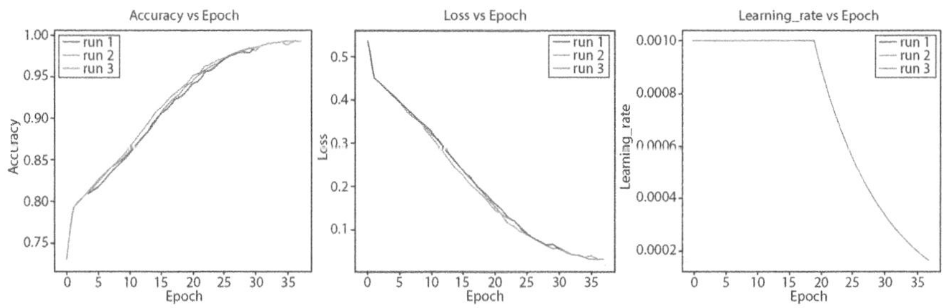


**Figure 9.2** Learning curves - LSTM V1.

### 9.7.2 CNN

Table 9.7 shows that the gap between the accuracies of the train and the test set of CNN V_0 is very high which suggests a potential overfitting issue. CNN V_1 with a smaller gap in accuracy may be more robust. Also, the test accuracy of CNN V_1 is slightly higher which makes it a better model.

**Table 9.7** Training and testing results for CNN models.

| **Model** | **Train accuracy** | **Precision** | **Recall** |
|---|---|---|---|
| CNN V_0 | 0.969 | 0.978 | 0.967 |
| CNN V_1 | 0.924 | 0.916 | 0.879 |
| Model | Test accuracy | Test precision | Test recall |
| CNN V_0 | 0.814 | 0.832 | 0.8214 |
| CNN V_1 | 0.821 | 0.903 | 0.778 |

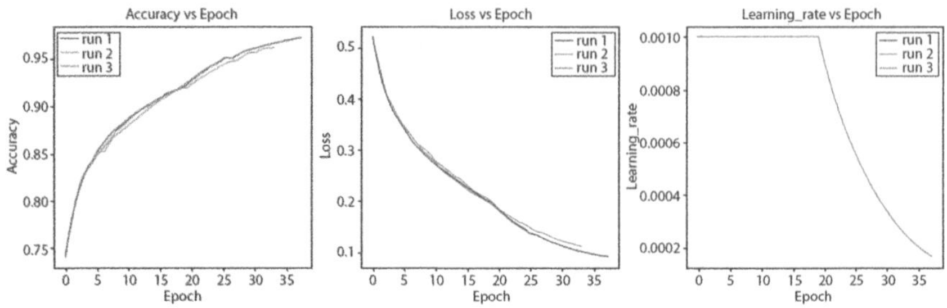


**Figure 9.3** Learning curves - CNN V0.

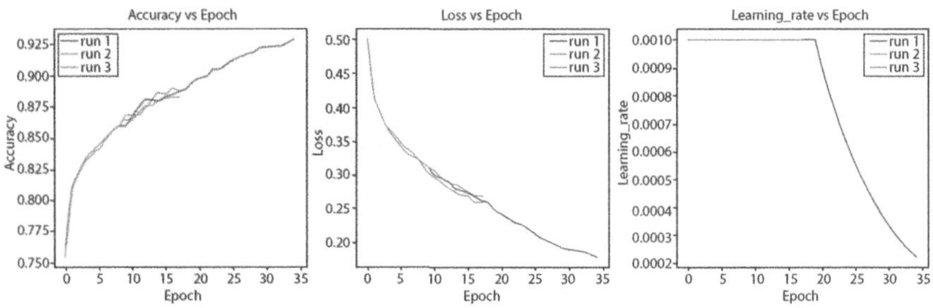


**Figure 9.4** Learning curves - CNN V1.

Figure 9.3 presents learning curves for CNN V0 exhibiting strong convergence to very high accuracies along with dropping losses in epochs. Figure 9.4 presents the learning curves for CNN V1. The trend is similar to that of CNN V0, but the variance across runs is slightly lower.

### 9.7.3 ConvoLSTM

Table 9.8 shows that both ConvoLSTM models seem to overfit the data.

Figure 9.5 shows learning curves for ConvoLSTMV0. Accuracy increases steadily, and loss decreases linearly.

Figure 9.6 shows learning curves for ConvoLSTM V1 - Consistent accuracy and loss trends across multiple runs.

**Table 9.8** Training and testing results for ConvoLSTM models.

| **Model** | **Train accuracy** | **Train precision** | **Train recall** |
|---|---|---|---|
| ConvoLSTM_V_0 | 0.985 | 0.990 | 0.977 |
| ConvoLSTM_V_1 | 0.992 | 0.993 | 0.986 |
| Model | Test accuracy | Test precision | Test recall |
| ConvoLSTM_V_0 | 0.839 | 0.853 | 0.851 |
| ConvoLSTM_V_1 | 0.845 | 0.873 | 0.838 |

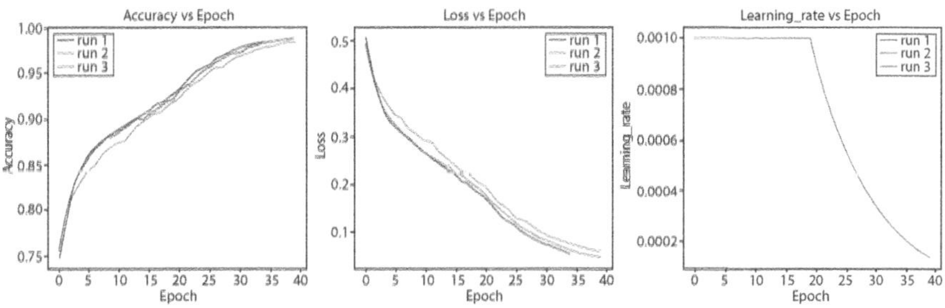


**Figure 9.5** Learning curves - ConvoLSTM V0.

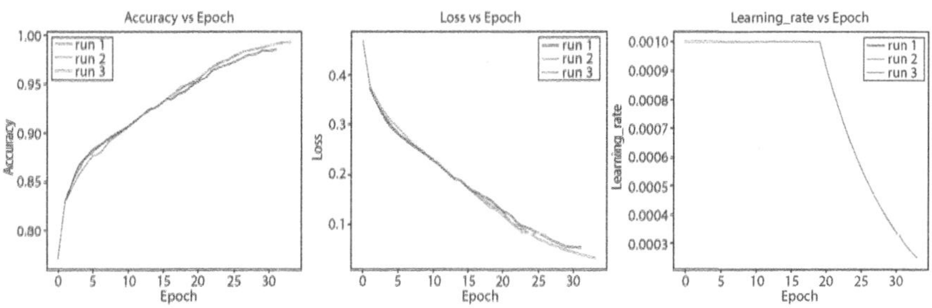


**Figure 9.6** Learning curves - ConvoLSTM V1.

### 9.7.4 WaveNet

Here, Table 9.9 shows that both models generalize the model well enough. Since WaveNet V_1 has a better recall than WaveNet V_0, it outperforms WaveNet V_0.

Figure 9.7: Learning curves for WaveNet V0: accuracy, loss, and learning rate for multiple runs.

Figure 9.8: The extended training performance displays consistent trends in accuracy improvement, loss reduction, and adaptive learning rate adjustments.

**Table 9.9** Training and testing results for WaveNet models.

| Model | Train accuracy | Train precision | Train recall |
|---|---|---|---|
| WaveNet_V_0<br>WaveNet_V_1 | 0.813<br>0.944 | 0.888<br>0.942 | 0.751<br>0.851 |
| Model | Test accuracy | Precision | Recall |
| WaveNet_V_0<br>WaveNet_V_1 | 0.811<br>0.886 | 0.906<br>0.945 | 0.747<br>0.848 |

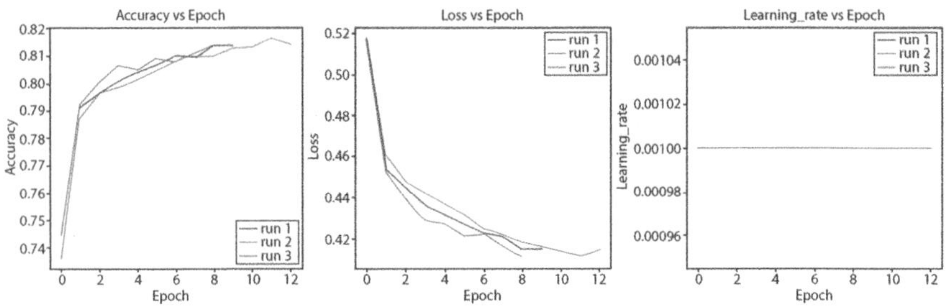


**Figure 9.7** Learning curves - WaveNet V0.

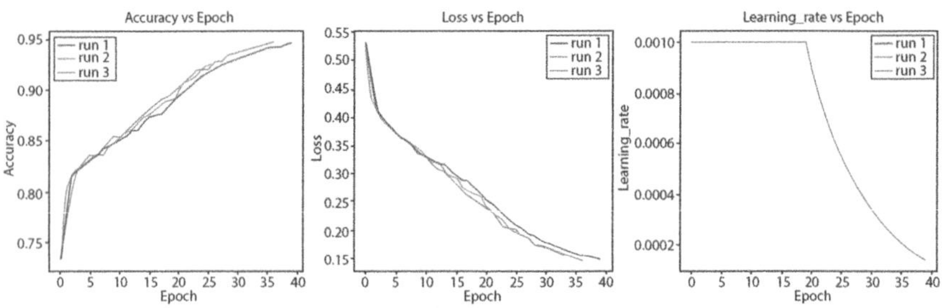


**Figure 9.8** Learning curves - WaveNet V1.

Among the deep learning models evaluated for the specific problem statement at hand, including LSTM V_0, CNN V_1, and WaveNet V_1, WaveNet V_1 has performed the best, particularly with regard to recall performance which is crucial in the context of the research problem.

Also, WaveNet V_1 exhibits this performance utilizing less than 20% trainable parameters and training time as compared to the other models. Thus, WaveNet V_1 emerges as the preferred choice.

**Table 9.10** Trainable parameters for different models.

| Model | Trainable parameters |
|---|---|
| CNN_V_0 | 7769 |
| CNN_V_1 | 7865 |
| ConvoLSTM_V_0 | 24,409 |
| ConvoLSTM_V_1 | 19,449 |
| LSTM_V_0 | 83,265 |
| LSTM_V_1 | 63,041 |
| WaveNet_V_0 | 2941 |
| WaveNet_V_1 | 16,653 |

**Table 9.11** Training time (in seconds) for different models.

| Model | Training time (seconds) |
|---|---|
| CNN_V_0 | 224 |
| CNN_V_1 | 175 |
| ConvoLSTM_V_0 | 248 |
| ConvoLSTM_V_1 | 266 |
| LSTM_V_0 | 665 |
| LSTM_V_1 | 597 |
| WaveNet_V_0 | 96 |
| WaveNet_V_1 | 224 |

Table 9.10 shows Trainable parameters for different models and Table 9.11 shows the Training time in seconds for each model.

## 9.8 Conclusion

In conclusion, this research project explores deep learning methodologies for classifying non-TATA promoters—a crucial aspect in unraveling gene regulation mechanisms.

By conducting a comprehensive comparative analysis of diverse deep learning architectures, valuable insights into the effectiveness and performance of different models for this significant task have been obtained.

We started our study by examining common sequence-based models like LSTM and GRU, which gave us a solid foundation for understanding how to process DNA sequences. Then, we expanded our analysis to include feature extraction methods and combined them with sequence modeling techniques. This allowed us to see the pros and cons of each approach. Additionally, we applied the WaveNet architecture, typically used for audio generation, to our specific application. This showcased its potential in effectively handling long one-dimensional sequences like DNA.

Throughout the experimental setup, we maintained a rigorous evaluation process, considering various metrics such as accuracy, precision, recall, computation time, and the number of parameters. Our analysis also included a comprehensive comparison within each class of models and an interclass evaluation, ultimately leading to the identification of the best-performing models within each category. The continuous advancements in deep learning and genomics research offer promising opportunities for unraveling the complexities of gene regulation and its implications for diverse biological phenomena.

## References


1. Guimaraes, R.C., Moreira, C.H.C., de Farias, S.T., A self-referential model for the formation of the genetic code. *Theory Biosci.*, *127*, 249–270, 2008.
2. Michaelian, K. and Padilla, N.S., UVC photon-induced denaturing of DNA: A possible dissipative route to Archean enzyme-less replication. *Heliyon*, *5*, 6, 2019.
3. Krawczak, M., Chuzhanova, N., Stenson, P., Johansen, B., Ball, E., Cooper, D., Changes in primary DNA sequence complexity influence the phenotypic consequences of mutations in human gene regulatory regions. *Hum. Genet.*, *107*, 362–365, 2000.
4. Tapia-Rojo, R., Mazo, J.J., Hernandez, J.A., Peleato, M.L., Fillat, M.F., Falo, F., Mesoscopic model and free energy landscape for protein-DNA binding sites:

analysis of cyanobacterial promoters. *PLoS Comput. Biol.*, *10*, 10, e1003835, 2014.

5. Marbach-Bar, N., Bahat, A., Ashkenazi, S., Golan-Mashiach, M., Haimov, O., Wu, S.Y., Chiang, C.M., Puzio-Kuter, A., Hirshfield, K.M., Levine, A.J., Dikstein, R., DTIE, a novel core promoter element that directs start site selection in TATA-less genes. *Nucleic Acids Res.*, *44*, 3, 1080–1094, 2016.
6. Park, D., Morris, A.R., Battenhouse, A., Iyer, V.R., Simultaneous map- ping of transcript ends at single-nucleotide resolution and identification of widespread promoter-associated non-coding RNA governed by TATA elements. *Nucleic Acids Res.*, *42*, 6, 3736–3749, 2014.
7. Umarov, R.K. and Solovyev, V.V., Recognition of prokaryotic and eukaryotic promot- ers using convolutional deep learning neural networks. *PLoS One*, *12*, 2, e0171410, 2017, https://doi.org/10.1371/journal.pone.0171410.
8. Alipanahi, B., Delong, A., Weirauch, M., *et al.*, Predicting the sequence specificities of DNA- and RNA-binding proteins by deep learning. *Nat. Biotechnol.*, *33*, 831–838, 2015, https://doi.org/10.1038/nbt.3300.
9. Umarov, R., Kuwahara, H., Li, Y., Gao, X., Solovyev, V., Promoter analysis and prediction in the human genome using sequence-based deep learning models. *Bioinformatics*, 35, 16, 2730–2737, August 2019.
10. Solovyev, V. and Umarov, R., Prediction of prokaryotic and eukaryotic promoters using convolutional deep learning neural networks, arXiv preprint arXiv:1610.00121, 2016.
11. Umarov, R., Kuwahara, H., Li, Y., Gao, X., Solovyev, V., Promid: human promoter prediction by deep learning, arXiv preprint arXiv:1810.01414, 2018.
12. Anderson, M., Thompson, S., Garcia, R., Exploring the Depths of WaveNet: A Comprehensive Literature Review on Theory, Application, and Optimization. *J. Signal Process. Mach. Learn.*, *15*, 2, 45–68, 2023.
13. Sherstinsky, A., Fundamentals of Recurrent Neural Network (RNN) and Long Short-Term Memory (LSTM) network. *Physica D*, 404, 132306, 2020, ISSN 0167-2789.
14. Li, Z., Liu, F., Yang, W., Peng, S., Zhou, J., A Survey of Convolutional Neural Networks: Analysis, Applications, and Prospects. *IEEE Trans. Neural Netw. Learn. Syst.*, 33, 12, 6999–7019, Dec. 2022, doi: 10.1109/TNNLS.2021.3084827.
15. Gu, J., Wang, Z., Kuen, J., Ma, L., Shahroudy, A., Shuai, B., Liu, T., Wang, X., Wang, G., Cai, J., Chen, T., Recent advances in convolutional neural networks. *Pattern Recognit.*, 77, 354–377, 2018, ISSN 0031-3203.

# 10

# Data Protection Regulation for E-Health Devices

**Satwika Dash[1], Kumash Patel[2] and Manivel Kandasamy[3]***

*[1]B.Sc. (Hons.) Computer Science, Unitedworld Institute of Technology, Karnavati University, Gandhinagar, Gujarat, India*
*[2]B.Tech Computer Science Engineering, Unitedworld Institute of Technology, Karnavati University, Gandhinagar, Gujarat, India*
*[3]Department of Computer Science and Engineering Unitedworld Institute of Technology, Karnavati University, Gandhinagar, Gujarat, India*

## *Abstract*

The special domain of data protection represents a fluid convergence of technological innovations, legal structures, and ethical imperatives, which are critical for the protection of personal data in the modern digital landscape. The fast proliferation of electronic health devices has extremely altered the healthcare model. However, this development brings forward significant challenges regarding the data protection of sensitive data and the conservation of privacy. This chapter investigates the complex interactions among these changes, underscoring the requirement for ongoing amendments to advancements in technology especially in data security and shifts in the regulatory frameworks. In addition, it meticulously scrutinizes the details of data protection regulation within the realm of e-health devices, focusing on essential regulatory frameworks such as the General Data Protection Regulation and the Health Insurance Portability and Accountability Act (HIPAA) along with other relevant national and international acts. The analysis includes the specific requirements for agreement, the criticality of informed consent, the implementation of data security protocols, and the implications of noncompliance. Additionally, it assesses the balance between technological innovation and regulatory frameworks, emphasizing case studies and best practices to ensure that the benefits of e-health devices are realized while maintaining patient privacy. Through a comprehensive analysis, this chapter aims to provide investors

**Corresponding author*: manivelk79@gmail.com

Ajay Kumar Vyas, Harleen Kaur, Sourabh Sharma and Bhavya Alankar (eds.) Metaverse Technologies, Security and Applications for Healthcare, (219–254) © 2025 Scrivener Publishing LLC

including healthcare professionals and new technology developers with essential insights and recommendations for effective navigation.

***Keywords***: E-health devices, data protection and regulation, data navigation

## 10.1 Introduction to E-Health Devices

Healthcare has come through a dramatic transformation in the 21st century, a shift in the pattern from curative to preventive care. This growth has been moved by the advancements in the defined e-health gadgets often referred to as the digital technology gadgets that act as a bridge between the virtual and the actual world. These gadgets which include simple tracking devices for physical activities to complicated implantable devices for the human body have become crucial tools in the quest of some of the most technologically advanced people seeking the best quality of healthcare and some medical practitioners themselves.

Physiological data acquisition, analysis, and transmission are the main features of e-health devices, and these require large-scale implementation [1]. It is essentially multisensory organ implants that constantly monitor everything that has to do with the patient's health and well-being, including his or her vital signs, physical activity, and sleep cycle, among many other things. Once obtained, this information undergoes an extensive analysis which provides important insight to enable the individual to make informed decisions to change the course of their health.

Personal health monitoring is not the only way that e-health gadgets are revolutionizing the healthcare sector. Such technologies prevent diseases from developing, allow for customizing the treatment process, and give care providers controlled access to patient information. The prospects for enhancing quality, decreasing the risk of chronic diseases, and effectively handling acute issues are immense. In addition, e-health devices have enormously enriched aggregate data available to medical researchers, thus enhancing the advancement of new therapies and interventions.

The prospects for implementing e-health devices are rising with the advancement of technology today [1], which proceeds at an unprecedented pace. It seems that the future IS bright indeed, including such advances as wearable tech as a personal trainer or coach, and implantable sensors for chronic disease management. However, the more everything progresses, the more it is necessary to regulate the issue of data protection, address such ethical questions, and ensure equal availability of such revolutionary technologies.

### 10.1.1 Definition of E-Health Devices

E-health devices are digital instruments that capture, manage, and transmit data with reference to health [2]. These can range from a simple fitness wristband to medical equipment that aids in tracking the health of a person and disease management, general health, and well-being is provided by the provision of data needed.

### 10.1.2 Scope and Trends in E-Health Devices

#### *10.1.2.1 Scope of E-Health Devices*

A wide range of technology instruments intended to track, control, and enhance health outcomes is included in the category of e-health equipment in below Figure 10.1.

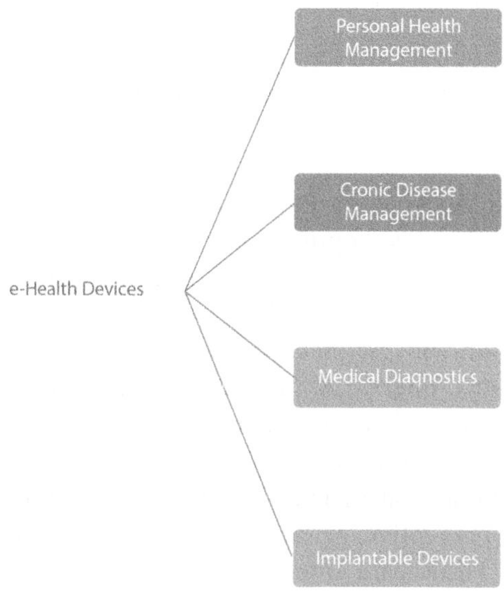


**Figure 10.1** Scope of e-health devices.

- **Personal Health Management:** E-health devices are portable health information devices that capture, store, process, and transmit information. These gadgets range from activity monitors to body fat scales, including medical devices, and are intended to help manage chronic diseases and achieve better health by offering health information.
- **Chronic Disease Management:** The use of glucose monitors, insulin pumps, and inhalers empowers patients to actively manage their chronic conditions.
- **Medical Diagnostics:** Diagnostic tools, such as portable analyzers for blood and urine, as well as other laboratory specimens, increase patients' access to healthcare services.
- **Implantable Devices:** Cardiac pacemakers, defibrillators, and other implantable medical devices provide constant surveillance and intervention [3].

#### 10.1.2.2 *Trends in E-Health Devices*

The environment of e-health devices is complex and dynamic in that it is influenced by technological advances and the altering face of healthcare.

Key trends include:

- Wearable Technology Expansion: Besides fitness tracking, wearables possess sophisticated sensors for the assessment of stress levels, mental conditions, and potential disease markers.
- Integration with Artificial Intelligence: Smart devices make suggestions, offer recommendations, and thereby generate forecasts and enhanced understanding of the analysis.
- Focus on Preventive Care: E-health gadgets are now used to screen diseases at their early stage, to encourage people to practice preventive measures and to practice a healthy life.
- Remote Healthcare Integration: Telehealth is used in the processes of remote consultations, medication monitoring, and chronic disease care due to the possibility of smooth interaction with telehealth platforms.
- Data Security and Privacy: To protect the confidentiality and privacy of the health data collected and shared, strong security features need to be incorporated for patient's trust through patient manufacturer devices.

- Miniaturization and Improved Battery Life: The gadgets have been made compact and more efficient allowing them to last longer than before, thus enhancing the comfort of the user.
- Consumerization of Healthcare: Technological devices and enabling tools used in e-health are becoming easy to use and available to people thus empowering individuals to take control of their health [4].

### 10.1.3 E-Health Devices in Healthcare and Important Roles

E-health gadgets have revolutionized patient and physician interactions with the system, making them crucial instruments in today's healthcare environment. These technologies are essential to many areas of healthcare:

#### *10.1.3.1 Patient Empowerment and Self-Management*

- **Chronic Disease Management:** Glucose monitors, insulin pumps, and inhalers empower patients in the management of chronic conditions leading to increased treatment adherence.
- **Fitness and Wellness:** Wearable devices use sensors to quantify physical activity, sleep patterns, and nutrition status promoting a healthier lifestyle for their users and helping them in making well-informed health decisions.
- **Early Detection:** Devices that can monitor vital signs and detect anomalies can help in the early detection of potential health issues, allowing for prompt interventions [5].

#### *10.1.3.2 Healthcare Provider Efficiency and Effectiveness*

- **Remote Patient Monitoring:** It refers to using remote monitoring technology equipment with the help of which healthcare provider can monitor patients at home and is also attributed to them if any kind of problem or consequences are detected.
- **Data-Driven Decision-Making:** E-health device data provides healthcare practitioners with valuable insights to make data-based decisions and offer personalized treatment plans.

- **Improved Patient Outcomes:** E-health devices improve patient outcomes and reduce hospitalizations by enabling early detection, remote monitoring, and personalized care.

#### *10.1.3.3 Healthcare System Optimization*

- **Population Health Management:** Data obtained from e-health devices at scale can be used to uncover health trends and patterns in societies which will direct public health policies such as resource allocation.
- **Cost Reduction:** E-health gadgets effectively diagnose and treat disease, thereby reducing healthcare costs by preventing complications or hospitalizations.
- **Access to Care:** Telemedicine and remote monitoring can improve access to health services which would be especially beneficial for those living in rural areas.

## 10.2 Importance of Data Protection Regulations

Data protection laws are essential to safeguarding the privacy of citizens, building trust, and further responsible data innovation. They keep personal info safe from breaches, reduce privacy risks by storing ownership data in the hands of individuals, and demonstrate an organization's commitment to doing things right. If businesses comply with these rules, they can prevent any monetary loss or legal repercussions and, of course, promote a safer sound digital space [6].

### 10.2.1 Overview of General Data Protection Regulation (GDPR)

The European Union (EU) has put into effect a comprehensive data protection law known as the General Data Protection Regulation (GDPR). It outlines firm rules for the collection, processing, and storing of personal data on EU citizens.

- Data Subject Rights: People have the right to access, correct, delete, and restrict the processing of their data.
- Accountability: People have the right to access, correct, delete, and restrict the processing of their data.

- Data Protection by Design and Default: Address privacy in the early stages of designing or developing systems, processes, and principles into products.
- Data Breaches: Report data breaches as soon as possible and inform individuals whose information has been exposed.
- International Data Transfers: The transfer of personal data outside the EU is regulated with rigorous laws.

### 10.2.2 Health Insurance Portability and Accountability Act (HIPAA)

Sensitive patient health information (PHI) cannot be disclosed without the informed consent of the patient thanks to US federal law known as HIPAA. It was passed in 1996 for:

- **Improve Healthcare Efficiency:** By standardizing e-health records and other data associated with health.
- **Protect Patient Privacy:** By granting patients control over their health information and establishing strong guidelines for how healthcare providers, health plans, and other covered entities must safeguard patient privacy.

**Key Components of HIPAA:**

- **Privacy Rule:** Creates nationwide guidelines for securing people's medical records and other sensitive health information.
- **Security Rule:** Establishes nationwide guidelines for securing electronic protected health information.
- **Breach Notification Rule:** In the event of a data breach, covered companies are required to notify affected persons as well as the Department of Health and Human Services.

### 10.2.3 Accountability Act and Relevant Regulations (CCPA and PIPEDA)

**California Consumer Privacy Act (CCPA)**

- Encourages the independence of Californians over their data.

- The right to data portability, the right to be informed, the right to erase, and the right to refuse the sale of personal data are important components.

**Personal Information Protection and Electronic Documents Act (PIPEDA)**

- The federal privacy law in Canada governs how personal information is collected, used, disclosed, and retained in the private sector.
- It emphasizes identifying purposes, accountability, disclosure, retention, consent, accuracy, limiting collection, safeguards, challenging compliance, and individual access.

### 10.2.4 Important Guidelines and International Standards

While there is no single "Accountability Act" that governs data protection worldwide, a number of international standards and legislation have emerged to provide a framework for data management and privacy.

**International Standards:**

- **ISO/IEC 27001:** With regard to information security management systems (ISMS), this is a generally recognized standard. It provides a logical approach to managing and protecting confidential company data.
- **NIST Cybersecurity Framework:** It was created as a voluntary framework for controlling cybersecurity risk by the National Institute of Standards and Technology, or NIST.

**Key Data Protection Regulations:**

- **General Data Protection Regulation (GDPR):** Strict guidelines are enforced by the EU for the processing of inhabitants' data.
- **California Consumer Privacy Act (CCPA):** Encourages the independence of Californians over their data.
- **Personal Information Protection and Electronic Documents Act (PIPEDA):** Canada's federal privacy law governs how personal information is collected, used, disclosed, and retained.

## 10.3 Security Principles and Data Privacy

Data privacy goes hand in hand with security, ensuring data confidentiality, integrity, and availability. It is provided by the security aspect which protects data against unauthorized access or modification and ensures its availability. Whether it is technical like encryption, firewalls, and access controls, or organizational like security awareness training and incident response planning [7].

By contrast, data privacy is about the right of individuals to retain control over their personal information and prevent it from being misused. These include principles such as data minimization, purpose limitation, accuracy in storage, and deletion of information amongst others. Privacy safeguards ensure that personal information is collected and used lawfully, fairly, and transparently while granting individuals control over their data.

Security, together with privacy, creates a holistic protection of data. Security provides the technical foundation for protecting data from threats, while privacy establishes the legal and ethical framework for its handling. A solid focus on both is necessary to build customer trust, comply with regulations, and protect against risk liability should a data breach occur. It means creating a joint security and privacy framework so that we can develop the data protection culture altogether for individuals as well as business organizations [8].

### 10.3.1 Overview of Data Minimization

The concept of data minimization concerns the collection, processing, and storage of only the information that is necessary to attain a specific purpose.

It is essential to data management and protection, especially in the recently developed privacy regulations like GDPR.

The main thought is not to gather as much information as possible but only the ones directly related to the performance of the task.

### 10.3.2 Data Integrity

Data integrity refers to the accuracy, consistency, and completeness of data throughout its life cycle. It ensures that data are reliable and trustworthy, free from errors, inconsistencies, or corruption.

**Maintaining data integrity is crucial for several reasons:**

- Decision-Making: Accurate and complete data are essential for making informed decisions.
- Compliance: Many regulations, such as HIPAA and GDPR, require data integrity.
- Reputation: Errors in data can damage an organization's reputation.
- Financial Loss: Inaccurate data can lead to financial losses due to incorrect calculations or decisions.

**To achieve data integrity, organizations employ various techniques, including the following:**

- Data Validation: Checking data for accuracy and consistency before it is stored.
- Data Cleansing: Identifying and correcting inaccurate, incomplete, or duplicate data.
- Data Backup: Regularly backing up data to prevent data loss.
- Access Controls: Limiting who can access and modify data.
- Data Encryption: Protecting data from unauthorized access and modification.

### 10.3.3 Data Confidentiality

Data confidentiality prevents information from being leaked, accessed by unauthorized personnel, or stolen unlawfully. This is also a fundamental component of information security and privacy. This protection is crucial for individuals, organizations, and governments alike in below Figure 10.2.

**Key Elements of Data Confidentiality:**

- **Protection of Sensitive Information:** This includes personal information, financial and banking details, business and trade secrets, among other information.
- **Prevention of Unauthorized Access:** Measures being taken in the process of gaining control and reducing access of data to only certain authorized person(s).
- **Data Encryption:** Data are converted into code to avoid unauthorized access.

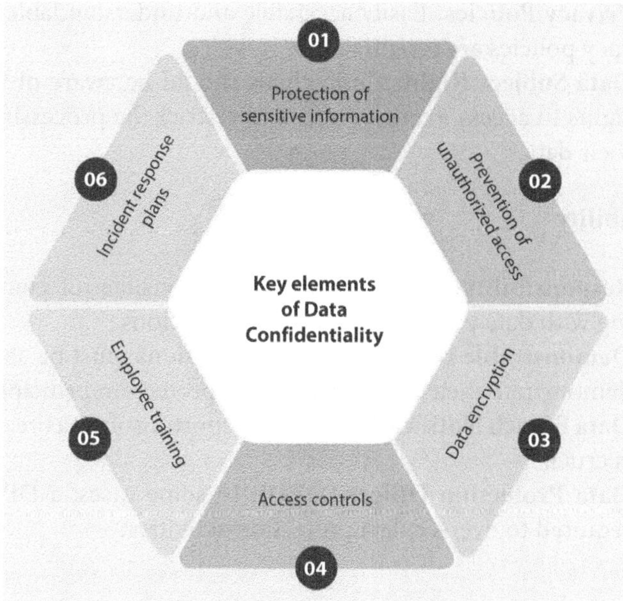


**Figure 10.2** Key elements of data confidentiality.

- **Access Controls:** Developing measures for restricting data access and changes.
- **Employee Training:** Formation of awareness programs for the employees on the need to preserve data and how to deal with such information.
- **Incident Response Plans:** Having a plan in place to respond to data breaches.

## 10.3.4 Transparency and Accountability of Data Privacy

**Transparency and accountability** are fundamental principles in data privacy. They ensure that individuals understand how their data are being handled and that organizations are responsible for their data practices.

### *10.3.4.1 Transparency*

- **Clear communication:** Organizations must clearly communicate their data practices to individuals, including how data are collected, used, shared, and protected.

- **Privacy Policies:** Easily accessible and understandable privacy policies are essential.
- **Data Subject Rights:** Individuals should be aware of their rights to access, rectify, erase, and restrict the processing of their data.

**Accountability**

- **Responsibility:** Organizations are responsible for complying with data protection laws and regulations.
- **Demonstrable Compliance:** Organizations must be able to demonstrate their adherence to data protection principles.
- **Data Breach Notification:** Timely reporting of data breaches is crucial.
- **Data Protection Officer (DPO):** In some cases, a DPO is required to oversee data protection activities.

### *10.3.4.2 Rights of Data Security*

**Data subject rights** are the entitlements granted to individuals whose personal data are being processed. These rights are enshrined in various data protection regulations, such as the GDPR (General Data Protection Regulation) and CCPA (California Consumer Privacy Act).

**Key Data Subject Rights**

**Right to be Informed:** Individuals have the right to be informed about the collection and processing of their personal data.

- **Right of Access:** Individuals have the right to obtain copies of their personal data.
- **Right to Rectification:** Individuals have the right to correct inaccurate or incomplete data.
- **Right to Erasure (Right to be Forgotten):** In certain circumstances, individuals can request the deletion of their personal data.
- **Right to Restriction of Processing:** Individuals can request a temporary or permanent halt to the processing of their data.
- **Right to Data Portability:** Individuals have the right to transfer their personal data to another organization.

- **Right to Object:** Individuals can object to the processing of their personal data.
- **Rights Related to Automated Decision-Making:** Individuals have rights related to decisions based on automated processing, including the right to human intervention.

## 10.4 Regulatory Requirements and Compliance Framework

Regulatory compliance is important in organizations that process or store personal information. Compliance management at an organization encompasses the recognition of relevant regulations, evaluation of the organization's practice, and putting in place adequate controls and monitoring. In this way, it is possible for various businesses to prevent some risks, ensure the protection of information, and gain the necessary trust of consumers. Some of these rules include GDPR, CCPA, HIPAA, and PCI DSS, which set out certain requirements that organizations must meet to protect data.

### 10.4.1 Data Preprocessing, Retention, and Storage

#### *10.4.1.1 Data Preprocessing*

Is the operation by which data are prepared for the purpose of the analysis it is going to suffer, which is the first step of the data preparation. Some of the data warehouse activities carried out during this process are data cleaning, data integration, data transformation, and data reduction.

#### *10.4.1.2 Data Retention*

Is understood as a procedure for storing data for a certain period of time. It will also be important for organizations to develop proper data retention policies to solve legal and oversee necessities and support the activity of organizations. One of the major challenges in information management is the tension between data availability and protection in retention processes.

#### *10.4.1.3 Data Storage*

Means that data may be stored for later use. Some of the storage solutions depend on aspects like the volume of data, how often the data are accessed, the level of security required, and the cost of the solution. These solutions span across the conventional types of storage such as hard drives to cloud storage platforms and data storage warehouses. Appropriate data management aims at data accessibility, accuracy, and security.

### 10.4.2 Data-Sharing Access

Data sharing is the process of sharing data and making it available to parties that are legally allowed to have access to it. It involves providing users with the necessary access to the data while, at the same time, preserving the essence of the data, its privacy, and its accessibility. The problem of data sharing is a critical part of collaboration, new ideas formation, and decision-making processes [9].

**Key Aspects of Data-Sharing Access:**

- Access Controls: Implementing robust mechanisms to determine who can access data, what data they can access, and what actions they can perform.
- Data Masking: Protecting sensitive information by obscuring or replacing it with nonsensitive data.
- Data Encryption: Safeguarding data by converting these into a code that can only be accessed with a decryption key.
- Data Governance: Establishing policies and procedures for data sharing, including data quality, security, and compliance.
- Data Usage Agreements: Defining the terms and conditions for data sharing, including responsibilities and liabilities.

### 10.4.3 Risk Assessment of E-Health Devices

The safety of e-health devices requires a risk assessment to evaluate the risks associated with the devices and put measures in place to counter any risk. These devices hold sensitive health data, exposing them to various cyber threats.

**Key Areas of Risk Assessment:**

- Data Privacy And Security: Protection of patient data from unauthorized access, disclosure, alteration, or destruction.
- Device Security: Ensuring the device itself is protected from malware, hacking, and physical damage.
- Data Integrity: Maintaining the accuracy and completeness of health data.

- Device Reliability: Ensuring the device functions correctly and consistently.
- User Safety: Protecting patients from harm due to device malfunction or misuse.
- Regulatory Compliance: Adhering to relevant regulations such as HIPAA, GDPR, and others.

**Risk assessment methodologies:**

- Threat Modeling: Identifying potential threats and vulnerabilities.
- Risk Matrix: Assessing the likelihood and impact of identified risks.
- Vulnerability Assessment: Identifying weaknesses in the device or system.
- Penetration Testing: Simulating attacks to discover vulnerabilities.

### 10.4.4 Data Protection and Privacy

Data protection and data privacy represent two aspects of the same problem but they denote two different aspects of data security. Data privacy as one of the basic human rights deals with ownership of an individual's information. It includes the right to find out what information is collected, the uses of the information, and the right to choose how the information will be used. This includes the right to access and obtain a copy of the data, the right to rectify data, or to erase the data.

Both these concepts are highly relevant to understanding the ways of increasing the level of trust between organizations and individuals. Stemming from the above discussion, the following conclusions can be made: Whenever data protection measures are well developed, people have more confidence in the way their information is processed. On the other hand, prescriptive privacy rights reinforce the ability of individuals to determine what ought to be done with their data, thus putting pressure on data protection measures, although not directly.

It is essential to recognize that data protection and privacy are not static concepts. Given the fact that technology is constantly evolving and that there are more and more data breaches and concerns over privacy, it is important to have a responsive one. The law affecting organizations is dynamic and issues of data protection are dynamic, hence, organizations have to be dynamic in ensuring they meet the requirements for the protection of these data [10].

In the end, the vision is for people to own their data and organizations to be responsible for data. Achieving this balance needs some form of data protection and privacy principles that are molded in a balanced manner.

### 10.4.5 Security Mechanisms for Regulatory Requirements

The technological and operational measures used to secure against unauthorized access, use, disclosure, disruption, alteration, or destruction of data and information systems are known as security mechanisms. Organizations must put in place a comprehensive set of security controls in order to comply with regulatory obligations.

**Key Security Mechanisms:**

- Access Control: Limiting user roles, permissions, and authentication-based access to systems and data.
- Authentication: Confirming the legitimacy of individuals or gadgets before allowing entry.
- Authorization: Deciding what can be done by users once they have been authenticated.
- Encryption: Transforming data into an unreadable format to protect its confidentiality.
- Data Integrity: Ensuring data accuracy and completeness through checksums, hashing, and digital signatures.
- Network Security: Utilizing virtual private networks (VPNs), intrusion detection and prevention systems, and firewalls to safeguard the network infrastructure.
- Endpoint Protection: Safeguarding devices (computers, laptops, and mobile devices) with antivirus software, antimalware, and intrusion prevention.
- Incident Response: Establishing procedures for identifying, handling, and recovering from security incidents.
- Business Continuity and Disaster Recovery: Ensuring the continuity of operations and data availability in case of disruptions.
- Aligning security mechanisms with regulatory requirements
- Identify Applicable Regulations: Determine which regulations apply to your organization based on industry, location, and data types.
- Conduct a Risk Assessment: Evaluate potential threats and vulnerabilities to identify critical assets and risks.

- Implement Controls: Select and implement security mechanisms that address identified risks and comply with regulatory requirements.
- Monitor and Review: Continuously monitor the effectiveness of security controls and make necessary adjustments.

**Examples of Regulations With Specific Security Requirements:**

- GDPR: Requires strong data protection measures, including data encryption, access controls, and data breach notification.
- HIPAA: Mandates security safeguards for electronic protected health information (ePHI), such as access controls, audit trails, and encryption.
- PCI DSS: Sets strict standards for handling credit card data, including encryption, vulnerability management, and access control.

## 10.5 Data Transfer and Standard Regulations

In today's interconnected world, data movement is arguably the most important activity and definitely one that presents numerous challenges. The world is more interconnected than ever with businesses and people linked up and data that have been growing at a frantic pace requires information to be easily transmitted. This can enable different companies to work effectively and share information better, hence improving their innovations.

However, most of these data are confidential, and thus, there must be strict guidelines in order to ensure privacy and security. It is a tricky balance: ensuring that during communication there is a free flow of data and yet at the same time ensuring the protection of the information. This balancing act has caused the formulation of a rather complex set of rules. To deal with all of it, it is important that you know the global guidelines of data sharing such as GDPR, CCPA, and HIPAA, and then incorporate a good security solution to manage all the processes and follow the rules.

### 10.5.1 Global Data Transfer and Legal Frameworks

The ability to move information freely across international borders has been one of the key components enabling globalization, helping businesses move efficiently and collaborate and innovate. However, as people got more knowledgeable of the fact that personal data are precious and important assets that can be leveraged, or abused, they have erroneously developed not a simple but rather a convoluted patchwork of data protection laws around the globe. CCPA of the USA has its own rules for the transfer of data, as well as the GDPR of the EU and LGPD of Brazil. They center on things such as people's rights, nonuse of data, data protection, and corporate responsibility. For organizations, it means that they must master these rules to avoid falling foul of the law. It becomes even more complicated, especially with new technologies and other forms of data. For instance, cloud computing, IoT devices, and big data analytics are posing new problems with data transfer. Furthermore, as supply chains become integrated across the world, protecting information is even more important. To address these challenges, firms employ different measures that include impact assessments for transfers, standard contract provisions, and mandatory internal regulation. In the future, globally standardized frameworks for data protection can facilitate cross-border data flows.

**Key Challenges in Global Data Transfer**

- **Conflicting Data Protection Laws:** Different countries have different levels of data protection, which can make compliance tricky.
- **Data Localization Requirements:** Some places require data to be stored locally, which can restrict data flow.
- **Emerging Technologies:** New techs like AI and IoT bring their own data transfer challenges.
- **Geopolitical Tensions:** International relations can affect data transfer rules and practices.

## 10.5.2 Binding Corporate Rules (BCR)

Binding Corporate Rules (BCRs) are a company's internal guidelines on the processing of personal data, especially when transferring them across borders outside the EU. They are meant to assist organizations to remain compliant with the EU data protection regulations such as the GDPR and protect personal data at all times and in every place within the corporate structure.

**Key Features of BCRs**

- Legally Binding: These rules apply to every part of the company in its operation.
- All-Encompassing: They range from the utilization of the data gathered, and how the data are sorted through to how these are transmitted and secured.
- Approved by Authorities: The EU's data protection authorities must first okay the use of BCRs before they are granted clearance.
- Enforceable Rights: Under these rules, people's rights about their data are legal.

**Benefits of BCRs**

- Legal Certainty: As such, they offer a sound legal framework for transferring data across the organization.
- Efficiency: It reduced the amount of microlevel checks that have to be made for each data transfer.
- Commitment: They demonstrate clear care of the company for the data of the users.
- Flexibility: They can be enthusiastically developed and designed to meet the particular needs of the company.

**Challenges of BCRs**

- Approval Hurdles: It takes time sometimes to get approvals from several authoritics.
- Ongoing Compliance: It can be ascertained that to meet all the BCR requirements, the process has to be ongoing and dynamic.
- Enforcement: Safety from everyday operations sometimes becomes nearly impossible as it becomes a daily challenge to ensure that all areas within a specific firm adhere to the laid rules.

### 10.5.3 Standard Contractual Clauses (SCC)

Standard Contractual Clauses (SCCs) are preapproved contractual clauses designed to facilitate lawful transfers of personal data from the EU to countries outside the EU (third countries) that do not have an adequacy decision. They serve as a mechanism to ensure that personal data continues to be protected in accordance with EU data protection standards even when transferred to countries with lower data protection standards.

Essentially, SCCs are a standardized contract between the data exporter (the entity transferring the data) and the data importer (the entity receiving the data) that outlines the obligations of both parties to protect the transferred data.

**Key Features of SCCs**

- Preapproved by the EU: SCCs are approved by the European Commission, providing legal certainty.
- Contractual Obligations: They impose specific obligations on both the data exporter and importer, including data protection measures, data subject rights, and dispute resolution mechanisms.
- Flexibility: SCCs can be adapted to specific data transfer scenarios.
- Complementary Measures: While SCCs provide a solid foundation, additional safeguards may be necessary depending on the specific circumstances of the data transfer.

Organizations can limit the risks associated with transferring personal data to third countries and establish compliance with the GDPR by adding SCCs to their data transfer agreements.

### 10.5.4 Decision-Making for Data Transfer

The selection of the best way of transferring information is always based on several factors. Key elements influencing this decision include the following:

**Data Characteristics**

- Sensitivity: Proposed level of security needed to maintain confidentiality of data.
- Volume: The size of data to be transmitted.
- Format: The kind of structure and the type of data that the company has (if it is structured, unstructured, etc.).

**Transfer Requirements**

- Speed: A clear indication of how fast transfer speed is required for business.
- Reliability: The requirement for data consistency and the possibility of it getting lost in the process of distribution.
- Security: The amount of protection needed for the information in transit.
- Cost: The amount of money that has been planned for data transfer.

## 10.6 Future Data Protection for the E-Health Sector

The e-health industry is on the verge of revolutionizing the manner in which healthcare services are provided; this is probably because of some new technological inclusion and data solutions [3]. When more tools are applied to the healthcare system and the data are gained from the patients, the question of patients' confidentiality arises. This growth is highly likely due to the increased number of Internet-of-Things devices such as wearables and implants which makes our trails larger for hackers to corrupt.

However, the above-discussed use of health data is desirable for research, public health, and system integration but comes with certain challenges. Rules and new strategies are being developed every time in an attempt to maintain the perfect balance between the creation of innovations and the violation of people's privacy. To manage these complexities, we require an approach that will address them fully. This entails adopting advanced technologies with additional privacy properties such as differential privacy and federated learning as well as employing blockchain technology, and enforcing cybersecurity measures alongside international cooperation. The future of e-health will then be shaped by the ability of an organization to balance innovation on technology and at the same time ensure that patient data are protected.

### 10.6.1 Future Technologies and Impact of the E-Health Sector

The rapidly advancing field of e-health is poised for a revolutionary period propelled by technological breakthroughs. These developments have the potential to transform the way healthcare is provided, improve patient outcomes, and boost productivity.

At the front of this change are **machine learning (ML)** and **artificial intelligence (AI)**. Utilizing these tools will speed up drug research, forecast disease outbreaks, provide individualized treatment regimens, and analyze enormous databases. Additionally, chatbots and virtual assistants driven by AI are improving patient interaction and doing preliminary triage.

**Wearable devices and IoT sensors** are producing an incredible amount of real-time health information. This information can be used to manage cases of chronic illnesses, to identify signs of certain diseases, or to encourage early screenings and check-ups. These devices when combined with AI are resulting in much more precise and tailored health-related information.

**Blockchain technology** provides possible solutions to some of the problems related to data security, integration, and openness. It can be used to protect data of patients' records, monitor the supply of drugs, and share data across the network.

**Virtual reality and augmented reality** are revolutionizing medical education, surgery preparation, and treatment delivery. Such technologies can contribute solutions for learning in healthcare, surgical training, patient encouragement, and physical therapy.

**3D printing** is the future of the manufacturing of healthcare products, such as medical equipment, artificial limbs, and even human organs. By means of customization and the ability to create prototypes out of the proper materials, this technology definitively helps to solve the problem and significantly decreases expenditures.

When all these technologies work together, they could build a healthcare system that is more focused on patients, efficient, and accessible. But we need to make sure that we also have strong data protection and ethical practices in place to balance the benefits with the risks.

### 10.6.2 Emerging Technologies in Data Protection

The rapid evolution of technology has profound implications for data protection. While these advancements present new challenges, they also offer innovative solutions to safeguarding sensitive information. Figure 10.3 shows key emerging technologies in data protection for future technologies and the impact of the e-health sector.

- **Blockchain:** This decentralized technology can enhance data security, transparency, and accountability. It can be used for creating immutable records, verifying data integrity, and managing access controls.

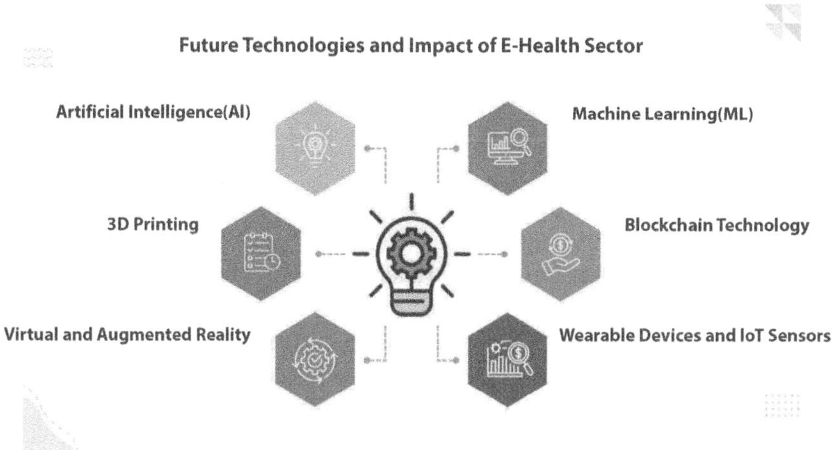


**Figure 10.3** Key Emerging technologies in data protection.

- **Artificial Intelligence (AI):** AI-powered systems can analyze vast amounts of data to identify anomalies, detect potential threats, and predict security breaches. However, AI itself must be protected from malicious attacks.
- **Homomorphic Encryption:** This sophisticated form of encryption allows data to be processed in an encrypted format meaning that privacy is kept as work on data is done.
- **Zero-Trust Architecture:** This security approach is based on the phrase "never trust, always verify," which aims at verifying who has access to information.
- **Biometrics:** Unique physical or behavioral characteristics can be used for strong authentication, replacing traditional passwords.

### Challenges and Opportunities

While these technologies hold immense potential for enhancing data protection, they also introduce new complexities. For instance, blockchain has the advantage of offering security given that it is unalterable, yet it has become a pathway for attacks. In addition, the AI systems have to be trained on fair datasets to avoid such unfair results.

However, for successful utilization of these technologies, organizations are required to develop research pertaining to these technologies and employ expert professionals. In addition, these technologies require a clear legal and regulatory framework to address new problems to meet the ethical use of the technology.

#### *10.6.2.1 AI and Machine Learning in Data Protection*

The advanced technologies of AI and ML are already starting to shift the strategy of data protection [7]. These are the technologies that can enhance security greatly, prevent threats and attacks, and preserve our privacy.

**Benefits of AI and ML in Data Protection**

- **Threat Detection and Prevention:** AI can analyze vast amounts of data to identify patterns indicative of cyberattacks, enabling proactive measures to be taken. ML algorithms can evolve to recognize new threats as they emerge.
- **Anomaly Detection:** By establishing baseline behaviors, AI can identify deviations that may signal a security breach or data loss.
- **Privacy Enhancement:** AI can be used to develop privacy-enhancing technologies like differential privacy, which allows for data analysis without compromising individual privacy.
- **Automation:** Data sorting and access can also be done through AI and this helps to minimize the chances of making errors which, in turn, makes everything flow smoothly.
- **Risk Assessment:** AI is in a position to diagnose threats that might be posed to your information and other systems, hence helping you prioritize key matters.

**Challenges and Considerations**

- **Data Quality:** AI and ML models are as precise as the datasets that feed them. Sometimes, the data collected may be biased or inaccurate, and hence, the results may tend to be wrong.
- **Explainability:** In the case of AI systems, the models themselves can often be very large and hard to interpret, hence the reason for decision justification drawbacks. This does so concerning transparency and accountability.
- **Adversarial Attacks:** Malicious actors can manipulate AI systems, leading to incorrect outputs or security breaches.
- **Ethical Implications:** The incorporation of AI in data protection still brings a lot of ethical issues such as bias, surveillance, and privacy.

#### *10.6.2.2 Role of Blockchain in Data Protection Management*

Blockchain, a distributed ledger technology, has emerged as a powerful tool in data protection management [8].

Its decentralized nature, immutability, and transparency offer significant advantages in safeguarding sensitive information.

**Key Benefits of Blockchain in Data Protection**

- **Immutability:** Once data are recorded on a blockchain, it cannot be altered or deleted, ensuring data integrity and preventing tampering.
- **Transparency:** All transactions are visible to network participants, enhancing accountability and trust.
- **Security:** Cryptographic techniques secure data and transactions, making it difficult for unauthorized parties to access or modify information.
- **Decentralization:** Data are distributed across multiple nodes, reducing the risk of data loss or corruption due to a single point of failure.
- **Auditability:** The blockchain provides a complete and auditable record of data interactions, facilitating compliance with regulations.

**Challenges and Considerations**

While blockchain offers significant benefits, challenges remain.

- **Scalability:** Blockchain technology might not allow for the management of very large datasets in the capacity as is practiced today.
- **Complexity:** Blockchain solutions application and management may require comparatively significant efforts and knowledge, especially when it initially starts.
- **Energy Consumption:** Some blockchain platforms have high energy consumption, raising environmental concerns.
- **Privacy:** While blockchain ensures data integrity, it can also expose sensitive information if not implemented carefully.

### *10.6.2.3 Data Protection Regulatory Evaluation*

A data protection regulatory evaluation is a comprehensive assessment of an organization's adherence to data protection laws and regulations. It involves a systematic examination of data handling practices, security measures, and compliance frameworks [5].

**Key Components of a Regulatory Evaluation**

- **Data Mapping:** Identifying and documenting all personal data processed by the organization.
- **Risk Assessment:** Assessing potential risks to data privacy and security.
- **Legal and Regulatory Compliance:** Evaluating adherence to applicable data protection laws (GDPR, CCPA, HIPAA, etc.).
- **Data Subject Rights:** Assessing processes for handling data subject requests (access, rectification, erasure, etc.).
- **Security Measures:** Evaluating the effectiveness of technical and organizational security controls.
- **Data Breach Response:** Assessing the organization's preparedness for and response to data breaches.

**Benefits of a Regulatory Evaluation**
Risk Mitigation: Identifies potential vulnerabilities and allows for proactive measures.
Compliance Assurance: Ensures adherence to data protection laws and avoids penalties.
Enhanced Reputation: Demonstrates a commitment to data protection and builds trust with customers.
Operational Efficiency: Streamlines data handling processes and reduces costs.

**Challenges and Best Practices**
Conducting a thorough regulatory evaluation can be complex and time-consuming. Organizations should consider engaging external experts to assist with the process.

**Best practices include the following:**
Regular Assessments: Conducting evaluations periodically to identify emerging risks.

Continuous Improvement: Implementing corrective actions based on evaluation findings.
Employee Training: Raising awareness of data protection obligations among employees.
Documentation: Maintaining comprehensive documentation of the evaluation process and findings.

### 10.6.3 Security Measures and Ethical Considerations

In the context of data protection, ethical considerations and security measures are inextricably intertwined. Security is concerned with preventing unauthorized access, use, disclosure, interruption, alteration, or destruction of data; on the other hand, ethics makes sure that these precautions are carried out in a way that upholds social norms and individual rights.

**Key Security Measures**

- **Access Controls:** Limiting the access by the people in terms of who gets the data and who does not get access to it.
- **Encryption:** To encode information in such a way that it is only accessible to a particular group of people keeping it secret.
- **Network Security:** Employing firewalls and "intrusion detection" and "intrusion prevention" systems to guard your network.
- **Endpoint Protection:** Protection of a device with antivirus and antimalware to protect it from threats.
- **Data Loss Prevention (DL):** Preventing users from filming confidential information thus transmitting them to the wrong channels or possessing them maliciously.
- **Incident Response Planning:** Developing strategies to respond to and recover from security breaches.

**Ethical Considerations**

- **Privacy:** Respecting individuals' rights to control their personal information.
- **Accountability:** Accepting the accountability for data and for any incursion that may be recorded.
- **Fairness:** Ensuring that security measures do not create unfair disadvantages for certain groups.

- **Human Rights:** This involves thinking of how the measures being put in place can interfere with certain basic liberties such as the right to free speech.

### 10.6.4 Enhancing the Protection Control over Personal Health Data

Protecting personal health data is paramount due to its sensitive nature. Several strategies can enhance control over this information:

- **Data Ownership and Control:** Share power to empower people and allow them to manage their data and control who may use it and for what purpose.
- **Data Portability:** One should be able to have a smooth transition of the health data from one healthcare provider to the other.
- **Transparent Consent:** Make sure that everybody gets it and agrees on how the data are going to be collected and processed.

#### Technological Advancements

- **Blockchain:** Utilizing blockchain technology for secure and transparent data management, ensuring data integrity and provenance.
- **Encryption:** Encrypt the data security so that it would remain secure in the database as well as while it is in transit.
- **AI-Powered Anonymization:** Employing advanced AI techniques to anonymize health data while preserving its utility for research.

#### Regulatory and Policy Frameworks

- **Comprehensive Legislation:** Enact strong and effective data protection laws that target the issues of dealing with health data.
- **Data Breach Notification:** Set a rule that notification to the concerned individuals must be done as soon as possible in case of data breaches.

- **Privacy by Design:** Incorporate data protection as an integral component of the formation of healthcare systems as well as the application.
- **Risk Assessment:** Conduct a frequent review of the exposures and ensure appropriate mitigations for the risks are implemented.
- **Employee Training:** Ensure that subordinate staff is well-trained on the rules and regulations needed to safeguard data.
- **Data Minimization:** Acquire and retain the minimum necessary health information and secure them for as short a time as is feasible.
- **Incident Response Plan:** In case of leakage, have a proper approach to how the occurrences should be dealt with.

### 10.6.5 Industry Standards in Data-Sharing Mechanisms

Industry standards play a crucial role in facilitating secure and efficient data sharing. These standards provide a common framework for data exchange, ensuring interoperability, data quality, and security.

**Key Industry Standards**

- Data Formats: Bates formatting, XML, JSON, and CSV are some of the standard formats that are employed for sharing the data to ensure that the data are consistent across different systems.
- Data Quality: Standardization of data elements for instance through ISO/IEC 11179 describes how it is understood to provide accuracy to the data that are collected.
- Metadata Standards: Other guidelines include Dublin Core and ISO 19115 which offer directions on how data resources could be described using metadata.
- Security Standards: Regulations such as ISO/IEC 27001 and the NIST Cybersecurity Framework explain how data can best be defended while in transit.
- Privacy Standards: Standards like GDPR and CCPA provide guidelines for handling personal data during sharing.
- Interoperability Standards: There is FHIR for healthcare and financial institutional messages for businesses that guarantee that data exchange functions optimally in individual sectors.

**Benefits of Industry Standards**

- Interoperability: It makes it possible for the various systems and applications to exchange data.
- Data Quality: They ensure that data are up to date and are retained in the proper format.
- Security: They provide procedures for securing information while the sharing of the information is in progress.
- Efficiency: It helps to make the process of using and exchanging data easier and often results in cost reduction.
- Compliance: They assist organizations in achieving compliance with legal standards.

**Challenges and Considerations**

- Adoption: Ensuring widespread adoption of standards can be challenging.
- Evolution: There is a need to synchronize standards with emergent technology and innovations.
- Complexity: When working with multiple sets of standards it may be not easy, time-consuming, and requires many resources.
- Balance: Striking a balance between standardization and flexibility is crucial.

### 10.6.6 Future Challenges and Solutions for Data Protection

The world is going digital, and this is rapidly changing the techniques and possibilities of protecting our information [10]. Even as we advance in technology, we are equally exposed to more threats as far as privacy and security are concerned.

**Emerging Challenges**

- **AI and Deepfakes:** AI can be misused in making deepfakes of a person and that results in big issues such as identity theft and fraudulence.
- **IoT and Data Privacy:** As more IoT devices fill our world, we can gather huge amounts of information and there are privacy issues and there is a higher susceptibility to cyber intrusion.

- **Cloud Security:** While cloud computing offers scalability and flexibility, it also introduces new security risks.
- **Data Breaches and Ransomware:** Clients' records hacked or their companies' ransomware attacked is not a rare case anymore, it is necessary to have adequate protection.
- **Regulatory Complexity:** There are numerous laws covering the protection of data across the world and they vary from one region to the other thus, observing them may be quite a herculean task.

**Possible Solutions**

- **Advanced Encryption Techniques:** Applying next-generation encryption methods that will help to protect organizations against future threats.
- **Privacy-Preserving Technologies:** Using technologies such as homomorphic encryption and differential privacy to preserve confidentiality or ownership rights of the data and yet being able to analyze the data for useful purposes.
- **AI for Cybersecurity:** Use of AI for identification and combating of cyber threats as they occur.
- **Blockchain:** Blockchain solution in the management of the data to enhance the security and transparency of the data being managed.
- **Data Minimization and Retention:** Collecting and further archiving only those data which, strictly speaking, are needed in order to limit risk.
- **Employee Training:** Organizing extensive courses that will make the concerned personnel realize possible risks and how they might be tackled.
- **Incident Response Planning:** Develop action checklists that contain proper strategies to react to information security incidents promptly.
- **International Cooperation:** Collaboration with other countries regarding the issues of data protection around the world.

### 10.6.7 Summary of the Data Protection

Data protection is a complex and dynamic area because it is marked by constant changes that occur due to technological developments, changes in legislation, and social norms. By understanding the complexities of global data transfer and implementing robust compliance strategies, organizations can mitigate risks, protect data, and maintain trust with customers and stakeholders.

We have examined basic concepts like privacy, security, and integrity of data and remainders of data protection. We have also evaluated some of the primary laws as the legal frameworks of data privacy, including GDPR, CCPA, and HIPAA which provide a legal framework for the protection of personal data. Moreover, we have analyzed how technology enhances and hinders the processing of data security, with reference to AI, ML, and blockchain.

Based on the analyzed case, the practical need for data protection requires the implementation of a multi-faceted strategy. This means legal, technical, and organizational solutions concerning a formulated hypothesis. An organization requires an effective security framework in place, good governance practices, and a culture shift toward data security within the firm.

Taking that into consideration, it would be pertinent to assert that data protection will also be dynamic with regard to future developments in technology as well as the risks that are yet to come. Businesses have to remain vigilant and assess risks, whereas the current pace and threat sophistication require in order to ensure the security of data.

Understanding the challenges in data protection and implementing the right strategies to deal with the situation enables organizations to establish trust with the customers, minimizing the risks hence contributing to the development of a safe digital environment.

#### *10.6.7.1 Applications of Data Privacy and Security in E-Health*

The e-health sector is at the forefront of data-driven innovation, with immense potential to improve patient outcomes. However, the sensitive nature of health data necessitates robust data privacy and security measures. Some of the key functions of data privacy and security in e-health are as follows:

**Patient Record Management:**
Secure storage of electronic health records (EHRs) to prevent unauthorized access.

- Implementing access controls to ensure only authorized personnel can view and modify patient information.

- Encrypting sensitive data to protect it from breaches.

**Telemedicine:**

- Secure transmission of patient data for remote consultations.
- Protecting patient privacy during video conferences.
- Ensuring the confidentiality of medical information exchanged digitally.

**Wearable Devices:**

- Secure data collection and transmission from wearable devices to healthcare providers.
- Protecting user privacy by minimizing data collection and providing clear consent options.

**Health Data Analytics:**

- Implementing data anonymization techniques to protect patient privacy while enabling valuable insights.
- Ensuring secure data sharing for research purposes.

**Mobile Health Apps:**

- Protecting user data through secure authentication and encryption.
- Complying with data privacy regulations (e.g., HIPAA and GDPR).

#### *10.6.7.2 Future Trends in Data Protection for E-Health*

Thanks to the new technology and new regulations, the e-health sector is standing on the threshold of radical changes. Looking into the future, maintaining health information security will also remain of the utmost importance, so the ideas for its protection should be searched for. Here is what is on the horizon:

**Key Trends**

- **AI and ML:** These technologies will play an increasingly important role in identifying and mitigating risks, detecting anomalies, and predicting potential breaches. However, ensuring the ethical and responsible use of AI in data protection will be critical.

- **Blockchain:** This could make a significant change to the transfer of data and handling of consent and make the practice more open and honest in healthcare.
- **Quantum Computing:** At the same time, it initiates new problems for encryption or opens up opportunities to devise new quantum-secure encryption methods for the preservation of data.
- **Privacy-Enhancing Technologies:** Techniques like differential privacy, homomorphic encryption, and federated learning will gain prominence in protecting sensitive health data while enabling data analysis.
- **Regulatory Evolution:** Data protection laws will continue to develop for new technologies, transfer of data, and rights of an individual.
- **Patient Empowerment:** The patient will get more active insights into his data and this will increase the need for better and easy-to-use tools as well as transparent data management.

The future of data protection in e-health presents both challenges and opportunities. Balancing innovation with security, ensuring data privacy while facilitating data sharing, and adapting to emerging threats will be critical. Organizations must invest in research and development, collaborate with industry peers, and build strong partnerships with regulators to navigate this complex landscape.

**Summary of this Chapter:**

Technological, legal, and ethical factors interact in a complex way inside the data protection landscape. Fundamentally, it is necessary to protect personal data from unwanted access, use, disclosure, interruption, alteration, or destruction. Technically speaking, the foundation of data protection is made up of security features including network security, access controls, and encryption. New technologies such as blockchain, AI, and ML provide creative answers to changing threats. These technologies do, however, also bring with them new difficulties that need serious examination of the ethical ramifications.

The legislative foundation for data protection is provided by legislative frameworks including the CCPA, GDPR, and HIPAA. In order to protect people's rights, these laws provide rules for data collection, processing, storage, and transmission. Observing these regulations is essential for businesses functioning in a globalized environment.

Data privacy, which stresses individual control over personal information, is a key component of data protection. In addition to the ability to stop its processing, these rights cover the ability to access, correct, or delete data. The requirement to safeguard individual privacy must be balanced by organizations with the necessity to use data for operational purposes.

In summary, the field of data protection is dynamic and necessitates constant adaptation to changes in the regulatory environment and technology. Encouraging companies and individuals to trust one another while protecting personal information requires a comprehensive strategy that takes legal, ethical, and technical factors into account.

## References


1. Stefaan Callens, A. and Cierkens, K., Legal aspects of E-Health, in: *Collaborative Patient Centred eHealth*, vol. 141, pp. 47–56, IOS Press, Amsterdam, Netherlands, 2008.
2. Cirillo, F., The Impact of the E-Health on Privacy and Fundamental Rights: from Confidentiality to Data Protection Regulation. *Eur. J. Privacy Law Technol.*, 2, 1–7, 2019.
3. Wilkowska, W. and Ziefle, M., Privacy and data security in E-health: Requirements from the user's perspective. *Health Inf. J.*, 18, 3, 191–201, 2012.
4. Amato, F. and Moscato, F., A model driven approach to data privacy verification in E-Health systems. *Trans. Data Privacy*, 8, 3, 273–296, 2015.
5. Liu, J., Xiong, L., Luo, J., Semantic Security: Privacy Definitions Revisited. *Trans. Data Privacy*, 6, 185–198, 2013.
6. Savic, D. and Veinovic, M., Challenges of General Data Protection Regulation. *International Scientific Conference on Information Technology And Data Related Research, SINTEZA 2018.*
7. El Mestari, S.Z., *et al.*, Preserving data privacy in machine learning systems. *Comput. Secur.*, 137, 1–22, February 2024.
8. Finck, M., Blockchain and the General Data Protection Regulation. *Int. Data Privacy Law*, 8, 2, 103–127, 2019.
9. Kairys, D., *International Encyclopedia of the Social & Behavioral Sciences (Second Edition)*, Elsevier, USA, 2015.
10. Bertino, E., Data Security and Privacy: Concepts, Approaches, and Research Directions. *IEEE 40th Annual Computer Software and Applications Conference (COMPSAC)*, Atlanta, GA, USA, pp. 400–407, 2016.

# 11

# An Extensive Review of Current Cybersecurity Trends in the Healthcare Sector

**Manoj Dhawan**[1]* **and Lalit Purohit**[2]

[1]*CSE Department, SGSITS, Indore, Madhya Pradesh, India*
[2]*Department of IT, SGSITS, Indore, Madhya Pradesh, India*

***Abstract***

Clinical treatment has relied more on computer technology over the past 10 years. The delivery of safe, dependable, and appropriate healthcare now necessitates the use of cybersecurity for healthcare information networks. A thorough analysis of the literature on healthcare and healthcare delivery was the goal of this research. This article's objective is to examine the literature on the steps taken by healthcare organizations to safeguard patients' private information, how breaches and vulnerabilities happen, and the effects on those organizations. A thorough search of peer-reviewed examination of English-language publications was conducted utilizing the Web of Science and PubMed databases. Chronological analysis, domain clustering, and text analysis were utilized to develop a comprehensive conceptual map, identifying key terms and their interconnections. Strengthening IT systems is crucial to ensuring reliability, protecting data, sustaining operations, and reducing risks from cyberattacks that threaten security and reputation. This article was mostly based on papers published between 2015 and 2020 on the topics of cybersecurity, cyberattacks, healthcare facilities, and patient health information. Cyberattacks are simple to carry out on devices with insecure IT or security systems.

***Keywords:*** Cybersecurity, bolstering information technology, attacks, healthcare, vulnerabilities

**Corresponding author*: manojreswork@gmail.com

Ajay Kumar Vyas, Harleen Kaur, Sourabh Sharma and Bhavya Alankar (eds.) Metaverse Technologies, Security and Applications for Healthcare, (255–276) © 2025 Scrivener Publishing LLC

## 11.1 Introduction

Cybersecurity is becoming an essential component of healthcare IT systems. From telemedicine and digital health records to mHealth apps for mobile devices and connected medical devices, the growing digitization of healthcare delivery raises cybersecurity issues [1]. The vulnerability of healthcare systems is one of the difficulties that they face. The digitization of medical records and the use of electronic equipment such as cell phones in telemedicine raise the danger of cybersecurity vulnerabilities. As part of their work, medical staff, such as doctors, nurses, and others, use a variety of mobile devices. These gadgets are one of the more natural ways for hackers to gain access to these institutions' databases. These individuals are in charge of safeguarding enterprises, with cybersecurity being a major worry. In 2019, an attack on a healthcare provider in a hospital in Georgia, USA, revealed over 278,016 individual records. The primary objective of the Privacy Rule is to ensure that an individual's health information is adequately protected while facilitating the necessary flow of information to deliver and achieve high-quality healthcare, thus safeguarding the well-being and health of the general public. In 1996, the United States Department of Health and Human Services (HHS) established the Privacy Rule to implement the provisions of the Health Insurance Portability and Accountability Act (HIPAA).

These flaws are of particular concern as healthcare cyberattacks have the potential to compromise highly sensitive personal data and interfere with the delivery of clinical care [2–5]. By compromising data integrity or interfering with the functionality of medical equipment, cyberattacks have the potential to endanger patient safety. The WannaCry and NotPetya ransomware attacks, as well as a bug in the programming of his Medtronic implantable cardiac device, are recent occurrences that had an impact on the effectiveness of healthcare service [6]. Cyber threats put healthcare institutions in grave danger. According to Verizon's 2018 Data Breach Investigations Report, 24% of all breaches investigated across various sectors occurred in the healthcare industry, making it the most affected. Furthermore, the Ponemon Institute discovered that almost 90% of participants had experienced data breaches in this sector, including employees from clearinghouses and health insurance firms as well as physicians who use electronic medical records, had dealt with a data breach in the two years prior [7]. I learned that more than 75% of medical information security professionals surveyed reported having lately dealt with security issues while working for healthcare organizations [8]. Human error and cultural issues are increasingly important determinants [9, 10]. There are many causes, and they affect both technology and humans. A recent study found that one in five healthcare workers still wrote down her ID and password on paper, despite initiatives to impart the best security practices through educational programs [6]. It is crucial to do a thorough analysis of the literature about the relationship between cybersecurity and healthcare, considering the increasing significance of cybersecurity in ensuring the secure, efficient, and reliable delivery of healthcare services. The results of 13 studies on cyber incident response in healthcare organizations and 31 papers on cyber threats in healthcare were recently summarized by a systematic analysis [10, 11]. A thorough examination of the present level of investigation into healthcare cybersecurity is essential to understanding existing trends, identifying knowledge gaps, and guiding future research efforts to enhance the security of healthcare systems. A significant literature review was conducted, highlighting the growing focus on cybersecurity within healthcare's IT infrastructure, including electronic medical records, telemedicine, mobile health (mHealth), and connected medical devices; the rapid digitization of healthcare is creating a cybersecurity gap. After all, a cyberattack in healthcare could reveal sensitive personal information or disrupt hospitals these vulnerabilities are especially concerning. Cyberattacks pose a significant risk to patient safety, especially when they disrupt the operation of medical devices or compromise essential data. Prominent instances of impaired healthcare services include the WannaCry and NotPetya ransomware attacks, alongside software vulnerabilities found in Medtronic's implantable cardiac devices.

Recent instances of interrupted healthcare services include the WannaCry and NotPetya ransomware outbreaks, along with programming flaws in Medtronic's implantable cardiology devices [7]. According to a different study of computer security professionals, more than 75% of healthcare organizations recently encountered a security incident [8]. Human error and societal factors aggravate the causes' multifactorial nature [9, 10]. Despite training programs promoting best-practice security behavior, one out of five healthcare employees still records their usernames and passwords on paper [6].

In light of the rising significance of cybersecurity in ensuring safe, effective, and reliable healthcare, it is crucial to evaluate the existing body of knowledge on this subject. Recent systematic evaluations combined knowledge of cyber threats from 31 articles with management strategies for cyber incidents in healthcare companies from 13 articles [10, 11]. We performed a thorough bibliometric analysis of the literature to chart the state of the field related to different facets of cybersecurity in healthcare. This initiative aimed to capture emerging trends, identify current weaknesses, and direct further studies to improve healthcare systems' security.

## 11.2 Related Work

Many healthcare organizations rely on the medical data they save, preserve, and communicate for their support and delivery. This information is the most vulnerable to cyberattacks and is the most likely to be made public. To address this problem, several security approaches have been created by researchers to shield data against nefarious attempts and breaches [8].

Three essential components are the security of information, security of data, and access control of big data security in the healthcare sector, according to Kim *et al.* [9]. They advised that companies secure the security of big data through the use of appropriate hardware and software for clinical and administrative data. Data retention, reuse, and auditing must all be done at the start of the project to ensure cost-effectiveness.

For knowledge generation, Yazan *et al.* [10] established a security architecture that includes data collecting, data storage, data processing, and data analysis. They provided a paradigm for the entire big data security life cycle.

Zhang and Liu [6] proposed an authentication-based security paradigm for data transfer over the Internet using the Transport layer and secure socket layer. It functions in a similar way as advanced web technologies such as online browsing, voice-over-IP (VoIP), electronic mail, Internet faxing, and so on. To authenticate the server, mutually trusted certificates can be utilized with secure socket later (SSL) or transport layer security (TLS).

Yang *et al.* [11] proposed a one-time pad algorithm–based authentication architecture that did away with the requirement for passwords between servers. The information about the consumer's identity and service providers must be validated every time access is granted, according to this paradigm.

To prevent unauthorized access to confidential healthcare data throughout the security life cycle, other encryption-based security models, such as DES, AES, RC6, 3DES, RC4, IDEA, RSA, Rijndael, and Blowfish, have also been proposed [6, 10, 12, 13]. The encryption key size varies based on how much data are being encrypted, which presents a major challenge for the researchers. By replacing sensitive data pieces with anonymous values, some academics have also used data masking technology to increase the security of big healthcare data. Then, in a de-identification method, these data elements are retrieved using quasi-identifiers.

To safeguard the identity of healthcare large data, Swaney and Samrati [14, 15] presented a k-anonymity strategy of data masking.

Truta *et al.* [16] enhanced this work by providing p-sensitive anonymity in the security framework by adding the attributes alongside the identification parameters. These approaches, on the other hand, were unable to perform well when dealing with high-dimensional dataset anonymity. Access control–based security techniques have also been suggested by healthcare researchers.

Attribute-based access control was presented by Mohan and Blough [17].

In addition, Zhou and Wen [18] suggested a cloud computing–based dynamic access control system that combined ciphertext and encryption techniques.

Wang *et al.* [19] suggested a framework for big data analytics for the healthcare industry using several big data methodologies. Large quantities of data are processed using parallel architectures such as Hadoop, MapReduce, pig Cassandra, HBase, Zookeeper, Oozie, Avro, Mahout, and others. Thanks to distributed design and parallel processing, the algorithm's complexity has been decreased.

Arellano *et al.* [20] examined policy publications on the common rule, HIPAA privacy and security laws, and governance, as well as patient perspectives, consent methods, and research ethics.

They recognized the major aspects of the revised common rule, as well as the most significant differences from the prior version.

Ive *et al.* [21] suggested a method for creating fictitious clinical papers. They analyze discharge summaries from intensive care units and a large mental health provider using this strategy. Additionally, they do a thorough intrinsic assessment that includes a variety of text preservation techniques, analyze the model's recall of training data, and use a human evaluation task to judge the resulting text's clinical validity.

Fine-grained access control predicates were proposed by Ulusoy *et al.* [22]. Each user can then view the files using this method after the user-specific predicates have been applied to them. The predicates individually execute the access control filters (ACFs) for individual records. According to the security policy, ACFs choose one of three actions: reject, grant, or amend.

Security considerations for the cloud computing warehouse where various stakeholders have access to the data were addressed by Guermazi *et al.* [23]. One of the first issues in the informatics field in 2007 was automated ICD-9 coding for radiological data. Two fundamental categories of techniques can be used to automatically give ICD-9 codes to clinical notes without any text. The first is founded on rules, and the second is based on learning. Experts in their particular fields create rule-based systems. In many cases, this strategy was more effective than other options [24]. This type of system, though, is challenging to maintain and expand to more widespread cases because it primarily relies on the physical assistance of medical professionals. Contrarily, learning-based systems depend on developing methods to determine the underlying distribution of datasets, so medical professionals are not required to possess any domain expertise [25]. In [27] and [28], the retrieval of information from written papers in the electronic health record (EHR) is thoroughly examined. Recently, end-to-end data-driven methodologies have grown in popularity. Deep learning–based algorithms have also shown cutting-edge success in a number of tasks, including computer vision, speech recognition, and natural language processing (NLP) [26].

Choi *et al.* [29] employed recurrent neural networks (RNNs) to predict heart failure in the clinical domain. Long short-term memory (LSTM) was used by Lipton *et al.* [30] to classify 128 illnesses based on 13 commonly but irregularly collected clinical measures retrieved from structured EHR data. Similarly, for diagnostic categorization, DoctorAI [31] and RETAIN [32] used RNNs on structured EHR data. To anticipate the diagnosis, many researchers employed deep learning on unstructured free text. For example, Bai suggested a deep transfer learning system for ICD-9 coding that made extensive use of MeSH domain knowledge [33].

Condensed memory neural networks and raw text from Wikipedia were used by Prakash *et al.* [34] to learn the diagnostic from Medical Information Mart for Intensive Care (MIMIC-III) data. Our findings were compared to their findings because they deal with situations that are comparable to ours. Zhang and Zhou [35] also contain an overview of contemporary deep learning algorithms for EHR.

Devlin *et al.* [36] suggested a unique transfer learning-based approach for efficient NLP. To process real-time linguistic data, the proposed study employs an encoder-based transfer learning system. BERT is the name of the suggested model, which uses a bidirectional model encoding strategy to extract the past and future values of the sequence in order to extract the text's context.

Perotte *et al.* [37] proposed a unique paradigm for encoding disease codes and assigning codes to reflect them in formal documentation. They have devised a system for determining the severity of diseases based on evaluation parameters and a variety of indicators.

Pestian *et al.* [4] combined the capabilities of the most recent NLP models with biological text data, referring to the technique as biomedical NLP.

The clinical data and ICD codes were combined to create a patient summary. On the basis of clinical text processing, a multi-label classification framework is suggested to discern the severity and seriousness of the condition.

On the basis of machine learning approaches, Pakhomov *et al.* [38] suggested an automatic diagnosis code assignment policy. They also extracted features from clinical text data and previous cases using a biological NLP technique.

Ling [39] has looked at a variety of mathematical modeling and analysis methodologies for clinical datasets. To support observations, a variety of datasets are used.

Krizhevsky *et al.* [40] proposed a novel deep learning configuration for clinical images, which utilized the convolutional neural network (CNN) for image classification. The ImageNet dataset is used to extract picture features and train the CNN for the appropriate categorization.

Graves *et al.* [41] took advantage of deep learning's promise for audio signal processing. To extract acoustic features and train and test the model with real-time data, the given study employs an RNN-based classification strategy.

Chiu *et al.* [42] looked into the more in-depth features of biomedical NLP and determined the key characteristics that are crucial in word embedding training in biomedical NLP. Many scholars have praised the effort because of the scarcity of a large corpus of biological and clinical data.

Huang *et al.* [43] evaluated the effectiveness of deep learning algorithms in automatically mapping clinical notes to ICD-9 medical codes. They focused on learning processes from beginning to finish without using human rules. The MIMIC-III collection has been subjected to both conventional machine learning algorithms and cutting-edge deep learning methods like RNN and CNN. With the MIMIC-III dataset, Nuthakki *et al.* [44] developed an NLP-based classification model. A framework for Hadoop Distributed File Systems was proposed by Reddy *et al.* [45]. The proposed framework provides a security paradigm that encrypts sensitive data and grants access tokens to authorized users. Theoretical foundations were provided, along with an objective function for managing user access to the database. The algorithms assist in the detection of an intruder. The access permissions and the resultant return value are included in the security model. The access authorization determines the return value.

To identify such data items, Kumar *et al.* [46] suggested a Sensitive Data Detection (SDD) methodology that uses data context, usage patterns, and data provenance. Airavat, a MapReduce-based security solution, was proposed by Srinath *et al.* [47]. A MapReduce-based solution that ensures strong security and privacy for sensitive data distributed computations. Customers can only access data within the bounds of the data providers' access rules, which are determined by the data providers and govern access to sensitive information.

Content Sensitivity Based Access Control (CSBAC), as developed by Kumar *et al.* [48], bases access choices on the content itself. Using the data to determine its sensitivity and implementing access control rules is a novel strategy in the Hadoop environment. The CSBAC framework also monitors variations in sensitivity when different datasets are linked. CSBAC is an automated system that requires very little user input and effort. It saves the Hadoop cluster's data owner and administrator a lot of time and work.

With the help of the below table, the author has given the detail of different authors.

| Ref. | Objectives | Methodology | Findings |
|---|---|---|---|
| [49] | To make improvements in the clinical notes encoding. | Used naive Bayes machine learning method for encoding experiment and experiment conducted on Weka tool. | • Used naive Bayes as a baseline method.<br>• Machine learning techniques have their limitations. |
| [22] | To authorize the files in the MapReduce model as per user categories. | Fine-grained access control predicates policy is used and the Vigiles system is implemented on the basis of Java security. | • Only the data owner's information is used in the process of finding sensitive information.<br>• According to the findings from Vigiles, the implementation that modifies the Hadoop source code has a 1% overhead. |

*(Continued)*

(*Continued*)

| | | | |
|---|---|---|---|
| [50] | To assess how well deep learning-based systems execute the automatic mapping of clinical notes to ICD-9 medical codes. | On the MIMIC-III dataset, modern deep learning techniques like RNN and CNN were used along with conventional machine learning algorithms. | • For forecasting the top 10 ICD-9 codes and categories, deep learning models fared better. |
| [51] | Predict final diagnoses by using NLP to link clinical notes to medical codes. | Pulled the necessary data from the MIMIC-III dataset after preprocessing. The necessary characteristics were then extracted using transfer learning in accordance with the demands of the language model. Finally, RNN was used to build the classifier models. | • Achieve good results.<br><br>Future work:<br>• Prediction with only a single model.<br>• To improve the speed and accuracy, some tweaks must be made. |
| [21] | To show a practical method for creating artificial clinical documents. | • Considered two datasets CRIS MHR and MIMIC III.<br>• Text generation with neural transformer model.<br>• BoW, LDA, and CNN are used as a text classification model. | • Able to generate artificial clinical data that may be disseminated to the broader research community, accelerating the creation of algorithmic methods utilizing medical data. |

(*Continued*)

(*Continued*)

| | | | |
|---|---|---|---|
| [45] | To avoid unauthorized access to sensitive data. | • The algorithms that govern unauthorized information are created by combining various hypotheses, definitions, propositions, and theorems. | • Implement the algorithms with the proper authorization rights to protect the organization's sensitive data. |
| [52] | By combining mandatory access control with differential privacy, end-to-end confidentiality, integrity, and privacy assurances are provided. | • First design a data collection process based on client-server architecture then categorize user groups for the data collection process.<br>• Interview and case studies for analyzing data.<br>• In the last work estimate the sensitive data and apply the most suitable security controls as per sensitivity level. | • Detected confidentiality issues with critical data categories in MHDCS.<br>• Estimated three degrees of sensitivity.<br>• A plug-in implementation of the data classification algorithm will be done in the future. |
| [46] | To suggest a framework for Hadoop access management that automates the manual process of manually identifying sensitive data items. | • Different key components introduce.<br>• Enhancing the meta-data generator.<br>• Putting the origin tracker into action.<br>• Estimating the measure of data similarity.<br>• Estimating the value of knowledge.<br>Locating confidential data elements. | The process of identifying sensitive data items is automated by the Sensitive Data Detection (SDD) framework that has been suggested.<br>SDD does not take into consideration differences in data sensitivity when combining multiple datasets. |

(*Continued*)

(*Continued*)

| | | | |
|---|---|---|---|
| [48] | To determine whether a dataset's individual data elements are sensitive or not. | The authors proposed different key components with different roles for the CSBAC framework: Enhanced Metadata Generator, Data Usage Tracker, Provenance Tracker, Data Similarity Analyzer, and Data Sensitivity Estimator. | • A novel Hadoop strategy involves estimating the data sensitivity and enforcing access control rules.<br>• The CSBAC framework detects sensitivity changes when numerous datasets are combined. |
| [20] | When sharing clinical data, which frequently holds sensitive information, privacy is a crucial factor to take into account. | Vital components of the updated common rule and the biggest adjustments since its prior iteration are noted in review policy articles. | • Patient privacy cannot be fully protected by the HIPAA privacy regulation, so ongoing vigilance through proactive policies and technological advancements is required. |
| [53] | The topic of risk assessment techniques is covered in depth, as is their applicability to IoMT. | Based on a quantified risk assessment approach. | Define a cutting-edge strategy or model for enhancing risk and trust management in the setting of e-health.<br>Future work will define an intelligent management strategy based on AI methods to check on the system's correct operation. |

## 11.3 Findings from the Review

The medical data that are saved, preserved, and sent by many healthcare organizations are critical to their support and delivery. This information is particularly sensitive to cyberattacks and is at risk of being made public. To address the problem, a number of researchers have developed several security models to protect data from malicious assaults and leaks [8].

Data protection, access management, and information safeguarding were identified as essential aspects of ensuring big data security within the healthcare industry [9]. They advised that enterprises protect the security of big data by using appropriate hardware and software for clinical and administrative data. To determine the cost-effectiveness of a project, it is necessary to do data retention, reuse, and auditing at the start.

For knowledge generation, Yazan *et al.* [10] proposed a security architecture that includes data collection, storage, processing, and analysis. They suggested a whole life-cycle model for large data security.

For data communication over the internet, Zhang and Liu [6] suggested an authentication-based security architecture using the transport layer and secure socket layer. It functions in a similar way as advanced web technologies such as online browsing, VoIP, electronic mail, and Internet faxing. The server can be authenticated using mutually trustworthy certificates through SSL or TLS.

Yang *et al.* [11] proposed a one-time pad algorithm–based authentication mechanism that eliminated the requirement for passwords between servers. The information about the consumer's identity and service providers must be validated each time access is granted, according to this approach.

Throughout the security life cycle, a number of encryption-based security models have been put out to stop unwanted access to private medical information, including RSA, Rijndael, AES and RC6, DES, 3DES, RC4, IDEA, and Blowfish [6, 10, 12, 13]. The researchers, on the other hand, face a significant hurdle because the size of the encryption key varies with the size of the data. Some academics have utilized data masking technology to improve the security of healthcare big data by substituting unidentifiable values for sensitive data items. These data pieces are then recovered using quasi-identifiers in a de-identification strategy.

To safeguard the identity of healthcare large data, Swaney and Samrati [14, 15] presented a k-anonymity data masking strategy.

Truta *et al.* [16] went on to propose p-sensitive anonymity in the security framework by integrating attributes with identification parameters. These approaches, on the other hand, were unable to cope with the anonymity of large datasets. Security techniques based on access control have also been proposed by healthcare researchers.

An attribute-based access control was proposed by Mohan and Blough [17].

Zhou and Wen [18] suggested a cloud-based dynamic access control system that combined ciphertext and encryption techniques.

By combining multiple big data methodologies, Wang *et al.* [19] proposed a framework for big data analytics in the healthcare sector. Hadoop, MapReduce, pig Cassandra, HBase, zookeeper, Oozie, Avro, Mahout, and other parallel architectures are used to process vast amounts of data. Parallel processing and distributed architecture have been used to reduce the algorithm's complexity.

Arellano *et al.* [20] examined policy publications on the common rule, HIPAA privacy and security laws, and governance, as well as patient perspectives, consent methods, and research ethics.

They recognized the revised common rule's essential elements as well as the most significant differences from the prior version.

Ive *et al.* [21] suggested a method for creating fictitious medical records. They use this method to analyze discharge reports from a major mental health provider and intensive care unit discharge summaries. After that, they carry out a thorough intrinsic assessment that uses a variety of text preservation measures to gauge how well the model retains training data and calculates the resulting text's clinical validity using a human evaluation task.

Fine-grained access control predicates were proposed by Ulusoy *et al.* [22]. Once the user-specific predicates have been applied to the files, each user can access them accordingly. The ACFs for individual records are run individually by the predicates. According to the security policy, ACFs conduct the following actions: refuse, grant, and modify. Security considerations for the cloud computing warehouse where various stakeholders have access to the data were addressed by Guermazi *et al.* [23].

Although numerous academics have provided several security frameworks for the fields of healthcare, the following are some of the most notable research works.

One of the initial issues in the informatics field in 2007 was automatic ICD-9 coding for radiological reports. For automatically allocating ICD-9 codes with clinical comments devoid of language, there are two basic groups of methods. The first is based on rules, whereas the second is based on learning. Human specialists develop rule-based systems [24]. In several circumstances, our procedure outperformed others.

However, because this kind of system mostly relies on medical personnel's physical involvement, scaling to larger applications and maintaining it is difficult. In contrast, learning-based systems utilize algorithms to identify the underlying distribution of datasets, eliminating the need for medical professionals to possess domain knowledge [25, 26]. Data extraction from textual records in the EHR is thoroughly examined by Goldstein *et al.* [27] and Meystre *et al.* [28]. In recent years, end-to-end data-driven approaches have become increasingly popular. NLP, computer vision, and speech recognition are just a few of the fields where recent improvements in deep learning algorithm performance have been seen [26].

Choi *et al.* used RNNs to predict heart failure in the clinical domain [29]. LSTM was used by Lipton *et al.* [30] to classify 128 diagnoses retrieved from structured EHR data using 13 commonly but irregularly sampled clinical measures. Similarly, RNNs were used on structured EHR data by DoctorAI [31] and RETAIN [32] to classify diagnoses. Deep learning was also employed by many researchers to predict the diagnosis using unstructured free text. Using a significant quantity of MeSH domain knowledge, Bai suggested a deep transfer learning architecture for ICD-9 coding [33].

Prakash *et al.* [34] used Wikipedia's raw text as a knowledge source, and condensed memory neural networks were utilized to extract the diagnosis from MIMIC-III data. Our findings were compared to theirs because they deal with difficulties that are comparable to ours. The work of Zhang and Zhou [35] also contains an overview of recent EHR deep learning approaches. Devlin *et al.* [36] suggested a unique transfer learning–based approach for NLP efficiency. To analyze real-time linguistic data, the proposed research uses an encoder-based transfer learning system. The proposed model is called BERT, and it uses a bidirectional model encoding approach to extract the text's past and future values.

Perotte *et al.* [37] proposed a new approach for illness encoding and assigning codes to represent them in formal documentation. They developed a system for determining the severity of diseases using numerous metrics and evaluation factors. Pestian *et al.* [4] combined the power of the most recent NLP models with biological text data and dubbed the technology biomedical NLP. A summary of the patient was created using clinical information and ICD codes. On the basis of clinical text processing, a multi-label classification framework is suggested to discriminate disease severity and seriousness.

On the basis of machine learning approaches, Pakhomov *et al.* [38] established an automatic diagnosis code assignment policy. They have also extracted features from clinical text data and previous examples using a biological NLP technique. Ling [39] investigated a variety of mathematical modeling and analysis strategies for clinical datasets. To justify observations, several datasets are used.

Krizhevsky *et al.* [40] employed CNN for image categorization and provided a novel deep learning configuration for clinical images. The ImageNet dataset is investigated in order to extract picture features and train the CNN for classification. Graves *et al.* [41] use deep learning for audio signal analysis. To extract acoustic features and train and test the model using real-time data, the reported study uses an RNN-based classification strategy.

Chiu *et al.* [42] looked into the more in-depth features of biomedical NLP and discovered the key characteristics that play a role in word embedding training in biomedical NLP. Many scholars have acknowledged the effort because of the scarcity of a large corpus of biomedical and clinical data. Huang *et al.* [43] investigated the efficacy of deep learning–based systems for mapping clinical notes to ICD-9 medical codes automatically. They concentrated on end-to-end learning approaches that did not rely on rules that had to be manually specified. The MIMIC-III dataset has traditionally been used to test machine learning algorithms and cutting-edge deep learning techniques like CNN and RNN.

The NLP-based classification model was developed with the MIMIC-III dataset by Nuthakki *et al.* [44]. For Hadoop Distributed File Systems, Reddy *et al.* [45] presented a framework. The proposed architecture includes a security paradigm that encrypts sensitive data and allows valid users access tokens. The theoretical underpinnings were supplied, as well as an objective function enabling user access to the database. Intruder detection is aided by the algorithms. Access privileges and the consequent return value are part of the security model. The value returned is determined by the level of access.

To identify such data items, Kumar *et al.* [46] suggested an SDD system, which uses data context, usage patterns, and provenance. Airavat, a MapReduce-based security system, was proposed by Srinath *et al.* [47]. A MapReduce-based system enables distributed computations on sensitive data while providing strong security and privacy assurances. Consumers can only access data within the boundaries of the data providers' access regulations for sensitive information. CSBAC, as developed by Kumar *et al.* [48], makes choices about access depending on the information itself. An innovative approach within the Hadoop environment involves using data to assess its sensitivity and applying access control restrictions accordingly. Moreover, the CSBAC framework reflects differences in sensitivity when different datasets are joined. CSBAC is a fully automated framework that requires very little human interaction. For the data owner and Hadoop cluster administrator, it saves a lot of time and work. Ksibi *et al.* [53] examined which risk assessment techniques are suitable for IoMT. Given its significant risk exposure, the authors suggested a paradigm to improve trust and aid in decision-making in e-healthcare situations. Based on a defined risk assessment methodology, the suggestion is as follows.

## 11.4 Limitations and Suggestions for Future Research

Imagine waking up every morning to a world in which your individual device precisely recommends the supplements you should take based on your previous week's nutrition, environment, activity, and stress levels. In order to achieve the common objective of enhancing the manner in which patients receive healthcare, the healthcare industry is entering a new era in which nearly everything is connected to digital technologies. There is no more guessing in this future; customers will be able to manage their own health on their own.

Cybersecurity lies at the heart of all of these exciting developments. As the healthcare industry's future develops, so will the risks associated with cybersecurity. The future of healthcare is increasingly tied to cyber technologies, bringing with it significant cybersecurity challenges. The problems with cybersecurity that go along with them, and the actions that leaders can take to deal with the changing threats posed by cybersecurity in healthcare [54].

**Expected in the Future**

- Fundamentally interoperable data that enable highly engaged customers to stay healthy.
- Always on sensors and platforms that collect data and platforms that collect, store, and drive insights.
- Proactive and predictive care that adapts to the needs of empowered consumers. In the future of health, data will be shared, collected, and analyzed on a larger scale. By using this information to increase operational efficiency and improve customer retention, healthcare organizations can create new value. As part of this transformation, businesses must pay more attention to data protection and modernize their data protection standards. They will also face pressure to improve cybersecurity threat awareness, detection, and response in the healthcare sector. As the future of healthcare evolves more rapidly than anticipated, largely due to the COVID-19 pandemic, leaders must brace for a swiftly

> changing risk landscape associated with advancements and innovation. It is essential to begin by recognizing the six factors that are expected to play a pivotal role in shaping the future of healthcare cybersecurity: agility, data, device ecosystem, AI, and usability. Typical healthcare privacy and cybersecurity practices are not known to be agile or adapt quickly to change [55]. These groups should be incorporated into pilot efforts being conducted by nontraditional departments within the organization. This allows them to benefit from insights and insights that make those people, processes, technologies, and data capabilities more agile and future-proof. This not only helps cyber adapt to fast-paced change but also enables more successful digital health-related innovations within organizations. Numerous seismic shifts are imminent in the healthcare sector. New risks will continue to be elevated and introduced by innovations and external factors. New healthcare services and solutions must be piloted and implemented with cybersecurity and privacy fully integrated by design now more than ever. In addition, players in the industry are obligated to responsibly embrace the forces driving change and the challenges that lie ahead, not only to fulfill the promise of the health of the future but also to make tomorrow safe and secure.

The search strategy's phrases were only found in papers with titles or abstracts that contained information; other articles were not recovered because they used different terminology. We also only incorporated tales that had cybersecurity at their core. Journal articles, conference papers, white papers, and reports issued by governments or other agencies were the only non-English language items we evaluated. In a more in-depth search, these sites might be used. The work being done in the areas of healthcare and computer security is largely administrative and operational rather than intellectual, which is significant. When it comes to cutting-edge diagnosis or treatments, IT security experts could rely less on academic material than doctors, preferring instead "on-the-job" expertise and industry standard practices. Furthermore, security considerations may prevent information security research done within the healthcare ecosystem from being published, such as the potential disclosure of internal vulnerabilities. A great way to start is by reading the literature that has already been published in this area. Anywhere research is done, transparency will benefit hospitals and patients.

## 11.5 Conclusion

The two major factors putting healthcare at risk from cyber threats are rapid technological advancement and shifting federal policy. Due to its difficulties in implementing new technologies and security procedures, hospital IT infrastructure is a common target for medical information stealing. While the government and security companies have made strides in reducing the frequency of cyberattacks, the healthcare sector continues to fall behind other major industries in protecting sensitive information. The rising threat of ransomware, which targets critical infrastructure and compromises private patient data, along with other emerging cybersecurity trends and threats, necessitates that healthcare continuously adapt its security measures. Maintaining and protecting the secrecy of patient data from unauthorized access, as well as the security of healthcare technology, require significant time and effort.

## References

1. Sharathkumar, S. and Jagadamba, G., Adaptive content-aware access control of EPR resource in a healthcare system. *2017 International Conference on Advances in Computing, Communications and Informatics (ICACCI)*, Udupi, pp. 205–210, 2017.
2. Dev Mishra, A. and Beer Singh, Y., Big data analytics for security and privacy challenges. *2016 International Conference on Computing, Communication and Automation (ICCCA)*, Noida, pp. 50–53, 2016.
3. Larkey, L.S. and Bruce Croft, W., Automatic assignment of icd9 codes to discharge summaries. Technical report, Technical report, University of Massachusetts at Amherst, Amherst, MA, 1995.
4. Pestian, J.P., Brew, C., Matykiewicz, P., Hovermale, D.J., Johnson, N., Bretonnel Cohen, K., Duch, W., A shared task involving multi-label classification of clinical free text, in: *Proceedings of the Workshop on BioNLP 2007: Biological, Translational, and Clinical Language Processing*, Association for Computational Linguistics, pp. 97–104, 2007.
5. Ribeiro-Neto, B., Laender, A.H.F., De Lima, L.R.S., An experimental study in automatically categorizing medical documents. *J. Assoc. Inf. Sci. Technol.*, 52, 5, 391–401, 2001.
6. Zhang, R. and Liu, L., Security models and requirements for healthcare application clouds, in: *IEEE 3rd international conference on cloud computing*, 2010.

7. Liang, X., Lu, R., Chen, L., Lin, X., Shen, X., Pec: A privacy preserving emergency call scheme for mobile healthcare social networks. *Commun. Networks J.*, 13, 2, 102–112, April 2011.
8. Mashima, M.A.D., Bauer, D., Blough, D., User-centric identity management architecture using credential-holding identity agents, in: *Digital Identity and Access Management: Technologies and Frameworks*, IGI Global, Hershey, PA, USA, December 2012.
9. Kim, S.-H., Kim, N.-U., Chung, T.-M., Attribute relationship evaluation methodology for big data security, in: *2013 international conference on IT convergence and security (ICITCS)*, IEEE, pp. 1–4.
10. Yazan, A., Yong, W., Raj Kumar, N., Big data life cycle: threats and security model, in: *21st Americas conference on information systems*, 2015.
11. Yang, C., Lin, W., Liu, M., A novel triple encryption scheme for hadoop-based cloud data security, in: *Emerging intelligent data and web technologies (EIDWT), 2013 fourth international conference on*, pp. 437–42, 2013.
12. Wu, X., Wu, G.Q., Ding, W., Data Mining with Big Data. *IEEE Trans. Knowl. Data Eng.*, 26, 1, 97–107, Dec. 2012.
13. Ghinita, G., *Privacy for location-based services synthesis*, Lectures on Information Security, Privacy, and Trust, University of Massachusetts, Boston, Tech. Rep, April 2013.
14. Sweeney, L., Achieving k-anonymity privacy protection using generalization and suppression. *Int. J. Uncertainty Fuzziness Knowledge Based Syst.*, 10, 571–88, 2002.
15. Samrati, P., Protecting respondents' identities in microdata release. *IEEE Trans. Knowl. Data Eng.*, 13, 1010–27, 2001.
16. Truta, T.M. and Vinay, B., Privacy protection: p-sensitive k-anonymity property, in: *Proceedings of 22nd international conference on data engineering workshops*, p. 94, 2006.
17. Mohan, A. and Blough, D.M., An attribute-based authorization policy framework with dynamic conflict resolution, in: *Proceedings of the 9th symposium on identity and trust on the internet*, 2010.
18. Zhou, H. and Wen, Q., Data security accessing for HDFS based on attribute-group in cloud computing, in: *International conference on logistics engineering, management and computer science (LEMCS 2014)*, 2014.
19. Wang, H., Yin, J., Perng, C.S., Yu, P.S., Dual encryption for query integrity assurance, in: *Proceedings of the 17th ACM conference on Information and knowledge management*, 2008, October, ACM, pp. 863–872.
20. Arellano, A.M., Dai, W., Wang, S., Jiang, X., Ohno-Machado, L., Privacy Policy and Technology in Biomedical Data Science. *Annu. Rev. Biomed. Data Sci.*, 1, 115–129, 2018 Jul, doi: 10.1146/annurev-biodatasci-080917-013416.
21. Ive, J., Viani, N., Kam, J., Yin, L., Verma, S., Puntis, S., Cardinal, R.N., Roberts, A., Stewart, R., Velupillai, S., Article: Generation and evaluation of artificial mental health records for Natural Language Processing. *npj Digital Med.*, 3, 69, 2020.

22. Ulusoy, H., Kantarcioglu, M., Pattuk, E., Hamlen, K., Vigiles: Fine-grained Access Control for MapReduce Systems. *IEEE International Congress on Big Data*, pp. 40–47, 2014.
23. Guermazi, E., *et al.*, Adaptive security for Cloud data warehouse as a service. *2015 IEEE/ACIS 14th International Conference on Computer and Information Science (ICIS)*, pp. 647–650, 2015.
24. Bhansali, A. and Gupta, N., Embedding Color Watermark by Adjusting DCT using RGB Gray Scale Watermarking. *IEEE InternationalEmerging Trends in Industry 4.0 (ETI 4.0)*, pp. 1–4, 2021.
25. Choi, E., Bahadori, M.T., Sun, J., Kulas, J., Schuetz, A., Stewart, W., Retain: An interpretable predictive model for healthcare using reverse time attention mechanism, in: *Advances in Neural Information Processing Systems*, pp. 3504–3512, 2016.
26. Gupta, N., Embedding Color Watermark in a Digital image by Adjusting DCT Coefficients through Back Propagation Neural Network using RGB Gray Scale watermarking and subsequent Union of RGB planes. *Test Eng. Manage.*, 82, 375–380, 2020.
27. Goldstein, I., Arzumtsyan, A., Uzuner, Ö., Three approaches to automatic assignment of ICD-9-CMcodes to radiology reports, in: *AMIA Annual Symposium Proceedings*, vol. 2007, American Medical Informatics Association, p. 279, 2007.
28. Meystre, S.M., Savova, G.K., Kipper-Schuler, K.C., Hurdle, J.F., *et al.*, Extracting information from textual documents in the electronic health record: a review of recent research. *Yearb. Med. Inform.*, 35, 128, 44, 2008.
29. Choi, E., Schuetz, A., Stewart, W.F., Sun, J., Using recurrent neural network models for early detection of heart failure onset. *J. Am. Med. Inf. Assoc.*, 23, Article ocw112, 2016.
30. Lipton, Z.C., Kale, D.C., Elkan, C., Wetzell, R., Learning to diagnose with LSTM recurrent neural networks, arXiv preprint arXiv:1511.03677, 2015.
31. Baker, S. and Korhonen, A., Initializing neural networks for hierarchical multilabel text classification, in: *BioNLP 2017*, Association for Computational Linguistics, Vancouver, Canada, pp. 307–315, 2017.
32. Zeng, M., Li, M., Fei, Z., Yu, Y., Pan, Y., Wang, J., Automatic icd-9 coding via deep transfer learning. *Neurocomputing*, 324, 43–50, 2019.
33. Lample, G. and Conneau, A., Cross-lingual Language Model Pretraining, ArXiv abs/1901.07291, 2019.
34. Prakash, A., Zhao, S., Hasan, S.A., Datla, V.V., Lee, K., Qadir, A., Liu, J., Farri, O., Condensed memory networks for clinical diagnostic inferencing, in: *AAAI*, pp. 3274–3280, 2017.
35. Zhang, M.-L. and Zhou, Z.-H., A review on multi-label learning algorithms. *IEEE Trans. Knowl. Data Eng.*, 26, 8, 1819–1837, 2014.
46. Devlin, J., *et al.*, BERT: Pre-training of Deep Bidirectional Transformers for Language Understanding, in: *NAACL-HLT*, 2019.

37. dutta, V. and Gupta, N., entimental analysis using Deep Learning techniques. *Int. J. Sci. Res. Publ.*, 12, 2, 550–575, 2022.
38. Pakhomov, S.VS., Buntrock, J.D., Chute, C.G., Automating the assignment of diagnosis codes to patient encounters using example-based and machine learning techniques. *J. Am. Med. Inf. Assoc.*, 13, 5, 516–525, 2006.
39. Ling, Y., Methods and Techniques for Clinical Text Modeling and Analytics. PhD thesis, Drexel University, 2017.
40. Krizhevsky, A., Sutskever, I., Hinton, G.E., Imagenet classification with deep convolutional neural networks, in: *Advances in neural information processing systems*, pp. 1097–1105, 2012.
41. Graves, A., Mohamed, A.-., Hinton, G., Speech recognition with deep recurrent neural networks, in: *Acoustics, speech and signal processing (ICASSP), 2013 IEEE international conference on*, IEEE, pp. 6645–6649, 2013.
42. Chiu, B., Crichton, G., Korhonen, A., Pyysalo, S., How to train good word embeddings for biomedical NLP. *Proceedings of the 15th Workshop on Biomedical Natural Language Processing*, pp. 166–174, 2016.
43. Huang, J., Osorio, C., Sy, L.W., An Empirical Evaluation of Deep Learning for ICD-9 Code Assignment using MIMIC-III Clinical Notes. ELSEVIER, *Comput. Methods Programs Biomed.*, 177, 141–153, August 2019.
44. Nuthakki, S., Neela, S., Gichoya, J.W., Purkayastha, S., Natural language processing of MIMIC-III clinical notes for identifying diagnosis and procedures with neural networks, Capstone Project that was accepted by the Faculty of Indiana University, arXiv:1912.12397.
45. Reddy, Y.B., Access Control for Sensitive Data in Hadoop Distributed File Systems. *The Third International Conference on Advanced Communications and Computation INFOCOMP 2013*, pp. 72–78.
46. TK, A.K., Liu, H., Thomas, J.P., Mylavarapu, G., Identifying Sensitive Data Items within Hadoop. *2015 IEEE 17th International Conference on High Performance Computing and Communications (HPCC), 2015 IEEE 7th International Symposium on Cyberspace Safety and Security (CSS), and 2015 IEEE 12th International Conf on Embedded Software and Systems (ICESS)*, pp. 1308–1313, 2015.
47. Roy, I., Setty, S.T.V., Kilzer, A., Shmatikov, V., Witchel, E., Airavat: Security and Privacy for MapReduce. *7th USENIX conference on Networked systems design and implementation NSDI 2010*, pp. 297–312.
48. T.K., A.K., Liu, H., Thomas, J.P., Hou, X., Content sensitivity based access control framework for Hadoop. *Digital Commun. Networks*, 3, 4, 213–225, November 2017.
49. Medori, J. and Fairon, C., Machine learning and features selection for semi-automatic icd-9-cm encoding, in: *proceedings of the NAACL HLT 2010 Second Louhi Workshop on Text and Data Mining of Health Documents*, Association for Computational Linguistics, pp. 84–89, 2010.

50. Huang, J., Osorio, C., Wicent Sy, L., An Empirical Evaluation of Deep Learning for ICD-9 Code Assignment using MIMIC-III Clinical Notes. *Comput. Methods Programs Biomed.*, 177, 141–153, August 2019.
51. Nuthakki, S., Neela, S., Gichoya, J.W., Purkayastha, S., Natural language processing of MIMIC-III clinical notes for identifying diagnosis and procedures with neural networks, Capstone Project that was accepted by the Faculty of Indiana University, arXiv:1912.12397.
52. Katarahweire, M., Bainomugisha, E., Mughal, K.A., Data Classification for Secure Mobile Health Data Collection Systems. *J. Dev. Eng.*, 5, 100054, June 2020.
53. Ksibi, S., Jaidi, F., Bouhoula, A., A Comprehensive Study of Security and Cyber-Security Risk Management within e-Health Systems: Synthesis, Analysis and a Novel Quantified Approach. *Mob. Netw. Appl.*, 24, 1232–1246, 2022, https://doi.org/10.1007/s11036-022-02042-1.
54. Jarrett, M., Cybersecurity-A Serious Patient Care Concern. *JAMA*, 318, 14, 1319–1320, 2017 Oct 10, doi: 10.1001/jama.2017.11986.
55. Kramer, D. and Fu, K., Cybersecurity Concerns and Medical Devices: Lessons From a Pacemaker Advisory. *JAMA*, 318, 21, 2077–2078, 2017 Dec 05, doi: 10.1001/jama.2017.15692.

12

# Implementation of Metaverse Technologies and Its Security

**Manas Tiwari[1*], Kamal Kumar Kushwah[2†], Hameed Khan[3] and Ajay Kumar Vyas[4]**

[1]*Department of Electrical Engineering, Jabalpur Engineering College, Jabalpur, Madhya Pradesh, India*
[2]*Department of Applied Physics, Jabalpur Engineering College, Jabalpur, Madhya Pradesh, India*
[3]*Department of Computer Science & Engineering, Jabalpur Engineering College, Jabalpur, Madhya Pradesh, India*
[4]*Department Information and Communication Technology, Adani University, Ahmedabad, Gujarat, India*


## *Abstract*

The metaverse—a developing digital space that combines virtual reality (VR), augmented reality (AR), and mixed reality (MR)—has the potential to drive significant innovations in healthcare. This study examines how the metaverse could transform healthcare delivery, focusing on areas such as telemedicine, medical education and training, patient engagement, and clinical research. Possible enhancements in a metaverse-enabled future include virtual health clinics, high-fidelity medical simulations, advanced patient support groups, and globally cooperative study environments that promote collective efforts. While the metaverse holds promise, it faces issues related to privacy, security, and technical access, making it difficult to implement in healthcare. It is necessary to overcome these roadblocks to fully realize the advantages of the metaverse. By overcoming these challenges, it will allow us to achieve personalized healthcare, improve productivity, and increase the accessibility of health and social services. The findings of this study highlight significant moral and technological obstacles when taking advantage of the metaverse to enhance healthcare, which requires nuanced ethical consideration. This evolution in the metaverse could indicate the future


*Corresponding author*: Manast619@gmail.com
†*Corresponding author*: kamal_kushwah2005@yahoo.com

Ajay Kumar Vyas, Harleen Kaur, Sourabh Sharma and Bhavya Alankar (eds.) Metaverse Technologies, Security and Applications for Healthcare, (277–296) © 2025 Scrivener Publishing LLC

landscape of healthcare, defined by a moment when the digital and physical worlds merge to expand capabilities for patient care delivery—driven by research and facilitated by technology.

***Keywords:*** Patient participation, virtual and augmented reality, healthcare education, multiverse, data protection

## 12.1 Introduction

The way we interact with people, use technology, and live our lives is being disrupted by a new digital domain known as the metaverse [1]. Consider stepping into a vast digital reality, where individuals can interact, learn, and collaborate remotely. While the metaverse remains a developing concept, it is obvious that healthcare, in particular, has the potential to be changed entirely. These are the basic experiences of virtual reality (VR), augmented reality (AR), and mixed reality (MR), which enable a more complete immersive experience. These three technology layers make up the elements that glue together what is known as the metaverse. VR headgear, controllers, and haptic devices are used in VR settings with exploratory behaviors for game users [2]. It differs from regular reality in that more layers of digital information are superimposed over our regular environment, adding "navigation" and other interactive enhancements to real-world objects. In contrast, mixed reality merges VR and AR, allowing virtual objects to coexist alongside the real environment [3]. Altogether, these technologies comprise the framework behind the metaverse, offering new ways for people to connect and engage that would have been unimaginable before. The metaverse gives us endless possibilities, including healthcare opportunities, opening up new pathways for conducting research, delivering care, and engaging patients. The need for improved, personalized care is especially timely with global healthcare systems grappling with issues of aging populations and escalating costs. The delivery of healthcare could be revolutionized by the metaverse. Training environments for medical students promote active, immersive learning, while virtual clinic 'care corners' leverage telemedicine tools for remote consultations [4]. One interesting use for the metaverse in healthcare is to improve telemedicine and enable remote consultations. The COVID-19 pandemic revealed the demand for telemedicine from locations with limited or no clinical assistance. The metaverse takes this further by creating digital healthcare campuses where patients and doctors can interact as if they are physically in the same place [5]. Imagine seeing a doctor via VR, examining full medical records, and even having physical examinations through advanced haptic feedback solutions. This could enhance patient-doctor relationships as well as the effectiveness of treatment—at scale. The use of the metaverse in medical education and training offers several potential advantages. Traditional approaches rely on empirical experience, which can be limited by access to resources or concerns for patient safety. The metaverse changes this by allowing professionals and students to create virtual simulations to practice procedures risk-free [6]. These simulations offer students a realistic approach to everything from regular physical examinations to the most unusual clinical conditions, preparing them for any situation in therapy. The metaverse could also play a major role in living organs and tissue banks. Chronic pain and anxiety are already treated with VR therapy [7]. This is complemented by the metaverse, which provides an even deeper wellness experience. For example, patients can join online support groups where they mingle with individuals undergoing similar challenges in a supportive and uplifting atmosphere. Moreover, the metaverse enables the deployment of extremely personalized care models that meet every patient's specific needs and result in better therapeutic outcomes across the board.

The metaverse in healthcare has its complexities. If we do not address the security and privacy of data, then patient health as well as consumer faith in AI-generated results may be compromised. It is also necessary to overcome technical challenges such as infrastructure and accessibility issues, in order for everyone to benefit from these improvements. Figure 12.1 shows

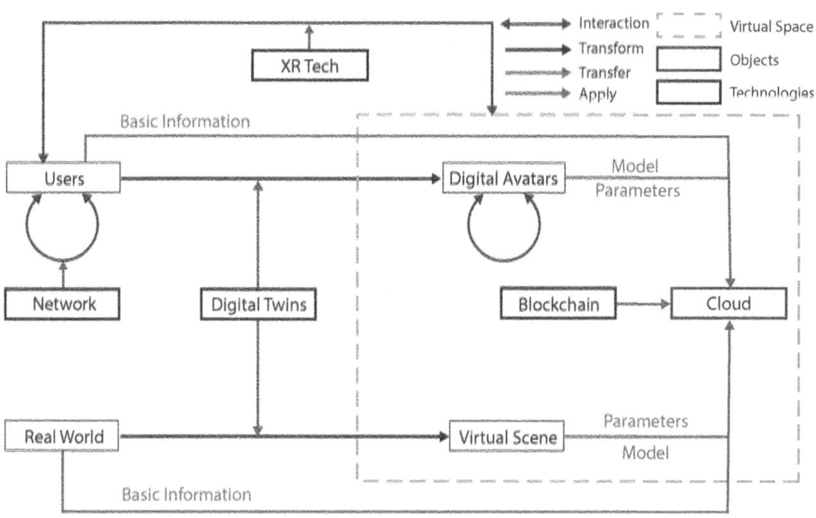


**Figure 12.1** The metaverse's general technological architecture.

the overview of the metaverse's general technological architecture, illustrating key components such as virtual environments, blockchain, AI integration, IoT connectivity, and user interface technologies. In this article, we will run a deep analysis of how the metaverse could change healthcare. Consideration for potential uses will be given to include patient involvement, medical research, and telemedicine, among others. It will also highlight the technical and ethical challenges that we must address as a society to ensure that this exciting future is just and humane.

The big idea is that the metaverse with its collaborative and immersive qualities holds unparalleled promise in revolutionizing healthcare—not as a magical tech solution looking for an ailment. The central idea is that the metaverse, with its collaborative and immersive qualities, holds immense potential to revolutionize healthcare—not as a one-size-fits-all solution, but as a tool requiring a balanced approach to challenges and opportunities. To navigate this emerging landscape, policymakers, technologists, and healthcare professionals must collaborate closely [8]. The metaverse in healthcare is more than just a vision of the future—it is on its way here and could change care delivery dramatically.

## 12.2 Unpacking the Metaverse and Its Key Ingredients

The metaverse refers to a virtual tech-scape that fuses several technologies to deliver an all-encompassing experience. This combination of VR, AR, and MR means that users are placed in an interactive environment for a more intensive experience. Figure 12.2 illustrates the three primary augmented reality (AR) technologies.

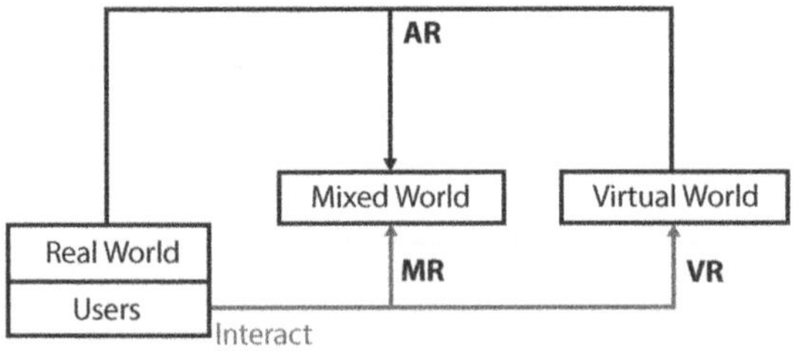


**Figure 12.2** A schematic representation of the three AR technologies.

### 12.2.1 Virtual Reality (VR)

VR transports users to completely virtual environments. As a result of headsets and bespoke hardware, we can immerse ourselves in 3D places so that the world continues to hold meaning.

### 12.2.2 Augmented Reality (AR)

AR adds digital elements to a live view of the current world, unlike VR. With the use of smartphones or AR glasses, individuals should be able to see and communicate with digital content in real time—blending it into their surroundings while mixing both realities.

### 12.2.3 Mixed Reality (MR)

MR merges the immersive nature of VR and AR to create a new world that contains both digital objects and actual items, in an interaction that transcends traditional user interface devices such as controllers or keyboards. Imagine users being able to interact with both physical and virtual worlds at the same time; it would be an incredibly immersive and seamless experience that neither VR nor AR can offer alone. The metaverse is built on these fundamental technologies, with unlimited potential for communication, teamwork, and innovation in many fields.

### 12.2.4 Metaverse Enables in Health Space

Medical services delivery could be a remarkable change that the metaverse brings about. For instance, telemedicine is significantly improved by allowing physicians and patients to interact in a fully interactive 3D setting. VR simulations are very useful for medical education as physicians can practice operations in a virtual environment, which is safe. While undergoing operations, AR can show surgeons pertinent details almost literally in front of their eyes. The metaverse could also bring an extreme and safest view of healthcare for all people. Rural individuals would be able to connect with well-known physicians and resources without even going anywhere. The convergence of VR, AR, and MR technology within the metaverse has great potential to revolutionize healthcare as a whole. With improved healthcare, redefined medical education, and access to care, we can achieve huge leaps in global healthcare delivery.

The integration of the metaverse into our healthcare system delivers the most fundamental shift in how medical services are delivered. Gone are the

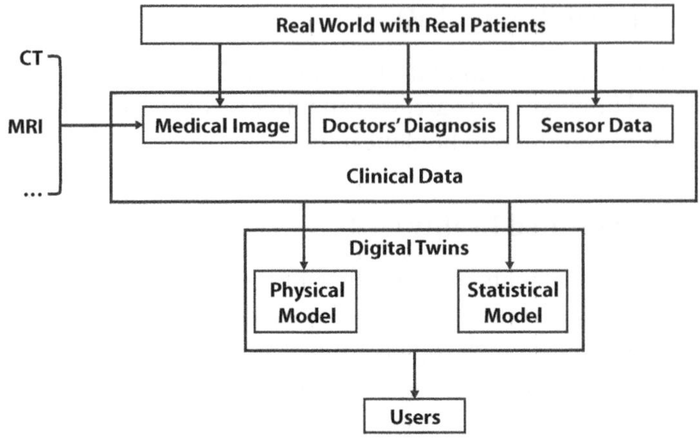


**Figure 12.3** Digital twins used in medicine in operation.

days when it was simply a best effort; revolutionary technologies, such as VR, AR, and MR, have been defining roles in innovation within the healthcare space. Due to the rapid development of telemedicine, patient-physician communication, and medical education, all are under the healthcare sector itself [9]. Figure 12.3 illustrates the application of digital twin technology in medicine, showing how real-time data from a patient's physical body is mirrored in a virtual model.

### 12.2.5 Telemedicine and Remote Consultations

Telemedicine is indispensable in addressing global health problems we face today within the existing healthcare scene. The metaverse is the next step, offering virtual clinics where patients can speak directly with doctors in 3D mode. This technology offers a more immersive experience than typical video conversations and helps patients feel more connected to their healthcare providers, even when they cannot be in the same place. Imagine patients consulting with doctors in these virtual clinics designed to alleviate the isolation often felt during remote sessions. These may look like real hospitals, or they could simply be made to appear so reassuring. For instance, something a person with disabilities can navigate through those virtual spaces without the barriers of reality.

Progress also benefits healthcare providers for tests; they will be able to use digital units for 3D patient data visualization with robust VR and AR performance. Specialized collaboration improved diagnostic accuracy and increased the provision of coordinated treatment irrespective of geography [10]. To put these virtual clinics into practice, it will require a solid technology infrastructure—fast Internet connections, modern VR and AR equipment, and secure forms of sharing private data. Ensuring the system is user-friendly and accessible to all is essential. Equally important is prioritizing patient data security, which is crucial for fostering trust and encouraging the adoption of these cutting-edge technologies.

This strategy could involve the metaverse—a concept that only a few hospitals are currently exploring. For example, XYZ Hospital introduced a virtual clinic that operates globally, enabling interactions between patients and doctors. This initiative significantly expanded access to care and may signal the future of telemedicine. As exciting as it sounds, this is a challenging transition. These problems are significant: sustaining outdated technology, ensuring the basic right to the Internet for everyone, and protecting people from data misuse. However, these challenges also allow opportunities for better user experiences and safer communication methods [11]. As the metaverse transforms medical education, we envision a future where aspiring healthcare professionals can undergo safe, highly effective, and impactful hands-on training. Imagine a student practicing surgery or emergency procedures in virtual reality, with no risk to real individuals. These methods are priceless to get hands-on experience simulating realistic cases of procedures and doctor-patient interactions by utilizing VR and AR technology. Research shows that students practicing with VR enhance their efficiency and self-assurance in contrast to relying only upon textbooks or lectures.

Students can make the program their own by participating in these types of experiences that allow them to tailor their education and focus on areas they struggle with. One of the most interesting aspects is haptic feedback, which provides a realistic sense similar to feeling through surgical operations. Consequently, trainees might be able to acquire skills and perform relevant exams that were previously not possible. They use AR to teach anatomy and VR for practical exercises in bathing. The growth of medical education will become greater in the future by these improvements that increase student engagement (Figure 12.4).

## 12.3 Patient Engagement and Therapy in the Metaverse

By utilizing virtual reality, innovative methods are being developed for therapeutic interventions across various dimensions, enabling greater

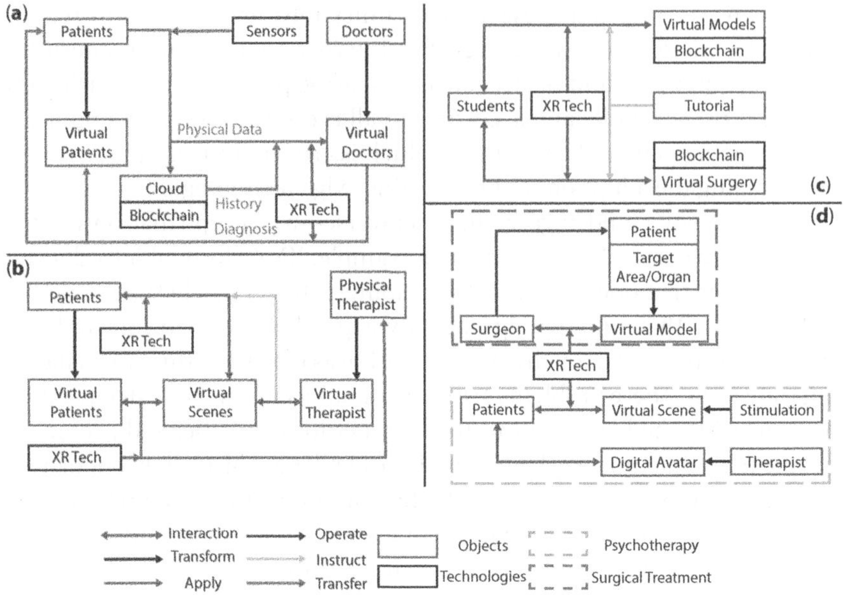


**Figure 12.4** The service architectures of metaverse are adaptable to many healthcare applications, each adapted to meet the unique requirements of distinct medical disciplines.

patient involvement in their care. The metaverse will revolutionize patient interactions with healthcare by making them more personalized and engaging, leading to improved outcomes and higher satisfaction.

## 12.3.1 Virtual Reality Treatment

The use of VR as a therapeutic tool is gaining recognition each year, with its applications in clinical areas ranging from mental health issues like anxiety to physical conditions such as chronic pain management, becoming increasingly well-documented by researchers [12]. Therapeutic movements that help patients relax and manage their symptoms more effectively are guided by carefully planned VR sessions. People with chronic pain can enjoy the calming, soothing environment as a form of comfort from attending places that they are comfortable with or are generally peaceful. These experiences are intended to occupy the mind in a way that reduces pain sensations and promotes healing rather than serve only as an escape from reality. VR can be employed to create protective spaces in the psychiatric domain, where people coping with phobias and panic can safely experience and manage their symptoms. They can be adjusted to each patient's comfort level and used for therapy, as well as forward-graded exposure, without any of the real-world risks.

### 12.3.2 Involved Patients and Personalized Therapy

The days are gone when patients were merely at the receiving end of passive care within this quickly changing digital realm. The metaverse is about unengaged involvement, where the people are just as participative in making their care plans and interventions happen. By collecting such personal data and adjusting plans accordingly, healthcare practitioners are more likely to alleviate symptoms in their patients. Come on in fact, this helps patients and providers bond but treatment is the responsibility of a team. In charge of health journeys patients may feel more empowered in their care, helping to motivate and adhere to regimens. When patients think that there is an element of cooperation and shared responsibility, it keeps them more active in their treatment which helps to build trust.

### 12.3.3 Establishing Networks and Communities

In addition to personalized care, the metaverse also promotes support groups and community-building. In the metaverse, there are online support groups where people who face similar problems come together to share stories and give feedback to each other. These networks are a lifeline for those who live with long-term illnesses, mental health disorders, or any other chronic issues. It emphasizes that we value connections between people, even with the Internet age, and a bit of optimism for more determination around mental health in this lotus field. Such interactions, where other people have gone through similar journeys, improve perspective, which has led to experiencing a complete touch of rehabilitation for mental health and better planning for therapy [13].

Today, clinical trials are limited by sample size and patient availability; the metaverse has much to offer in solving this issue with virtual groups of patients who can test novel drugs faster than ever. With greater safety and effectiveness records, derived from simulated real-world circumstances, calculated through these virtual trials, researchers can access the maximum amount of data for selling products in actual clinical areas before they are brought into practice.

**Virtual Collaboratory Platforms:** The metaverse breaks geographical limits, bringing the possibility of researchers and healthcare experts working together in real time from around the world. Using tools such as virtual whiteboards, 3D models, and simulations, experts can work together on projects in this collaborative environment. The relative ease with which this complementary work has been shared, such as through virtual conferences and meetings, makes it possible for researchers across domains to interact with one another and move medical care forward.

## 12.4 Case Study for the Global Health Initiative

- The researchers involved in the Global Health Initiative—which aims to develop a vaccine for an unfamiliar virus—come from diverse regions, including Asia, Europe, and the United States of America, which again is another proof of how you could utilize the metaverse to conduct research. IoT technology (Table 12.1) could also allow the coordination of data between different research centers as well as real-time simulation to create the vaccine much faster. This collaboration was vital for curtailing the outbreak and is indicative of the way that a metaverse can enable rapid international health crisis responses [14].
- **Security and Privacy:** The metaverse has the potential to collect a vast amount of data on each individual as well as encourage people's participation, raising serious concerns about both data security and privacy. In today's digital era, securing confidential information (private and health-related) is vital.
- **Data Privacy:** The metaverse has leveled up personal data to previously unseen levels where the users exchange their detailed daily lifestyle, including health records. Data

**Table 12.1** This table shows how our design compares to previous research in the healthcare metaverse.

| **AI** | | **Blockchain** | | **Input data types** | | |
|---|---|---|---|---|---|---|
| **XAI/ Grad, CAM** | **XAI/ LIME** | **Transaction info.** | **Decentralized technology** | **Medical image-based** | **NLP-based** | **Sensor/ clinical-based** |
| × | × | √ | √ | × | √ | √ |
| × | × | × | × | √ | × | × |
| √ | √ | √ | √ | √ | √ | √ |

Note: √ denotes yes; × denotes no.

breaches also lead to some serious problems. This is associated with complications in maintaining anonymity across different metaverse platforms.

- **Cybersecurity Protocols:** To address these concerns, advanced cybersecurity measures are essential. Enhancing data security can be achieved through strategies such as implementing end-to-end encryption, securing login processes, and establishing real-time threat monitoring. One prospective solution is employing blockchain technology to provide immutably logged data transfers and ensure that patient information remains protected from outsider attacks [15]. Biometrics and multi-factor authentication (MFA) can protect user accounts from unauthorized access. Figure 12.5 carries out the most important analysis of blockchain structure here.
- **Ethical Considerations:** Integrating the metaverse with healthcare can present a range of ethical dilemmas, including those related to technology use in patient care.
- **Informed Consent and Patient Autonomy:** Ensuring that people understand what they are signing up for when contributing their data to the metaverse is an important ethical dilemma. In virtual care settings, patients in the healthcare

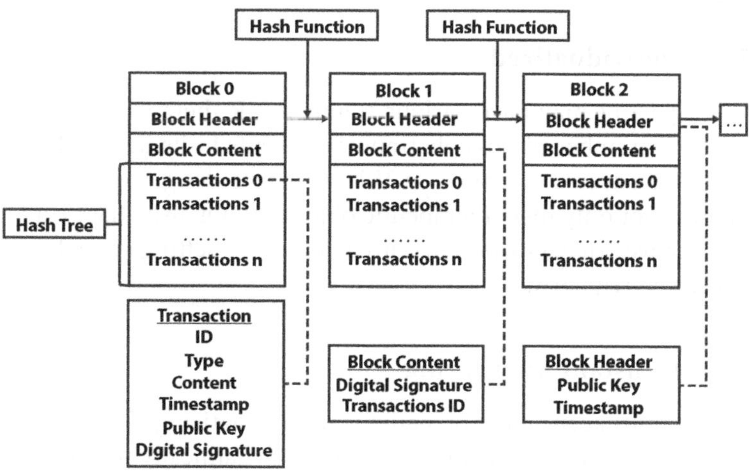


**Figure 12.5** Blockchain fundamental composition and structure.

space should be well-informed participants as to how their data are being used. Transparency is essential to respect the privacy of patients and ensure that their choices are truly informed because how these digital environments are designed can subtly bias assessments.
- **VR's Moral Use in Healthcare:** The biggest promise lies in utilizing VR in patient care, allowing an opportunity for new modes of treatment and reaching out to patients, ultimately improving their daily lives. That said, if this automation and standardization is ever to be fully realized, ethical obligations alongside the technology-driven hurdles need strong consideration.

## 12.5 Ethical Factors in VR Therapy

### 12.5.1 Informed Consent

It is important to be well-informed about the nature and consequences of applying VR therapy. Patients should be informed of potential emotional triggers or disturbing aspects of the VR sessions. The result is that everyone knows exactly what the membership entails, and they can make an informed decision on their participation.

### 12.5.2 Individualized

Since the patient may have various traumas, VR therapy should be sensitive to any number of possible traumatic events in its design. Given the potential for adverse outcomes in VR, therapists designing these experiences must not only meet therapeutic objectives but also adapt content to protect against triggers where required, adjusting settings based on feedback received regularly.

### 12.5.3 Constant Monitoring

Therapists must keep an eye on patients while practicing VR sessions. This real-time monitoring allows for therapy to be dynamically adjusted quickly ensuring that it is safe and effective.

## 12.6 Technological Challenges and Solutions

- **Digital Divide:** High-speed Internet seems to be ready, but its accessibility, combined with cutting-edge hardware, is still only for those truly interested in VR. Such a digital divide idiosyncratically decrees which patients have the unprivileged of undergoing VR therapy.
- **Cost Barriers:** The hefty price tag that comes with VR technology is a huge obstacle to the mass use of it in healthcare. Most likely, the costs will prevent many healthcare providers and patients from using them.
- **Investments in Infrastructure:** Erasing the digital divide will involve making a substantial investment in digital infrastructure, with special attention being paid to areas that may be underserved. Ensuring the broad availability of high-speed Internet is necessary for VR therapies to reach a wide patient base.
- **Cost Reduction Plans:** The introduction of plans such as subsidies, bulk purchasing programs, and innovation sustainment projects has the potential to reduce costs in the production of VR technologies. Furthermore, as new cloud-based VR platforms require cheaper hardware, experiences will become more accessible.
- **Embracing Next-Generation Technologies:** The integration of new technologies like 5G and AI can dramatically improve VR features. 5G can offer the speed and reliability required for a frictionless VR session, while AI could help improve onsite experiences to be more personable and immediate.

### 12.6.1 The Metaverse's Potential for Healthcare

The metaverse is in the process of being created, and as Figure 12.6 shows, the potential impact on healthcare of new technologies is significant.

- **Incorporation of AI:** With artificial intelligence, virtual environments can be converted to maximize their creativity and response. AI-powered avatars and virtual assistants can provide live support to patients and healthcare providers, enhancing immediate meetings while personalizing care.

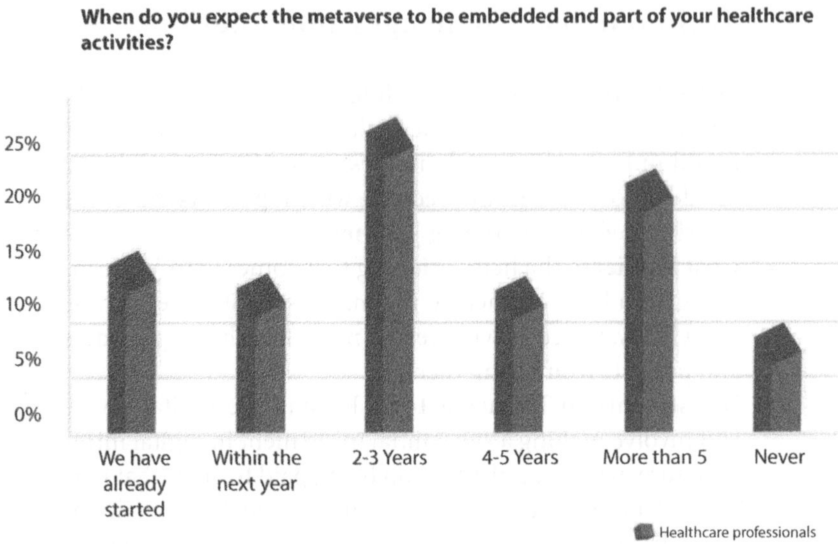


**Figure 12.6** Survey of medical experts on their expectations for the integration of the metaverse into healthcare efforts.

- **Decentralized Platforms:** Blockchain technology creates a safe and transparent platform where medical data are traded. Decentralized platforms offer smoother transfers of information within disparate systems, strengthening healthcare teamwork and productivity.

A study referenced in Figure 12.6 questioned medical experts when they anticipated the metaverse to be an aspect of their healthcare efforts.

### 12.6.2 Prospective Applications in the Future

- **Virtual Hospitals:** This truly has the potential to completely change how treatment is delivered. These hyper-realistic virtual environments might offer everything from basic physical examinations to complex surgical treatments, allowing patients to consult with physicians anywhere in the world without ever having to set foot outside their homes. They refer to two specific types of digital twins: one tailored specifically for an individual's health and made using precision health data [16]. For a gravity-dependent marker such as fractional excretion of sodium, one may expect that models

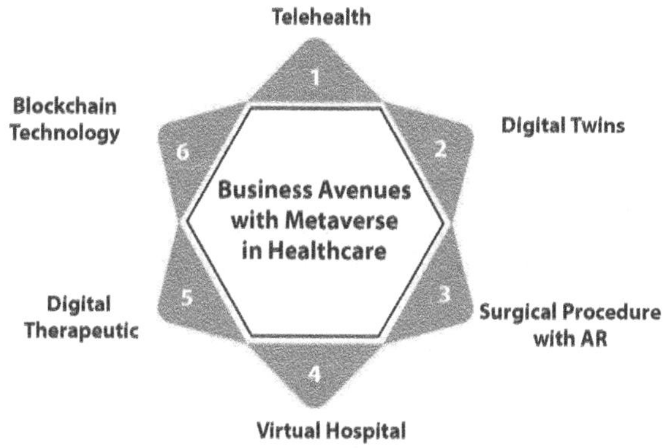


**Figure 12.7** Possible commercial opportunities using the metaverse in healthcare.

could help physicians tailor their treatment and optimize these possibilities based on whether they believe patients might or might not respond.

- **International Health Initiatives:** Instead of having to travel around the globe, researchers can "meet" virtually on sustainability and global projects dealing with everything from disease control measures. Global teams of scientists may collaborate in real-time to communicate data and plan responses to pandemics [17]. The Figure 12.7 demonstrates various commercial opportunities for integrating the metaverse into healthcare sector.
- **Paradigms in Healthcare Delivery:** The integration of the metaverse into healthcare will bring with it a lot of changes to traditional paradigms. By utilizing technologies including VR, AR, and MR, the metaverse introduces exciting new possibilities around patient access to care, which patients see, and the quality of treatment [18].
- **Access:** The goal is to create an inclusive system that allows patients to receive relevant healthcare from anywhere in the world, overcoming geographical barriers to physical healthcare facilities. This will particularly benefit individuals in rural or underserved areas who often lack access to healthcare [19].
- **Educated Choices:** Allowing individuals to conduct their research can help people make informed decisions about the types and quality of treatments offered in this virtual world. Connecting with different healthcare providers in virtual

worlds could allow patients to make better judgments based on the services and skills that are accessible.

- **Tailoring the Service to Individuals:** In dealing with a metaverse of health, patients can reach optimal resources and services that work with them as individuals. Patients can be better because the treatments online are tailored to their needs and health conditions, and their lives will be happier from any side.
- **Cost Efficiency:** The metaverse, by improving access to care and focusing on outputs rather than purely volume numbers, is likely going to reduce overall healthcare costs. Virtual monitoring, simplified treatment protocols, and remote consultations may reduce hospital stays and the demand for face-to-face interactions, enabling cost-effective care delivery [20].

### 12.6.3 Potential Limitations and Challenges

- **Integration with Legacy Systems:** Careful planning is crucial when incorporating metaverse technology into healthcare systems, as these systems were not originally designed for such applications. A critical part of this transition is ensuring seamless integration with existing medical equipment and electronic health records.
- **Technology Adoption:** Mitigating high prices, ensuring that they are fairly available to individuals who need the gear and connection necessary for metaverse technologies [21, 22].
- **Security and Confidentiality:** For the systems storing patient data, considerable attention will have to be given to ensuring robust security and privacy protection inside the metaverse. Data protection should be paramount to the existing healthcare and metaverse-based solutions with elements of building trust [23, 24].

## 12.7 Conclusion

The metaverse has a massive potential to change healthcare in innovative and novel ways, enhancing patient care all over the world by conducting medical research or international collaborations. We have witnessed that telemedicine, medical education, and patient engagement are driven by this digital new frontier. Increasing access to care, improving the quality and effectiveness of healthcare services delivered in traditional settings, or being reconstructed into VR/AR/MR technology-based environments with a backbone goal. The metaverse is revolutionizing healthcare—spawning virtual clinics, dynamic support networks, and immersive training environments among others. As we traverse through this new landscape, it will be critical that privacy, security, and technology access hurdles are met.

This potential the metaverse offers can be used wisely and strategically to improve patient outcomes, speed up medical procedures, and encourage greater international cooperation between different countries. The metaverse is a movement, and it is luring medical order. The sign refers to a world where the digital and physical will come closer together, presenting tremendous opportunities for change that we have never seen before. Achieving this requires collaboration among technologists, legislators, and healthcare experts. We will ensure that the metaverse, once fully implemented, transforms the concepts of ease and comfort in healthcare, paving the way for a new era of patient experiences and healthcare innovation through the use of advanced data analytics and technologies.

## References

1. Flavián, C., Ibáñez-Sánchez, S., Orús, C., Barta, S., The dark side of the metaverse: The role of gamification in event virtualization. *Int. J. Inf. Manage.*, 75, 102726, 2024, https://doi.org/10.1016/j.ijinfomgt.2023.102726.
2. Yang, L., Xu, Y., Hui, P., Metaverse Identity: Core Principles and Critical Challenges, arXiv.org, 2024, https://arxiv.org/abs/2406.08029.
3. Chen, K., Meng, Z., Xu, X., *et al.*, Real-Time Interactions Between Human Controllers and Remote Devices in Metaverse, arXiv.org, 2024, https://arxiv.org/abs/2407.16591.
4. Skalidis, I., Muller, O., Fournier, S., CardioVerse: The cardiovascular medicine in the era of Metaverse. *Trends Cardiovasc. Med.*, 33, 471–476, 2023, https://doi.org/10.1016/j.tcm.2022.05.004.
5. Shao, L., Tang, W., Zhang, Z., Chen, X., Medical metaverse: Technologies, applications, challenges and future. *J. Mech. Med. Biol.*, 23, 2023, https://doi.org/10.1142/s0219519423500288.
6. Mystakidis, S., Metaverse. *Encyclopedia*, 2, 486–497, 2022, https://doi.org/10.3390/encyclopedia2010031.
7. Ouyang, W., Wang, B., Tian, L., Niu, X., Spatial deprivation of urban public services in migrant enclaves under the context of a rapidly urbanizing China: An evaluation based on suburban Shanghai. *Cities*, 60, 436–445, 2017, https://doi.org/10.1016/j.cities.2016.06.004.

8. Carl, B., Bopp, M., Saß, B., *et al.*, Spine Surgery Supported by Augmented Reality. *Global Spine J.*, 10, 41S–55S, 2020, https://doi.org/10.1177/2192568219868217.
9. Queen Mary students receive first lecture in the metaverse, Queen Mary University of London, 2022, https://www.qmul.ac.uk/media/news/2022/pr/queen-mary-students-receive-first-lecture-in-the-metaverse.html.
10. Alawa, K.A., Nolan, R.P., Han, E., *et al.*, Low-cost, smartphone-based frequency doubling technology visual field testing using a head-mounted display. *Br. J. Ophthalmol.*, 105, 440–444, 2019, https://doi.org/10.1136/bjophthalmol-2019-314031.
11. Khan, H., Kushwah, K.K., Singh, S., *et al.*, Smart technologies driven approaches to tackle COVID-19 pandemic: a review. *3 Biotech*, 11, 2021, https://doi.org/10.1007/s13205-020-02581-y.
12. Roy, E., Bakr, M.M., George, R., The need for virtual reality simulators in dental education: A review. *Saudi Dent. J.*, 29, 41–47, 2017, https://doi.org/10.1016/j.sdentj.2017.02.001.
13. Srivastava, S., Exploring the Opportunities, Expenditure, and Steps to Develop Metaverse in Healthcare, Appinventiv, 2024, https://appinventiv.com/blog/metaverse-in-healthcare/.
14. Bhatt, T. and Bhatt, T., Metaverse in Healthcare Industry: Applications, Advantages, Challenges, and More, Intelivita, 2023, https://www.intelivita.com/in/blog/metaverse-in-healthcare/.
15. Baccour, E., Erbad, A., Mohamed, A., *et al.*, A Blockchain-Based Reliable Federated Meta-Learning for Metaverse: A Dual Game Framework. *IEEE Internet Things J.*, 11, 22697–22715, 2024, https://doi.org/10.1109/jiot.2024.3383096.
16. The Future of Healthcare in the Metaverse, PwC, https://www.pwc.com/m1/en/industries/healthcare/the-future-of-healthcare-in-the-metaverse.html.
17. Vyas, A.K., Ganwar, R., Kumar, S., Elliptical air hole PCF-based low-cost sensor for refractive index and temperature detection: Design and analysis. *Opt. Fiber Technol.*, 73, 103060, 2022.
18. Jiang, Y., Cao, J., Yu, C., Dog Heart Rate and Blood Oxygen Metaverse Interaction System, arXiv.org, 2024, https://arxiv.org/abs/2406.04466.
19. Aydin, O., Karaarslan, E., Narin, N.G., Artificial Intelligence, VR, AR and Metaverse Technologies for Human Resources Management, arXiv.org, 2024, https://arxiv.org/abs/2406.15383.
20. Thomason, J., Metaverse, token economies, and non-communicable diseases. *Global Health J.*, 6, 164–167, 2022, https://doi.org/10.1016/j.glohj.2022.07.001.
21. Khazanchi, D., Kumar Vyas, A., Kant Hiran, K., Padmanaban, S., *Blockchain 3.0 for Sustainable Development*, De Gruyter, Berlin, Boston, 2021, https://doi.org/10.1515/9783110702507.

22. Kant Hiran, K., Khazanchi, D., Kumar Vyas, A., Padmanaban, S., *Machine Learning for Sustainable Development*, De Gruyter, Berlin, Boston, 2021, https://doi.org/10.1515/9783110702514.
23. Vyas, A.K., Balamurugan, S., Hiran, K.K., Dhiman, H.S. (Eds.), eds., *Artificial Intelligence for Renewable Energy Systems*, John Wiley & Sons, 2022, ISBN: 9781119761693.
24. Tiwari, S., Vyas, A.K., Dixit, Y., Bale, A.S., Dixit, A., Refractive index sensing of human blood using patterned photonic crystal containing defects. *Int. J. Mod. Phys. B*, 38, 20, 2450261, 2024.

13

# Metaverse Technologies, Security, and Applications for Healthcare

**Shilpi Jindal[1]*, Shristi Chaudhary[2], Shalini Sharma[1], Meenu Rani[3] and Sonia Bajaj[4]**

[1]*Department of Physics, Chandigarh University, Gharuan, Mohali, Punjab, India*
[2]*UCRD, Department of Physics, Chandigarh University, Mohali, Punjab, India*
[3]*Department of Physics, Hindu College Sonipat, Sonipat, Haryana, India*
[4]*Department of Mathematics, Chandigarh University, Gharuan, Mohali, Punjab, India*

### *Abstract*

Metaverse has transformed several industries, including healthcare with the amalgamation of revolutionary new technologies like virtual reality (VR), augmented reality (AR), artificial intelligence (AI), blockchain, and the Internet of Things (IoT). Through this chapter, the impact of metaverse technologies is examined on healthcare, with a major focus on upcoming technologies with the growing level of applications related to security systems and the transformational potential. The metaverse creates environments that are immersive, interactive, and are well patient-focused; it virtually offers an incomparable prospect, which further improves patient care, and advanced medical education and also improves healthcare delivery. The chapter also explores the ethical corollary of upcoming technologies in healthcare systems, highlighting the major focus on patient permission, data privacy, and the digital divide. The chapter further emphasizes the crucial thorough legal frameworks and the moral principles and standards that further regulate virtual technology to protect patient safety and assist in maintaining their confidence within the swiftly changing digital healthcare environment. The further discussion in the chapter sways emphasis on the critical strike on maintaining the balance between the ethical duties of developers and the professionals working under healthcare systems with the advancement of technological systems.

**Corresponding author*: shilpi.85jindal@gmail.com

Ajay Kumar Vyas, Harleen Kaur, Sourabh Sharma and Bhavya Alankar (eds.) Metaverse Technologies, Security and Applications for Healthcare, (297–312) © 2025 Scrivener Publishing LLC

***Keywords*:** Virtual reality, augmented reality, blockchain security, tele medicine, digital twins, healthcare data privacy, AI in healthcare, immersive patient care

## 13.1 Introduction to the Metaverse

In recent years, the blend of technologies like virtual reality (VR), augmented reality (AR), blockchain, and artificial intelligence (AI) particularly has led to the advancement of metaverse among customers, which further assists their businesses and tech enthusiasts. The combination of the technologies creates an accessible digital world and connects in the prevailing environment where people carry out different tasks simultaneously. At present, metaverse has potentially been used in many industries; similarly, the healthcare industry has also been a promising area for using advanced digital systems [1–3].

**Secure Access in an Ever-Evolving Metaverse**

In-depth security systems are an important call in the healthcare sector, which needs special focus and attention. It is particularly important to maintain security systems due to the high consideration of individual personal data which comes with the stringent regulatory requirements. The personal nature of data needs to be protected or to be dealt with by the concerned person only, therefore, needs to be secured. The chapter further reviews the underlying technologies of the metaverse, the security systems and the challenges involved in the practice, and the transformative applications that can be perched and poised to reshape the industry.

## 13.2 Metaverse Technologies: Back to the Basics and Beyond

Several advanced technologies support the metaverse to make it immersive and interconnected. Understanding these technologies in depth is essential to harness the metaverse's potential in healthcare.

### 13.2.1 Virtual Reality (VR) and Augmented Reality (AR)

The metaverse cannot exist without VR and AR—VR provides complete immersion in another environment, whereas AR superimposes digital elements over the real world. In medicine, VR is used in therapeutic contexts, medical training, and patient education. AR can enhance real-world medical procedures, providing real-time data and 3D models over a surgeon's field of view during operations [4].

### 13.2.2 Blockchain and Decentralized Technologies

Transactions are secure and transparent within the metaverse thanks to blockchain technology. In healthcare, it can protect electronic health records (EHRs), support trusted exchanges of medical information across organizations, and manage digital identities. Decentralized systems empower patients by granting them greater control over their data and facilitating the formation of global, interoperable health networks [5].

### 13.2.3 AI and ML

AI and ML personalize each user's experience within the metaverse, making it a more interactive space. In healthcare, AI uses big data for diagnostics, screens patient records for treatment options, and predicts outcomes. AI-driven avatars in the metaverse can provide real-time health monitoring and serve as virtual personal wellness coaches [6].

### 13.2.4 5G and Edge Computing

High-speed, low-latency networks are essential to the metaverse's operation, especially in healthcare applications that depend on real-time data flow [7]. 5G technology and edge computing altogether amalgamated further enhance the connection in the device and assist the practitioners of healthcare systems to access rapid information with less latency.

### 13.2.5 Innovations in Human-Computer Interaction (HCI)

The current innovations and development of technology have labeled the metaverse more approachable and a blessing to human-computer interactions (HCI). Recent innovations such as brain-computer interfaces and feedback systems primarily require updated fast digital interpretations. The advancements in AI or aided technologies offer realistic and captivating simulations to healthcare and activate various senses which add positive impact on patients who undergo rehabilitation. This may also aid in improving the quality of life of paralyzed patients as they may use gadgets solely to engage themselves [8, 9].

## 13.3 Security Challenges in the Metaverse for Healthcare

There are potentially many challenges faced by healthcare organizations in procuring data; for these security issues, there are many possibilities that can be explored through the metaverse. The novel technologies innovated recently reflect the weaknesses that malevolent entities may leverage and this further endangers the patient's privacy, invasion of information, and security [10].

### 13.3.1 Data Privacy and Confidentiality

Data breaches are so common and are likely even in the metaverse as it has interconnections. Healthcare data is particularly vulnerable to intrusions because of its sensitivity. Therefore, strong encryption and safe authentications are required in the procedures to be followed to procure the data in the systems and a proper call for adherence to laws needs to be incorporated in the system to ensure patient privacy and protect the data. The laws like Health Insurance Portability and Accountability Act (HIPAA) in the United States are imbibed in the units to protect the data invasion [11].

### 13.3.2 Identity Management and Authentication

Metaverse users communicate with digital identities using the internet which is easily hacked or stolen. The undesired intrusion in data needs to be safeguarded, and unwanted access needs to be protected in the healthcare services; for this, there is a need to identify the management systems effective in protecting against the invasion of privacy data. To improvise the systems, techniques already in use biometric verification, decentralized identity systems (DID), and multi-factor authentication (MFA) are equally effective [12].

### 13.3.3 Cybersecurity Threats and Attack Vectors

The metaverse has the nature of interconnections, and therefore, the invasions of data have become a major cyber threat to data procurers. The blockchain system integrates with other domains, it poses extra hazards. Similar hazards occur when VR and AR technologies are integrated into healthcare, much as the Internet of Things (IoT) is connected to medical devices, and the same in VR and AR technologies [13]. It is critical to adopt comprehensive cybersecurity strategies inside healthcare organizations. Smart strategies like sophisticated threat intelligence, intrusion detection systems (IDS), and regular vulnerability assessments need to be mandatory and incorporated into healthcare concerns.

### 13.3.4 Data Integrity and Reliability

Data procuring in the healthcare industry is very critical to be handled. It is well organized with blockchain technology which is a tamper-proof ledger for keeping the medical records of the patients. Although the healthcare data is reliable and requires data quality if it is segregated, careful consideration of consensus, smart security, and data provenance is necessary to ensure data uniformity throughout decentralized networks [14, 15].

### 13.3.5 Compliance with Regulatory Requirements

There are strict regulations and guidelines in the healthcare industry formulated to govern and keep the records of patients with the patient consent and promising of data to be protected. The current laws demand compliance and then authorize the incorporation of metaverse technologies for record keeping. The news guidelines can be called for the procurement of data and handling of the difficulties aroused by the virtual world [16].

**Digital Health Transformation**

The goals of healthcare systems' technical innovations are to maintain, improve, and restore patient care. Patient-physician interactions have been profoundly altered by the quick development of digital health services that make use of the Internet and digital tools. These changes are being driven by technologies like blockchain, AR, and VR, which are improving prescription adherence, patient satisfaction, and health monitoring [17–19].

With the integration of digital diagnostics, self-service applications, virtual care, and remote monitoring, healthcare is taking a more comprehensive approach to well-being. AI, cloud computing, AR, VR, and other innovations are improving accessibility, operational effectiveness, and patient experiences. The metaverse uses these technologies to provide customized healthcare solutions through its immersive and personalized services [20].

**Artificial Intelligence and the Metaverse in Healthcare**

Emerging technologies like AI and metaverse apps present fresh possibilities for developing an immersive, interactive healthcare setting. Incorporating blockchain, AI, AR, VR, and cloud computing into the metaverse has the potential to transform healthcare in several ways.

1. **Enhanced Access**: Regardless of location, it makes it easier for patients and doctors to connect.
2. **Improved Precision**: Advances in diagnostic and surgical technologies.
3. **Cost Reduction**: Lowers healthcare delivery, education, and administrative expenses.
4. **Data Management**: Streamlines storage and distribution of various healthcare data.
5. **Increased Satisfaction**: Enhances patient and provider satisfaction with novel services.
6. **Operational Efficiency**: Improves recruitment, training, and payment processes.

**Examples of Metaverse Applications in Healthcare**

- **Virtual Reality**: Employed in medical education, mental health treatments, and pain management [21].
- **Augmented Reality**: Enhances surgical procedures, imaging, and patient education.
- **Blockchain**: Provides supply chain verification, data security, and streamlined payments.
- **M-Worlds**: Platforms for medical training, meetings, and conferences.

While the role of metaverse in healthcare is still developing, its potential is substantial. The market is anticipated to grow as new use cases emerge, though challenges such as ethical, legal, and technical issues must be addressed [22–25].

**Digital Health and the Metaverse**

Digital healthcare, integrating tools like e-prescriptions, telemedicine, and digital radiology, is increasingly blurring the lines between traditional and digital health services. The COVID-19 pandemic has accelerated the adoption of digital solutions, highlighting the need for innovative tools to address healthcare challenges [26].

**Blockchain in Digital Healthcare and the Metaverse**

Blockchain technology has transformative potential for digital healthcare and the metaverse by providing a secure, decentralized network for managing healthcare data and transactions. Key applications include the following [27–29]:

1. **Supply Chain Transparency**: Tracks and ensures the quality and authenticity of medical products.
2. **Patient-Centric EHRs**: Enables secure, patient-controlled EHRs.
3. **Smart Contracts**: Automates insurance claims and payments, enhancing efficiency and trust.
4. **Medical Staff Credential Verification**: Provides secure records of medical qualifications.
5. **IoT Security**: Protects remote monitoring devices and patient data from cyber threats.

**Genome Editing in Healthcare**

Genome editing allows scientists to modify DNA, offering personalized treatment options and improving intervention effectiveness for chronic conditions. The technology has evolved significantly, reducing both the time and cost of genome sequencing, and continues to advance rapidly [30].

**Applications of Genome Editing in Digital Healthcare**

1. Customized Therapies: Thanks to genome editing, specific therapies based on a patient's genetic composition can be created. This includes developments in precision medicine, gene therapy, and cell therapy, which target particular genetic variables that are particular to each patient.
2. Biomarkers as Diagnostic Tools: Devices like liquid biopsies, clustered regularly interspaced short palindromic repeats (CRISPR)-based detection techniques, and digital polymerase chain reaction (PCR) are developed through genetic data. The diagnostic tools are good for continuing surveillance and also assist in the identification of early symptoms of illness.
3. Infectious Diseases Management: Novel vaccinations, antiviral medications, and immunological modulators are precautionary aids that help in preventing infectious diseases [31].

4. Recuperating Safety and Efficacy: With the blend of blockchain, AI, and machine learning (ML), genome editing has become more perfect and accurate and it helps in addressing safety concerns with an effect on improvised treatment outcomes [32].

Genome editing is a potential revolution in the healthcare division. The ethical and social concerns along with the regulatory issues are to be considered hypothetically to come up with equitable application of the said applications and tools.

**Applications of Metaverse Technologies in Healthcare**

Patient care is handled with numerous applications available on the metaverse. People get medical education and operational effectiveness updated versions in the metaverse.

1. Tele-Medicine and Virtual Consultations: Today's generation easily meets immersive virtual consultations and seeks professional medical advice. Metaverse has improved the level of interaction and the three-dimensional environment in telemedicine consultation. Enhancing patient-doctor contacts and facilitating easy access to healthcare are the main objectives, especially for underprivileged groups and people living in remote or far-off places [33].
2. Medical Training and Simulation: AR and VR technological aids have revolutionized medical education completely. Many simulations are offered as surgical procedures in emergencies. The introductions avoid the crucial in-person practice and the dangers and assist the practitioners minutely in handling the situations [34].
3. Physical Therapy and Rehabilitation: Metaverse has made it possible for patients to participate in interactive exercises, for the patients who are healing from ailments feel it easy to practice the exercises through VR rehabilitation programs. This supports the patients individually and tailors their needs as per their requirements hereby increasing the count of participation further increases the progress monitoring.
4. Mental Health and Therapy: Metaverse VR environment exposure therapy is used to treat anxiety issues of the patients, PTSD, and other phobias of individuals. AI avatars

support and supervise patients' mental health 24/7 and are rated highly by the users.

5. Remote Monitoring and Chronic Disease Management: Metaverse is also assisting in the monitoring of chronic illnesses in real time while facilitating wearable technology and the IoT. The abnormalities and malformations are well identified through metaverse and it offers healthcare doctor consultation along with timely solutions to patients. The complete AI operates the data records and analysis the same [35–37].
6. Virtual Health Communities and Support Groups: Metaverse supports virtual communities for the patients to interact with people and endow with the support system with comparable medical issues. Social networking involves patients and they feel connected to the world and easily get swayed away from their sufferings; they feel less alone. It is a good chance for patients struggling with mental disorders, mental health, and other chronic conditions.

**Case Studies and Real-World Implementations**

1. VR in Surgical Training: VR-based surgical pieces of training guide the doctor interns to easily practice the different methods and procedures followed up in medical school. Interns easily enhance their performance and confidence through these trainings.
2. AR in Physical Therapy: AR assistance in individual physical therapy guides the patients comfortably, and at their own pace, they may practice. The strategy in comparison to the traditional method seems to be more engaging and satisfactory, increasing the engagement of the patients with faster recuperation.
3. Blockchain for Medical Record Management: The healthcare network manages the EHRs, which are connected through the blockchain, and facilitates the improvisation in accessibility and security checks of data. It also grants ownership to the patients with access to their medical records.
4. AI-Driven Mental Health Support: AI allows patients with anxiety issues and depression to access mental health facilities. The AI avatar monitors the different emotional states and later offers the mechanisms to cope with the natural

language processing system. The avatars work on the patients and help them lessen their symptoms and increase their interest and belief in the usage of healing therapy.

## Future Trends and Challenges in the Metaverse for Healthcare

1. AI in Personalized Medicine: By evaluating large datasets to customize therapies based on unique genetic profiles, lifestyles, and environmental factors, AI will progressively contribute to personalized healthcare.
2. Ethical Issues and Patient Permission: It will be essential to address ethical concerns about patient autonomy and permission as the metaverse becomes more immersive. Processes for informed consent and clear norms will be required.
3. Interoperability and Standardization: Effective integration of metaverse technologies requires interoperability between platforms and standardized data formats, communication protocols, and security measures.
4. Effect on Healthcare Workforce: By necessitating the acquisition of new skills and possibly leading to job displacement, the adoption of metaverse technologies may affect the healthcare workforce. It will be crucial to have ongoing instruction and training.
5. Sustainability and Environmental Considerations: As the metaverse expands, its environmental impact must be managed, including the energy consumption of data centers and VR/AR devices. Sustainable practices and energy-efficient solutions should be explored [38].

## Transforming Healthcare Through Digital Tools and Emerging Technologies

Digital healthcare is rapidly advancing, supported by innovations like AI and the metaverse, which are reshaping clinical decision-making, administrative support, and overall healthcare delivery:

1. **Clinical Decision-Making Tools:**
   - Clinical Decision Support Systems (CDSS): Platforms that analyze health data to provide alerts, guidelines, and diagnostic assistance.

- AI and Machine Learning Tools: Algorithms that help in identifying patterns and making predictions for better clinical decisions [39].
- Visual Communication Tools: Illustrations and animations that make difficult information easier for people to comprehend and process.

2. **Administrative Support:**
   - Automation and AI: Reducing repetitive tasks and enhancing efficiency.
   - Training and Education: Preparing healthcare workers for new roles and responsibilities [40].
   - Well-being and Resilience: Supporting healthcare professionals to regulate stress and prevent burnout.

**Overcoming Barriers in Developing Nations**

Developing countries face challenges in adopting digital health solutions, such as policy gaps, workforce readiness, and funding limitations. Addressing these issues requires strengthening regulations, enhancing workforce training, and scaling successful pilot projects to build a robust digital health ecosystem [41–49].

**Conclusion**

The metaverse presents a transformative opportunity for healthcare, offering new ways to improve patient care, education, and operational efficiency. However, successful adoption requires addressing challenges related to security, privacy, and ethics. By embracing these technologies thoughtfully and collaboratively, the healthcare industry can create a more connected, efficient, and patient-centered system.

## References

1. Riva, G. and Wiederhold, B.K., What the Metaverse is (really) and why we need to know about it. *Cyberpsychol. Behav. Social Network.*, *25*, 6, 355–359, 2022, https://doi.org/10.1089/cyber.2022.0124.
2. Lee, J., Park, S., Park, H., Augmented reality and virtual reality applications in medicine. *Front. Med.*, *8*, 693026, 2021, https://doi.org/10.3389/fmed.2021.693026.

3. Kim, J. and Lee, K., The role of artificial intelligence in the Metaverse: A case study in healthcare. *J. Healthcare Inf. Res.*, *5*, 3, 489–506, 2021, https://doi.org/10.1007/s41666-021-00124-0.
4. Zhu, E., Lilienthal, A., Shluzas, L.A., Masiello, I., Zary, N., Design of mobile augmented reality in health care education: A scoping review. *JMIR mHealth uHealth*, *8*, 4, e15628, 2020, https://doi.org/10.2196/15628.
5. Dubovitskaya, A., Xu, Z., Ryu, S., Schumacher, M., Wang, F., Secure and trustable electronic medical records sharing using blockchain. *AMIA Annu. Symp. Proc.*, *2020*, 1, 650–659, 2020, https://doi.org/10.1136/amiajnl-2019-000567.
6. Esteva, A., Robicquet, A., Ramsundar, B., Kuleshov, V., DePristo, M., Chou, K., Cui, C., Corrado, G.S., Thrun, S., Dean, J., A guide to deep learning in healthcare. *Nat. Med.*, *25*, 1, 24–29, 2019, https://doi.org/10.1038/s41591-018-0316-z.
7. Mouradian, C., Naboulsi, D., Yang, C., Glitho, R.H., Desprats, T., A comprehensive survey on fog computing: State-of-the-art and research challenges. *IEEE Commun. Surv. Tutorials*, *20*, 1, 416–464, 2018, https://doi.org/10.1109/COMST.2017.2771153.
8. Perez-Paredes, P., Del-Pino, R., Pons, J.L., Prieto, A., Haptic feedback technology for rehabilitation: A review of the state-of-the-art. *J. NeuroEng. Rehabil.*, *18*, 89, 2021, https://doi.org/10.1186/s12984-021-00894-0.
9. Lebedev, M.A. and Nicolelis, M.A., Brain-machine interfaces: Past, present, and future. *Trends Neurosci.*, *29*, 9, 536–546, 2006, https://doi.org/10.1016/j.tins.2006.07.004.
10. Kuo, T.T., Kim, H.E., Ohno-Machado, L., Blockchain distributed ledger technologies for biomedical and health care applications. *J. Am. Med. Inf. Assoc.*, *24*, 6, 1211–1220, 2017, https://doi.org/10.1093/jamia/ocx068.
11. Subramanian, S. and Abdul, S.S., Cybersecurity in the healthcare sector: Exploring the cybersecurity and technological challenges in healthcare. *Int. J. Comput. Appl.*, *178*, 44, 11–16, 2019, https://doi.org/10.5120/ijca2019918598.
12. Pereira, E., Lopes, N., Melício, F., Virtual and augmented reality: A systematic review and security concerns in healthcare. *Sensors*, *21*, 6, 2225, 2021, https://doi.org/10.3390/s21062225.
13. Chang, S. and Trewin, S., Challenges and recommendations for secure telemedicine in healthcare. *J. Med. Internet Res.*, *22*, 9, e20916, 2020, https://doi.org/10.2196/20916.
14. Sahi, P.K., Mishra, S., Singh, K., Srivastava, A., Cybersecurity issues in healthcare data management in the Metaverse: Challenges and future directions. *Health Technol.*, *12*, 1, 1–12, 2022, https://doi.org/10.1007/s12553-022-00637-3.
15. Barsom, E.Z., Graafland, M., Schijven, M.P., Systematic review on the effectiveness of virtual reality training for surgeons. *Surg. Endoscopy*, *30*, 2, 417–427, 2016, https://doi.org/10.1007/s00464-015-4205-9.

16. Sielhorst, T., Feuerstein, M., Navab, N., Advanced medical displays: A literature review of augmented reality. *J. Disp. Technol.*, *4*, 4, 451–467, 2008, https://doi.org/10.1109/JDT.2008.2002123.
17. Mallari, B., Spaeth, E.K., Goh, H., Boyd, B.S., Virtual reality as an analgesic for acute and chronic pain in adults: A systematic review and meta-analysis. *J. Pain Res.*, *12*, 2053–2085, 2019, https://doi.org/10.2147/JPR.S200498.
18. Dunn, P., Saredakis, D., Barnett, A., Telepresence: Immersive virtual reality in health care. *J. Med. Internet Res.*, *19*, 8, e295, 2017, https://doi.org/10.2196/jmir.5869.
19. Wood, D., Sherwood, D., Bickle, M., The use of augmented reality to teach anatomy: Study design and pilot results. *MedEdPublish*, *7*, 1, 68, 2018, https://doi.org/10.15694/mep.2018.0000055.1.
20. Laver, K.E., Lange, B., George, S., Deutsch, J.E., Saposnik, G., Crotty, M., Virtual reality for stroke rehabilitation. *Cochrane Database Syst. Rev.*, *11*, CD008349, 2017, https://doi.org/10.1002/14651858.CD008349.pub4.
21. Azaria, A., Ekblaw, A., Vieira, T., Lippman, A., MedRec: Using blockchain for medical data access and permission management. *2016 2nd International Conference on Open and Big Data (OBD)*, pp. 25–30, 2016, https://doi.org/10.1109/OBD.2016.11.
22. Bibault, J.E., Chaix, B., Guillemassé, A., Cousin, S., Escande, A., Perrin, M., Nectoux, P., A chatbot versus physicians to provide information for patients with breast cancer: Blind, randomized controlled noninferiority trial. *J. Med. Internet Res.*, *21*, 11, e15787, 2019, https://doi.org/10.2196/15787.
23. Latif, S., Qadir, J., Farooq, S., Imran, M.A., How 5G wireless (and concomitant technologies) will revolutionize healthcare? *Future Internet*, *9*, 4, 93, 2017, https://doi.org/10.3390/fi9040093.
24. Caserman, P., Garcia-Agundez, A., Goebel, S., Göbel, S., Evaluating the potential of immersive virtual reality systems for motor rehabilitation in patients with Parkinson's disease: A systematic review. *J. NeuroEng. Rehabil.*, *17*, 1, 135, 2020, https://doi.org/10.1186/s12984-020-00729-8.
25. Cohen, I.G., Amarasingham, R., Shah, A., Xie, B., Lo, B., The legal and ethical concerns that arise from using complex predictive analytics in health care. *Health Aff.*, *33*, 7, 1139–1147, 2014, https://doi.org/10.1377/hlthaff.2014.0048.
26. Pormeister, K., Genetic data and the GDPR: A legal analysis of the compliance challenges. *Comput. Law Secur. Rev.*, *35*, 1, 47–67, 2019, https://doi.org/10.1016/j.clsr.2018.11.003.
27. Mantovani, F. and Castelnuovo, G., Virtual reality in psychological and medical treatments: A mapping review. *Clin. Psychol. Psychotherapy*, *27*, 4, 446–464, 2020, https://doi.org/10.1002/cpp.2441.
28. Miller, D.P., Johnson, C.T., Whittington, J., Smith, C., HIPAA considerations for healthcare facilities using wearable and mobile technology. *Am. J. Health Syst. Pharm.*, *75*, 3, 123–128, 2018, https://doi.org/10.2146/ajhp170148.

29. Martin, G., Koizia, L., Kooner, A., Cafferkey, J., Ross, C., Purkayastha, S., Darzi, A., Use of the artificial intelligence chat bot for patient education and adherence support: Evaluation in a national health service blood and transplant site. *J. Med. Internet Res.*, *22*, 11, e20769, 2020, https://doi.org/10.2196/20769.
30. Zulkifly, M.A., Pan, J.S., Othman, M.A., Mohamad, A.R., Virtual reality in surgical training: A comprehensive review of surgical VR applications. *Surg. Innov.*, *25*, 5, 549–560, 2018, https://doi.org/10.1177/1553350618798682.
31. Chen, J., Wang, Y., Xu, J., Zhang, C., Wu, Y., Augmented reality-based rehabilitation interventions for patients following total knee arthroplasty: A systematic review and meta-analysis of randomized controlled trials. *J. Rehabil. Res. Dev.*, *57*, 3, 621–634, 2020, https://doi.org/10.1682/JRRD.2020.03.0043.
32. Ateniese, G., Fu, K., Green, M., Hohenberger, S., Improved proxy re-encryption schemes with applications to secure distributed storage. *ACM Trans. Inf. Syst. Secu. (TISSEC)*, 9, 1, 1–30, 2006.
33. Fulmer, R., Joerin, A., Gentile, B., Lakerink, L., Rauws, M., Using psychological artificial intelligence (Tess) to relieve symptoms of depression and anxiety: Randomized controlled trial. *JMIR Mental Health*, *5*, 4, e64, 2018, https://doi.org/10.2196/mental.9782.
34. Topol, E.J., High-performance medicine: The convergence of human and artificial intelligence. *Nat. Med.*, *25*, 1, 44–56, 2019, https://doi.org/10.1038/s41591-018-0300-7.
35. Goodman, K.W., Ethics and health informatics: User-centered design and sustainable innovation. *Int. J. Med. Inf.*, *141*, 104230, 2020, https://doi.org/10.1016/j.ijmedinf.2020.104230.
36. Mandel, J.C., Kreda, D.A., Mandl, K.D., Kohane, I.S., Ramoni, R.B., SMART on FHIR: A standards-based, interoperable apps platform for electronic health records. *J. Am. Med. Inf. Assoc.*, *23*, 5, 899–908, 2016, https://doi.org/10.1093/jamia/ocv189.
37. Schwamm, L.H., Rosenthal, E.S., Hirshberg, A., Schaefer, P.W., Little, E.A., Koroshetz, W.J., Virtual technologies and the healthcare workforce: Opportunities and challenges. *Stroke*, *48*, 12, 3354–3360, 2017, https://doi.org/10.1161/STROKEAHA.117.018341.
38. Andrae, A.S.G. and Edler, T., On global electricity usage of communication technology: Trends to 2030. *Challenges*, *6*, 1, 117–157, 2015, https://doi.org/10.3390/challe6010117.
39. Smith, M.D. and Graham, K.M., Teaching with VR: Application in medical education. *Med. Teach.*, *41*, 9, 1054–1058, 2019, https://doi.org/10.1080/0142159X.2019.1581106.
40. Freeman, D., Haselton, P., Freeman, J., Spanlang, B., Kishore, S., Albery, E., Slater, M., Automated psychological therapy using immersive virtual reality for treatment of fear of heights: A single-blind, parallel-group, randomised controlled trial. *Lancet Psychiatry*, *5*, 8, 625–632, 2018, https://doi.org/10.1016/S2215-0366(18)30226-8.

41. Labrique, A., Vasudevan, L., Kochi, E., Fabricant, R., Mehl, G., mHealth innovations as health system strengthening tools: 12 common applications and a visual framework. *Global Health Sci. Pract.*, *1*, 2, 160–171, 2013, https://doi.org/10.9745/GHSP-D-13-00031.
42. Ozair, F.F., Jamshed, N., Sharma, A., Aggarwal, P., Ethical issues in electronic health records: A general overview. *Perspect. Clin. Res.*, *6*, 2, 73–76, 2015, https://doi.org/10.4103/2229-3485.153997.
43. Nakanjako, D., Namagala, E., Semeere, A., Kigozi, J., Sempa, J., Ddamulira, J., Kamya, M., Global health leadership training in resource-limited settings: A collaborative approach by academic institutions and local health care programs in Uganda. *Hum. Resour. Health*, *15*, 1, 88, 2017, https://doi.org/10.1186/s12960-017-0263-0.
44. Wamai, R.G., Alemu, K., Adego, M.A., Hogan, M., Health systems capacity building: Review of the literature. *BMC Health Serv. Res.*, *17*, 1, 328, 2017, https://doi.org/10.1186/s12913-017-2262-0.
45. Khazanchi, D., Kumar Vyas, A., Kant Hiran, K., Padmanaban, S., *Blockchain 3.0 for Sustainable Development*, De Gruyter, Berlin, Boston, 2021, https://doi.org/10.1515/9783110702507.
46. Kant Hiran, K., Khazanchi, D., Kumar Vyas, A., Padmanaban, S., *Machine Learning for Sustainable Development*, De Gruyter, Berlin, Boston, 2021, https://doi.org/10.1515/9783110702514.
47. Vyas, A.K., Balamurugan, S., Hiran, K.K., Dhiman, H.S. (Eds.), *Artificial Intelligence for Renewable Energy Systems*, John Wiley & Sons, New Jersey, 2022, ISBN: 9781119761693.
48. Khatri, N., Vyas, A.K., Abdul-Qawy, A.S.H., Rene, E.R., Artificial neural network based models for predicting the effluent quality of a combined upflow anaerobic sludge blanket and facultative pond: Performance evaluation and comparison of different algorithms. *Environ. Res.*, 217, 114843, 15 January 2023.
49. Pathmudi, V.R., Khatri, N., Kumar, S., Abdul-Qawy, A.S.H., Vyas, A.K., A systematic review of IoT technologies and their constituents for smart and sustainable agriculture applications. *Sci. Afr.*, 19, e01577, 2023.

14

# Leading-Edge Key Management Techniques in the Cryptography: The Metaverse-Driven Strategy

**Devendra Kuril[1]*, Manoj Dhawan[2] and Lalit Purohit[3]**

*[1]Department of Information Technology, Shri Vaishnav Vidyapeeth Vishwavidyalaya, Indore, Madhya Pradesh, India*
*[2]School of Engineering, Avantika University, Ujjain, Madhya Pradesh, India*
*[3]IT Department, SGSITS, Indore, Madhya Pradesh, India*

## *Abstract*

Employing innovative methods for encryption techniques to protect the information, identification, and interaction in virtual realms serves the purpose of securing the metaverse. In the metaverse-driven strategy, asymmetric encryption using leading-edge key infrastructure allows secure interaction among users, or systems for cryptography can emerge. It validates the identities of the system or users in addition to the interaction and various operations in the digital signature that can emerge. Also, audio and video interactions secured the realism interaction in the virtual world. Addressing these shortcomings necessitates the integration of an indispensable key enhancement mechanism to mitigate these challenges emerging in the metaverse. Assure that a certain amount of information transferred throughout the metaverse is protected during interaction; utilize complete security methods to avoid vulnerabilities. In the absence of the metaverse, prior analyses have underscored the inadequacy of typical methodologies, as they remain susceptible to numerous anomalies. Toward the framework of the metaverse, the present chapter examines and assesses for various techniques eliminating underlying hazards and augmented cryptography durability.

However, the cryptography using the leading-edge key manages and encounters the challenge of modulating matrices during computation, swiftly resolved by the system. Documentation indicates to evaluate the progressive cryptography, specifically designed to address the singular key issue through integration with a

**Corresponding author*: dev.kuril19@gmail.com

Ajay Kumar Vyas, Harleen Kaur, Sourabh Sharma and Bhavya Alankar (eds.) Metaverse Technologies, Security and Applications for Healthcare, (313–324) © 2025 Scrivener Publishing LLC

robust system. While they prove inadequate for handling entirely null values within respective blocks of the cryptosystem, the analysis suggests that virtual cryptography can be enhanced. The expansion of the proposed system is justified through key matrix generation approaches that pose relative complexity in recognition.

***Keywords*:** The metaverse, leading-edge key, cryptography, public key infrastructure

## 14.1 Introduction

One of the primary goals for many researchers in the context of technical advancement is to enhance organizational services for reviewing and improving end-user satisfaction. Security encounters unprecedented challenges and opportunities within the metaverse, an interconnected simulated environment created through a combination of substantially enhanced realism and augmented reality. Information confidentiality, integrity, and authenticity are increasingly crucial for users as they participate, deal with, and interact in such realistic environments.

Throughout the metaverse, cryptography plays a vital role in protecting confidential information, maintaining security for transactions, and validating authenticity. In rapidly developing technological environments, effective cryptography approaches by advanced automated virtual environments are crucial to protection.

In the present era, such architecture serves as essential in securing significant information spanning a variety of organizations, including finance, communication, and healthcare using the metaverse (Kürtünlüoğlu *et al.*, 2022) [4]. The leading-edge key matrix cryptography is designed to secure against unauthorized access, tempering, and interception, ensuring the privacy, authenticity, and integrity of information.

Risks arising from illegal access to unauthorized decryption activities; In short, the implementation of many crypto systems is an example of current research and advancement in revolutionary technology to overcome security features and prevent the secrets of encrypted information from being shared in the virtual world, which prevents the threats that are increasing every day.

In advanced cryptography executions, two kinds of cryptosystems persist and often operate within computerized frameworks of the metaverse. The relationship enables comprehensive secured features for versatile and significant processes of encryption. This sophisticated method might have irregular vulnerabilities in existing cryptography, although it featured security abilities (Shi *et al.*, 2023) [5].

## 14.2 Association of Sections

The remaining content is summed up in the following order. Section 14.3 explores the significance and consequences of the leading-edge key matrices utilizing the cryptographic framework. Section 14.4 explores the fundamental concepts that guide the recommended approaches. Section 14.5 explains the efficient methodology of cryptology which has enabled metaverse key elements and processes regarding the generation of the leading-edge key matrix, converging on concert matrices, measurement of the secured computation, and its effectiveness. Section 14.6 presents the observation and examination of the suggested approaches. Lastly, section 14.7 shows features work and summarization entails describing the key aspects and methodologies of the study, whereas summarizing work and, concentrates on distilling those components into understandable.

## 14.3 Significant and Consequence of the Leading-Edge Key Management

Managing communications in the metaverse—a technological state that integrates enhanced and virtual realities—involves leading-edge cryptographic approaches. The leading-edge cipher techniques, which are the foundation of cryptography, enable an effective structure within the virtual universe. Highlighting this study shows the significant role of the leading edge in modern cryptography techniques by executing its application and function driven by the metaverse technology.

An overview of the leading-edge key management in cryptography provides the mathematical underpinnings and insights into its past evolution. This explanation details how ciphers use matrices to generate keys, offering more information and facilitating necessary actions (Paragas *et al.*, 2019) [6].

In the metaverse, sophisticated cryptographic solutions are required, combining augmented and virtual realities, by the vase digital space to guarantee strong protected data security and interactions. In the security infrastructure or cryptography process, the leading-edge key management provides the essential part which is automated and generated by the user and is used in the virtual world to encrypt the information and vice versa. This research provides an extensive examination of cryptography with leading-edge key management inside the metaverse, describing its architecture, functions, vulnerabilities, and potential development (Kuril *et al.*, 2023) [3].

Encipher and decipher play a vital function in the consideration and deployment of cryptology using key processes. Such an algorithm operates within the framework of linear cipher structures which are distinguished by the utilization of matrices comprising information including symbols or characters. Using the leading-edge key system, the decryption of encrypted text necessitates the identification of a key matrix. This pivotal step involves determining whether the inverse matrix exists by assessing the determinant's value. If the computation deviates from unity or equals zero, then the matrix loses its composition. In these criteria, an optionally leading-edge key matrix is generated to perform the enciphering method (Shi *et al.*, 2023) [5].

In manual input processes, discrepancies can arise from potential inherent issues, particularly as these processes expand within a metaverse system. The integration of the metaverse into the cryptography techniques boosts resilience and efficiency, maximizing the safety of confidential data in parallel and minimizing the probability of mistakes. Professionals can adeptly and accurately maneuver through the intricacies of encryption and decryption procedures through the integration of metaverse technologies into cryptography techniques. The metaverse system ensures that the appropriate matrix constraints are fulfilled through a minimum of user input, which ensures the intended decrypted plaintext output. The implementation of constraints boosts the correctness as well as dependability of cryptography methods by offering security against any vulnerability or deviations from the available encryption process (Kim *et al.*, 2021) [7].

In addition, the metaverse improves performance by carrying out activities while they are truly required, reducing the requirement for extraneous information that may take place in manual processes. Minimizing unnecessary inputs and a suitable approach to encrypting and decrypting data with accuracy and discretion, instead of traditional manipulation where an authenticate user can input information as needed into each information block.

This simplified approach lets you perform effortless encryption and decryption across a wide range of datasets and circumstances, while additionally improving the efficiency of cryptographic techniques and the whole system performance. Cryptographic systems can achieve upgraded levels of dependability, scalability, and security by utilizing the mentioned system to control input restrictions and optimize the execution of tasks. These approaches ensure the integrity and secrecy of critical information in today's data-driven environments.

By analyzing the mentioned strategy to supervise input constraints and maximize the performance of the task, systems can cryptographically achieve an enhanced degree of scalability, reliability, and privacy. This streamlined approach improved the overall system performance and effectiveness of cryptographic algorithms while activating similar enciphering and deciphering across a huge range of datasets and conditions (Huynh-The *et al.*, 2023) [2].

## 14.4 Recommended Approaches

The arrangement of the associated cryptography offers security against potential vulnerability during the enciphering process through the inclusion of a further randomization model. The logical cryptosystem provides strong computation concepts, as illustrated by its techniques of enciphering and deciphering.

To cut down on unnecessary complexity and simplify the process, the encryption approach starts the encryption process with the generation of a single random numeral. Every single piece of data is then encoded starting with this first random number. Furthermore, a series of matrix regressions is used to consistently compute the real arbitrary number block linked to each data component during the encryption process. The block diagram in Figure 14.1 illustrates a high-level overview of the principal activities or global processes across the metaverse system utilized the previous defined approach. Although it offered a simple visualization, it attempts to reflect the intricacy and complexities of the various procedures and operations involved. Such procedures work on a metaverse basis & encompasses involve a range of interrelated activities required for functioning of the system's, which are explained extensively during the all process (Paragas *et al.*, 2019) [6]. The most recent authenticity represents that usual matrices are favored during the deciphering operation. By using arbitrary numbers as

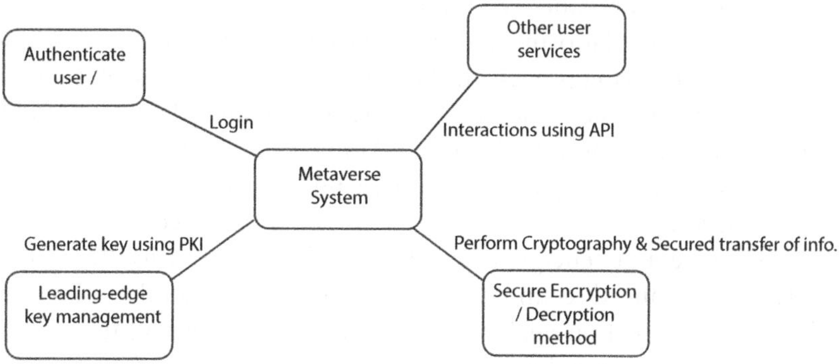


**Figure 14.1** Block diagram of enabled cryptography techniques using metaverse.

blocks and matrix regressions in the encipher operation, the cryptosystem makes ease of creation and preserves its strength while reaching a higher degree of cryptography.

The fact that key management within a matrix cannot always be statistically validated under most circumstances highlights a significant modification in metaverse systems. To create resilient cryptographic algorithms and computing systems, it is necessary to take into account and communicate the duties through singular matrices (Dr Kingslin, 2018) [8].

In the fields of cryptography and metaverse, the frequency of leading-edge key management matrices beyond computational has been acknowledged as both an advancement and an impediment, which emphasizes the evaluation of ongoing exploration and implementation efforts. It promotes the exploration of various tactics and approaches. This offers to minimize the impacts of usual key matrices, which is beneficial for the generation of mentioned systems that are more relevant and complicated (Seo, 2024) [9].

In the context of the majority of advanced ciphering, the vulnerability resulting from zero computation in a singular matrix poses a serious risk to the security of encrypted text. Employing the sophisticated resolutions recommended by the metaverse efficiently addresses this problem usually to dynamically alter encryption and decryption processes in response to the presence of leading-edge key matrices. By integrating metaverse-driven techniques, indicating a potential vulnerability of the cryptosystem can automatically identify situations when the computation of a matrix is null.

According to the projected approach, if a matrix's computation is null, the overall process identifies the flaws and highlights them through landmark strategies based on the metaverse. The framework develops a distinctive enhanced code for enciphering and deciphering when the mechanism of responding becomes apparent.

In addition, features and trends identified in encoded data may be modified by metaverse platforms and user devices to mitigate vulnerabilities during the enciphering process. If the singular matrix is present, then it is ensured that the encipher method's quality of dynamic adaption would be sufficiently robust to prevent decoding (Wang *et al.*, 2022) [1].

In a nutshell, the integration of the expanding technology with the linear substitution cipher with a leading-edge key matrix led to an important improvement in enciphering and deciphering security. Employing such type of advanced technology, leading-edge matrices offer robust and sophisticated protection against unwanted users, sustaining the secured and association of enciphered information in an easy and trustworthy manner (Huynh-The *et al.*, 2023) [2].

## 14.5 An Extremely Efficient Encipher/Decipher Suggested Algorithm

Within the realm of the metaverse, cryptography also ensures the integration of information as well as a secure transaction in a virtual environment.

### 14.5.1 Essential Key Elements

- **5.1.1 Authentic Individual:** Users employ various devices to communicate throughout the realm of the metaverse.
- **5.1.2 Platform of the Metaverse:** Cloud services and servers that comprise the infrastructure of the virtual world.
- **5.1.3 Algorithm related to cryptography: A** sophisticated substitution cipher process or method used for enciphering and deciphering.
- **5.1.4 Trusted Environments:** The communication channel that ensures the security and privacy of information.
- **5.1.5 Nodes Toward the Boundary and Outside Services:** The system in a distributed environment for additional analytics and characteristics (Wang *et al.*, 2022) [1].

### 14.5.2 Approaches in the Process of Encipher/Decipher

- **5.2.1 Verified Legitimate User:** Utilizing protected credential information including username, password, and multifactor identification user can access the platform of metaverse using OpenID or OAuth (Zhang *et al.*, 2023) [10].
- **5.2.2 Generation of Leading-Edge Key:** Throughout the user's terms, the key of cryptography created is done by the combination of public key infrastructure which is more secure in the virtual environment. Generation of key protocol among substitution cipher may be utilized to share securely through the users.
- **5.2.3 Encipher of Information and Secured Communication:** A proposed method of leading-edge key encrypts the simple information prior to getting delivered to another user. The secure path within the metaverse serves for communicating the enciphered information or encrypted text. These steps ensure the security and confidentiality of information whenever it is being processed through standards like SSL/TLS. To secure interactions in the metaverse, it is necessary that all communication between legitimate

users, services, and avatars are encoded. This framework provides security against intermediate assaults, unauthorized access, and even espionage. Secret information, sensitive data, and conversations in real-time are adequately protected against breakthrough by the use of strong encryption framework. Such approaches enhance assurance between users and features while ensuring the virtual environment's secrecy and integrity (Kim *et al.*, 2021) [7].

- **5.2.4 Getting the Leading-Edge Key Matrix:** Retrieve the leading-edge key that was used for encryption; it is shared among users by avatars in the virtual world and is also required for deciphering. This leading-edge key is required to be distributed and stored securely.
- **5.2.5 Produce Leading-Edge Key Matrices Through Regular Matrix:** In contrast to regular cryptology procedures, rules utilize the identical matrix, simple matrix, or singular matrix which has diligently generated the most advanced methodology. Those grids include broad fluctuates of information which also have distinctive signs, numeral figures, and data in specified boundaries. Through a collaboration of multiple elements, encoding procedures achieve a level of complexity that hinders opponents' efforts to gather information.

  Despite prior procedures of encoding, the framework is constructed utilizing leading-edge key matrices which are properly created through complicated but secured techniques. Such structure of a matrix comprises a broad quantity of algebraic information which is not simple and extends outside established limits. The encoding mechanism merges multiple pieces of information, making efforts to decode those failures because of its outstanding complications.
- **5.2.6 Received Information Decipher:** The secure mechanism for obtaining accessible information that is enciphered and rendered suitable alongside the virtual world is known as decoding. In order to secure the information processed under the encipher and decipher, the metaverse comprises a digital virtual environment that offers secure and strong cryptography to process the information. It offers an in-depth description of the deciphering method, i.e., relevant to the metaverse (Patan, 2023) [11].
- **5.2.7 Retrieval of Information:** Content that is encoded can be obtained through a variety of resource information,

including simulated interactions, activities, as well as system storage. Following that, ensure whether the details are obtained from a trustworthy system by verifying the authenticity and extent of credibility linked to the assets.

- **5.2.8 Deciphering Process in the Metaverse Framework:** The procedure of deciphering and enabling the model of the metaverse involves an environment that is intelligent with the ability to get the information that has been encoded and transform its normal conventional shape. The structure depends upon the system pointed out previously and has become strong to decode, requiring enciphering information along with moves for the remaining steps. The goal of the system we implemented would be to reverse the encoded procedure to retrieve the original data.

## 14.6 Observation and Examination

### 14.6.1 Considering an Instance as All Factors Remained Null During Leading-Edge Key Generation

The architecture recognized the potential causes posed through a null matrix key generated and an environment supporting multiple facets for a secured process. When an authorized individual has just unintentionally adjusted each component to null, the framework must rapidly recognize and fix such types of vulnerabilities. The framework frequently redefines the vital grid by employing advanced powered by metaverse computational method, therefore eliminating underlying vulnerabilities in security and improving durability toward attacks (Wang *et al.*, 2022) [1].

## 14.7 Summarization and Future Work

Regular strategies are challenged by the leading key production of vital frameworks using the application of metaverse integrative evolutionary tactics. In an effort to render the process of encoding less susceptible to the attack of cryptanalysis, a randomized factor was added to the collection of obtainable matrices key. All were thoughtfully chosen to utilize blocks of text and already determined multiplying elements. Utilizing leading-edge matrices key generated in virtual technology improved the exposers of enciphering recognized usable or under-stable data and an extensive evaluation. Considering continuous growth facilitated through smart virtual technology, however, the encryption protocol develops as it works through its shortcomings as well as offers encipher transformation commitment and improved authenticity.

Through the utilization of leading-edge key techniques with a public key infrastructure powered by the metaverse, the security-associated encipher strategy gets improved. Through implementing encipher strategies and enhancing the security of information, this framework shields over specific hazards.

Leading-edge key management techniques powered by the metaverse illustrate an entirely distinct idea behind the process of encryption. Through employing revolutionary vital techniques regarding the assessment influenced by metaverse strategies, such particular ways elevate the standard of security of information toward formerly impossible degrees of robustness and complexity. When exploring the framework and principle of secure communication, such as cryptology, it is important to point out how such methods integrate seamlessly into rapidly evolving systems. The specialist work to ensure the confidentiality, integrity, and validity of secret information. The analysis of Cryptology addresses new vulnerabilities while simultaneously providing security outcomes that outperform established strategies. This proactive strategy ensures that secure information is safeguarded from potential breaches, giving users a more strong and dependable safeguard in a dynamic and threat-prone environment (Zhai *et al.*, 2024) [12].

## References

1. Wang, Y., Su, Z., Zhang, N., Xing, R., Liu, D., Luan, T.H., Shen, X., A Survey on Metaverse: Fundamentals, Security, and Privacy. *IEEE Commun. Surv. Tutor.*, 25, 1, 319–352, 2022, doi: 10.1109/COMST.2022.3202047.
2. Huynh-The, T., Gadekallu, T.R., Wang, W., Yenduri, G., Ranaweera, P., Pham, Q.-V., da Costa, D.B., Liyanage, M., Blockchain for the metaverse- A Review, *Future Gener. Comput. Syst.*, 143, 401–419, June 2023, (http://creativecommons.org/ licenses/ by/4.0/), doi: doi.org/10.1016/j.future.2023.02.008.
3. Kuril, D., Dhawan, M., Shrivastava, G., The Advance method of Polygraphic substitution cipher using an automation system for non invertible matrices key, in: *Robotic process Automation*, pp. 329–338, scrivener Publishing, 100 Cummings Center Suite 541J, Beverly, MA 01915, United States, 2023, (https://onlinelibrary.wiley.com/), https://doi.org/10.1002/9781394166954.ch22.

4. Kürtünlüoğlu, P., Akdik, B., Karaarslan, E., Security of Virtual Reality Authentication Methods in Metaverse: An Overview. 5, 2022, (cs.CR) ACM classes: H.m., doi: 10.48550/arXiv.2209.06447.
5. Shi, F., Ning, H., Zhang, X., Li, R., Tian, Q., Zhang, S., Zheng, Y., Guo, Y., Daneshmand, M., A new technology perspective of the Metaverse: its essence, framework and challenges. *Digital Commun. Networks*, 1, 1–20, 2023.
6. Paragas, J., Sison, A.M., Medina, R., A New Variant of Hill Cipher Algorithm Using Modified S-Box. *Int. J. Sci. Technol. Res.*, 8, 10, 615–619, October 2019.
7. Kim, H., Lim, J., Lee, J., Kang, M., Secure Data Sharing for IoT and Metaverse Integration Using Physical Unclonable Function. *IEEE Access*, 9, 106387–106398, 2021.
8. Kingslin, S. and Saranya, R., Evaluative Study on Substitution and Transposition Ciphers. *IJCRT*, 6, 1, 155–160, January 2018, ISSN: 2320-2882.
9. Seo, J. and Park, S., SBAC: Substitution cipher access control based on blockchain for protecting personal data in metaverse. *Future Gener. Comput. Syst.*, 151, 85–97, February 2024, doi: 10.1016/j.future.2023.09.022.
10. Zhang, T., Shen, J., Lai, C.-F., Ji, S., Ren, Y., Multi-server assisted data sharing supporting secure deduplication for metaverse healthcare systems. *Future Gener. Comput. Syst.*, 140, 299–310, 2023.
11. Patan, R. and Parizi, R.M., Securing Data Exchange in the Convergence of Metaverse and IoT Applications, in: *The 18th International Conference on Availability, Reliability and Security (ARES 2023)*, p. 8, 2023, doi: 10.1145/3600160.3605019.
12. Zhai, H., Deng, M., Wu, H., Elliptic Curve Cryptography-Based Identity Authentication Scheme Suitable for Metaverse Environment, *Symmetry*, 16, 891, 1–21, 2024, doi: 10.3390/sym16070891.

# Part III

# APPLICATIONS OF METAVERSE

# 15

# Implementation of Metaverse for Healthcare System Modeling

**Naureen Afrose, Rideb Chakraborty, Ahana Hazra, Pratibha Bhowmick and Mithun Bhowmick***

*Bengal College of Pharmaceutical Sciences and Research, Basu Sarani, Bidhannagar, Durgapur, West Bengal, India*

***Abstract***

Through the use of hyper-connected, intelligent new technology, the physical, digital, and biological worlds combine in the 3D transcendent reality referred to as the metaverse, which has an impact on every business and economy. A significant prospect to completely transform healthcare system models has been presented by the emergence of the metaverse service, which consists of the five key technologies of virtual reality (VR), mixed reality (MR), extended reality (XR), augmented reality (AR), and artificial intelligence (AI). Healthcare system modeling has been influenced by patient pathway simulation, healthcare facility design, and epidemiological forecasts using metaverse. VR technology has been used in rehabilitation treatment programs to help patients who have had brain surgery, Parkinson's disease, stroke, or other recognized brain disorders regain their lost movement abilities. VR technology and song gesture recognition technology have also been used to enhance the cognitive abilities of high-risk groups with mild cognitive dysfunction and dementia. The application of MR technology has been seen in situations such as the visualization of patient anatomy data needed for heart surgery. XR technology is being employed in many different contexts, such as patient care, telemedicine, surgical procedures, and healthcare professional education and training. The primary applications of XR are in the fields of medical education and rehabilitation. Additionally, it is used to virtually represent the patient's state in

**Corresponding author*: drmithunbhowmick@gmail.com; ORCID: 0000-0002-7776-5744
Naureen Afrose: ORCID: 0000-0001-8334-9053
Rideb Chakraborty: ORCID: 0009-0007-3931-8349
Ahana Hazra: ORCID: 0000-0002-4850-2769
Pratibha Bhowmick: ORCID: 0000-0003-0445-5910

Ajay Kumar Vyas, Harleen Kaur, Sourabh Sharma and Bhavya Alankar (eds.) Metaverse Technologies, Security and Applications for Healthcare, (327–350) © 2025 Scrivener Publishing LLC

order to pinpoint the precise surgical site for care. Implementations of AR have been found in spinal surgery support systems and in situations such as operating rooms, where they are used to immediately monitor extra surgical information on the afflicted area in order to increase surgical accuracy and attention. AI technology has been used in situations where patients are tracking their health using AI-based systems, which enables them to do so without scheduling doctor's visits or physically visiting any hospitals. The VR, MR, XR, or AR environments have integrated pertinent healthcare data sources, such as electronic health records (EHRs), medical imaging, patient demographics, and facility layouts, through the use of metaverse implementation. In order to better visualize patient paths, optimize healthcare facility layouts, and simulate complex medical processes in a virtual environment, the metaverse has proven useful in healthcare modeling. In order to better understand how metaverse technology can be applied to healthcare system modeling, the chapter discusses its areas of implementation and clarifies how it can be used to improve patient outcomes, make better decisions, and allocate resources more efficiently.

***Keywords***: Metaverse, healthcare system modeling, virtual reality, extended reality, augmented reality, mixed reality, artificial intelligence

## 15.1 Introduction

With the introduction of the metaverse, the technological landscape is changing dramatically. This immersive 3D environment combines the physical and digital worlds into a hyper-connected tapestry. Its effects are destined to reverberate throughout our lives, including the basic foundation of healthcare institutions.

The revolutionary potential of metaverse services is driven by a convergence of five important technologies: virtual reality (VR), mixed reality (MR), extended reality (XR), augmented reality (AR), and artificial intelligence (AI) [1, 2]. These technologies, while powerful separately, become game changers when coupled within the metaverse framework. Historically, healthcare systems have been somewhat isolated. However, the metaverse represents a new frontier with the potential to transform healthcare modeling. The metaverse has the potential to transform how we approach patient care, facility design, and even illness predictions by combining immersive simulations with data integration.

This chapter discusses the different ways in which healthcare systems can use the metaverse. We will look at specific applications of VR, MR, XR, and AR, demonstrating how they may improve rehabilitation programs, optimize surgical planning, and give real-time information in operating

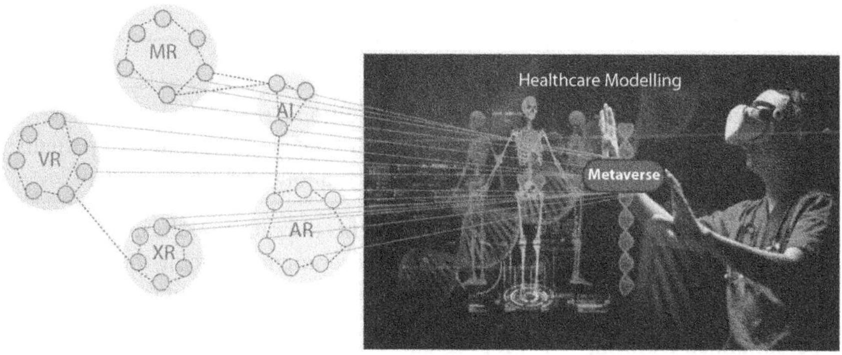


**Figure 15.1** Metaverse in healthcare modeling.

rooms. In addition, we will look at how AI may help individuals control their own health and help healthcare professionals make decisions.

Finally, the purpose of this chapter is to demonstrate how metaverse implementation can be used to enhance patient outcomes, assist improved decision-making, and promote increased efficiency within healthcare systems. Understanding the metaverse's potential allows us to usher in a new era of healthcare modeling, one that prioritizes patient well-being and optimizes resource allocation for a healthier future. Metaverse and its key technologies involved in the healthcare modeling system are illustrated in Figure 15.1.

## 15.2 Key Technologies of the Metaverse for Healthcare

### 15.2.1 Virtual Reality (VR)

VR is a cornerstone technology in the metaverse healthcare revolution. It develops immersive 3D environments in which patients can participate in virtual activities, providing a revolutionary approach to rehabilitation including cognitive therapy. VR has been used to provide a safe and regulated setting for patients recuperating from brain surgery, Parkinson's disease, stroke, and other neurological illnesses [3–5]. Consider a patient practicing walking or reaching for things in a virtual grocery store to aid in motor skill development and recovering lost mobility. VR also aids with cognitive enhancement, such as when paired with technology such as song recognition for gestures, VR can potentially address cognitive loss. Consider a patient with mild cognitive problems navigating a virtual maze loaded with

**Table 15.1** The benefits of VR therapy.

| Benefits | Scenario |
|---|---|
| **Increased engagement** | In contrast to traditional methods, VR settings are intrinsically engaging ensuring that patients are motivated and following therapy plans. |
| **Improved safety** | VR enables patients to practice skills in a safe and controlled environment, reducing the danger of falls or accidents during rehabilitation. |
| **Personalized training** | VR programs can be adapted to a patient's exact needs and abilities, enabling personalized therapy regimens for optimal rehabilitation. |
| **Data collection and analysis** | Virtual reality environments can assess patient development in real time, enabling therapists to analyze performance and change treatment regimens accordingly. |

musical signals, which stimulates brain function and may slow the spread of dementia. The benefits of VR therapy are highlighted in Table 15.1.

The potential of VR stretches beyond physical rehabilitation. According to studies, VR can help alleviate symptoms of depression, anxiety, and even post-traumatic stress disorder (PTSD) [6]. As VR technology evolves and integrates with other metaverse components such as AI, the opportunities for personalized and successful treatment will only grow. Furthermore, combining VR and AI could result in personalized therapy regimens that adapt to each patient's unique progress. VR is poised to become a strong tool for healthcare practitioners, providing novel approaches to improving patient outcomes and revolutionizing rehabilitation and cognitive treatment. Some examples of VR applications are as follows:

- **Stroke Rehabilitation:** Patients can practice activities of daily living (ADLs) in a simulation home setting to restore lost abilities and boost confidence [7].
- **Phobia Treatment:** VR may expose individuals to their phobia in a controlled atmosphere, allowing them to face their concerns in a safe and healing way [8, 9].
- **Pain Management:** VR can give distraction and relaxation strategies, helping people manage chronic pain more successfully [10].

### 15.2.2 Mixed Reality (MR)

MR appears as a game changer in the metaverse healthcare scene, particularly in surgical planning. Consider a surgeon wearing an MR headset that does not replace their perspective of the real world, but rather superimposes essential data directly onto the patient's anatomy. This demonstrates the potential of MR in action, providing unmatched anatomical data visualization for better surgical planning. It has revolutionized surgical planning through 3D visualization of patient anatomy. MR enables surgeons to examine a patient's data from medical imaging (CT scans and MRIs) as a 3D holographic model superimposed on the patient's body [11–13]. This provides previously unknown levels of detail about important structures like organs, blood arteries, and nerves. It additionally enhanced preoperative planning.

Surgeons can methodically arrange surgical procedures ahead of time when they have a clear visualization of the patient's anatomy. This allows for more precise incisions, reduces the danger of inadvertent harm to neighboring tissues, and, ultimately, improves patient outcomes. It also improved communication and collaboration. MR improves communication among surgeons, enabling them to exchange information and visualize surgical plans more clearly [14]. This promotes collaboration and guarantees that everyone involved with the procedure has the same information. The benefits of MR therapy are highlighted in Table 15.2.

**Table 15.2** Benefits of MR-assisted surgery.

| Benefits | Scenario |
|---|---|
| **Increased accuracy and precision** | Surgeons can visualize important structures in real time, which leads to more precise incisions and a lower chance of complications. |
| **Minimally invasive procedures** | MR enables fewer and more precise incisions, resulting in shorter patient recovery periods and less postoperative pain. |
| **Improved patient outcomes** | By improving surgical planning and allowing for more precise treatments, MR eventually leads to improved patient outcomes and speedier recovery periods. |

Some examples of MR Applications in surgery are as follows:

- **Cardiac Surgery:** MR allows for 3D visualization of the heart and adjacent structures, facilitating precise preparation of complex cardiac treatments [15].
- **Brain Surgery:** MR can offer a detailed image of the brain, allowing surgeons to navigate fragile brain tissue during tumor excision or other neurological treatments.
- **Orthopedic Surgery:** MR may be used to see the joints and bones in 3D, which aids in the planning of complex orthopedic surgery such as replacements of joints or fracture repairs [16].

### 15.2.3 Extended Reality (XR)

XR is a powerful umbrella term that includes both VR and AR. Within the metaverse healthcare ecosystem, XR provides a holistic solution that transforms patient care, telemedicine, and healthcare training for professionals. It has significantly transformed patient care, as seen in Enhanced Understanding. Consider a patient having a difficult surgery and virtually "walking through" the procedure beforehand. XR simulations can help to clarify difficult medical procedures, reduce anxiety, and promote informed consent. It also focuses on pain-management techniques [17, 18]. XR environments may offer immersive diversions and relaxation techniques, giving patients an effective tool for managing chronic pain or anxiety during treatments. It can also be used for postoperative rehabilitation. XR can be utilized to develop engaging and participatory rehabilitation routines, which promote speedier recovery.

It has significantly revolutionized telemedicine, such as in remote patient assessments. XR enables healthcare providers to conduct virtual consultations with patients and examine them remotely using real-time 3D visualizations [19]. It improved diagnostic accuracy. XR can be used to exchange medical imaging data and communicate with professionals in real time, resulting in more accurate diagnoses and better patient outcomes. It also shows remote procedural guidance. XR enables healthcare experts to remotely guide medical treatments carried out by on-site personnel, especially in rural or underserved locations with limited access to specialists.

XR has also optimized healthcare professional training. XR creates immersive learning environments. XR simulations may generate realistic scenarios in which medical students and trainees can practice operations,

**Table 15.3** Benefits of XR in healthcare.

| Benefits | Scenario |
|---|---|
| **Increased accessibility** | XR enables remote healthcare services for underserved communities. |
| **Improved communication** | XR improves interaction among patients and healthcare personnel, resulting in more cooperative and informed care. |
| **Enhanced training** | XR provides an exciting and efficient way for healthcare workers to learn and practice their abilities. |

develop their abilities, and acquire vital experience in a secure and controlled setting. Standardized training protocols are designed. XR ensures that all learners get consistent and standardized training experiences, regardless of their location or available resources. It is useful for practicing complex procedures. XR enables trainees to simulate complex surgical operations before conducting them on actual patients, resulting in increased confidence and competence [16]. The benefits of MR therapy are highlighted in Table 15.3.

Some examples of XR Applications in the healthcare system are as follows:

XR combines VR with AR, providing a wide range of applications in the healthcare system. Below are some particular examples of how XR has changed in many areas:

- **In Patient Care:** XR can enhance physical therapy with interactive activities, resulting in speedier healing and increased motor abilities after surgery [16].
- **Telemedicine:** Doctors can use XR to provide virtual meetings with patients in remote regions. Specialists can examine patients remotely using 3D visualizations provided by on-site medical workers, resulting in speedier diagnosis and better care coordination. XR enables remote procedural guidance for healthcare providers in underdeveloped locations or with limited resources. Consider a surgeon in a major city utilizing AR to guide tricky procedures performed by a rural doctor.
- **Healthcare Professional Training:** XR provides authentic surgical simulation for medical learners to practice

procedures safely. This helps them develop their skills and acquire vital experience before applying them to actual patients. Standardized training regimens can be created and provided via immersive XR simulations. XR enables trainees to simulate complex surgical operations without performing them on actual patients [16, 20]. This promotes more confidence and expertise among healthcare practitioners.

### 15.2.4 Augmented Reality (AR)

AR emerges as a valuable tool in the metaverse healthcare landscape, particularly for surgeons who want to achieve unmatched accuracy during treatments. Unlike VR, which entirely immerses the user in a virtual setting, AR overlays digital information in the real world. In the operating room, this means that a surgeon's field of view is enhanced by important information presented directly on the patient's anatomy. It has revolutionized surgical accuracy in a variety of ways, including delivering real-time information. Consider a surgeon executing an intricate procedure with vital signs, imaging data, or even surgical directions superimposed on the surgical field. AR offers this level of real-time information overlays, enabling surgeons to make informed choices in the present [21]. It also improves the visualization of critical structures. AR may overlay a patient's 3D medical imaging information (CT scans and MRIs) directly onto their anatomy, emphasizing important elements such as blood arteries, nerves, and organs [22]. This enables surgeons to operate with more precision while reducing the danger of inadvertent injury. Additionally, it has enhanced surgical guidance. AR can display detailed surgical instructions or even highlight the best surgical path based on the patient's anatomy. This can be especially useful for difficult or minimally invasive operations. The benefits of AR therapy are outlined in Table 15.4.

Some examples of AR applications in surgery are as follows:

- **Orthopedic Surgery:** AR can be used to show a 3D model of the patient's bone structure throughout a joint replacement procedure, ensuring precise implant placement.
- **Brain Surgery:** AR technology can reflect a patient's MRI scan onto their brains during tumor removal, enabling surgeons to visualize important areas while minimizing damage to healthy tissue.
- **Laparoscopic Surgery:** AR can aid surgeons in least invasive laparoscopic surgeries by revealing critical organs and appropriate surgical pathways within the belly [22].

**Table 15.4** Benefits of AR-assisted surgery.

| Benefits | Scenario |
|---|---|
| **Increased accuracy and precision** | Real-time data overlays and improved visualization of vital components lead to more accurate incisions and a lower risk of complications. |
| **Minimally invasive procedures** | AR can help surgeons do minimally invasive procedures, resulting in smaller incisions, shorter patient recovery times, and less postoperative pain. |
| **Improved communication and collaboration** | AR can help surgeons communicate better by enabling them to share data and view the operating field in real time. |

## 15.2.5 Artificial Intelligence (AI)

AI symbolizes a transformational force in the metaverse healthcare environment. AI enables both patients and healthcare providers in meaningful ways by deploying machine learning algorithms and massive volumes of medical data, as seen in Empowering Patient Self-Management [23]. It has helped with personalized health data tracking. AI-powered programs can examine a patient's health information via wearable devices or medical records. This enables personalized insights and early diagnosis of potential health risks, potentially avoiding avoidable hospitalizations. It can also aid with chronic disease management. AI can help patients with chronic illnesses such as diabetes or heart disease by reminding them to take their medications, monitoring their vital signs, and providing personalized food and exercise advice. It was also utilized to provide mental health support. AI-powered chatbots can provide basic behavioral support and self-management tools, making them an easily accessible resource for patients suffering from anxiety, depression, or other mental health issues [24]. In addition, it has been shown to play a vital role in offering decision support for healthcare professionals. It has proven useful in precise evaluation and therapy planning. AI algorithms can analyze massive volumes of medical data, such as patient records, medical imaging, and clinical research, to help healthcare providers make more accurate diagnoses and create personalized treatment regimens [25]. Improved risk classification is another application of AI. AI can identify patients who are more likely to develop specific diseases, allowing healthcare providers to focus on preventative medicine and interventions. AI is also utilized to streamline administrative tasks. AI can automate monotonous administrative chores such as

Table 15.5 Benefits of AI for patient self-management and decision support.

| Benefits | Scenario |
|---|---|
| **Improved health awareness** | AI enables patients to take an active part in their health by delivering personalized insights and data-driven suggestions. |
| **Early detection of health issues** | AI can analyze health data to detect potential problems at an early stage, when these issues are often simpler to cure. |
| **Improved quality of life** | By offering continuing assistance with management techniques for chronic diseases, AI may significantly enhance a patient's standard of life. |
| **Enhanced clinical decision-making** | AI helps healthcare personnel optimize patient care by providing data-driven insights. |
| **Improved efficiency** | It automates administrative duties, freeing up time to focus on patients. |
| **Reduced healthcare costs** | AI has the potential to lower overall healthcare costs by allowing for more accurate diagnosis, earlier interventions, and better treatment planning. |

appointment scheduling, medical record processing, and report generation, allowing healthcare workers to devote more time to patient care. The benefits of AR therapy are outlined in Table 15.5.

Some examples of AI applications in surgery are as follows:

- AI-powered drug research and development
- Personalized treatment based on a patient's genetics
- AI-driven robotic surgery for precise and minimal invasiveness

## 15.3 Metaverse Implementation in Healthcare Modeling

Immersive modeling, real-time data integration, and powerful visualization tools can all help healthcare systems that integrate both the digital and physical worlds [26]. The use of the metaverse in healthcare modeling holds enormous potential for the future of healthcare delivery as shown in Table 15.6.

**Table 15.6** Metaverse implementation in various healthcare scenarios.

| Area | Current application | Metaverse potential |
|---|---|---|
| Mental health | VR exposure therapy for anxiety disorders | Immersive virtual environments are used for experiential therapy and other behavioral therapies. |
| Surgical training | VR simulators for surgical practice | Collaborative virtual training programs for surgeons in multiple places. |
| Preoperative planning | 3D imaging for surgery planning | Integrated 3D models into the metaverse for realistic preoperative planning. |
| Telehealth | AR overlays for telehealth Consultations | AR and AI integration improves communication and diagnosis during remote consultations. |
| Physical therapy | VR exercises for rehabilitation | Augmented VR exercises for physical treatment, complete with immediate feedback and therapist instruction in the metaverse. |
| Chronic disease management | Remote patient monitoring with wearables | Wearable data along with real-time patient avatars are integrated into the metaverse to provide personalized chronic disease treatment. |
| Medical education | VR dissections and 3D anatomy models | Interactive virtual labs allow medical students to practice dissections, study 3D models of tissues and systems, and engage with teachers in the metaverse. |
| Drug discovery | Virtual simulations for drug testing | Virtual avatars with unique genetic profiles are being created within the metaverse to aid in personalized drug testing and speed drug development. |

By developing immersive simulations, supporting full data integration, and enabling breakthrough visualization tools, the metaverse lays the path for enhanced outcomes for patients, better decision-making for healthcare professionals, and increased healthcare system efficiency.

### 15.3.1 Integrating Healthcare Data Sources: EHRs, Imaging, Demographics, and Facility Layouts

One of the key components of a successful metaverse deployment in healthcare modeling is the smooth integration of multiple healthcare data sources. This provides a comprehensive understanding of a patient's health, facility operations, and resource allocation.

**Electronic Health Records (EHRs)**

EHRs are the backbone of modern healthcare, retaining detailed information about a patient's medical history [27]. This includes previous diagnoses and treatments, medications and allergies, vaccination records, laboratory test results, vital signs, and clinical observations.

Integrating EHR data within the metaverse framework provides healthcare practitioners with a comprehensive view of a patient's particular health journey. This allows many scopes as follows:

- Personalized care plans
- Tailoring treatment plans to a patient's specific medical history and risk factors
- Improved clinical decision-making
- Having access to a patient's complete medical record at the point of care allows for more informed decisions
- Reduced medical errors
- Eliminating the need to search for scattered medical records across different systems minimizes the risk of errors.

**Medical Imaging**

Modern medicine relies heavily on diagnostic imaging. Integrating data from medical images such as X-rays, CT scans, MRIs, and ultrasound scans into the metaverse allows for the creation of 3D reconstructions of a patient's anatomy [28, 29]. This allows for:

- Enhanced surgical planning
- Surgeons can visualize a patient's anatomy in 3D, leading to more precise and minimally invasive procedures

- Improved diagnosis and treatment
- 3D visualization of medical images can aid in diagnosing complex conditions and planning targeted treatments
- Better patient education
- Patients can gain a clearer understanding of their medical condition by viewing 3D models of their anatomy.

**Patient Demographics**

Patient demographics include age, gender, socioeconomic level, lifestyle behaviors, and family medical history. Integrating these data into the metaverse allows for:

- Identification of at-risk populations
- By analyzing demographic data, healthcare systems can identify individuals at higher risk for certain diseases and implement preventive measures
- Targeted public health interventions
- Tailoring public health campaigns to specific demographics can improve their effectiveness
- Development of personalized healthcare programs
- Considering demographics alongside medical history can lead to more personalized healthcare approaches.

**Facility Layouts**

The metaverse enables the integration of architectural blueprints for clinics, hospitals, and other healthcare institutions [30]. This 3D visualization of the design of a facility can be used for the following:

- Optimize patient flow
- Simulate patient movement within the facility to identify bottlenecks and improve efficiency
- Enhance resource allocation
- Visually analyze the placement of equipment and personnel to optimize resource utilization
- Improve disaster preparedness
- Conduct virtual drills and emergency response simulations within the metaverse replica of the facility.

### 15.3.2 Patient Pathway Simulation: Optimizing Care Delivery and Patient Flow

Patient route simulations in the metaverse represent a game-changing approach to healthcare delivery. These simulations enable healthcare workers to model and optimize a patient's whole path through the healthcare system, from diagnosis to treatment and recovery. This results in considerable improvements to care delivery and patient flow.

**Optimizing Care Delivery**

Preoperative planning includes things like virtual simulations that can simulate surgical procedures beforehand. This enables surgeons to plan the most effective surgical approach considering a patient's specific anatomy and medical history, detect and deal with potential complications before they arise in the operating room, and practice complicated surgeries in a safe virtual setting before performing them on real patients. This rigorous preoperative planning inside the metaverse leads to better surgical outcomes and more accurate and effective surgeries resulting in shorter patient recovery times and lower complication rates. This approach also reduces healthcare expenditures by minimizing surgical errors and complications, which leads to cheaper healthcare costs.

Personalized rehabilitation using VR environments can offer patients engaging and tailored rehabilitation exercises. This approach allows for targeted therapies that focus on specific areas of weakness or injuries based on each patient's individual needs. Additionally, VR environments enhance patient involvement by making rehabilitation more participatory and entertaining, which can lead to better adherence to therapy regimens. Ultimately, these personalized and engaging rehabilitation programs result in quicker patient recovery and improved functional capacities. Telemedicine consultations in the metaverse allow for real-time, comprehensive telemedicine consultations [31]. This allows for better access to healthcare. Patients in remote places or with restricted movement can connect with healthcare experts remotely. Reduced wait times, such as in telemedicine consultations, can expedite patient treatment and shorten in-person appointment wait times, as well as improve patient-provider communication.

**Patient Flow Optimization**

Simulating hospital operations: By generating a virtual version of a hospital, the metaverse may imitate patient flow around the facility. This helps in identifying bottlenecks, as virtual simulations can reveal regions of congestion within the medical facility and identify opportunities for improvement.

Analyzing patient flow data allows for optimal resource allocation, enabling better deployment of workers and equipment to suit patient demands. Improving patient experience via shorter wait times and a simpler patient journey results in a more optimistic overall healthcare experience. Pre-admission education allows patients to take virtual tours of the hospital and become acquainted with preoperative procedures. This can help in understanding what to expect ahead of time helps reduce patient worry, boost patient confidence, and improve patient preparation.

### 15.3.3 Healthcare Facility Design: Virtual Prototyping for Improved Efficiency

The metaverse uses virtual prototyping to transform healthcare facility design. Consider developing and testing a healthcare facility plan in a virtual setting, involving patient flow simulations and equipment layout. The unique technique provides significant benefits for enhancing efficiency in healthcare settings, such as optimized patient flow. Virtual simulations enable architects and healthcare experts to analyze patient flow within the institution. This enables the identification of bottlenecks and congestion locations, such as congested waiting areas or narrow hallways; testing multiple layout configurations to optimize patient flow and reduce wait times [32]; and streamlining the flow of patients, workers, and equipment across the facility.

This also contributes to improved ergonomics and workflow, such as virtual prototypes allowing you to test equipment placement, facility layouts, and personnel movement patterns. This promotes ergonomic design by arranging equipment and workstations for staff comfort and ease of use, lowering the risk of musculoskeletal injuries. Simulating staff movement helps optimize productivity by strategically arranging supplies and equipment, as well as improving patient and worker safety. Identifying potential safety issues in the virtual model enables modifications before the building begins.

### 15.3.4 Epidemiological Forecasting: Simulating Disease Spread and Resource Allocation

The metaverse provides an effective tool for revolutionizing epidemiology predictions. Healthcare workers can better plan and respond by constructing virtual simulations of large populations that mimic the transmission of infectious diseases, predict pandemics, and optimize resource allocation.

**Simulating Disease Spread**

The metaverse aids in disease propagation by generating virtual populations [33]. Here, researchers can develop virtual populations in the metaverse that mirror real-world population demographics, relationships, and travel routines. It can simulate disease transmission. Scientists can imitate the development of disease in the virtual world by introducing a virtual virus into these communities. This enables analyzing transmission dynamics through studying aspects such as incubation period, transmission pathways, and population immunity, which can provide useful insights into disease spread. It also predicts outbreak trends. Researchers can forecast the potential size and direction of an outbreak by simulating several scenarios with alternative actions [33]. It can also be used to test other public health treatments, such as vaccination programs or social distancing measures. There are certain advantages to simulated disease spread, such as improved outbreak preparedness. Accurate estimates of disease transmission enable healthcare systems to plan for contingencies and store vital supplies while implementing preventative measures in advance. It is also useful in targeted healthcare interventions. Simulated outbreaks can identify vulnerable populations in the model, enabling more targeted healthcare interventions and allocation of resources. It also helps to improve disaster response. Simulations can assist healthcare workers prepare for and fine-tuning their response methods in the case of a real-life outbreak.

**Resource Allocation Planning**

The metaverse enables the modeling of the influence of disease breakouts on healthcare resources, as seen in hospital capacity [34, 35], where simulations may forecast probable upsurge in hospital admissions, enabling preventive actions such as raising bed capacity or levels of staffing. It also helps with medical supply distribution. Predicting the locations that would be most affected allows supplies such as respirators, PPE, or testing kits to be pre-allocated to guarantee effective distribution. It is effective for vaccine rollout strategies. Simulations can help establish optimal vaccination campaign plans by prioritizing high-risk populations and increasing immunization coverage. Improved efficiency is one of the positive aspects of resource allocation modeling. Effective resource allocation makes sure healthcare systems are ready to address outbreaks while minimizing interruption. It also leads to lower healthcare costs. Efficient resource utilization reduces waste and maximizes expenditure on healthcare during outbreaks. It leads to improved public health outcomes. Targeted resource allocation improves epidemic control while minimizing public health damage.

## 15.4 Benefits of Metaverse for Healthcare System Modeling

The use of the metaverse in healthcare system modeling represents a huge opportunity to transform patient treatment, allocation of resources, and overall healthcare delivery. Below is an in-depth investigation of how the metaverse may lead to.

### 15.4.1 Improved Patient Outcomes

The metaverse contributes to better patient outcomes, such as enhanced rehabilitation. The metaverse enables immersive and interactive rehabilitative experiences. Patients can participate in VR-based workouts that are targeted, personalized, and tailored to meet specific needs and restrictions based on a patient's condition. Engaging and motivating make rehabilitation more fun, resulting in greater compliance to therapy plans, as well as improved feedback and monitoring since real-time data from VR workouts allow therapists to evaluate progress and alter rehabilitation programs accordingly. These qualities ultimately lead to speedier healing rates, higher functional capacities, and a more positive patient experience.

The metaverse also contributes to early intervention. The metaverse may be utilized to analyze massive volumes of healthcare data, such as medical history, demography, and lifestyle choices [36]. This enables the identification of at-risk people by proactively identifying those who are more likely to develop specific diseases. Simulations can also aid in the early identification of health issues, as prospective problems are frequently easier to treat and control at this stage. It also plays a part in preventative healthcare efforts. Early detection enables early interventions and preventative actions to slow the spread of diseases. By targeting early detection, the metaverse can help improve long-term patient outcomes while also lowering healthcare expenses related to late-stage treatment.

In personalized care, the metaverse enables a more personalized approach to healthcare through the integration of various data sources such as EHRs, which provide an in-depth examination of a person's medical history, imaging data, which allows for 3D visualization of a patient's anatomy, and lifestyle and environmental factors, which are integrated into the model for a broader awareness of a patient's health. This detailed patient data enables healthcare practitioners to adjust treatment regimens to particular patient needs, resulting in greater efficacy and favorable outcomes.

### 15.4.2 Better Decision-Making

Data-driven insights in the metaverse aid in better decision-making. The metaverse allows for the integration and evaluation of massive volumes of healthcare data. This enables the recognition of trends and patterns. Identifying previously unknown patterns in data can provide fresh insights into illness progression and risk factors. By analyzing past data and present patterns, Predictive modeling in the metaverse can help anticipate potential health outcomes and resource needs. Additionally, evidence-based decision-making allows healthcare practitioners to make better educated and effective patient care decisions using data-driven insights. This emphasis on factual information rather than intuition leads to improved decision-making throughout the healthcare system.

### 15.4.3 Increased Efficiency

In resource optimization, the metaverse is capable of being used for simulating and modeling resource allocation in healthcare environments. This allows us to identify bottlenecks and inefficiencies. Virtual simulations can help identify places where resources are underutilized or overstretched. It also aids in optimizing staffing and equipment distribution. Data-driven insights can help guide resource allocation decisions, ensuring optimal utilization. It also promotes cost-effective care delivery. The metaverse can help cut healthcare expenses by optimizing resource allocation without sacrificing patient care. Improved allocation of resources ensures that medical facilities are ready to address patient needs and provide the best possible treatment.

Streamlined operations in the metaverse can be used to model and optimize healthcare facility workflows, hence enhancing operational efficiency. This streamlines workflows, focuses on critical tasks, improves communication, reduces wait times, and improves patient flow. Increased efficiency means less waste, a greater level of patient, and better use of healthcare resources.

Reduced costs are one of the reasons for higher efficiency. Several aspects contribute to reduced healthcare costs during metaverse implementation, including improved resource allocation, which minimizes waste and optimizes expenditure on equipment, supplies, and manpower. Early intervention reduces the need for expensive and invasive therapy later on, while enhanced rehabilitation leads to shorter recuperation periods and fewer hospital stays. By focusing on effectiveness and mitigation, the metaverse has the potential to significantly reduce healthcare costs.

## 15.5 Challenges and Considerations

While the metaverse shows great promise for healthcare system modeling, there are many obstacles and issues that must be addressed before widespread application.

There are ethical concerns with data privacy. The metaverse generates a massive amount of personal health data [37]. Protecting patient privacy will require effective data security measures along with informed consent for data use. Data security is also a concern. The interconnected nature of the metaverse raises issues related to data breaches and unauthorized access to critical medical information. Robust cybersecurity protocols and laws are necessary to address these issues; besides, access and equity are also a challenge. Not everybody has access to the technology and infrastructure needed to engage in the metaverse [37, 38]. Providing fair availability of healthcare services in the metaverse will prove to be a continuing problem.

Technical challenges also pose a challenge. Healthcare systems use a wide range of software and data types. Ensuring seamless data transmission between multiple platforms inside the metaverse is critical for effective healthcare modeling. Standardizing data types and protocols for communication across the metaverse will be critical for enabling interoperability and seamless data integration. Infrastructure requirements are one of them. The metaverse necessitates extensive processing power and rapid connectivity to Internet access. Providing extensive access to these infrastructures will be critical for increased adoption.

User adoption and integration are equally challenging. Healthcare workers and patients alike will need training to navigate the metaverse and properly use its functions in healthcare settings. Changing mindsets can be a challenge here since integrating the latest technology into current healthcare procedures necessitates dealing with possible resistance and issues from healthcare providers and patients. To enable universal acceptance, the platform for the metaverse must be user-friendly and intuitive, accommodating users of diverse technical expertise. However, following certain considerations can help overcome these challenges.

- However, setting up explicit data governance rules would ensure correct data processing and patient protection.
- Implementing strong cybersecurity measures, such as encryption and multi-factor authentication, will protect critical data.

- Creating accessible and reasonably priced technological alternatives will be key to closing the digital gap and ensuring equal access.
- Creating standardized data types and communication protocols will allow for smoother data interchange throughout the metaverse healthcare community.
- Investing in the construction of infrastructure, particularly in underprivileged areas, is required to enable the fair availability of metaverse healthcare solutions.
- Involving healthcare stakeholders in the development and execution phase helps alleviate worries and build a collaborative culture.
- Prioritizing user experience by creating an intuitive and consumer-friendly metaverse platform that serves a wide spectrum of users.

## 15.6 The Future of Metaverse in Healthcare System Modeling

The metaverse is an unprecedented idea for healthcare system modeling, with the potential to alter patient care, the provision of healthcare, and medical research. Remote surgery is one of the applications in which surgeons will be able to execute intricate surgeries remotely utilizing powerful haptic technology that creates the sensation of touch within the virtual setting [39]. This will allow increased availability to specialized surgeons: Patients in remote places can benefit from surgeons' expertise from anywhere in the world. Enhanced training and teamwork will be implemented. Surgical teams can practice and collaborate in a virtual setting before executing real-world treatments. Reduced patient trauma will occur when surgical treatments performed in the metaverse using robotic arms commanded by surgeons will result in minimal invasion [39].

Patients in this scenario can participate in interactive and engaging instructional sessions through the metaverse environment. It will also help with genetic analysis. Integrating genetic information can aid in predicting possible health concerns and tailoring prevention strategies. Furthermore, incorporating data on nutrition, exercise, and environmental factors enables personalized treatment strategies. Virtual models for testing drugs with individual genetic histories have the potential to transform drug research and development by enabling personalized medical techniques [40].

## 15.7 Conclusion

The metaverse has the possibility to cause an abrupt shift in how we conceptualize and deliver healthcare. The metaverse can improve patient outcomes through early intervention, personalized care plans, and enhanced surgical techniques, optimize resource allocation, streamline workflows, reduce healthcare costs, provide greater access to specialized care for patients in remote locations, and foster patient education and involvement with their own healthcare. Healthcare experts, technological professionals, policymakers, and patients will all need to work together to make the metaverse-integrated healthcare system a reality. By solving the difficulties and seizing the opportunities, we can unleash the metaverse's transformational potential and design a more efficient, egalitarian, and patient-centered healthcare future.

## References


1. Mystakidis, S., Metaverse. *Encyclopedia*, 2, 1, 486–497, 2022.
2. Venugopal, J.P., Subramanian, A.A.V., Peatchimuthu, J., The realm of metaverse: A survey. *Comput. Anim. Virtual Worlds*, 34, 5, e2150, 2023.
3. Canning, C.G., Allen, N.E., Nackaerts, E., Paul, S.S., Nieuwboer, A., Gilat, M., Virtual reality in research and rehabilitation of gait and balance in Parkinson disease. *Nat. Rev. Neurol.*, 16, 8, 409–425, 2020.
4. Patil, V., Narayan, J., Sandhu, K., Dwivedy, S.K., Integration of virtual reality and augmented reality in physical rehabilitation: a state-of-the-art review, in: *Revolutions in Product Design for Healthcare: Advances in Product Design and Design Methods for Healthcare*, pp. 177–205, 2022.
5. Truijen, S., Abdullahi, A., Bijsterbosch, D., van Zoest, E., Conijn, M., Wang, Y., Struyf, N., Saeys, W., Effect of home-based virtual reality training and telerehabilitation on balance in individuals with Parkinson disease, multiple sclerosis, and stroke: a systematic review and meta-analysis. *Neurol. Sci.*, 43, 5, 2995–3006, 2022.
6. De Jesus Junior, B.J., Perreault, L., Lopes, M.K., Roberge, M.C., Oliveira, A.A., Falk, T.H., Using Multisensory virtual reality nature immersion as a therapeutic modality for improving HRV and cognitive functions in post-traumatic stress disorder: a pilot-study. *Front. Virtual Reality*, 4, 1261093, 2023.
7. Long, Y., Ouyang, R.G., Zhang, J.Q., Effects of virtual reality training on occupational performance and self-efficacy of patients with stroke: a randomized controlled trial. *J. NeuroEng. Rehabil.*, 17, 1–9, 2020.

8. Freitas, J.R.S., Velosa, V.H.S., Abreu, L.T.N., Jardim, R.L., Santos, J.A.V., Peres, B., Campos, P.F., Virtual reality exposure treatment in phobias: a systematic review. *Psychiatric Q.*, 92, 4, 1685–1710, 2021.
9. Lv, S., Zhang, Q., Wang, L., VR virtual reality technology and treatment progress. *SID Symp. Dig. Tech. Pap.*, 51, 35–38, 2020, July.
10. Prabhu, V.G., Stanley, L., Morgan, R., A biofeedback enhanced adaptive virtual reality environment for managing surgical pain and anxiety. *Int. J. Semantic Comput.*, 14, 03, 375–393, 2020.
11. Lu, L., Wang, H., Liu, P., Liu, R., Zhang, J., Xie, Y., Liu, S., Huo, T., Xie, M., Wu, X., Ye, Z., Applications of mixed reality technology in orthopedics surgery: a pilot study. *Front. Bioeng. Biotechnol.*, 10, 740507, 2022.
12. Wake, N., Rosenkrantz, A.B., Huang, W.C., Wysock, J.S., Taneja, S.S., Sodickson, D.K., Chandarana, H., A workflow to generate patient-specific three-dimensional augmented reality models from medical imaging data and example applications in urologic oncology. *3D Print. Med.*, 7, 1–11, 2021.
13. Wong, K.C., Sun, E.Y., Wong, I.O.L., Kumta, S.M., Mixed reality improves 3D visualization and spatial awareness of bone tumors for surgical planning in orthopaedic oncology: a proof of concept study. *Orthop. Res. Rev.*, 13, 139–149, 2023.
14. Sánchez-Margallo, J.A., Plaza de Miguel, C., Fernández Anzules, R.A., Sánchez-Margallo, F.M., Application of mixed reality in medical training and surgical planning focused on minimally invasive surgery. *Front. Virtual Reality*, 2, 144, 2021.
15. Ismail, T.F., Strugnell, W., Coletti, C., Božić-Iven, M., Weingaertner, S., Hammernik, K., Correia, T., Kuestner, T., Cardiac MR: from theory to practice. *Front. Cardiovasc. Med.*, 9, 826283, 2022.
16. Mathew, P.S. and Pillai, A.S., Role of immersive (XR) technologies in improving healthcare competencies: a review, in: *Virtual and Augmented Reality in Education, Art, and Museums*, pp. 23–46, 2020.
17. Wong, K.C., Sun, Y.E., Kumta, S.M., Review and future/potential application of mixed reality technology in orthopaedic oncology. *Orthop. Res. Rev.*, 14, 169–186, 2022.
18. Cascella, M., Cascella, A., Monaco, F., Shariff, M.N., Envisioning gamification in anesthesia, pain management, and critical care: basic principles, integration of artificial intelligence, and simulation strategies. *J. Anesthesia Analg. Crit. Care*, 3, 1, 33, 2023.
19. Girishan Prabhu, V., Stanley, L., Morgan, R., Shirley, B., Designing and developing a nature-based virtual reality with heart rate variability biofeedback for surgical anxiety and pain management: evidence from total knee arthroplasty patients. *Aging Mental Health*, 28, 5, 738–753, 2024.
20. Zhang, J., Lu, V., Khanduja, V., The impact of extended reality on surgery: a scoping review. *Int. Orthop.*, 47, 3, 611–621, 2023.

21. Innocente, C., Ulrich, L., Moos, S., Vezzetti, E., Augmented reality: Mapping methods and tools for enhancing the human role in healthcare HMI. *Appl. Sci.*, 12, 9, 4295, 2022.
22. Campisi, C.A., Li, E.H., Jimenez, D.E., Milanaik, R.L., Augmented reality in medical education and training: from physicians to patients, in: *Augmented Reality in Education: A New Technology for Teaching and Learning*, pp. 111–138, 2020.
23. Iqbal, J., Jaimes, D.C.C., Makineni, P., Subramani, S., Hemaida, S., Thugu, T.R., Butt, A.N., Sikto, J.T., Kaur, P., Lak, M.A., Augustine, M., Reimagining healthcare: unleashing the power of artificial intelligence in medicine. *Cureus*, 15, 9, 44658, 2023.
24. Zafar, F., Alam, L.F., Vivas, R.R., Wang, J., Whei, S.J., Mehmood, S., Sadeghzadegan, A., Lakkimsetti, M., Nazir, Z., The Role of Artificial Intelligence in Identifying Depression and Anxiety: A Comprehensive Literature Review. *Cureus*, 16, 3, 56472, 2024.
25. Rajpurkar, P., Chen, E., Banerjee, O., Topol, E.J., AI in health and medicine. *Nat. Med.*, 28, 1, 31–38, 2022.
26. YongQi, Z., Chan-Bormei, S., Miri, H., Transforming Healthcare with Immersive Visualization: An Analysis of Virtual and Holographic Health Information Platforms, in: *International Conference on Haptics and Virtual Reality*, 2023, December, Springer Nature Switzerland, Cham, pp. 81–104.
27. Srividhya, G., Electronic health records: a transitional view, in: *The Internet of Medical Things (IOMT) Healthcare Transformation*, pp. 289–300, 2022.
28. Chengoden, R., Victor, N., Huynh-The, T., Yenduri, G., Jhaveri, R.H., Alazab, M., Bhattacharya, S., Hegde, P., Maddikunta, P.K.R., Gadekallu, T.R., Metaverse for healthcare: a survey on potential applications, challenges and future directions. *IEEE Access*, 11, 12765–12795, 2023.
29. Lastrucci, A. and Giansanti, D., Radiological Crossroads: Navigating the Intersection of Virtual Reality and Digital Radiology through a Comprehensive Narrative Review of Reviews. *Robotics*, 13, 5, 69, 2024.
30. Yang, E., Implications of immersive technologies in healthcare sector and its built environment. *Front. Med. Technol.*, 5, 1184925, 2023.
31. Mohammed, Z.K., Mohammed, M.A., Abdulkareem, K.H., Zebari, D.A., Lakhan, A., Marhoon, H.A., Nedoma, J., Martinek, R., A metaverse framework for IoT-based remote patient monitoring and virtual consultations using AES-256 encryption. *Appl. Soft Comput.*, 158, 111588, 2024.
32. Alnahari, M.S., Exploring the Potential of Blockchain Technology for Improved Management and Safety of Underground Utilities (Doctoral dissertation), Arizona State University, 2023.
33. Sun, M., Xie, L., Liu, Y., Li, K., Jiang, B., Lu, Y., Yang, Y., Yu, H., Song, Y., Bai, C., Yang, D., The metaverse in current digital medicine. *Clin. eHealth*, 5, 52–57, 2022.

34. Kerdvibulvech, C., Exploring the impacts of COVID-19 on digital and metaverse games, in: *International Conference on Human-Computer Interaction*, 2022, June, Springer International Publishing, Cham, pp. 561–565.
35. Rejeb, A., Rejeb, K., Treiblmaier, H., Mapping metaverse research: identifying future research areas based on bibliometric and topic modeling techniques. *Information*, 14, 7, 356, 2023.
36. Nguyen, H.S. and Voznak, M., A bibliometric analysis of technology in digital health: Exploring health metaverse and visualizing emerging healthcare management trends. *IEEE Access*, 12, 23887–23913, 2024.
37. Wang, Y., Su, Z., Zhang, N., Xing, R., Liu, D., Luan, T.H., Shen, X., A survey on metaverse: Fundamentals, security, and privacy. *IEEE Commun. Surv. Tutorials*, 25, 1, 319–352, 2022.
38. Letafati, M. and Otoum, S., On the privacy and security for e-health services in the metaverse: An overview. *Ad Hoc Networks*, 150, 103262, 2023.
39. Tan, T.F., Li, Y., Lim, J.S., Gunasekeran, D.V., Teo, Z.L., Ng, W.Y., Ting, D.S., Metaverse and virtual health care in ophthalmology: Opportunities and challenges. *Asia-Pac. J. Ophthalmol.*, 11, 3, 237–246, 2022.
40. Singh, A.V., Chandrasekar, V., Paudel, N., Laux, P., Luch, A., Gemmati, D., Tisato, V., Prabhu, K.S., Uddin, S., Dakua, S.P., Integrative toxicogenomics: Advancing precision medicine and toxicology through artificial intelligence and OMICs technology. *Biomed. Pharmacother.*, 163, 114784, 2023.

# 16

# 5G Speeds for Metaverse Healthcare Promises and Challenges

**Mamta B. Savadatti[1], Ajay Sudhir Bale[1]*, Achyutesh Dixit[2] and Subhashish Tiwari[3]**

*[1]Department of ECE, New Horizon College of Engineering, Bangalore, Karnataka, India*
*[2]Department of Physics, Muzaffarpur Institute of Technology, Muzaffarpur, Bihar, India*
*[3]Department of Electrical, Electronics & Communication Engineering GITAM University, Bangalore, Karnataka, India*


## *Abstract*

Immersive virtual worlds and virtual care services are set to revolutionize medical care in the wake of the metaverse and advances in extended reality technologies. Nevertheless, the network infrastructure will face significant demands from several healthcare applications in the metaverse regarding latency, dependability, connection density, and speeds. The only network architecture that can feasibly enable massive use of the metaverse for healthcare is 5G, which provides wireless connections with latency as low as 1 ms and download rates of up to 20 Gbps. 5G networks can capture and analyze patient data streams in real time, facilitate high-fidelity visualization and simulation, allow multi-party collaboration in virtual worlds, and enable sophisticated metaverse experiences employing haptic technologies. But getting 5G infrastructure up and running to make this dream a reality is still no picnic. To reap the benefits of metaverse healthcare applications, the rate of network coverage expansion, spectrum allocation, technical obstacle overcoming, and 5G connection affordability must match the rate of progress in these areas. This chapter takes a look at the potential benefits and potential pitfalls of 5G, the technology that will open the door to healthcare metaverse adoption. Various kinds of metaverse healthcare systems have their quantitative performance goals and benchmarks established. The analysis's overarching goal is to examine potential risks and uncertainties related to 5G's potential to enable


**Corresponding author*: ajaysudhirbale@gmail.com

Ajay Kumar Vyas, Harleen Kaur, Sourabh Sharma and Bhavya Alankar (eds.) Metaverse Technologies, Security and Applications for Healthcare, (351–378) © 2025 Scrivener Publishing LLC

next-generation virtual care and to provide recommendations and expectations in this regard.

***Keywords***: Metaverse, healthcare, 5G issues, smart technologies

## 16.1 Introduction

The logical step for two cutting-edge technologies that have been created to improve the accessibility, convenience, and productivity of their users' lives is the confluence of fifth-generation (5G) technology with the World Wide Web of Things. With the advent of 5G, among the most widely used technologies, new possibilities will open up for businesses thanks to the integration of Industry 4.0, Internet of Things (IoT) devices, smart cities, and improved global cfonnection. An ever-expanding ecosystem, the Web of Things is a vast network of interconnected devices that can gather vital statistics and perform sophisticated analyses with the help of cloud-based tools. For many players in many fields, this technology represents a fantastic opportunity. The IoT and connectivity are quickly becoming the focal points of future product and service development for many enterprises. Picking the best main or supplementary connection option for an IoT deployment depends on several criteria, including expenses for deployment, ranges, interference, and the abilities of IoT devices. For some aspects of smart building controls, Wi-Fi 6 or Zigbee will do, but for really mobile wide-area usage, they will be completely worthless. Also, in cases where 5G is accessible but has not achieved a big enough market scale to provide comparable endpoints or network services, it may be much more cost-effective to use older technologies like Wi-Fi, Bluetooth, Zigbee, or RFID. There is room in some frequency bands for 5G and other services, according to technical research. Without properly adjusted and not too restricted technical circumstances, 5G service pricing, coverage, and operational quality might be negatively impacted [1].

Several sectors rely on IoT services, such as healthcare, manufacturing, and transportation. In these areas, dependable and efficient connection is vital to the success of IoT components and business operations. Reducing productivity, increasing downtime, and decreasing customer satisfaction are all possible outcomes for firms that fail to handle noise and bandwidth concerns. For this reason, it is critical to optimize 5G networks for IoT services and resolve interference issues so that companies may reap the advantages of IoT services and IoT devices with dependable and efficient connections. So, this study's impetus is to survey current efforts to optimize IoT services for 5G and mitigate interference from these technologies. To guarantee dependable and effective connection for the IoT devices necessary for the correct running of business models, it is crucial to optimize and mitigate interference with 5G networks in IoT services. Businesses may maximize the advantages of 5G networks and IoT services by optimizing network performance and employing interference control measures. The primary takeaway from this analysis is the potential for a paradigm shift in human interaction brought about by the coming together of 5G networks with IoT services. But there are obstacles in this union, and one must conquer them if they are to realize the revolutionary technologies' full potential [2]. Every device is linked, and all events are smooth, thanks to the integration of 5G and the IoT. This opens the door to a new age of creativity. This study lays out the primary obstacles that will prevent 5G networks and IoT services from reaching their maximum potential without first integrating them seamlessly. In order to provide customers with high-speed, low-latency services, this paper emphasizes that 5G services are powered by IoT technologies and that their compatibility is vital. Also, it highlights the fact that interference is a major issue for manufacturers; in order to provide suitable and dependable services, they need to think about it. The ultimate goal of this chapter is to help the industry make sure that 5G and the IoT operate well together so that new opportunities for innovation and advancement may be realized. In Figure 16.1, one can see how 5G and the IoT might collaborate and open up new possibilities in many industries. The first use case is smart cities, where the IoT sensors can monitor things like energy use, air quality, and traffic patterns in real time. City operations and residents' quality of life may both be enhanced with the use of these data. The reduced latency and abundant bandwidth made possible by 5G networks make them ideal for these kinds of applications. Industrial automation makes use of IoT devices to keep tabs on production machinery and processes in real time. Efficiency and downtime may both be enhanced with this. These applications may be supported by 5G networks, which provide the capacity, stability, and low latency that are needed. One potential use of the IoT in healthcare is the facilitation of real-time communication and remote patient monitoring. Both patient outcomes and healthcare expenditures may be improved in this way. These applications may be supported by 5G networks, which provide the capacity, low latency, and dependability that are needed. When it comes to transportation, the IoT can optimize traffic flow and increase safety by providing real-time data on traffic systems including the performance of vehicles. With the capacity, low latency, and dependability offered by 5G networks, these applications can run smoothly. By keeping tabs on crops and animals in real-time, IoT devices can optimize productivity while reducing waste in

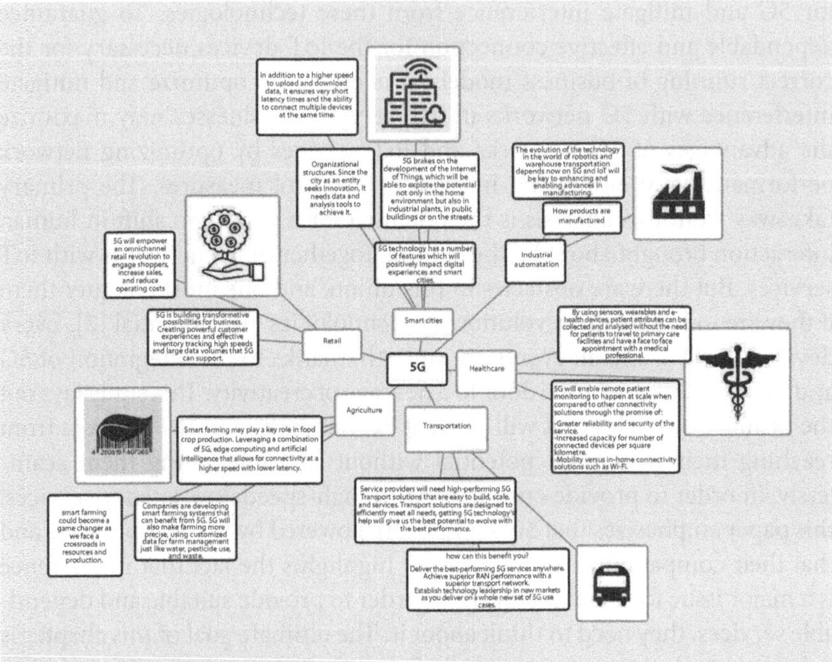


**Figure 16.1** 5G applications impacted by IoT devices [2].

agriculture. With the capacity, dependability, and minimal latency offered by 5G networks, these apps can run smoothly. Retailers can optimize shop operations and enhance the consumer experience by collecting real-time data on inventory levels and customer behavior using IoT devices [2]. These applications may be supported by 5G networks, which provide the capacity, stability, and low latency that are needed. Overarchingly, the chapter demonstrates how the IoT and 5G technology might collaborate to facilitate various applications across many domains. The capacity to gather and analyze data in real time, made possible by 5G networks' ample bandwidth, minimal latency, and dependability, has the potential to boost productivity, save expenses, and improve people's quality of life across many industries.

## 16.2 5G Network Requirements for Metaverse Healthcare

Figure 16.2 lays out the specifications needed for 5G which is the most recent iteration of the said networks, and it is made to provide a huge

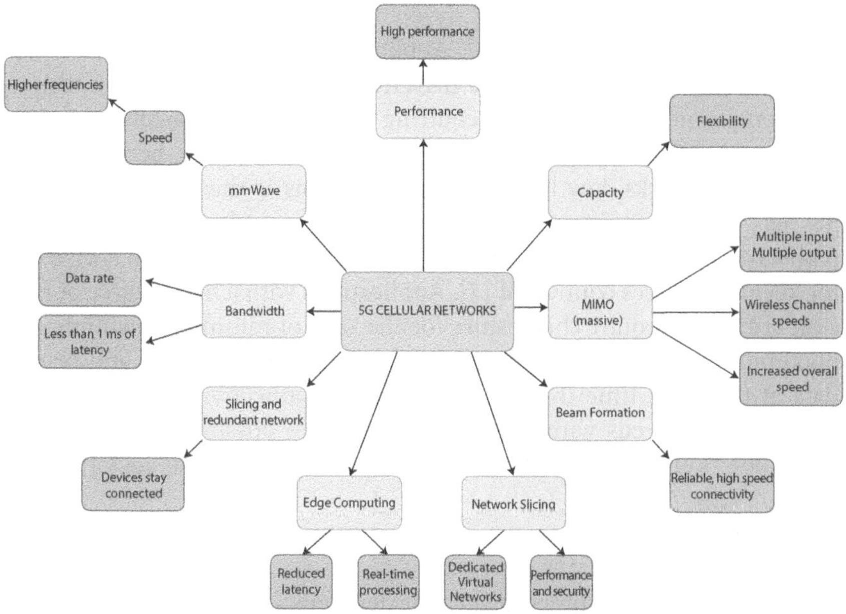


**Figure 16.2** 5G implementation requirements [2].

performance boost, capacity increase, and flexibility boost over its predecessors. 5G networks use many critical technologies to accomplish these enhancements. Millimeter wave (mmWave) frequencies are one such technology; these higher-frequency bands may provide more bandwidth and quicker communication speeds. The transmitter and receiver must be in a direct line of sight to communicate at these frequencies because of their short wavelengths. Massive MIMO (multiple input, multiple output) technology is another component of 5G networks; it employs a multitude of antennas to boost the wireless channel's efficiency and expand the number of spatial streams. Both the data transmission rates and the total capacity of the network may be enhanced in this way. One of the most important technologies utilized by 5G networks is beamforming, which employs sophisticated methods to direct a stronger radio signal onto a particular device while simultaneously decreasing interference [1, 2]. Providing dependable, high-speed connection in a dynamic, congested environment is made possible by this technology. An additional capability of 5G networks is network slicing, which enables the creation of specialized virtual networks to address the unique needs of various applications. This allows devices more control over the resources and services made available to them by the network, which improves both performance and safety. With the help of edge computing, 5G networks can analyze and analyze data in real time right at the network's periphery [3, 4]. Applications that rely on accurate timing, like virtual reality (VR) and driverless cars, may benefit from this as it lowers latency. Applications requiring real-time data transfer and reaction, such as unmanned cars and remote patient surgery, benefit greatly from 5G networks' low latency. Less than 1 ms is the target latency for 5G networks [5, 6]. Features like network slicing and redundant network pathways contribute to 5G networks' high dependability, which is essential for keeping devices connected [7]. Applications with a high degree of mission criticality require this feature for the sake of minimal downtime and maximum availability [8]. With 5G networks, you may send and receive data at the same time thanks to full duplex connectivity. Increased data transmission speeds with decreased latency are possible because of this technology's ability to boost the network's efficiency and capacity [9, 10].

### 16.2.1 Low Latency

The following are the prerequisites for deploying 5G networks, according to the specifications mentioned earlier [2]:

- Technology that uses massive MIMO (multiple input, multiple output) to increase the count of spatial streams and boost the efficiency of the wireless channel.
- Using beamforming, the radio signal may be directed toward a particular device, enhancing its intensity and decreasing interference.
- Improving network speed and security, network slicing facilitates to creation of specialized virtual networks to suit the individual needs of various applications.
- Reduce latency and boost the efficiency of applications that are time-sensitive using edge computing, which allows for real-time analysis and processing of data at the network's edge.
- The goal in [2] is to attain a delay of less than 1 ms for immediate interaction and reaction.
- Extremely dependable for mission-critical applications, guaranteeing little downtime and maximum uptime.
- Improved efficiency, capacity, and latency are all results of two-way communication, which facilitates the transmission and receiving of data at the same time.

- From IoT services to high-bandwidth applications like VR and AR, the integration of wireless technologies in 5G networks may allow a broad variety of extended work.
- In order to facilitate the expansion of the IoT ecosystem and usher in a new age of connectivity, 5G networks strive to provide the essential performance metrics required by these applications.

### 16.2.2 Key Performance Indicators for 5G Healthcare

The variety and heterogeneity of 5G applications necessitate the incorporation of new sets of key performance indicators (KPIs) for assessing the sufficiency and effectiveness of 5G-enabled services, in addition to the commonly used ones such as data rate, accessibility, reliability, and mobility. The taxonomy in Figure 16.3 shows how many 5G network KPIs there are. This taxonomy divides 5G KPIs into four groups: network, service,

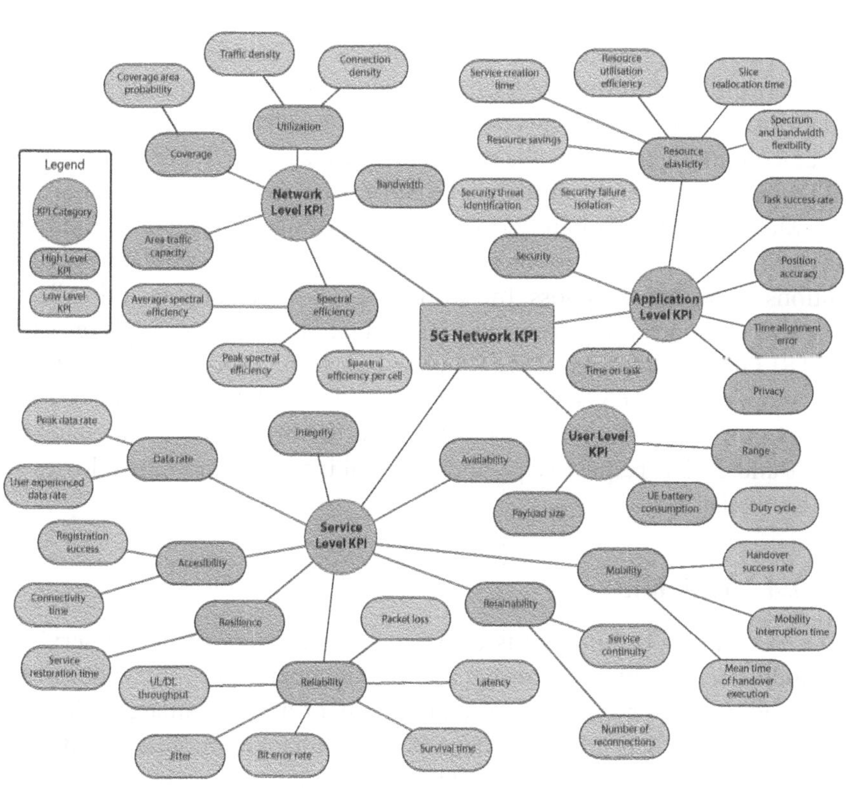


Figure 16.3 Taxonomy of 5G network KPIs [6].

application, and user. It draws inspiration from and incorporates domain expertise. With each grouping are both high- and low-level key performance indicators. On the one hand, there are high-level ones that calculate the network's overall performance using metrics specified by standardization groups like the 3GPP. Unfortunately, these broad KPIs often only attempt to describe the cellular system or service in general. To further concretize certain needs, additionally, low-level KPIs underneath each high-level one are provided. Depending on a certain set of KPIs to perform its role, a 5G-enabled healthcare application may be insensitive to others [6].

### 16.2.3 High Connection Density

Energy sustainability and environmental conservation have become global problems due to the growing demand for energy and the impacts of climate change. Smart grid advancements have disproved the notion that private, conventional electricity grids can handle the loads seen in manufacturing. The development of future smart grids will be propelled by the IoT, which is crucial to the growth of the 5G network sector. In addition to supplying the network architecture for smart grid edge computing, this sophisticated platform will include metaverse platforms. In order to build a long-term edge-computing network, it is crucial to optimize the IoT. For the IoT with 5G capabilities in environmentally friendly smart grid edge computing and the Metaverse, the work in [7] focuses on the design, production, and testing of a brand new, highly efficient GSM triplexer. In order to find the conditions for minimizing loss, the work looks at the resonator and collects a scattering matrix. For low-band 5G and GSM, the works triplexer runs at 0.81 GHz; for mid-band 5G, it operates at 1.58 GHz; and for mid-band 5G, it operates at 2.65 GHz. This triplexer has a small footprint of $0.007\ \lambda g^2 = 555\ mm^2$, large fractional bandwidths at the first and second channels (20% and 27.2%, respectively), and minimal insertion and return losses at all channels [7].

### 16.2.4 Reliability

The 5G cellular technology is enhancing the delivery of health services including treatment, monitoring, and remote operations. The widespread availability of 5G has spurred the development of more smart healthcare applications, which take advantage of 5G's enhanced mobile broadband (eMBB) and ultra-reliable low latency communications (URLLC) capabilities to create healthcare systems that reduce the need for patients to interact with healthcare providers in person at hospital centers. With this robust network, one may enjoy faster data transfers, far lower latency, and more capacity than 4G. By facilitating the use of Internet of Medical Things (IoMT) equipment, 5G cellular technology is anticipated to provide high-quality medical care.

### 16.2.5 Architecture of Smart Healthcare System

The primary components and overall design of the 5G-based smart healthcare network are shown in Figure 16.4. Assisted living, telemedicine, better medication, asset management in hospitals, remote monitoring, behavioral change monitoring, treatment compliance monitoring, and the IoT

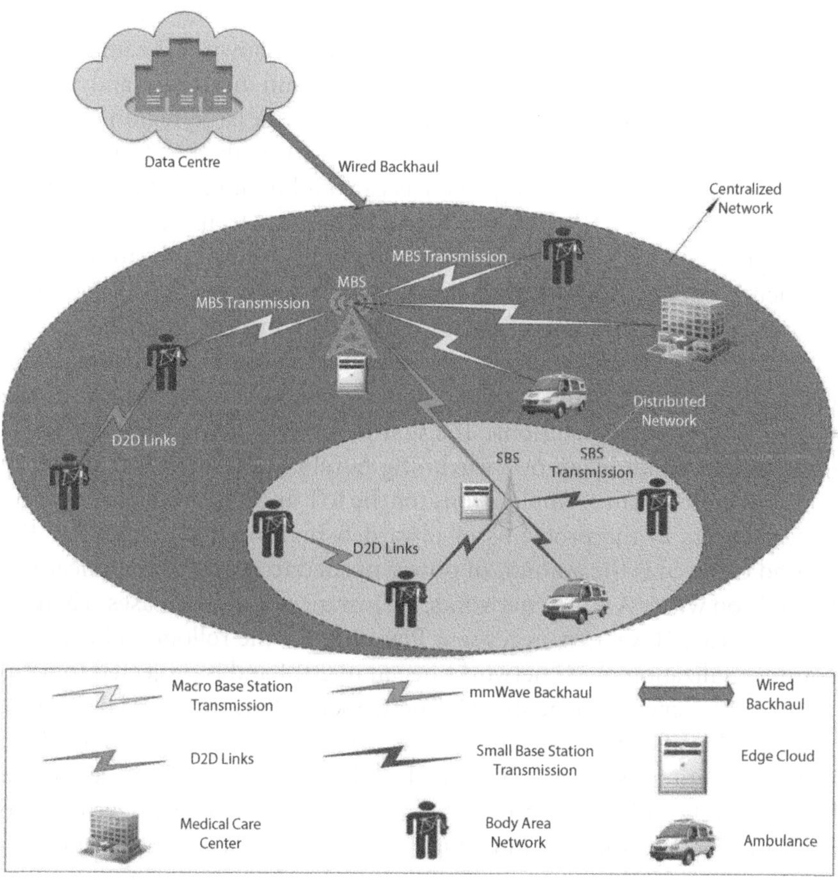


**Figure 16.4** A general architecture of a smart healthcare network based on 5G [12].

may all enhance various applications in smart healthcare. In the healthcare industry of the future, these applications will be crucial. The healthcare industry's IoT market is projected to reach over $117 billion by 2020 [6]. Numerous suggestions are made for the integration of online services, e-health, and mobile communication. The authors in [8] propose a mobile health app that can detect pressure sores using electronic health records. In [8], the goal is to create a smart health app that can evaluate and check dietary habits. The author proposes a fresh approach to mobile health apps. For the home, the authors also suggest wearable options that might aid with movement. For smart support in a mobile health setting, an IoT app is built on the mobile gateway [11]. According to [12], the IoT is a crucial component of any effective e-health platform. Wearable gadgets are suggested for healthcare inspection in a sensor-based wireless network. Smart antennas are crucial in 5G network communication. In order to increase the capacity and coverage of 5G, smart antennas make use of several important technologies. In one such invention, known as beamforming, RF energy is concentrated into a narrow beam and directed exactly where it is needed, rather than being spread out across a large region. Because higher-frequency mmWave RF deteriorates with authentication loss and distance due to things striking (such as cars and buildings), beamforming is very useful for 5GNR. The likelihood of optimal transmission capacity and signal quality is increased with a better-coordinated beam of radio frequency energy. Beamforming locations of interest are diminished with attenuation, therefore line of locate remains a concern. Smart healthcare in 5G networks is anticipated to be built on top of machine-to-machine (M2M) connectivity and the IoT. Two significant obstacles stand in the way of the proposed solutions. The first is the very dense network topology brought about by an overwhelming number of terminals (e.g., about 106 connections/km$^2$). Applications for the IoT and M2M communication need answers to the problems of ultra-densification and scalability. The second concern is the amount of power needed to power IoT applications that rely on wireless sensor networks; for instance, in certain cases, a battery life of at least 10 years is necessary. Planning for the rollout and eventual commercialization of 5G networks began in 2014 and is projected to wrap up by 2020. Expected benefits of 5G networks include increased data rates, network densification, and compatibility for a vast array of IoT devices. New applications, such as IoT smart healthcare applications, necessitate a high data rate and other features that 5G networks are being developed to support. These features include huge connectivity, wide deployment, reliability, reduced latency, energy efficiency, and wide-range communication.

## 16.3 Enabling Metaverse Healthcare Applications with 5G

Remote monitoring, telemedicine, remote surgery, and mobile medical support are the primary uses of smart healthcare. 4G technology has formed the foundation for the implementation of innovative applications in healthcare in recent years, with resources from earlier generations also being used. Unfortunately, technical limitations including poor transfer speeds, excessive latency, and restricted bandwidth have prevented them from meeting the actual expectations of the smart health industry [13].

Despite 4G's use in IoMT applications for linking a variety of physical devices—including smartphones, cardiovascular monitors, body sensors, and wearables—it encounters a plethora of problems as the number of connected devices grows. Consequently, a more advanced connection than 4G is necessary to fulfill the requirements of IoMT in regards to latency, data storage capacity, support for many devices connected at once, and speed [14]. Because it is more efficient than the 4G network, the 5G network seems like a fantastic option to fix this issue. 5G will make all of the present restrictions obsolete. Healthcare innovation will be made possible by networks with capacities greater than 4G, ultralow latency, improved mobile broadband, and high transmission speed. An ambulance, for instance, may facilitate remote and diagnostic procedures with the use of ultralow latency communication. On top of that, smart healthcare is anticipated to have a substantial 12.5% growth by 2025. Not only may smart healthcare's 5G technology improve treatment for the ill, but it also makes preventative care easier to implement. It also offers real-time remote device control, interactive video, and mass medical data transmission and management [15]. For the technology to handle the demands of several consultations, these data might be stored or sent between patients and doctors. Also, thanks to digital networks, patients will be able to have instantaneous access to their unique medical records regardless of their location or time of day. Patients might provide professionals with huge X-ray (XR) picture files, like magnetic resonance images, for evaluation; for instance, more and more medical research is demonstrating that 5G will be able to handle a wider range of clinical conditions as its deployment progresses. Platforms, methods, and applications have been developed to enhance healthcare via the use of telesurgery, teleconsultation, sanitary help, diagnostics, and preventative care. There is more current scientific material in this area due to the surge in technology solution development. Because of this, it is necessary to do a thorough analysis so that academics and developers who are interested in the topic may have access to a resource that is both practical and easy to comprehend. This resource will tell them how far along the solutions are and what new difficulties need to be addressed [8].

### 16.3.1 Real-Time Patient Monitoring

The term "remote care" refers to the delivery of medical treatment by trained professionals over the Internet [9]. With this, sensors and IoMT devices may share physiological data, which opens the door to remote diagnostics, surgeries, and treatments for patients. A teleoperated robot doing surgery remotely is seen graphically in Figure 16.5. In order to better understand the topic of application, this graphic is provided as a reference. Teleoperated robots aid in remote surgery [10, 11].

One aspect of the remote clinic is the use of the diagnostic and treatment system, which allows patients to avoid hospital visits altogether. A surgical robot and a control center housing the expert are essential components of a system for remote surgery. Despite the technology being discussed, there have been no documented surgeries as of yet because of the unresolved operational risk. Teleophthalmology, a laser instrument, a platform for remote computer control (TeamViewer GmbH), and a platform for teleconsultation via videoconference (Cisco Systems Inc.) are all part of the system. The inferior vena cava, heart, lungs, and blood arteries are all checked out by the system. It consists of two distinct ecosystems:

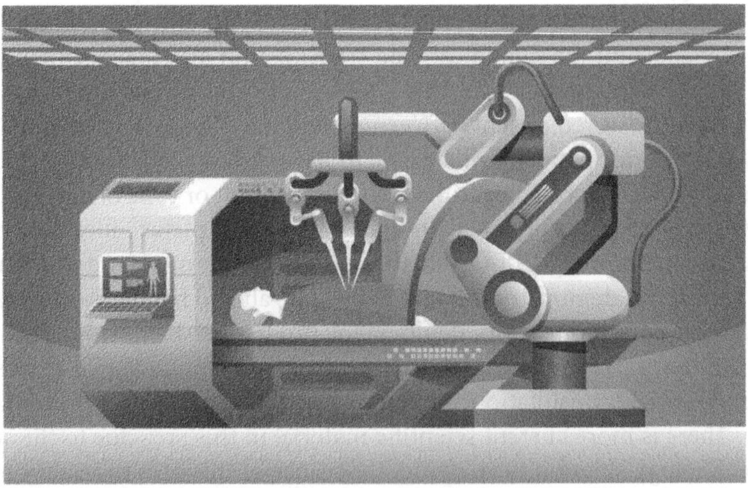

**Figure 16.5** Teleoperated robots aid in remote surgery [11].

A transducer, image displays, a console, and workstations make up the first, which is situated where the doctor is. In the second setting, the patient lies inside an ultrasonic (US) system that is augmented with a force sensor and transducers employing a six-degrees-of-freedom robotic arm [12]. A patient at Zhongnan Hospital, 700 km away from the sonographer, was the subject of the ultrasound [5].

### 16.3.2 High-Fidelity Medical Visualization

Modern volumetric modeling techniques enhance the ability of clinicians to diagnose and plan treatments by generating more lifelike depictions of patients' physical states compared to standard 2D photographs. Nevertheless, other constraints contribute to the imbalance between feasible options for training and education as well as for surgical preparation and other situations that need exceptional picture quality and stringent data management. Users are now limited to seeing 3D volumetric data on 2D screens, which hampers their capacity to do computations, such as measuring ranges between objects. Additionally, interactivity with the data is restricted to conventional input devices like a mouse and keyboard [13]. Mixed reality technology is now used in many capacities within the field of medicine. In the field of higher learning, the use of VR and AR is utilized for teaching anatomy. Immersive solutions are used in the instruction for healthcare learners, such as in PathoGeniusVR, where a serious game strategy is employed. Additionally, surgery simulators are employed using pre-processed models or actual scanning images [14, 15]. In the field of medicine, staff training utilizes it, and compares their approach with comparable ones. Surgical planning is a very impactful field in terms of public health, requiring high-quality images, accuracy, and strong interactive capabilities. VR is also extensively explored, particularly if haptic feedback is needed [16–18]. Recently, VR has been used for telerobotics and robot-assisted invasive structures. Undoubtedly, realistic healthcare simulations are a lot desired, as shown by many studies discussing the current status of these systems. VR is used in other situations, such as psychiatric treatment or rehabilitation, when the patient-as-user approach is used. Non-educational VR is utilized more often for two primary purposes: the development of extremely realistic simulators and the creation of highly dynamic medical data visualization workstations [19]. These applications are primarily intended for surgical planning. To be suitable for a system to qualify for being used in a medical setting, it must be capable of accommodating diverse clinical information (rather than already processed general

3D human models) and also be compatible with the data formats utilized by industry-standard electronics.

### 16.3.3 Virtual Collaborative Environments

The advent of 5G will be virtual consultations and the use of virtual meetings such as Skype, Teams, or Facetime, which have been in existence for some years. Nevertheless, the use of these technologies may result in the patient experiencing a sense of detachment from the clinician [20–22]. VR reduces the perceived distance between individuals by creating a highly immersive environment, which facilitates more intimate and personal conversations. VR prototypes designed for virtual medical consultations have been in existence for some years, including the Virtual Health Consultation program. The counseling supervisors interact with those taking part in different virtual locations. Such software might be integrated into a broader metaverse, enabling patients to get health help and counsel from the comfort of their own homes. Virtual consultations are time-saving for doctors and very beneficial for patients who have limited mobility. They might be included in a digital platform, allowing both the individual and the physician to see a virtual depiction of the patient during discussions about the patient's health, thus enhancing the patient's comprehension of the illness. The metaverse has the potential to provide healthcare personnel with online instruction and simulated events, enabling them to enhance their abilities via practice, while eliminating any potential harm to patients [23, 24]. VR has been suggested as a method for conducting surgical scenarios as early as the last century. Presently, there are several technologies available that enable training and simulation in VR. The Precision VR platform developed by Surgical Theatre generates patient-specific 360° VR models from volumetric scans like as CT and MRI. These models can be easily edited and seen from any angle using a display with touchscreens or a simulated reality headset with controls [25]. The MetaMedicsVR platform offers VR training for patients, including nurses, and doctors, along with additional medical experts. Educational VR systems provide a significant benefit by providing prompt and tailored information to students. Sandrone [26] demonstrates that metaverse games, which employ avatars to simulate healthcare situations, have been effectively tested in various medical domains, including preliminary and health education. These games have been shown to enhance educational results and foster greater interest, involvement, and partnership among medical students within an ideal setting for decision-making. The advancement of immersive educational technology is progressing quickly and has the potential to revolutionize the teaching of medicine shortly. Recent research indicates that a growing number of academic students increasingly choose cyber-physical institutions over traditional institutions. In addition to training and simulation systems, there are also VR reference works available. Medical Augmented Intelligence (MAI) developed a 3D VR tool called "BodyMap" [27], which provides a realistic depiction of the human body and can be edited for medical teaching.

### 16.3.4 Haptic Feedback and Immersion

Due to haptic feedback, a new technology that enables remote touch, physicians, doctors, and healthcare professionals may now remotely access, manipulate, and visualize 3D imaging data of patients with equivalent or even superior precision compared to being physically there. Consequently, they may get a more accurate clinical assessment, identifying any consequences resulting from a condition or infectious illness, such as COVID-19. Furthermore, by incorporating artificial intelligence (AI) into the system, it becomes capable of "learning" the actions performed by the controller during operation. Therefore, it will have the capability to execute operational tasks with little or no human supervision or intervention. 5G mobile networks are anticipated to address the considerable technological challenge of reducing latency among applications for telemedicine and master controllers. The primary objective of 5G systems is to maintain transmission latency within acceptable limits. This is crucial because skilled surgeons may remotely manage robotic surgical tools, even when they are positioned several kilometers farther from the patient. 5G networks are crucial for ensuring consistent connection stability and achieving minimal latency to effectively transmit haptic data. Furthermore, the enhanced data speeds of 5G networks will provide superior visualization and greater dexterity, leading to a more precise surgical procedure [28]. Applying novel technology in medicine to address epidemic illnesses presents several hurdles. Therefore, it is crucial to implement a highly efficient plan that incorporates state-of-the-art technology in order to accomplish this objective. The model involves integrating the following developing technologies to create a powerful framework that will enhance the diagnosis of problems and increase surgical operating skills.

VR and AR innovations, together with advancements in human-computer interface methods, enable the retrieval of volumetric data inside a 3D environment. Three-dimensional photographs provide an additional anatomical depiction of the human body compared to traditional 2D photos. Doctors may get precise information about a patient's health by using

VR/AR glasses. Thanks to haptic technology, a surgeon may perform a surgical procedure using a haptic device without having to remain in the same clinic as the patient. Using 5G networks, the surgeon may control a piece of robotic equipment from any location, allowing for simultaneous and accurate interaction with the surgeon's movements. By integrating AI with the interface between the haptic instrument and the robotic machines, the system can function autonomously by observing and learning from the movements of the surgeon.

The effective real-time interplay of actuator and touch requires an ultra-reliable and ultra-responsive connection of networking for haptic data transfer. The objective of Tactile Internet is to facilitate this kind of connectivity [29, 30]. It will revolutionize several aspects of society via remarkable technologies and fundamentally alter the current understanding of the Internet, shifting its focus from content to the transmission of haptic experiences. Haptic networking will provide a new and unique kind of Internet that enables interaction between machines and humans [31]. This technology provides high dependability, a little delay, enhanced security, and wider coverage of the network, all of which are crucial for real-time systems that interact. Haptic interaction is an emerging technology that is seeing tremendous growth. It has many uses in several fields, including learning, recreation, telerobotics, and the development of accurate emulators for intricate surgical operations. Haptics has the potential to enhance surgical planning by providing clinicians with simulated tools necessary for completing surgeries [32]. Consequently, a surgeon can physically perceive and manipulate the patient's skeletal structure, muscular system, and vital organs. Furthermore, contact pressures assist the surgeon in preventing the overlapping of body parts that may be hard to see. The use of haptic feedback to replicate certain surgical procedures enhances realism for educational purposes. Using sensory input in recreating particular surgical techniques for instructional reasons would enhance realism [33]. A haptic interface offers enhanced accuracy and faster job completion with fewer technical mistakes, while a visual-haptic interaction offers a sophisticated method for performing force-sensitive activities [34]. Therefore, the combination of haptic data with low latency networks will enable the development of VR headsets that may aid surgeons and physicians in performing remote surgical procedures, offering several advantages [35]. Figure 16.6 demonstrates how the Tactile Web will enhance the transfer of touch and grab abilities [28]. The use of this technology will enhance the physical capacities of healthcare practitioners to provide accurate remote diagnosis and treatment. The transfer of haptic data, which includes the sensation of

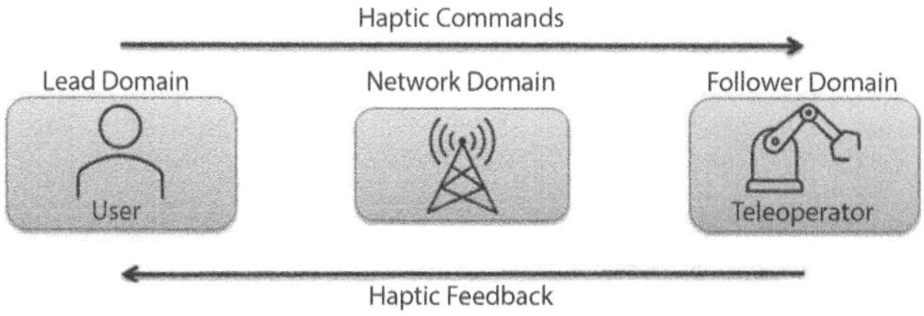


**Figure 16.6** Tactile network connectivity zones [28].

touch, is expected to improve real-time distant contact and consultation. Furthermore, VR and AR have the capability to be employed for virtual treatment by providing a deeply engaging user experience. The distinctive characteristics of e-health listed above are the primary drivers that will revolutionize the healthcare sector in the foreseeable future, providing several advantages and capacities [36]. 5G will improve the chances for remote instructional courses for medical professionals by including visual and tactile feedback. This will result in an Internet of medical abilities, in which medical professionals will be enabled to transmit their knowledge and exchange their expertise while overcoming the barrier of distance via the use of robotics and haptic technologies. Thus, one major benefit is that hobbyist surgeons will be able to go to and observe surgical operations performed by professional physicians, even if they are situated in different locations. Furthermore, surgeons will handle robots using tactile gloves or gadgets that can provide haptic input to the operative physician from a distance. This futuristic surgical surgery will be possible because of 5G's 1 ms latency.

The increasing use of VR and AR methods, together with advancements in human-computer interface methodologies, help the retrieval of volumetric data in a three-dimensional setting. More sophisticated visualization technologies and engagement techniques, such as VR, AR, AI, and haptic feedback, make it simpler to manipulate and potentially diagnose 3D images. Numerous solutions have been tested employing tactile stimulation sensors for collaborating with volumetric information during VR and AR environments. Despite having the ability to interact with volumetric data in 3D, these approaches use one-point haptic controllers.

The integration of VR, AR, AI, and haptics may provide surgeons with a multimedia approach to improve their practice. Because there is little danger of illness spreading among doctors, they may examine patients despite needing them to be present in the medical center or operation room. This approach may be especially useful when patients are struggling

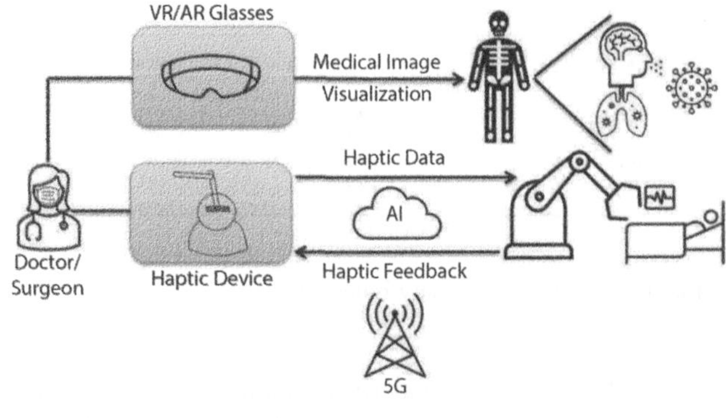


**Figure 16.7** Healthcare image visualization using AI-based tactile engagement [28].

with infectious diseases. Figure 16.7 depicts a doctor or surgeon using VR/AR glasses, which allow them to inspect the patient's body in 3D and gain a thorough understanding of the illness they have. Furthermore, haptics allows the surgeon to do a surgical operation by directing a haptic device that alters the surgery robot or slave equipment on the other end. This implies that the surgeon and the patient may be separated by distance rather than sharing the same operational room. Thus, any surgeon may be able to engage in surgical procedures all over the globe without leaving their permanent domicile. Using AI between the haptic and slave devices, the whole thing will be capable of self-learning by "observing" the doctor's activities, allowing it to develop completely free of human contact.

## 16.4 Challenges in 5G Rollout for Healthcare Metaverse

There are a lot of challenges in 5G which are with respect to the healthcare metaverse. The following subsections discuss this.

### 16.4.1 Network Coverage

For responsive and immersive experiences, you need a connection that is fast, has low latency, and has a lot of capacity, which is what both 6G and 5G networks provide. Enabling complete immersion in the metaverse relies heavily on connectivity [5]. 5G is playing a vital role in the evolving metaverse, according to Mischa Dohler, the chief architect at Ericsson Silicon Valley. 5G and 6G networks provide several benefits to the healthcare

**Table 16.1** Metaverse networks need and features.

| Factors | Features |
|---|---|
| Metaverse access for all multiverses in the universe | Capabilities to roam for easier access on a global scale |
| | Reliable coverage and ability |
| Portable and easy-to-use virtual reality headsets for use in the metaverse | Availability of low-latency, high-throughput computing at the edge |
| | Thanks to devices' reliable connections and minimal latency, additional jobs may be rendered at the edge using edge streaming |
| Edge-cloud and cloud capabilities | The render detail level has been improved |
| | Reduce processing load to prolong battery life |
| Consistent interfaces | Metaverse norms |
| | extended reality (XR), tactile, and holographic |
| | Telecom industry norms |
| Developers may quickly access packages | Make use of 5G's "network platform" by integrating its application programming interfaces (APIs) with existing developer tools and business logic |

industry, including speed, range, dependability, latency, and more—all of which are particularly important in the metaverse. A number of benefits, including the ability to teach medical professionals in the metaverse, perform aided metaverse telesurgery, and assure online consultations via patients' and physicians' avatars, will result from this connectedness. The 5G/6G technology has taken into account the characteristics and needs listed in Table 16.1 to guarantee the maximum flow of communication in the metaverse [4].

### 16.4.2 Spectrum Allocation

Although 6G has replaced 5G, 5G technologies are still needed. The wireless telecommunications industry still relies on 4G for consumer usage. 5G is progressively replacing this obsolete technology, with most installations taking place in densely populated areas. In 2009, the 4G/LTE technology revolutionized handheld devices by enabling faster connection rates and allowing users to stream HD movies, play multiplayer games online, and communicate large quantities of data at up to 33 Mbps. 5G surpasses 4G by employing microwave and mmWave technologies to achieve speeds of 900 Mbps or more. More rapid speeds and bandwidth are equivalent to commercial providers of internet service, allowing for other purposes beyond streaming video. IoT and edge computing will be equipped with real-time sensor abilities, allowing for immediate data collection via the cloud. 5G technology has uses in retailing and business, as it allows for quicker calculations to diagnose and treat patients in the healthcare sector. The benefits of 5G technology are many, but its entirety will not be realized until it is widely applied [36, 37]. While AR/VR technology has been around for a few years, its widespread adoption relies on 5G/6G technology and edge computing. 5G/6G technology requires low latency and high bandwidth to support certain use applications. Private 5G/6G services enable industry and corporate clients to perform essential procedures using the necessary resources. Private 5G/6G systems offer the necessary abilities for applications that are vital, whereas public networks may not provide appropriate coverage or a stable level of performance.

The metaverse has significant promise for guaranteeing the future of AR/VR/MR technology. The system enables users to create a fully featured virtual environment with specified rules without relying on platform developers or risking exposure to their vulnerabilities. Several AR/VR/MR applications might benefit from 6G technology, as described below.

- 6G networks provide terahertz communication in the submillimeter range with ultralow latency. Simulated services set in 6G improve management abilities and facilitate virtual communication beyond geographical borders. XR technology enables real-time 3D images and autonomous driving.
- Trusted decentralization across several nodes is crucial for data security in AR/VR uses, allowing for large-scale data exchange.
- Due to CPU and memory restrictions, AR/VR assets rely on a local primary server for quick picture and video interpretation.
- Due to the high data and bandwidth consumption of AR/VR apps, the central server may get overwhelmed by many asynchronous connections among the devices.

- Blockchain technology enhances security for army and combat uses by sharing private information and facilitating law enforcement and public safety efforts.
- The customized ecosystem of metaverse for collecting and distributing AR content may help commercialize AR gadgets.
- Connecting devices can let consumers and developers share and download information, build new apps, and establish markets for AR/VR/MR gadgets, increasing their economic viability.

### 16.4.3 Technical Obstacles

Medical data, especially that obtained via electronic anti-aging healthcare in the metaverse surroundings, is in high demand and necessary. Criminals pose a danger to privacy because they are always looking for methods to get access to illicit internet sites in order to steal data, despite the safety measures used by legitimate owners. Health data are large amounts of excellent information that are a goal for hackers; therefore, using the IoT for health data transmission introduces a new set of issues that must be solved. In addition, growing volumes of patient data raise protection concerns. The safety of data, like that of other online services, may be jeopardized. The virtual world hospitals must be outfitted with enhanced security measures to keep patients' data safe, allowing only authorized healthcare workers to access it [38]. The Health Insurance Portability and Accountability Act

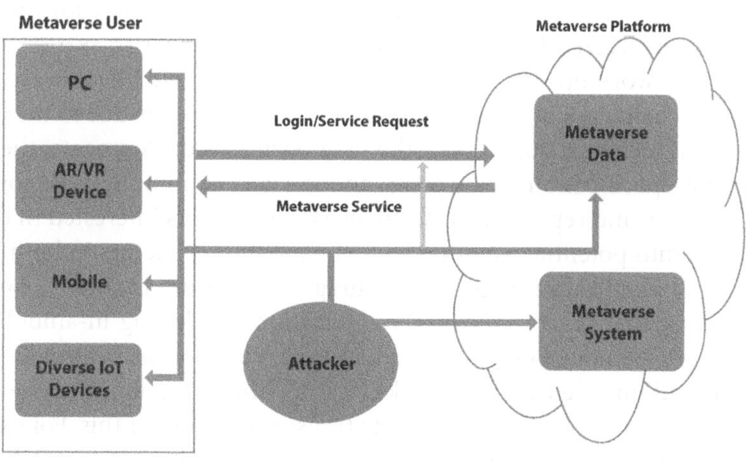


**Figure 16.8** Concerns regarding security and privacy in the metaverse [4].

(HIPAA) establishes concrete standards that can be modified about how much data can be distributed in the metaverse. Distinct nations have distinct data standards, and physicians are only licensed to practice in certain geographic areas, limiting their ability to operate in a metaverse with global patients [39–41]. It is reported that healthcare when combined with the metaverse, has the potential to make the world a more appealing place and unconventionally produce value. In Figure 16.8, the metaverse's confidentiality and safety problems are shown, emphasizing how an attacker (threat) is attempting to breach the metaverse user's equipment and framework [38].

## 16.5 Risks and Uncertainties

Some of the limitations of the research in the 5G speeds for metaverse healthcare include the limited number of network configurations tested, the short coverage area, and the lack of spatiotemporal heterogeneity in the laboratory trials. There is a gap in the research about a critical evaluation of the failure modes of 5G networks and how they may affect healthcare use cases that are 5G-enabled. For instance, the literature only covers the linked ambulance use case's success. But in cases of very high mobility, dense users, a mass evacuation of ambulances to a single location, a cell failure, or the existence of several important traffic flows in the network, this use case can be badly affected [40]. In addition, key performance indicators (KPIs) in networks are sometimes vendor-specific, meaning that different vendors of network equipment use different counters and naming standards to define performance measurements. Problems with managing nonstandardized key performance indicators may arise as a result of this. 5G network operators and end users of 5G-enabled healthcare systems face challenges in managing service level agreements due to the large number of technical counters in the heterogeneous deployments, the use of vendor-specific monitoring tools, and the lack of a unified data format for collecting and reporting performance data. Readers interested in delving more into potential ways to tackle the mentioned factors in both academic and practical settings are encouraged to consult. Lastly, it is worth mentioning that several healthcare applications, including in-ambulance therapy and remote robotic-assisted surgery, may benefit from real-time systems and time-sensitive networks (TSNs). The technological aspects of 5G, such as its near-instantaneous data transfer, may bolster this. For example, little latency between the robot and the remote physician has allowed for telerobotic spine procedures to be performed utilizing 5G-enabled robots. Research and study of real-time systems and TSNs, as well as their function in facilitating healthcare applications, should therefore be part of future 5G-enabled healthcare concerns. Even smaller healthcare institutions, such as those in rural regions, may benefit from 5G's ability to enable linked healthcare applications.

## 16.6 Conclusion and Future Directions

Innovation and progress in healthcare will be ushered in by new doors opened by the metaverse's progress. Technologies like digital twins, AI, blockchain, VR, and 5G form the foundation of the metaverse ecosystem [42–45]. This work presented a healthcare metaverse ecosystem that uses blockchain technology and AI in this study. There are three distinct settings: the one the doctor works in, the one the patient is in, and the metaverse. Using their domains, the doctor and patient access the metaverse using augmented, virtual, and XR technology. Both patients and physicians may fully immerse themselves in a virtual world in a metaverse healthcare system. There may be several upsides to incorporating healthcare services into the metaverse setting. This research set out to demonstrate, by the use of the metaverse, the efficacy of digital anti-aging in healthcare. Combining AI, blockchain, and the IoT may improve healthcare delivery in several ways: more personalized, efficient, and secure; less expensive; and longer patient life expectancy. To overcome potential obstacles and fully use metaverse technology in digital anti-aging and healthcare, ongoing investment in R&D is necessary going forward. Metaverse technology, if properly funded and used in tandem with other fields, might drastically alter the healthcare system, enhancing the lives of people everywhere. The only way to achieve the goals is for the standard to be widely adopted and for the major use cases to be put into action.

## References

1. Lee, C.W., Application of Metaverse Service to Healthcare Industry: A Strategic Perspective. *Int. J. Environ. Res. Public Health*, *19*, 13038, 2022, https://doi.org/10.3390/ijerph192013038.
2. Pons, M., Valenzuela, E., Rodríguez, B., Nolazco-Flores, J.A., Del-Valle-Soto, C., Utilization of 5G Technologies in IoT Applications: Current Limitations by Interference and Network Optimization Difficulties—A Review. *Sensors*, *23*, 3876, 2023, https://doi.org/10.3390/s23083876.

3. Ali, S., Abdullah, Armand, T.P.T., Athar, A., Hussain, A., Ali, M., Yaseen, M., Joo, M.-I., Kim, H.-C., Metaverse in Healthcare Integrated with Explainable AI and Blockchain: Enabling Immersiveness, Ensuring Trust, and Providing Patient Data Security. *Sensors*, *23*, 565, 2023, https://doi.org/10.3390/s23020565.
4. Mozumder, M.A.I., Armand, T.P.T., Imtiyaj Uddin, S.M., Athar, A., Sumon, R.I., Hussain, A., Kim, H.-C., Metaverse for Digital Anti-Aging Healthcare: An Overview of Potential Use Cases Based on Artificial Intelligence, Blockchain, IoT Technologies, Its Challenges, and Future Directions. *Appl. Sci.*, *13*, 5127, 2023, https://doi.org/10.3390/app13085127.
5. Wang, J., Peng, C., Zhao, Y., Ye, R., Hong, J., Huang, H., Chen, L., Application of a Robotic Tele-Echography System for COVID-19 Pneumonia. *J. Ultrasound Med.*, 40, 385–390, 2021.
6. Qureshi, H.N., Manalastas, M., Ijaz, A., Imran, A., Liu, Y., Al Kalaa, M.O., Communication Requirements in 5G-Enabled Healthcare Applications: Review and Considerations. *Healthcare*, *10*, 293, 2022, https://doi.org/10.3390/healthcare10020293.
7. Wu, P., Chen, D., Zhang, R., Topic prevalence and trends of Metaverse in healthcare: A bibliometric analysis. *Data Sci. Manage.*, 7, 2, 129–143, 2024.
8. Elhenawy, I., AL-baker, S.F., Mohamed, M., Intelligent Healthcare: Evaluation Potential Implications of Metaverse in Healthcare Based on Mathematical Decision-Making Framework. *Neutrosophic Syst. Appl.*, 12, 9–21, 2023.
9. Ye, J., The Role of Health Technology and Informatics in a Global Public Health Emergency: Practices and Implications From the COVID-19 Pandemic. *JMIR Med. Inform.*, 8, e19866, 2020.
10. Moztarzadeh, O., *et al.*, Metaverse and healthcare: Machine learning-enabled digital twins of cancer. *Bioengineering*, 10, 4, 455, 2023.
11. Peralta-Ochoa, A.M., Chaca-Asmal, P.A., Guerrero-Vásquez, L.F., Ordoñez-Ordoñez, J.O., Coronel-González, E.J., Smart Healthcare Applications over 5G Networks: A Systematic Review. *Appl. Sci.*, *13*, 1469, 2023, https://doi.org/10.3390/app13031469.
12. Ahad, A., Tahir, M., Aman Sheikh, M., Ahmed, K.I., Mughees, A., Numani, A., Technologies Trend towards 5G Network for Smart Health-Care Using IoT: A Review. *Sensors*, 20, 4047, 2020, https://doi.org/10.3390/s20144047.
13. Pires, F., Costa, C., Dias, P., On the use of virtual reality for medical imaging visualization. *J. Digital Imaging*, 34, 4, 1034–1048, 2021.
14. Gallo, L. and Placitelli, A.P., High-Fidelity Visualization of Large Medical Datasets on Commodity Hardware. *Int. Sch. Res. Not.*, 2013, 1, 892967, 2013.
15. Manners, C.P. and Gent, S.P., Data Analysis and Visualization for High Fidelity CFD Models for Medical Device Realization. *ASME International Mechanical Engineering Congress and Exposition*, vol. 58363, American Society of Mechanical Engineers, 2017.

16. Zhang, Q., Eagleson, R., Peters, T.M., Volume visualization: a technical overview with a focus on medical applications. *J. Digital Imaging*, 24, 640–664, 2011.
17. Tadeja, S.K., *et al.*, Immersive presentations of real-world medical equipment through interactive VR environment populated with the high-fidelity 3D model of mobile MRI unit. *Comput. Graphics*, 120, 103919, 2024.
18. Xu, Y., *et al.*, MedSyn: Text-guided Anatomy-aware Synthesis of High-Fidelity 3D CT Images. *IEEE Trans. Med. Imaging*, 43, 10, 3648–3660, 2024.
19. Gasciauskaite, G., *et al.*, Human-centered visualization technologies for patient monitoring are the future: A narrative review. *Crit. Care*, 27, 1, 254, 2023.
20. Encarnacion Ramirez, M., *et al.*, Development of a 3D printed brain model with vasculature for neurosurgical procedure visualisation and training. *Biomedicines*, 11, 2, 330, 2023.
21. Conesa, J., Mula, F.J., Bartlett, K.A., Naya, F., Contero, M., The Influence of Immersive and Collaborative Virtual Environments in Improving Spatial Skills. *Appl. Sci.*, 13, 8426, 2023, https://doi.org/10.3390/app13148426.
22. Bale, A.S., Ghorpade, N., Hashim, M.F., Vaishnav, J., Almaspoor, Z., A Comprehensive Study on Metaverse and Its Impacts on Humans. *Adv. Hum. Comput. Interact.*, 2022, 3247060, 11, 2022, https://doi.org/10.1155/2022/3247060.
23. Bale, A.S., Javed, S., Mishra, P., Savadatti, M.B., R, B.C., Joy, S., Psychological Approach based on Virtual Reality (VR) For Creating Successful Encounters to Improve Mobility for People with Disabilities. *J. ReAttach Ther. Dev. Divers.*, 6, 9s(2), 182–190, 2023, Retrieved from https://jrtdd.com/index.php/journal/article/view/1222.
24. Bale, A.S., Solanki, R.S., Mouneswari, V., Sanamdikar, S., Gulati, P., Trivedi, P.U., Psychological Confidence by AI: Enhancement Quality & Future of Mobility For People With Disabilities of Neurological Impairment. *J. ReAttach Ther. Dev. Divers.*, 6, 8s, 62–75, 2023, Retrieved from https://jrtdd.com/index.php/journal/article/view/859.
25. Hulsen, T., Applications of the metaverse in medicine and healthcare. *Adv. Lab. Med./Av. Med. Lab.*, 5, 2, 159–165, 2024, https://doi.org/10.1515/almed-2023-0124.
26. Sandrone, S., Medical education in the metaverse. *Nat. Med.*, 28, 2456–2457, 2022, https://doi.org/10.1038/s41591-022-02038-0.
27. Jang, S., Huang, L.-Y., Bartipan, T., BodyMap: Medical Virtual Reality Education and Simulation, in: *ACM SIGGRAPH 2021 Immersive Pavilion (SIGGRAPH '21)*, Association for Computing Machinery, New York, NY, USA, Article 9, pp. 1–2, 2021, https://doi.org/10.1145/3450615.3464527.
28. Minopoulos, G.M., Memos, V.A., Stergiou, K.D., Stergiou, C.L., Psannis, K.E., A Medical Image Visualization Technique Assisted with AI-Based

Haptic Feedback for Robotic Surgery and Healthcare. *Appl. Sci.*, 13, 3592, 2023, https://doi.org/10.3390/app13063592.
29. Kim, K., *et al.*, Metaverse wearables for immersive digital healthcare: a review. *Adv. Sci.*, 10, 31, 2303234, 2023.
30. Rostami, S. and Maier, M., The metaverse and beyond: Implementing advanced multiverse realms with smart wearables. *IEEE Access*, 10, 110796–110806, 2022.
31. Qi, J., *et al.*, HaptGlove—untethered pneumatic glove for multimode haptic feedback in reality–virtuality continuum. *Adv. Sci.*, 10, 25, 2301044, 2023.
32. Huang, Y., *et al.*, Recent advances in multi-mode haptic feedback technologies towards wearable interfaces. *Mater. Today Phys.*, 22, 100602, 2022.
33. van Wegen, M., *et al.*, An overview of wearable haptic technologies and their performance in virtual object exploration. *Sensors*, 23, 3, 1563, 2023.
34. Hsu, M.-H. and Chang, Y.-C., Haptic and force feedback technology in dental education: a bibliometric analysis. *Int. J. Environ. Res. Public Health*, 20, 2, 1318, 2023.
35. Moon, H.S., Orr, G., Jeon, M., Hand tracking with vibrotactile feedback enhanced presence, engagement, usability, and performance in a virtual reality rhythm game. *Int. J. Hum.-Comput. Interact.*, 39, 14, 2840–2851, 2023.
36. Liu, J.Y.W., *et al.*, The effects of immersive virtual reality applications on enhancing the learning outcomes of undergraduate health care students: systematic review with meta-synthesis. *J. Med. Internet Res.*, 25, e39989, 2023.
37. Zawish, M., *et al.*, AI and 6G into the metaverse: Fundamentals, challenges and future research trends. *IEEE Open J. Commun. Soc.*, 5, 730–778, 2024.
38. Bale, A.S., Joy, S., R., B.C., S., R.R., N., V., 4 Augmented reality in cross-domain applications, in: *Augmented and Virtual Reality in Social Learning: Technological Impacts and Challenges*, R. Kumar, V. Jain, A.A. Elngar, A. Al-Haraizah (Eds.), pp. 43–62, De Gruyter, Berlin, Boston, 2024, https://doi.org/10.1515/9783110981445-004.
39. Ullah, H., *et al.*, Exploring the potential of metaverse technology in healthcare: Applications, challenges, and future directions. *IEEE Access*, 11, 69686–69707, 2023.
40. Jahankhani, H., Kendzierskyj, S., Hussien, O., Approaches and Methods for Regulation of Security Risks in 5G and 6G, in: *Wireless Networks: Cyber Security Threats and Countermeasures*, pp. 43–70, Springer International Publishing, Cham, 2023.
41. Bale, A.S., Purohit, T.P., Hashim, M.F., Navale, S., Blockchain and Its Applications in Industry 4.0, in: *A Roadmap for Enabling Industry 4.0 by Artificial Intelligence*, Chatterjee, J.M., Garg, H., Thakur, R.N. (Eds.), 2022, https://doi.org/10.1002/9781119905141.ch16.
42. Khazanchi, D., Kumar Vyas, A., Kant Hiran, K., Padmanaban, S., *Blockchain 3.0 for Sustainable Development*, De Gruyter, Berlin, Boston, 2021, https://doi.org/10.1515/9783110702507.

43. Kant Hiran, K., Khazanchi, D., Kumar Vyas, A., Padmanaban, S., *Machine Learning for Sustainable Development*, De Gruyter, Berlin, Boston, 2021, https://doi.org/10.1515/9783110702514.
44. Vyas, A.K., Balamurugan, S., Hiran, K.K., Dhiman, H.S. (Eds.), *Artificial Intelligence for Renewable Energy Systems*, John Wiley & Sons, 2022, ISBN: 9781119761693.
45. Singh, S., Arya, R.K., Sahana, B.C., Vyas, A.K. (Eds.), *RF Circuits for 5G Applications: Designing with mmWave Circuitry*, John Wiley & Sons, 2023.

# 17

# Incorporating Digital Twin Technology in Healthcare: Prospects and Constraints

**Krupa Purohit**

*Adani University, Khodiyar, Gujarat, India*

## *Abstract*

Utilizing the digital twin technology, it is possible to bring new real-time data, advanced analytics, and simulations to change healthcare systems. Metaverse technology makes it possible to explore virtual three-dimensional structures, conduct small-group activities and collaborations, learn through individual self-directed instruction, and teach teamwork skills. Its rapid implementation in the healthcare sector is poised to fast-track digitization breaking through surgery and medical education. The metaverse can offer so many benefits for patient diagnosis and care. It results in better quality patient care, predictive analytics, more efficient clinical operations, and invaluable training and simulation tools. The healthcare industry is using digital patient twins (a virtual copy of a physical system) to continuously analyze, model, and monitor the data in real time. Sixty-six percent of healthcare executives also expect investment in digital twins to increase more than twofold over the next 3 years, according to Accenture. An important aspect is that digital twins can continuously learn and evolve through new data, which, in turn, enables part of their reasoning and rebuilding models for better decision-making. For these characteristics, they are recognized as important healthcare instruments for proactive management and personalized care, with direct impacts on patient assistance and promoting early identification of disease leading to prevention. Capable of ingesting and analyzing large volumes of patient data from multiple sources, digital twins can deliver personalized treatment plans using up-to-the-minute biometric characteristics gleaned from a patient's personal health history. Machine learning algorithms lead to the early identification of health risks and actions are taken beforehand, which gives way to predictive analytics and preventive interventions as well. Additionally, they are a critical piece of the puzzle to enhancing clinical operations and consequently bettering patient care by meticulously

*Email*: krupa.dave24@gmail.com

Ajay Kumar Vyas, Harleen Kaur, Sourabh Sharma and Bhavya Alankar (eds.) Metaverse Technologies, Security and Applications for Healthcare, (379–392) © 2025 Scrivener Publishing LLC

analyzing workflows and resource distribution. Digital twin technology relies on AI-ready models and Internet of Things sensor data streaming in from a growing number of sources. So in a way, this method assists the digital twin of the patient by learning insights from historical data to select proper drug treatment or forecast the impact that surgery conducted under certain conditions will have over time as well as managing chronic disease effectively. The primary objective of this article is to explore the many use cases and issues around digital twin technology in current healthcare, augmenting them with additional real-world applications. The final section of the chapter addresses several open research questions that require further investigation.

***Keywords*:** Digital twin, artificial intelligence (AI), internet of things (IoT)

## 17.1 Introduction

The healthcare industry is at the cusp of a new era with digital innovation [1]. The concept of digital twins is an exciting technological improvement, with a wide range of developments [2]. Digital twin is, in simple words, you can say - A virtual version of an existing real-world thing where data-driven by Internet-of-Things has made this possible. This intricate digital twin provides a comprehensive view of the health status of an individual through aggregating real-time data coming from different sources such as wearable sensors, medical imaging devices, and electronic health records (EHRs) [3].

Healthcare has seen faster integration of the metaverse. The outbreak of the 2019 coronavirus has only heightened the urgency for healthcare organizations to accelerate their digital transformation. Targetoid identification and envision display are novel applications of augmented-mixed reality coupled with the metaverse in image-guided procedures using a similar principle [2–4]. The metaverse allows for true-to-life consultations through our avatars, which are networked and personalized. One application of avatars that can be personalized is the area of patient education. By creating a virtual patient illustration, healthcare professionals can help patients with their medical conditions and available treatments.

Overcoming the four challenges to the digital twin promise, most of these issues relate to security holes, privacy concerns regarding customer data, and the problems embedding different healthcare systems [2]. In this review article, we explore the promising prospects of healthcare applications using digital twin technology. In particular, we are investigating how digital twins could revolutionize patient-tailored healthcare, and treatment plans as well as improve care of the patients [4].

Via the metaverse, medical trainees can perform better [3, 4]. Metaverse will revolutionize medical education by making it more adventurous, stimulating, and practical for students. Improving their skills, reducing medical errors, and preparing them for the real-world challenges of clinical practice are some [7–9]. The metaverse can be used to apply active learning methods in a hybrid learning environment [3]. This list will continue to grow as there are countless applications for the metaverse in education and healthcare, among others, because technology is always evolving.

Referring to the literature, there are many digital twins (DTs) demonstrating how the DT concept changed. Originally, the DT was designated as nothing in exchange for what should be called a static digital replica of an actual-world system. However, as the notion progressed, other permutations came in: "shadow twin," which looks like you from a different angle, "mirror twin," and more recently "clever twins," etc. [3].

The objective of this review is to identify the inner nature of this novel technique and how it can revolutionize the field of medicine by scientifically dissecting its pros and cons, here we discuss digitally twinning its Majority may be diverse from positive in numbers but exact according to healthcare [2].

This chapter aims to provide readers with a comprehensive overview of this new technology and its future impact on healthcare, and for that purpose, we will objectively look at the pros as well as cons of employing digital twins in the medical domain [4].

The healthcare sector is turning into a paradigm shift in patient care delivery, treatment optimization, and medical research catalyzed by digital twin technology integration. Digital twins, the virtual representation of any other object or system in technology from design to operation, may revolutionize healthcare by enabling it more dynamic and personalized. This chapter presents a review of the capabilities and shortcomings in implementing digital twin technology, specifically for healthcare applications [3, 4].

## 17.2 Leveraging Digital Twin Technology to Enhance Patient Care

With digital twin technology, customers will enhance the patient experience through trait providers utilizing real-time data integration and next-level advanced analytics with unmatched specific insight. By using these, healthcare providers can also gather and analyze patient data via wearables or health monitors, medical devices, EHRs, genetics, and other forms of relevant information.

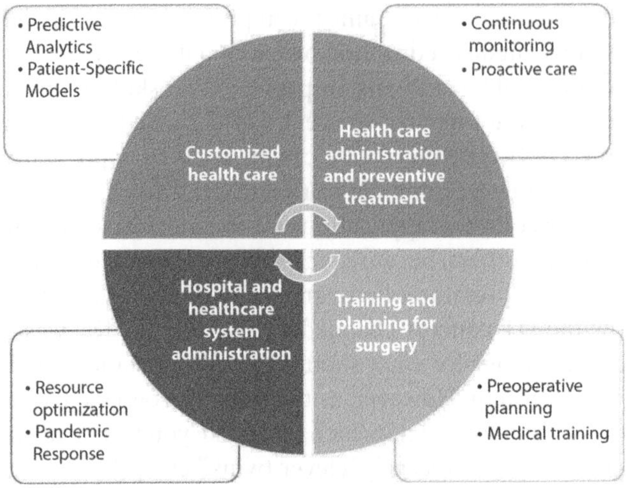


**Figure 17.1** Digital twin in patient care [5].

Digital twins combine real-time, continuous biological signals with prior clinical history to create an individualized (virtual) patient model that synthesizes quantitative physiological data integrated across scales [5].

The application of digital twin technology—where a virtual version is created for any real physical object or system—has vast potential to optimize patient care in healthcare as shown in Figure 17.1. Below, you may use the same:

### 17.2.1 Customized Healthcare

Patient-Specific Models: Digital twins of a patient use unique medical information, e.g., genetics, lifestyle, and environmental attributes. Instead of providing a one-size-fits-all-all regimen, personalized treatment plans are created for each patient based on their specific needs and conditions.

Healthcare professionals will be able to use predictions from predictive analytics and computer modeling of different treatment options for a patient's digital twin.

### 17.2.2 Healthcare Administration and Preventive Treatment

Real-Time Health History: Digital twins can evaluate long-term illnesses like diabetes or heart disease and continuously collect data to be reported on demand by a healthcare practitioner. This allows for rapid intervention and early recognition of problems.

Proactive Care: With the help of real-time data, digital twins model health scenarios for the future. It helps in early diagnosis of risk factors and recommending preventive measures that ultimately prevent diseases [3].

### 17.2.3 Training and Planning for Surgery

Presurgery Planning: Digital twins can provide surgeons with facilities in preoperative simulation for a complicated surgical operation. This allows them to anticipate possible problems and improve surgical outcomes.
Medical Assistance: Similar to training, digital twins can also be used as an element for practice and skill enhancement without putting into risk lives [4].

### 17.2.4 Hospital and Healthcare System Administration

Optimizing Resources: The powerful definition of hospital beds, medical equipment, personnel, or other resources used in the optimized way through digital twins that predict information. This can result in better patient care and more efficient management.
Pandemic Response: Digital twins can go a long way in simulating the spread and intervention impact on diseases during pandemics. It will reduce manual resource allocation and decision-making.

## 17.3 Prospects and Constraints

The digital twin can revolutionize healthcare and enhance patient outcomes. Digital Twins: A digital twin is a virtual replica of an object, disease, or even global healthcare system that simulates the properties and behaviors of its real-world counterpart entities [6, 7].

In healthcare, digital twin models could allow for personalized physiology of an organ (for example, the heart or liver) in providing new ways to study disease progression and tune treatment regimens. For instance, a digital twin of the heart has been developed by researchers that replicates electrical activity and can predict cardiac arrhythmia resulting in more individualized treatment for heart rhythm disorders [3, 4].

### 17.3.1 Prospects

- **Personalized Medicine:** With the aid of a digital twin, doctors can develop personalized care plans for every patient and predict how different drugs or treatments might affect them [4].

- **Improved Forecasting:** Experts might predict future health problems and take preemptive measures more precisely by evaluating data from the digital twin.
- **Remote Patient Monitoring:** With a digital twin, it is easier to intervene promptly in the case of emergencies or if symptoms are getting worse.
- **Patient Education:** Patients can engage with their digital twin to learn about their conditions and the treatments available [2].
- **Treatment Optimization:** Constantly updating digital twin models with real-time patient data allows healthcare professionals to flex treatment plans as patients evolve their health conditions. This approach may prevent any unfavorable effects and increase treatment efficacy.
- **Healthcare Professional Education and Training:** Digital twins can be a valuable tool for healthcare professionals. The diagnosis techniques, treatment protocols, and surgical methods can be practiced by medical experts or learners while interacting with virtual patient models helping them to enhance their clinical skills.
- **Development and Research:** Digital twins allow drug development or medical research to come out of the confines of costly physical experiments into feasible virtual experimentation or hypothesis testing. By using this method, researchers can anticipate outcomes and risk factors by simulating how novel therapies or interventions affect the virtual patient models and make treatment or therapy innovations.
- **Telemedicine and Remote Monitoring:** Digital twins can help in tracking patients' health stats/vital signs remotely, making it easier to intervene swiftly and pre-emptive care for preventative measures on long-term issues. This has the potential to provide wider access in general and may be of value for patients particularly those dwelling in remote or underprivileged places [5].

### 17.3.2 Constraints

- Data security and privacy: One of many challenges in health applications due to the large amounts of patient data needed

for digital twins. Ensuring both patient confidence as well as legal compliance necessitates stringent safeguards to ensure that their information is not misused, or accessed by unauthorized third parties.
- Interoperability: Integrating digital twin technology with existing systems and devices in the healthcare ecosystem brings interoperability issues. Standardization of Data Formats and Protocols: To enable networking between different platforms over heterogeneous networks with compatible systems, we need the data formats to be standardized such that their use is supported on various types.
- Model Accuracy and Validation: The accuracy of the model, which also comes with some limitations, is determined by input data quality; assumed behavior on specific components may not be always correct. However, even when digital twins are designed effectively to mimic the real-life physiology and pathology of a given patient population, there is still the potential for making inferences or treatment decisions from them that may be completely wrong requiring strict validation/verification.
- The use of digital twins raises ethical questions related to consent, autonomy, and responsibility The gathering, using, and sharing of patient data for digital twin modeling raise complex ethical issues that healthcare practitioners need to navigate in the interest of transparency, fairness, and patients' rights/privacy [3, 4].
- Cost and Resource Burden: Cultivation of this digital twin technology in the healthcare sector requires a high level of isolated proficiency with a heavy financial burden for setup as well as maintenance. For many healthcare organizations, initiatives such as these will be hard to scale and fund, particularly if not an already funded statutory compliance requirement.

## 17.4 Healthcare Facilities Utilizing Digital Twins

Patient-centered focused community engagement is a prerequisite for precision medicine and should incorporate personalized patient-centric modeling. Considering the rapid evolution and further development, it qualifies DT for the medical field, due to the activation of add-to-many promising generations. This results in an expanded real network connectivity provided that IoT [10] gadgets are getting simpler and more economical to implement. A DT healthcare was a suggested innovative medical simulation and it is a method of implementation of powerful, accurate, and effective care with multi-physics and technology in an interdisciplinary context and multi-scale characteristics. Artificial intelligence [11] and other state-of-the-art technologies are applicable for discrete identification of what causes. There have been many pilot studies in the past that set a foundation.

| **Utilizing digital twins for medical applications** | **Description** |
|---|---|
| Babylon's digital twin | The industry-leading platform for enabling people to view their medical records and other health information in their entirety is Babylon's digital twin for E-medical records. The system uses deep learning techniques and cutting-edge AI technology to deliver vital information on organ status and disease risk factors. Although the platform only covers 20 diseases at the moment, it will eventually be able to catch over 80 disorders. The growing significance of personal health data in helping people manage their health and well-being is confirmed by Babylon's digital twin. |
| Hospital ward management | Digital Twin of Mater Hospital - Dublin: An example of how digital twinning in healthcare can optimize the functioning and operations of hospitals or any other healthcare institute is present at The Mater Hospital -Dublin. The western aspect of the Mater Hospital Dublin used 3D visualizations to review basic ward operations from the radiography department. From this, it became clear that the digital twin project resulted in a significant reduction in patient wait times for life-critical CT and MRI examinations, which represented an actual improvement in patient experience. Workflow simulation with digital twins cut CT or MRI scan wait times to almost 240 minutes at Mater Hospital. This improvement in patient turnover time reduced the amount of MRI and CT scans issued. |

| Utilizing digital twins for medical applications | Description |
|---|---|
| Strengthening hospital logistics | Digital companions can also be applied for numerous commercial enterprises within a health center and thus help in any extensive development inside the entire surrounding. The model exhibits an inherent characteristic, and this could simulate different hospital processes, including human resources, patient movements, and equipment management. It tracks the location of people, systems, and resources. A high-quality AI model would produce more accurate impedance, and it could avail the real-time metrics from all touchpoints of a hospital. The model approach to help doctors in decision-making can be summarized based on laboratory diagnosis results, whether imaging or non-imaging. Researchers can test in the shop before putting life and money at risk on roads with digital twins. Digital twins have been a tool for engineers and manufacturers for quite some time now, but can these ideas even be applied to the field of medicine? |
| Boost the inventiveness of medicine | Medical advancements through better innovation and regulatory clearance by digital twins in the healthcare sector. In the future, should researchers further refine this process, doctors may even be able to fine-tune personalized therapeutic regimens for their patients. They could use digital twins to facilitate doctors bringing life-saving products more efficiently, cheaper, and safer on the market. These digital twins are built by inputting population and individual data into computational or *in silico* models. That knowledge is translated into computational models of human physiology that can be used to predict the impact of diseases and treat them, craft surgeries, and design medical devices. Preventing life-threatening patient emergencies, like "code blues" cardiopulmonary and respiratory arrest, through the use of digital twins could save lives. |

(*Continued*)

| Utilizing digital twins for medical applications | Description |
|---|---|
| The most effective therapeutic regimen | The digital twin can predict the outcome of a surgery. This can be useful when choosing which medication is the best option for a specific patient. Even in the bare bones state, digital twins can be extremely useful, with utilities already seeing success across reducing non-chargeable outflow meter outputs and bearing wear to pump impellers along marine propellers. Essentially, enabling technology will work with paired physical equipment inside the digital twin and data from IoT devices in real time to enable a digital tween. Digital twin provides all types of health data from images, test results, and genetics to be used in diagnosis. The clinical data will next be employed to recreate the patient's status in more sophisticated versions of these models and a whole-patient model. |
| Opportunities for rapid screening and therapy | Patients should be examined with scientific systems, and the patients do not need to carry human held bulky system in their hands for diagnostics or have a whole body scan that diagnoses more accurately. Now, one drawback of these technologies is that they involve relatively high radiation doses and costs, which makes them carcinogenic. For the most part, technologies are transitioning to digital twins and AI-based exams. They offer convenient and safer tests instead of the traditional way that might be riskier for diagnostic care. Digital twin systems are connected to IoT sensors and make sure the big data flows in real time for businesses to process them and catch failures on their systems before they occur. This technology helps businesses do a better job of predicting maintenance needs estimating OEE and minimizing unplanned downtime while getting a global real-time view of anchoring all the physical systems. |

| Utilizing digital twins for medical applications | Description |
|---|---|
| Assist patients remotely | Using fast-stream technology's digital twin patients, doctors can observe their patients from remote locations. It utilizes strong analytics and adaptive algorithms to deliver accurate results, in addition to its ever-improving capabilities for collecting and curating data. We can monitor the patients through smart wearables. These will be smaller wearables equipped with sensors that communicate real-time data to our cloud-based digital twin. Consequently, with an accurate understanding of the spread of the disease and the permanent retrieval of patient records can be done through fitness trackers. The hospital is using a digital twin to essentially model the whole organization and that has been successful. Thanks to a digital twin of the healthcare complex hospital, managers/personnel will be able to get data in real time on which and how patients are located or any ongoing surgical operations. |
| Administration of vital patient data | Now, digital twins are already found in the healthcare sector, where they can be used to monitor and control single individual vital signs using a biophysical model. Cloud-based analytics combined with sensor data enables medical professionals to remotely monitor and manage patient health while delivering therapy effectively. This enables the surgeon to collaboratively review medical issues and simulate procedures within a patient organ with all other healthcare personnel in controlled conditions. The digital twin is the perfect agent for visualizing all sorts of aspects/properties from physical or IoT devices. IoT is made easy with the shared model that digital twin provides. Therefore, a digital twin is a replica of the real object that can perform all its functions. Amidst the arrival of Industry 4.0, digitalization or connection everything has become vital in every industry. The digitization of physical equipment using IoT has influenced numerous sectors by increasing efficiency, improving user experiences, and enabling smarter decision-making point in this case is the notion of a "digital twin" that forecasts future outcomes for an operating object or product. Digital twin approach leads to reduced costs of production, higher performance and productivity, lower operating expenses (OPEX), and more accurate predictions. When integrated with state-of-the-art analytical tools and machine learning, the digital twin will transform equipment analysis and condition monitoring its operation post-deployment. |

## 17.5 Prospective Avenues for Further Investigation

In the end, digital twins might bring benefits to all sectors. With all of this done properly, digital twins pave the way to automated and iterative production on a scale fit for modernity. For years, digital twins were only found in their specific parts of the organization disconnected from operations, maintenance sales, or service finance and marketing would access everything they needed via a single real-world data source for design analysis using feedback pricing adjustment. Shortly, digital twins will largely help the industrial marketplace become digitized and change/shape the political landscapes of many countries. Beyond symptom treatment and environmental considerations, digital twins have the potential to address several healthcare-related problems [4, 5].

- **Acquiring and Integrating Data:** Resolving the issues of real-time data integration and interoperability is essential to creating digital twins in the healthcare industry. The seamless exchange and use of medical data will be made possible by the development of standards and standardized data formats, which will eventually improve patient care and operational effectiveness.
- **Security and Confidentiality of Information:** To guarantee patient privacy, data encryption, secure storage, and adherence to pertinent data protection regulations, stringent procedures must be implemented.
- **Infrastructure for Computation:** In theory, healthcare professionals and researchers might employ AR/VR (augmented reality/virtual reality) technologies to interact more naturally and immersively with digital twins. Ultimately, data privacy could be improved by storing and transferring information in a decentralized, transparent, and safe manner using blockchain and DLT (distributed ledger technology).
- **Data Impartiality and Bias:** A further issue is data bias. The representativeness, completeness, and quality of the data are essential to the effectiveness of DTs. A data model based on a balanced dataset that allows the comparison of every individual's data is necessary for DT accuracy. However, there are several ways that health data might be biased, including being skewed toward particular illnesses or demographics (such as ethnicity, gender, or other demographic causes of bias).

- **Ethics-Related Issues:** There are many ethical issues to be addressed when creating digital twins for medical purposes. A few examples of ethical issues are getting people's informed consent before collecting and using their data for the creation of digital twins, handling data ownership and management, granting patients autonomy, and recognizing legal restrictions.
- Maintaining healthcare equity is also necessary to prevent DTs for health from exacerbating already-existing health disparities. Developing health-related DTs should adhere to ethical norms for responsible and secure data sharing, data anonymization, and informed permission to promote ethical practices and trust. Furthermore, as was already indicated, eliminating biases in models and guaranteeing data accuracy are essential to averting negative effects on specific people.

## References

1. Turab, M. and Jamil, S., A comprehensive survey of digital twins in healthcare in the era of metaverse. *Biomed Inf.*, 3, 3, 563–584, 2023.
2. Suh, I., McKinney, T., Siu, K.C., Current perspective of metaverse application in medical education, research and patient care. *Virtual Worlds*, 2, 2, 115–128, MDPI, 2023, April.
3. Katsoulakis, E., Wang, Q., Wu, H., Shahriyari, L., Fletcher, R., Liu, J., Deng, J., Digital twins for health: a scoping review. *npj Digital Med.*, 7, 1, 77, 2024.
4. Vallée, A., Digital twin for healthcare systems. *Front. Digital Health*, 5, 1253050, 2023.
5. Sun, T., He, X., Song, X., Shu, L., Li, Z., The digital twin in medicine: a key to the future of healthcare? *Front. Med.*, 9, 907066, 2022.
6. Haleem, A., Javaid, M., Singh, R.P., Suman, R., Exploring the revolution in healthcare systems through the applications of digital twin technology. *Biomed. Technol.*, 4, 28–38, 2023.
7. Kaul, R., Ossai, C., Forkan, A.R.M., Jayaraman, P.P., Zelcer, J., Vaughan, S., Wickramasinghe, N., The role of AI for developing digital twins in healthcare: The case of cancer care. *Wiley Interdiscip. Rev.: Data Min. Knowl. Discovery*, 13, 1, e1480, 2023.
8. Khazanchi, D., Kumar Vyas, A., Kant Hiran, K., Padmanaban, S., *Blockchain 3.0 for Sustainable Development*, De Gruyter, Berlin, Boston, 2021, https://doi.org/10.1515/9783110702507.

9. Kant Hiran, K., Khazanchi, D., Kumar Vyas, A., Padmanaban, S., *Machine Learning for Sustainable Development*, De Gruyter, Berlin, Boston, 2021, https://doi.org/10.1515/9783110702514.
10. Pathmudi, V.R., Khatri, N., Kumar, S., Abdul-Qawy, A.S.H., Vyas, A.K., A systematic review of IoT technologies and their constituents for smart and sustainable agriculture applications. *Sci. Afr.*, 19, e01577, 2023.
11. Vyas, A.K., Balamurugan, S., Hiran, K.K., Dhiman, H.S. (Eds.), *Artificial Intelligence for Renewable Energy Systems*, John Wiley & Sons, New Jersey, 2022, ISBN: 9781119761693.

# 18

# Application Perspectives of Digital Twin in Healthcare Using Metaverse

**Bablu Kumar Singh**[1] **and Ajay Kumar Vyas**[2*]

[1]*Information and Communication Technology, Pandit Deendayal Energy University, Gandhinagar, Gujarat, India*
[2]*Information and Communication Technology, Adani University, Ahmedabad, Gujarat, India*

***Abstract***
The technology transformation has tremendously changed the world in the past decade, but it cannot be denied that the COVID pandemic has shaken the foundations in every manner. In the medical sector, it is essential to build systems that are sustainable and sensitive and facilitate reframing, redesign, interoperability, and scalability to ensure that they are more efficient and more informative for humankind. The system was put together by integrating numerous technologies, such as holographic construction emulation, virtual reality (VR) integration, and VR connection with medical science, and there is always an opportunity for enhancement. Consequently, the metaverse VR, augmented reality (AR), and related technologies will make significant contributions to healthcare. This chapter described the technologies of the metaverse and its capability as digital twin applications in the healthcare sector.

***Keywords*:** Metaverse, digital twin, healthcare, medicine cloud, VR, AR

## 18.1 Introduction

The virtual world has become the cover story of every platform, and the most prominent activity is the use of social media. At present, there are approximately 4.26 billion social media users worldwide, and by 2027, the

**Corresponding author*: ajay.vyas@adaniuni.ac.in

Ajay Kumar Vyas, Harleen Kaur, Sourabh Sharma and Bhavya Alankar (eds.) Metaverse Technologies, Security and Applications for Healthcare, (393–408) © 2025 Scrivener Publishing LLC

number of users is projected to reach about 6 billion [1]. In October 2021, Facebook officially changed its name to Meta to align social networks and three-dimensional (3D) virtual worlds to follow a new standard known as a metaverse [2]. 3D models, augmented reality (AR), virtual reality (VR), and various additional technologies have all contributed to the development of the metaverse. The wearable devices, avatars, and blockchain, AR, VR and 3D model are the parts of metaverse technology as mentioned in Figure 18.1. The next big thing there is much discussion about is what the metaverse will look like and how it will impact everyday lives; however, it is still more of a concept than reality [3]. In this stage, what might the metaverse look like and how could it impact healthcare in the coming decade? Many believe that the metaverse will become an extension of what we currently view as VR and AR [4]. People would enter the metaverse using a headset and find themselves in a connected digital environment that could be used for work, leisure, or socializing in recent years [5]. The formation of the metaverse technology is a combination of various technologies, as mentioned in Figure 18.1.

Robotics are already used in the surgical healthcare sector, which means that there is already a solid basis on which VR and AR can develop in the metaverse by being used in increasingly sophisticated surgical procedures [6]. Real-time guidance and imaging data are already being provided to surgeons using AR to give them data streams that assist them optimize their surgical procedures and sterilize the operating room [7]. While this is going on, more useful applications could be employed in a variety of clinical and

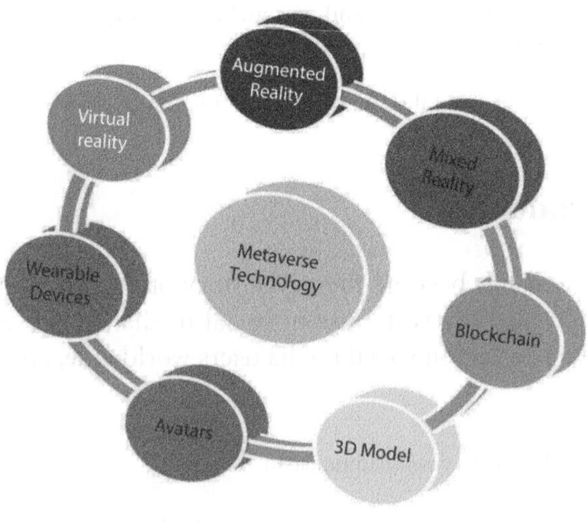


**Figure 18.1** Formation of metaverse technology.

surgical contexts, from straightforward operations to far-challenging surgeries, such as removing tumors and carrying out complex and complicated spinal surgery. Improved healthcare training in the metaverse is one of healthcare's big attractions [8]. Metaverse in healthcare is the feeling that anything is possible; for example, it could become a training environment for the next generation of surgical robots to understand and learn how to operate on humans through artificial intelligence (AI) and machine learning (ML) as with the surgical environment. Metaverse-friendly technologies are already widely used in the training of healthcare professionals [9–12]. VR headsets give doctors and medical staff unprecedented virtual access to the human body, helping them visualize conditions and allowing procedures to be replicated within a virtual clinical setting for students to cells into the surgical setting. They were the surgeon themselves; the metaverse could transform well-being, and fitness fighters will be able to connect remotely with patients and provide them with opportunities to offer well-being and fitness classes. Currently, any VR or AR technologies within the fitness arena are primarily limited to various mobile applications [13]. AR delivers workout guidance from instructors virtually, meaning that service users and fitness professionals can work remotely and be more innovative with their technology and time. It might be conceivable to give dementia patients access to the metaverse so they can interact with environments that aid in memory stimulation and reestablish connections with other users of the system [14]. Digital health will let us keep track of the health of an individual, and telemedicine hospitals will empower patients to access healthcare remotely. Considering the importance of caution from an alternative perspective, we could fix all these challenges, and it may be possible to redesign the future of hospitals layer by layer [2, 15–17]. Human tends to imagine future hospital buildings as massive science fiction with no changes in their functionality, but the purpose itself will be acceptable in the digital era [18–20].

The AR-based medical system will be very helpful in developing a sustainable future healthcare model, including surgical assistive tools, Microsoft HoloLens, and speed surgical procedures. It would also be utilized to get preoperative images from diagnostic machines like CT, MRI, and 3D sonography; essential real-time measurements like temperature, heart rate, respiration rate, and blood pressure are viewed using AR headsets. Figure 18.2 displays a few of the visualization algorithms.

The metaverse is an amalgamation of various digital environments that combine AR and VR to build a massive virtual healthcare network that runs on blockchain and allows for avatar-based interaction between medical professionals, patients, and other organizations. The healthcare industry is going to experience a transformation as an outcome of this technology.

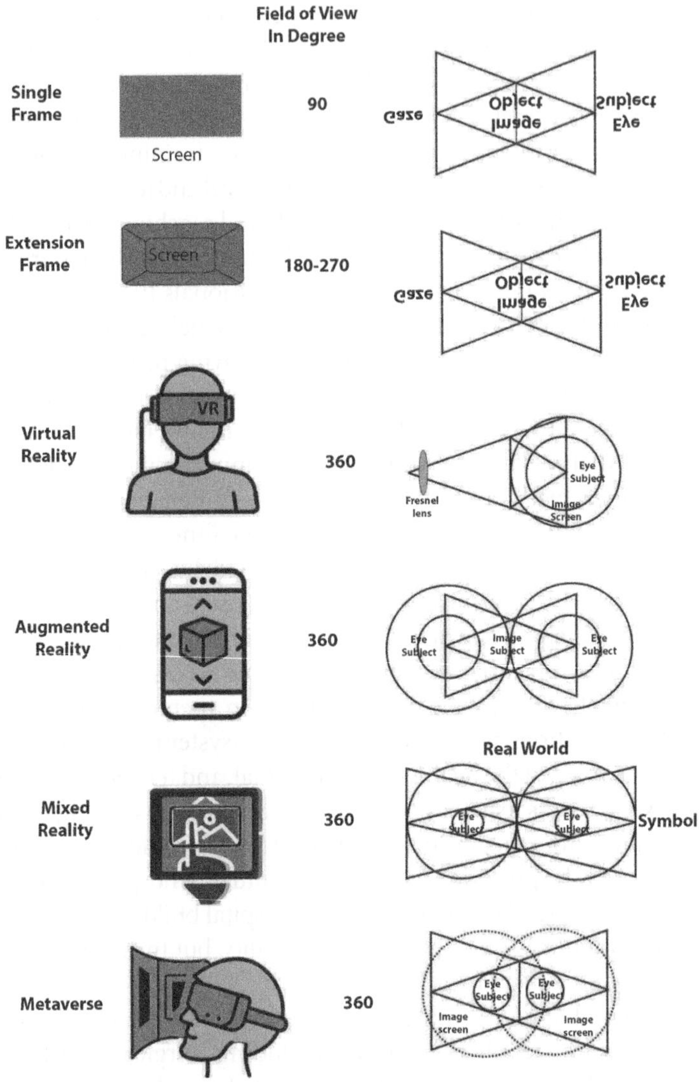


**Figure 18.2** Different visualization algorithms.

A digital twin is a platform of intelligent technology that synchronizes physical objects into digital objects that imitate virtually in real time, analyze situations for different purposes, and predict the behavior of physical objects based on analysis results. The digital twin offers a variety of models for resolving real-world issues by translating physical objects, i.e., people, places, things, systems, and processes to digital world objects. To create a safer and more effective real world by identifying the best solution and implementing it there, the digital twin is therefore the amalgamation of different technology platforms. The various goals of employing digital twin technology are as follows:

i. Process optimization: Based on equipment, component, production, and procedural change scenarios, the digital twin's behavior models can assist in identifying improved operation processes [21].
ii. Cause analysis: A digital twin's behavior models can mimic the things that happen to its physical equivalent. Analysis of the causes of these events can be assisted by reproductive simulation outcomes based on historical and previously incurred log information [21].
iii. To identify risk factors and prevent real-world problems before they arise, historical and present data collected from the actual world are investigated in a virtual environment.
iv. Efficient product design: Digital twin product design simulations can facilitate design iterations, better-informed engineering and design choices, and overall roadmap enhancement through the integration of real-world data obtained from the current machinery products performed and processes over a period [22].
v. Multidisciplinary decision making: By merging the inter-working of digital twins, it can be less complicated to analyze co-relationships and mutual effects among the industrial domains, pinpoint root causes of co-related and composite problems, and cooperate with stakeholders across the industrial ecosystem [22].

## 18.2 Need for Digital Twin for Healthcare

The digital twin is a digital replica of a physical object whose virtual data model matches its functionality and communicates with another physical object to create a seamless transition between the physical objects and virtual worlds. To establish the convergence between the physical and virtual worlds, a digital twin is an imitation of a physical asset in the virtual world whose data model replicates its actions and interaction with other physical assets. Making a digital asset out of actual things and actions would be beneficial. Significant changes in people's lifestyles have been sparked by the COVID-19 pandemic throughout the world. As a result, healthcare systems had to redesign patient care to cut back on in-person consultations, prioritize cases requiring immediate medical attention, postpone non-urgent appointments, and implement fresh infection prevention strategies. Although the IoT-based platforms (i.e., MIoT) support us, there are still many opportunities to get around MIoT's limitations. These issues fueled the need and possibilities for digital transformation, which aimed to boost healthcare systems' productivity, save time spent on getting facilities, and decentralize care with fewer physical contact points. The Figure 18.3 shows the framework of a digital twin for healthcare.

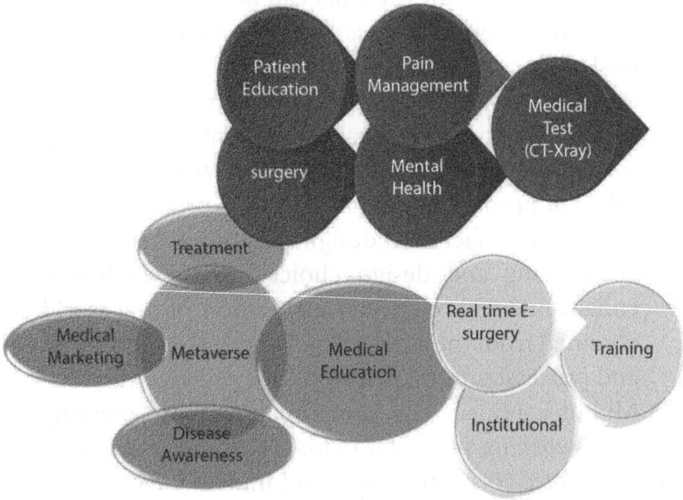


**Figure 18.3** Framework of a digital twin for healthcare.

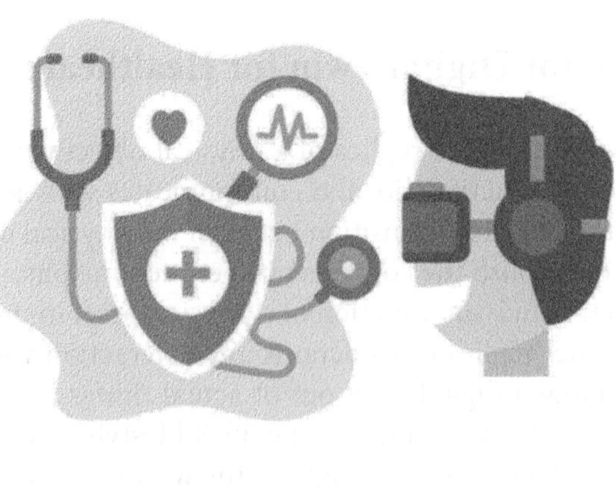

## 18.3 Opportunity

The various critical and necessary opportunities of metaverse with the use of technology like 5G, 6G, AR, VR, Internet edge computing, and IoT could revolutionize the healthcare sector which includes the use of remote surgery, telepresence of doctors or patients, AR real-time surgery with the help of IoT and robotics. To aid in education, diagnosis visualization, preventive medicine, as well as patient education, 3D human anatomy models are being developed. Visualization of massive medical databases for treatment planning, medical therapy, and pain control are very useful for healthcare sector. Even Psychotherapy through VR one of power instrument for treatment planning.

## 18.4 Applications

The metaverse provides revolutionary prospects in healthcare. It renders medical training easier by offering practice in actual environments free from physical restraints through virtual simulations. Remote diagnostics and immersive consultations are two advantages of telemedicine that increase access to healthcare services around the world. With personalized and interactive interventions, VR therapies provide cutting-edge care for mental health issues and rehabilitation. Moreover, medical education trains future doctors well using virtual classrooms and simulations. In this way, the healthcare industry introduces a new era of easily accessible, interactive, and effective healthcare solutions that, also improve patient care and outcomes while promoting continuous innovation in medical practices [23–31]. This chapter will consider some of the applications below:

i. Telemedicine Using Metaverse:

The ability of the metaverse to revolutionize telemedicine lies in offering consumers and medical professionals a more immersive and interactive experience. The metaverse enables doctors to see patients from everywhere while the patients can be seen by doctors anywhere. Through it, people who lack physical access to doctors' offices like those who live in remote areas or have transportation difficulties could also get medical aid [28]. Additionally, specialized care can also be provided through the metaverse. While receiving treatment, individuals can gain knowledge about their wellness with the help of this technology. In addition, all sorts of diseases, treatments, and medications may be examined on the Internet. Moreover, other patients can chat with them and learn from them. They should, therefore, make an informed decision about their health since they are well versed in it. Although it is still developing, telemedicine will probably be altered completely if things go as planned for the metaverse one day. This could enhance access, specialization, and teaching.

ii. Ophthalmology Applications:
In ophthalmology, the metaverse could be used to improve patient care in several ways. For example, it would be possible for telemedicine consultations with ophthalmologists to occur through the metaverse. This implies that individuals living in rural areas or requiring eye checkups but facing travel problems can receive the best medical care. Moreover, using the metaverse, it is also possible for the training of ophthalmologists and other eye caregivers to take place. Consequently, learning new techniques and procedures will be easier without attending a conference or training center. Furthermore, different diagnostic and treatment tools can be developed via the use of metaverse. Such as already some researchers are trying to develop virtual models of eyes that can help in diagnosing diseases as well as planning treatments via metaverse. Broadly speaking though, there is the likelihood of enormous effects on ophthalmology by the metaverse which would influence patient care significantly, enabling ophthalmologists to keep pace with modern methods easily and foster the invention of alternative diagnostic and therapeutic tools. The future of eye care could have some beneficial impacts from the metaverse. Remote consultations: Eye doctors would be able to use virtual worlds to interact with patients in a remote manner. Some individuals reside in rural areas or are handicapped and find it difficult to be on the road to visit an ophthalmologist. Training: The metaverse could serve as a platform for the training of ophthalmologists as well as other eye specialists. That way, they will not need to go to seminars and conferences since they will access the new techniques and procedures online.

iii. Diagnostics:
Researchers have been exploring how the metaverse could facilitate the creation of virtual models of eyes that can be used for diagnosed purposes and treatment plans. This may make it possible for such conditions as myopia to be diagnosed earlier than is at present possible thus increasing response rates regarding treatment. Treatments: Ophthalmology has the chance to create new forms of treatment for certain kinds of diseases affecting the eyes in metaverse. One example is research that uses VR that acts directly on the eye surface by providing treatment using VR technology

while avoiding invasive techniques that may result in lower efficiency levels while treating eye problems.

iv. Clinical Applications:
Clinical Trials: The metaverse can be utilized in clinical trials increasing their efficiency and success. This means that researchers might create virtual realities or areas where patients may participate in clinical trials without being physically present.

v. Metaverse in Fetal Medicine and Gynecology:
To start with, the metaverse could be used for prenatal care: both the patients residing in remote areas and those who find it difficult to access a medical facility can get prenatal care via metaverse using high-speed internet technology. In this way, even when patients are not required to travel, they will have an opportunity to interact with their doctor as well as see ultrasound images enabling them to consult on issues concerning diagnosis and any possible therapy. The use of such technologies is also useful in diagnosing and treating fetal defects. Another example is connecting pregnant women through metaverse to other expecting moms or groups that provide information about pregnancy such as what should be done during emergencies.

vi. Skin:
The possibilities are unlimited because the metaverse is still evolving into an idea of what will eventually be actualized. Although it may seem strange to conceive of skin care in a virtual environment, particularly one that will be filled with personalized or NFT avatars, this also gives skin care brands the chance to be innovative and make it simpler to communicate their messages in an unlimited and borderless environment. This can motivate someone to achieve their ideal physical appearance, discover the greatest skincare products, and benefit from recent developments in the beauty world. Skin care may also depend on creating a virtual community that is more about ideation and sharing in an unbounded creative space than it is about e-commerce and results in real-world innovation. By receiving skincare guidance directly from the product manufacturers, learning in-depth information about individual skin-tone requirements, or using cryptocurrency for in-person real-time purchases, the metaverse empowers users to realize all that is possible for their ideal skincare regimen. With silky-smooth skin and effective washing for all skin tones, user can use the natural environment even more as they engage in their metaverse exploration [29].

vii. Dental Application:
Diverse industries have begun to invest actively and investigate its potential applications, ranging from high-tech and business to art and real estate. The next industry to investigate this ground-breaking technological advancement that promises to revolutionize the medical industry, including cardiovascular medicine, is the healthcare industry. By giving patients and dentists a more immersive and interactive experience, the metaverse has the potential to revolutionize dentistry. The metaverse could be used, for instance, to deliver dental care to patients who reside in remote locations or have trouble getting to a dentist's office. Customers can consult their dentist virtually, and they can see a 3D model of their teeth and have a chance to ask questions. Viewing and diagnosing oral health problems: Dental professionals could assess patients' teeth by scanning and sharing information with other professionals through the metaverse. Educational service provision hence involves teaching dentists and dental students. The personnel of dental clinics and dental schools may benefit from the metaverse tools as they could simulate the process of practicing dentistry or master new dental procedures. Help patients who suffer from dental phobia: Patients who have dental phobia may be able to book a meeting with their dentist, but this can be done in the metaverse securely. However, one must understand that the metaverse is still in a somewhat early stage of development, but it can become a game changer in the future of dentistry. The metaverse has the potential to significantly enhance patient care by offering a more immersive and interactive experience.

viii. Cancer Treatment:
The cancer patient requires extra care and precaution. The digital platform can provide the evaluation of drug interactions with the patients. By obtaining the patient's medical records, we can pinpoint the precise purpose of the required treatment. Various hardware and software are needed to create 3D virtual data that create a 3D virtual world. The best technique attainable in the metaverse VR and AR is used to create and identify the necessary medical data. This method can be applied to the planning stage of the treatment and ultimately helps with execution [30–34]. The use of the metaverse in cancer treatment includes VR therapy, which can assist cancer patients in controlling their symptoms and side effects. VR can benefit patients by managing pain, reducing anxiety, and promoting better sleep. Rural consultation: This way, using the metaverse, cancer patients who live in rural areas or cannot easily physically arrive at the doctor's office can get remote consultations. Virtual surgery: Real patients can undergo surgery in the given simulation and the surgeons can get trained

for cancer treatment procedures in the metaverse created by such environments. By doing this, the chances of complications during the surgery will be brought down.

ix. Patient Monitoring and Rehabilitation:
The future of patient monitoring and rehabilitation in the healthcare sector appears vast with the incorporation of metaverse. Wearable devices can also be integrated into the simulated conditions to provide accurate information on patient's health status to remotely assess patients' condition and manage necessary changes to the treatment plan. The lack of human interaction, however, is not an issue with these virtual interfaces making it easier to execute home-based rehabilitation programs because they control and lead patients to do their exercises and therapies in ways that are less intimidating and more fun. Immersive technology is a great way to improve the involvement of care providers in the patient's health improvement process in combination with the feedback and monitoring of the progress achieved. Such an approach does not only expand the range of services provided to the patients but also empowers them to promote their recovery being an active part of the process after leaving the 'medical' sphere. The promising area where it is possible to enhance utilizing virtual environment for monitoring and rehabilitation of patients is the promising area in terms of enhancing the efficiency of the healthcare service delivery [33].

x. Medical Training and Education:
The metaverse is revolutionizing medical learning and training in virtual simulations and with 3D models. These 3D models help medical practitioners improve their efficiency as well as the ability to reason in appropriate situations as well as in inappropriate detailed settings. Students and professionals can study and comprehend complex anatomical structures and physiological processes in a detailed and captivating way by using interactive 3D models of anatomy and physiology. To ensure that healthcare workers are competent and prepared to provide high-quality patient care in actual clinical settings, the metaverse bridges the gap between theoretical knowledge and practical application [34].

## 18.5 Metaverse: Challenges and Opportunity

All nations and authorities should make investments in preventive measures and expand access to preventive care. Typically, hospital rooms have a prison-like appearance. The future should resemble tiny apartments and be entirely devoted to the healing process. Patients and their families should receive variable devices to better monitor their vital signs, it should be monitored for two-way videoconferencing between patients and caregivers, and disinfectant robots could clean hospital rooms more effectively. More significantly, they could end the horrifying fact that one in every 20 patients acquired an infection. Certain difficulties that a metaverse is expected to face have been foreseen. The major concerns include the security and privacy of patients, hospitals, and doctors and authenticating the identities of entities moving across the virtual world disguised as digital avatars. As a result, an unauthorized person can access the data or information under the hide of an individual, swindle other clients, or misuse the information. Concerning diagnosis, AR and VR may assist patients in recognizing vision-related disabilities [35], comprehending how loss of vision can impact function and quality of life [36], and evaluating the relationship between vision loss and the visual field in functional vision [37]. VR has also been utilized to evaluate visual functions in patients with strabismus and amblyopia [38, 39], as well as to help identify visual field limitations in glaucoma patients in association with the Humphrey perimeter [33, 34, 40]. The viability of showing optical coherence tomography pictures in a VR setting using a head-mounted display has also been investigated in the field of the retina and they may offer a platform for patient involvement, medical education, professional training, and other purposes for the next generation of optical coherence tomography image presentation mode [41–44].

## 18.6 Conclusion

Now, it does not seem like a far-fetched dream, and those who do manage screenings and take other preventive measures pay big bucks for it. In future COVID-like situations, hospitals will be relieved of the terrible burden they have undergone. Once the metaverse is fully implemented, then medical stresses will be streamlined. While we are in the hospital, the truth is that at our core, hospital rooms still function the way we did past 20 to 30 years. Patients are, by no means, the center of these systems. They are more like a burden, and we still use the term discharge for patients who get released without question. The metaverse is a collective system of virtual tools to integrate and enhance the digital, physical, and reality systems in open space for stakeholders of the medical sector. The metaverse will provide a decentralized, persistent, interoperable, and collaborative system in the healthcare sector, and these models will help humankind and a better life for people.

## References


1. Soava, G., Mehedintu, A., Sterpu, M., Analysis and Forecast of the Use of E-Commerce in Enterprises of the European Union States. *Sustainability*, 14, 14, 8943, 2022.
2. Aburbeian, A.M., Owda, A.Y., Owda, M., A Technology Acceptance Model Survey of the Metaverse Prospects. *AI*, *3*, 2, 285–302, 2022.
3. Thomason, J., MetaHealth-How will the Metaverse Change Health Care? *J. Metaverse*, *1*, 1, 13–16, 2021.
4. Wiederhold, B.K., Metaverse Games: Game Changer for Healthcare? *Cyberpsychol. Behav. Soc. Netw.*, *25*, 5, 267–269, 2022.
5. Dewi, Y.S. and Darma, G.S., Shifting Business Strategy of International Standard Hospital in Metaverse Era. *JMMR (J. Medicoeticolegal Manajemen Rumah Sakit)*, *11*, 1, 30–43, 2022.
6. Chen, D. and Zhang, R., Exploring Research Trends of Emerging Technologies in Health Metaverse: A Bibliometric Analysis. *SSRN Electron. J.*, 1, 1–32, 2022, Available at SSRN 3998068.
7. Yang, D., Zhou, J., Chen, R., Song, Y., Song, Z., Zhang, X., Bai, C., Expert consensus on the metaverse in medicine. *Clin. eHealth*, *5*, 1–9, 2022.
8. Keshmiri Neghab, H., Jamshidi, M.B., Keshmiri Neghab, H., Digital Twin of a Magnetic Medical Microrobot with Stochastic Model Predictive Controller Boosted by Machine Learning in Cyber-Physical Healthcare Systems. *Information*, 13, 7, 321, 2022.
9. Huynh-The, T., Pham, Q.V., Pham, X.Q., Nguyen, T.T., Han, Z., Kim, D.S., Artificial Intelligence for the Metaverse: A Survey, arXiv preprint arXiv:2202.10336, 2022.
10. Khazanchi, D., Kumar Vyas, A., Kant Hiran, K., Padmanaban, S., *Blockchain 3.0 for Sustainable Development*, De Gruyter, Berlin, Boston, 2021, https://doi.org/10.1515/9783110702507.
11. Kant Hiran, K., Khazanchi, D., Kumar Vyas, A., Padmanaban, S., *Machine Learning for Sustainable Development*, De Gruyter, Berlin, Boston, 2021, https://doi.org/10.1515/9783110702514.
12. Vyas, A.K., Balamurugan, S., Hiran, K.K., Dhiman, H.S. (Eds.), *Artificial Intelligence for Renewable Energy Systems*, John Wiley & Sons, New Jersey, 2022, ISBN: 9781119761693.
13. Xi, N., Chen, J., Gama, F., Riar, M., Hamari, J., The challenges of entering the metaverse: An experiment on the effect of extended reality on workload. *Inf. Syst. Front.*, 25, 1–22, 2022.
14. Liu, Z., Ren, L., Xiao, C., Zhang, K., Demian, P., Virtual reality aided therapy towards health 4.0: a two-decade bibliometric analysis. *Int. J. Environ. Res. Public Health*, *19*, 3, 1525, 2022.
15. Skalidis, I., Fournier, S., Hammilos, M., Kaldasch, M., El Idrissi, B., Kirsch, M., Maurizi, N., Feasibility of using the Metaverse as a Telecardiology

platform: Remote Follow-up of a patient with Vasospastic Angina. *Can. J. Cardiol.*, 38, 11, 1768–1769, 2022.
16. Thomason, J., Metaverse, Token Economies, and Chronic Diseases. *Global Health J.*, 1, 1, 13–16, 2022.
17. Sun, M., Xie, L., Liu, Y., Li, K., Jiang, B., Lu, Y., Yang, D., The Metaverse in Current Digital Medicine. *Clin. eHealth*, 5, 52–57, 2022.
18. Marzaleh, M.A., Peyravi, M., Shaygani, F., A revolution in health: Opportunities and challenges of the Metaverse. *EXCLI J.*, 21, 791–792, 2022.
19. Mesko, B., The promise of the metaverse in cardiovascular health. *Eur. Heart J.*, 43, 28, 2647–2649, 2022.
20. Yang, J.O. and Lee, J.S., Utilization Exercise Rehabilitation Using Metaverse (VR· AR· MR· XR). *Korean J. Sport Biomech.*, 31, 4, 249–258, 2021.
21. Dixit, A., Tiwari, S., Vyas, A.K., Kumar, R., Pandey, A., Optimization of Hexagonal Boron-Doped Silicate Photonic Crystal Fiber To Obtain Near Zero Flattened Dispersion For Nonlinear Waves By Finite Difference Method. *Quantum Opt. Electron*, 54, 9, 565, 2022.
22. Vyas, A.K. and Dhiman, H.S., Predication of negative dispersion for photonic crystal fiber using extreme learning machine. *J. Opt. Commun.*, 45, 2, 000010151520210124, 2021, https://doi.org/10.1515/joc-2021-0124.
23. Vyas, A.K., Multiple rings based photonic crystal fiber for terahertz application. *Optik*, 231, 166424, 2021.
24. Vyas, A.K., Hiran, K.K., Dhiman, H., Modelling of symmetrical quadrature optical ring resonator with four different topologies and performance analysis using machine learning approach. *J. Opt. Commun.*, 44, 1, 000010151520200270, 2021, https://doi.org/10.1515/joc-2020-0270.
25. Kim, Y.-W., Yoo, S., Lee, H., Han, S., Characterization of digital twin, May 2021.
26. The Promise of a Digital Twin Strategy, Feb. 2017, [online] Available: https://info.microsoft.com/The-promise-of-a-digital-twin-strategyBestpractices-for-designers-Registration-FormininBody.html.
27. Jagatheesaperumal, S.K., *et al.*, Semantic-Aware Digital Twin for Metaverse: A Comprehensive Review. *IEEE Wireless Commun.*, 30, 4, 38–46, August 2023, doi: 10.1109/MWC.003.2200616.
28. Bansal, G., Rajgopal, K., Chamola, V., Xiong, Z., Niyato, D., Healthcare in Metaverse: A Survey on Current Metaverse Applications in Healthcare. *IEEE Access*, 10, 119914–119946, 2022, doi: 10.1109/ACCESS.2022.3219845.
29. Mozumder, Md.A., Sheeraz, M., Athar, A., Aich, S., Kim, H.-C., Overview: Technology Roadmap of the Future Trend of Metaverse based on IoT, Blockchain, AI Technique, and Medical Domain Metaverse Activity, 2022, 10.23919/ICACT53585.2022.9728808.
30. Content available at https://www.univarsolutions.com.

31. Pathmudi, V.R., Khatri, N., Kumar, S., Abdul-Qawy, A.S.H., Vyas, A.K., A systematic review of IoT technologies and their constituents for smart and sustainable agriculture applications. *Sci. Afr.*, 19, e01577, 2023.
32. Khatri, N., Vyas, A.K., Abdul-Qawy, A.S.H., Rene, E.R., Artificial neural network based models for predicting the effluent quality of a combined upflow anaerobic sludge blanket and facultative pond: Performance evaluation and comparison of different algorithms. *Environ. Res.*, Elsevier, 217, 114843, 2023
33. Chengoden, R., Victor, N., Huynh-The, T., Yenduri, G., Jhaveri, R., Alazab, M., Bhattacharya, S., Hegde, P., Reddy, P., Gadekallu, T., Metaverse for Healthcare: A Survey on Potential Applications, Challenges and Future Directions, 2022.
34. Al-Elq, A.H., Simulation-based medical teaching and learning. *J. Fam. Commun. Med.*, 17, 1, 35–40, 2010 Jan, doi: 10.4103/1319-1683.68787. PMID: 22022669; PMCID: PMC3195067.
35. Lam, A.K., To, E., Weinreb, R.N., Yu, M., Mak, H., Lai, G., Use of virtual reality simulation to identify vision-related disability in patients with glaucoma. *JAMA Ophthalmol.*, 138, 490–498, 2020.
36. Jones, P.R., Somoskeöy, T., Chow, W.B.H., Crabb, D.P., Seeing other perspectives: evaluating the use of virtual and augmented reality to simulate visual impairments (OpenVisSim). *NPJ Digital Med.*, 3, 1–9, 2020.
37. Gopalakrishnan, S., Jacob, C.E.S., Kumar, M., Karunakaran, V., Raman, R., Comparison of visual parameters between normal individuals and people with low vision in a virtual environment. *Cyberpsychol. Behav. Soc. Netw.*, 23, 171–178, 2020.
38. Miao, Y., Jeon, J.Y., Park, G., Park, S.W., Heo, H., Virtual reality-based measurement of ocular deviation in strabismus. *Comput. Methods Programs Biomed.*, 185, 105132, 2020.
39. Panachakel, J.T., Ramakrishnan, A.G., Manjunath, K.P., VR glasses-based measurement of responses to dichoptic stimuli: a potential tool for quantifying amblyopia?, in: *42nd Annual International Conference of the IEEE Engineering in Medicine & Biology Society (EMBC)*, vol. 20–24, pp. 5106–5110, July 2020.
40. Alawa, K.A., Nolan, R.P., Han, E., Arboleda, A., Durkee, H., Sayed, M.S., Low-cost, smartphone-based frequency doubling technology visual field testing using a head-mounted display. *Br. J. Ophthalmol.*, 105, 440–444, 2021.
41. Dixit, A., Tiwari, S., Vyas, A., Singh, V., Maity, G., Investigation of Wave Propagation Characteristics in Photonic Crystal Micro-structure Containing Circular Shape with Varied Nonlinearity. *Opt. Quantum Electron.*, 56, 10, 1–15, 2023, DOI: 10.1007/s11082-023-04700-8.
42. Vyas, A.K., Dixit, A., Tiwari, S., Khatri, N., Design of double V-groove shape-based PCF sensor for cancer detection using RI technique. *Optik*, 305, 171783, 2024, https://doi.org/10.1016/j.ijleo.2024.171783.

43. Vyas, A.K., Dixit, A., Tiwari, S., Khatri, N., Investigation of crosstalk and BER in multicore fiber optic transmission link for Space Division Multiplexing. *Results Opt.*, 2022, https://doi.org/10.1016/j.rio.2022.100251.
44. Bale, A.S., Vinay, N., Tiwari, S., Dixit, A., Vyas, A., Pandey, A., Dixit, Y., Exploring Specialty Optical Fiber for Astrophotonics Applications. *Results Opt.*, 11, 1, 100380, 2023, DOI: 10.1016/j.rio.2023.100380.

19

# Optimizing DHD for Healthcare Applications in the Metaverse

**Vrunda Patel[1*], Mansvi Patel[1], Khush Patel[1] and Jignesh Thaker[2]**

[1]*Information and Communication Technology, Adani Institute of Infrastructure and Engineering, Ahmedabad, Gujarat, India*
[2]*Mechanical Engineering Department, Adani University, Ahmedabad, Gujarat, India*

***Abstract***
The present article comprehensively investigates the optimal algorithms for phase-only hologram (POH) and their methodologies. Holographic display technology, widely used in various laboratories, is explored with a focus on enhancing wearability, display, and overall outlook. This paper encapsulates experimental studies involving dynamic holographic displays through a comparative analysis of photorefractive materials (CsPbBr3, PVCz, and PATPD/CAAN) and liquid-crystal films. Furthermore, the implementation of computer-generated hologram (CGH) is detailed, employing a combination of U-Net and ResNet structures to achieve higher-quality reconstructed images. The integration of these advanced techniques within the convolutional neural network (CNN) methods is discussed in terms of the training process and its modifications. The overall optimization of hologram technology is highlighted to overcome zero-order intensity distortion, enormous computational time, and noise from the coherent light source as well as from the system. These optimizations in holographic display technology contribute significantly to diverse fields including healthcare, gaming, data storage, and interactive communication displays. Furthermore, a thorough evaluation of the metaverse has been conducted, encompassing its pivotal technologies, and various uses in the medical and healthcare fields, such as emergency response education, practical experience in anatomy education, ophthalmology, drug research, and so forth.

**Corresponding author*: vrundapatel.ict21@aii.ac.in

Ajay Kumar Vyas, Harleen Kaur, Sourabh Sharma and Bhavya Alankar (eds.) Metaverse Technologies, Security and Applications for Healthcare, (409–430) © 2025 Scrivener Publishing LLC

***Keywords***: Optimization, hologram technology, computer-generated hologram (CGH), convolutional neural network (CNN), dynamic holographic display (DHD), applied holography in healthcare

## 19.1 Introduction

Holographic display technology has a wide range of applications often utilized in data storage, telecommunications, and security purposes. Most prominently in the healthcare, education, surgical experiments, data analysis and enhancement, and medical awareness. Numerous research studies and experiments based on holography technology have been conducted in the scope of noise reduction, image reconstruction, and hologram-generating methods. Computer-generated hologram (CGH) can be classified into two categories, namely, phase and amplitude. Phase-only hologram (POH) shows correlatively higher diffraction potential aside from sacrificing the

**Table 19.1** Literature on holographic display technology utilized by various researchers.

| Year | Author | Outcome | Technology |
|---|---|---|---|
| 2019 | Gao *et al.* [13] | Silver nanoparticles are used with nanoparticle-doped liquid crystal films to get superfast hologram refresh speed as a real-time dynamic holographic medium. | Holographic display based on liquid crystal films doped with silver nanoparticles |
| 2021 | Wu *et al.* [14] | They proposed that perovskite NC doped with nematic LC was a better material for the display of the dynamic holographic image as it received better and faster photography illumination than previous materials [7]. | Holographic display based on liquid crystal films doped with perovskite nanocrystal |
| 2022 | Chen *et al.* [1] | When the network is trained through CNN, a better-optimized constant phase can be obtained. | High-speed computational system |

space bandwidth product (SBP) [1]. Table 19.1 represents a few pieces of literature on holographic display technology utilized by various researchers.

Reconstruction of high-quality images by POH is a challenging task and faces numerous challenges. Consequently, a multitude of optimization algorithms have been developed to ensure the production of high-quality CGH and images free from noise. Optimization algorithms are performed either iteratively or non-iteratively. The iterative approach includes the Wirtinger algorithm [2], the Gerchberg-Saxton (GS) algorithm [3], and the gradient descendent algorithm [4]. Iterative methods are time-consuming as they consume hours to implement the calculations. Instead, the non-iterative approach is less time-consuming and mainly includes complex-amplitude modulation (CAM) and error diffusion. CAM provides high-quality images with a reduction in SBP [5].

A hologram is a compound of intensities generated by scattering an electromagnetic wave through a study object. The computation of the studied object's wavefront, which is broken down into layer-based method (PSM) [6], source-based method [7], and polygon-based method [8], is a crucial component of recording. Among these, PSM is broadly used because it works on the decomposition of study objects to various point sources to later superimpose them into the final image. PSM can construct sharp structures, and it can be easily modified to give visual effects to the output. PSM uses either CAM or the random phase method (RPM) [9, 10] for image encoding. RPM is less complicated and does not theoretically reduce SBP. Furthermore, its reconstruction produces unwanted noise, which disrupts the process. The display must accurately replicate the color, light intensity, and depth cue of a three-dimensional image. Holography is a literal 3D display technique for the reconstruction of the phase information and intensity of the object without any special eyewear [11, 12].

## 19.2 Materials Used in Dynamic Holography Display

In the preceding years, various materials have been proposed (photorefractive, photochromic polymer, photosensitive crystal, doped liquid crystal, etc.) for the display of dynamic holography. Due to the low refresh rate, the holographic televised display of narrow field and large computing potential has not been instigated in real-world applications. To a greater extent, there is a need to enhance the execution of dynamic holographic displays (DHDs), which can procure little power exhaustion, better response time, and high resolution. Table 19.2 summarizes the research carried out in terms of two different materials for creating DHD. First, DHD is created using photorefractive materials, and second, DHD is created using doped liquid crystal materials.

Photorefractive materials constitute quick response property with better power exhaustion to secure high frame rate DHD. A few photorefractive materials, photorefractive polymers, and LC-doped films are tabulated in Table 19.2. However, after using these materials, the refresh rate was found to be insufficient for televising, and the response time proposed by Tsutsumi *et al.* [16] was 59 ms. It is still negligible for high-frame holographic displays. Furthermore, the diffraction efficiency is a crucial parameter that pertains to graphics video and graphics features and is firmly based on refractive index modulation. Large electric fields can be controlled by this modulation, in turn, for increased sufficiency, but photorefractive polymers are not suitable for real-world use.

Photorefractive materials are, therefore, inappropriate to use with DHD. Some researchers have chosen doped liquid crystal materials with large diffraction efficiency, which elevated the birefringence index to a smaller electrical field, received a better response time, and sensitized photoconductivity to overcome this issue. Recently, significant research has been reported on doped liquid crystals using different materials such as ferroelectric LC-doped, nematic LC, silver nanoparticles (AgNPs), and perovskite ($CsPbBr_3$) nanocrystal (NC)–doped LC films. The comparison of all these materials is tabulated in Table 19.2. The present work aims to compare two different materials (perovskite NC and silver nanoparticles doped in liquid crystal film) and determine which is more efficient and suitable for DHD.

**Table 19.2** Comparative study on various refreshable photorefractive materials, polymers, and liquid crystal–doped films.

| Author | Materials | Outcome |
|---|---|---|
| Blanche *et al.* [15] | 6-phenyl-C61-butyric acid methyl ester (PCBM):photorefractive polymer material tetraphenyldiaminobiphenyl (TPD):9-ethylcarbazole (ECZ):fluorinated dicyanostyrene (FDCST) (0.5:49.5:20:30 wt%). | The refresh rate found following this method was 0.5 Hz at 7 kV; however, this is insufficient for holographic televised display. |

*(Continued)*

**Table 19.2** Comparative study on various refreshable photorefractive materials, polymers, and liquid crystal–doped films. (*Continued*)

| Author | Materials | Outcome |
|---|---|---|
| Tsutsumi *et al.* [16] | Carbazolyl ethyl propionate (CzEPA):poly (N-vinylcarbazole) (PVCZ):2,4,7-trinitro-O-fluorenone (TNF):4-azacycloheptylbenzylidene-malonitrile (7-DCST), 1 wt% of (20:44:1:35 wt%) | As a result of this method, diffraction efficiency is 68% at 45V/μm, but still, it needs to be reduced for better performance. |
| Sasaki *et al.* [17] | 3T-2MB:trinitrofluorenone (TNF) (10:0.1) wt% | The response time was found to be 8 ms at an electrical field of 1 V/μm. |
| Li *et al.* [18] | Quantum dots (ZnS/InP) with nematic LC (4,4-n-pentylcyanobipheny 1, SCB) | The diffraction efficiency was obtained at 30%; still, it is a low-high-frame display. |
| Gao *et al.* [11] | 5CB doped along carbon dots | 30% diffraction efficiency was observed at an electrical field of 0.2 V/μm. |
| Wu *et al.* [14] | Perovskite (CsPbB13) NC–doped LC film | The response time was found to be 5.5 ms at an electrical field of 0.45 V/μm and the diffraction rate was observed at 18%. |
| Gao *et al.* [13] | LC-doped with silver nanoparticles (AgNPs) | The response time was found to be 0.1 ms at an electrical field of 0.12 V/μm. |

### 19.2.1 Experimental Details

Two experiments are reported in the present article, as shown in Figures 19.1 and 19.2. In the year 2021, an experimental method (as shown in Figure 19.1) was proposed by Wu *et al.* [14] which introduced a groundbreaking concept by integrating perovskite ($CsPbBr_3$) NCs doped into liquid crystal (5CB) films. This DHD based on CsPbX3-doped (X=BR, I) liquid crystal films examines the potential development of a new type of holographic display based on NC-doped liquid crystal films.

Perovskite materials have gained significant attention for their composition and exclusive molecular structure. Also, it exhibits peak optoelectrical power conversion efficiency and peak carrier mobility which improves the photoconductivity of the liquid crystal under laser illumination. This results in 18% of utmost diffraction efficiency and 5.5Ms of less response time. In addition, this work reports the possibility of combining nanotechnology, organic chemical synthesis, and liquid crystal technology to create a new type of compact and high-resolution display.

In the second experiment illustrated in Figure 19.2, Gao *et al.* [13] proposed using LC films doped with Ag NPs as a dynamic hologram display. This material was prepared with a mixture of 5CB of nematic LC with Ag NPs. The material is then heated to 80°C in a vacuum oven for a whole 12-hour period using an electrical field and an optical field application to

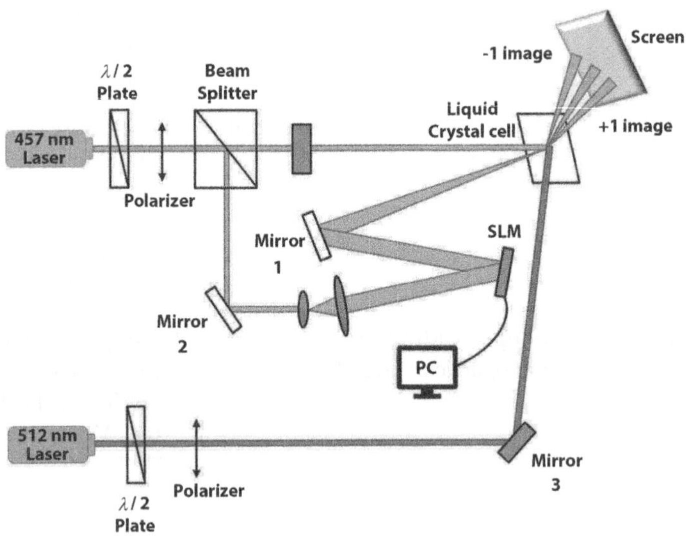


**Figure 19.1** Experimental setup of holography display based on CsPbB3 doped along liquid crystal films doped.

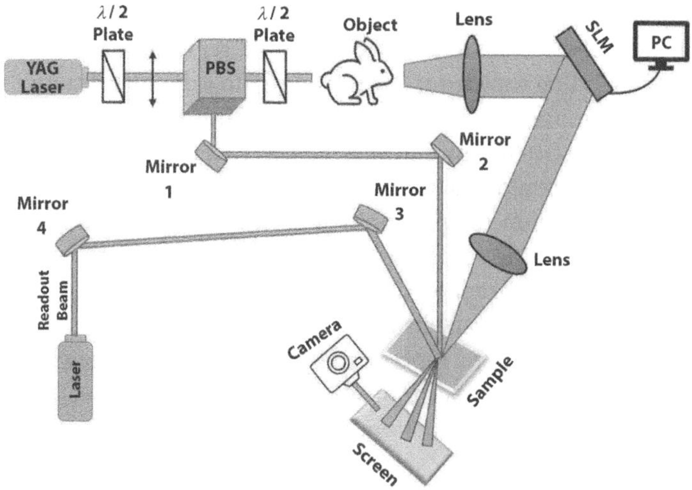


**Figure 19.2** Experimental setup of holographic display based on Ag NPs doped with LC films [13].

improve compatibility. After so many experiments, they found that 0.03 wt% was an optimum concentration and the thickness of the crystal layer was 25μm. In Figure 19.2, two polarized beams (457 lasers as an object light and 532 lasers as a reference light) are used, whose wavelengths are transformed by the λ/2 plate. A beam splitter is used to divide a lesser beam into two parts: a lesser reflection on an LC cell via an attenuator and a second lesser reflection on a mirror to a spatial light modulator (SLM). These reflect a second LC cell and generate a screen display.

The result of this experiment concludes that the maximum diffraction efficiency reaches 50% under 0.12 V/μm electric voltage values so that they get a minimum response time of 0.1 ms, which means that 5000 Hz is the maximum point for refresh rate. The diffraction efficiency is calculated based on two factors: polarization direction and energy of recording light. The polarization angle is kept as 40° and the reference light and intensity ratio recording are 2:1. Hence, the liquid crystal film doped with Ag NPs exhibits better capability to recognize polished holography display. Overall, this material turns out to be self-sufficient for real-world applications.

Ultimately, it was determined that in terms of reduced response time and increased diffraction efficiency, holographic displays based on Ag NPs doped with LC films were more effective compared to LC films doped with CsPbB3. Future improvements in the diffraction capacity and display time are still required.

Holographic display technology is considered for modulating light through diffractive components to encode and reproduce the wavefront. It focuses on encoding wavefront to get CGH from a digital refractive pattern into the superimposed holographic display. Thus, the test object can be inclusively reconstructed by showcasing the CGH on SLM and its subsequent luminescence along a light source.

Hologram works on the principle of light diffraction and interference. Mostly, the lasers are used as the illuminating source ascribed for coherence necessity by holographic display. Still, the usage of laser prevails over the specky sound which reflects into a crude intensive pattern overlapping over the image. Hence, to repress specked sound, it is suggested to use three strategies they are superimposition, temporal coherence destruction, and spatial coherence construction.

## 19.3 How to Train Network Through CNN for the Optimization of Phase-Only Hologram

Chen *et al.* [1] introduced the concept of optimized constant phases (OCPs). These OCPs can be utilized to optimize the POH. The first important element for the recording of the study object is the wavefront. The reversibility of the light principle allows one to construct an image of the study object by flipping the light path when light beams are projected on it from various angles. Additionally, the study object may disperse into different point sources when the light beam strikes it through PSM. These point sources are termed to be information carriers as they carry the information about the wavefront. As shown in Figure 19.3, each point source helps in the formation of the wavefront where five wavefronts are formed in the x- and y-axis of the same size. These wavefronts were superimposed and formed a 2D image. The area where all wavefronts exist is termed a common area and the hologram can be viewed above it. Hence, the term holographic viewing window (HVW) was coined. However, recently created holograms by PSM are not visible on top of the HVW. They are made up of a variety of sub-holograms and a range of zone plates. The reconstructed image is viewed from the perspective produced by an eyepiece. Deep learning has been applied to holographic displays in recent times soon to expand their potential and enable quick and accurate reconstruction of final images where OCP can be involved. Nevertheless, unsupervised learning can be used on the PSM and POH to map the target image of OCPs and ultimately produce an optimized POH. In conclusion, there is no way to train the OCPs.

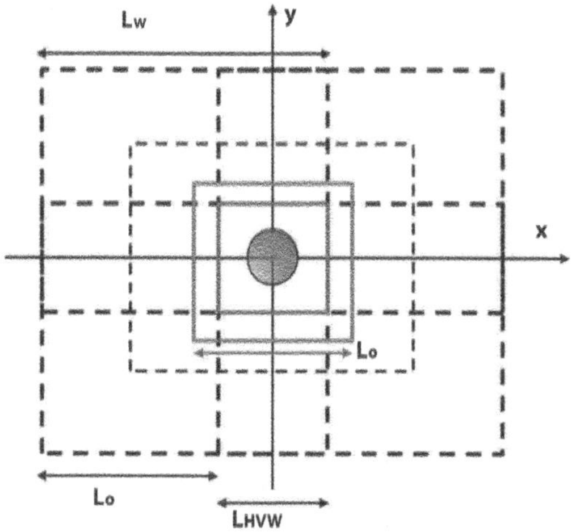


**Figure 19.3** Superimposed wavefront through various individual light sources.

CNN is prone to be precise and powerful in resolving categorization problems. OCPs instruct the network on how to incorporate the desired image into CNN. On the other hand, ANNs are dominant in situations where limited data sets are used, and image input is not always necessary. Conclusively, CNN has the capability of visualizing images as data. Hence, it is more widely used in the field of holographic display. In CNN, vector problems mostly involve the conversion of images into vectors. In U-net an image is transformed into a vector and then returned to its original form using the same mapping. The basic concept is as follows: After the image is captured, the U-net gradually breaks it up into different stages. U-net is divided into two sections. In the first half, the input image is simply divided into different levels, but all the information pertaining to each level can be also mapped. Five downsample blocks and five upsample blocks are shown in Figure 19.4. Each of these sample layers consists of two batch normalization layers, two convolution layers, two activation layers, and one single pooling layer. In order to achieve equal-sized matrices for both input and output images, a convolution layer is finally added subtly to increase the resolution. It is ensured that the size of the common area should be doubled, U-net also has a loss function that allows to recovery of lost data. Several architectures can be used as the backbone of the U-net framework. Res-blocks, or residual blocks, make up ResNet. ResNet's primary function is to create skipping connections which allows for the direct formation of jumps from one input to the next. The amalgamation of U-net with ResNet being the backbone would turn out to be an efficient framework.

The computation of loss value is measured by rechecking with identity value. This combination would aid in creating a more accurate and potent image.

Considering the convolution operation can double the size of the targeted picture from the primary one. Moreover, zero padding is utilized to result in the generation of a complicated field. The rebuilt picture is then retrieved using POH Fresnel diffraction. Additionally, U-net updates the parameters constantly to minimize the loss of weights and biases. When the MSE and NMSE are compared, it may be inferred that the NMSE oscillates less and converges more quickly and sharply.

Exciting results were obtained from the training process, which involved 3000 test images. The retrieved images were of higher quality and had significantly less speckle noise. However, the graph shows little variation due to the tiny batch size. Performance can be raised with a larger training set and better hardware appliances. The fluctuations in the loss value gradually stabilize after 1000 epochs or roughly 15 hours. After 13.5 seconds, the optimal POH is also achieved. The results demonstrate that the data obtained are not as impressive as the specific optimization given the poor quality of

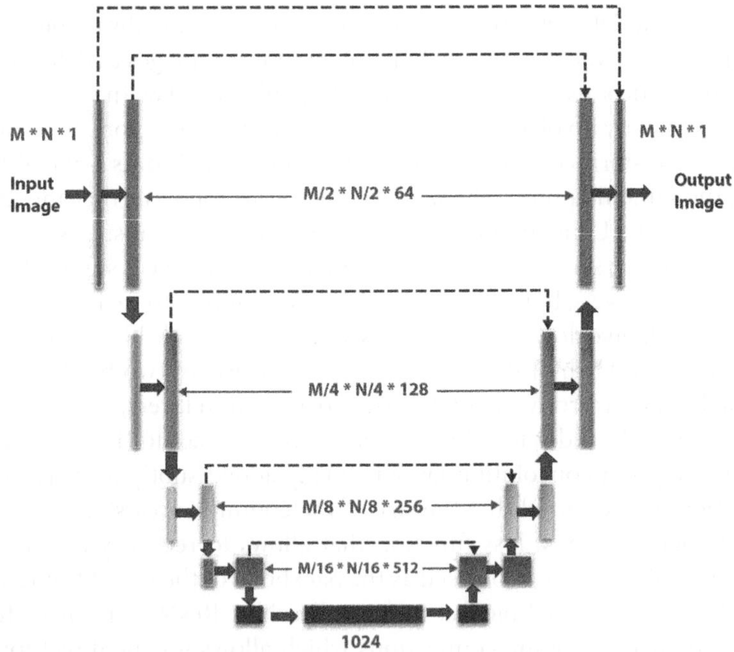


**Figure 19.4** Suggestion of the amalgamation of U-net with ResNet being the backbone for better consistency.

the constructed image acquired based on the generalization of the batches. To enhance the quality of the image, the POH can be optimized via groups, but this will demand a significant amount of time. Additionally, the trained CNN can be used to predict OCPs for study photos directly, which results in newly produced images with low quality. Thus, better optimization of the design and parameters will be needed for the best outcomes.

## 19.4 Metaverse Technology in Healthcare with Holographic Display

The metaverse is an advanced digital environment that has recently gained international attention for its ability to offer patients and medical professionals a vast array of health services. Given the rising strain on healthcare systems, it is imperative to investigate the most recent and economical approaches that can deliver dependable and prompt medical care. Therefore, the purpose of this study is to investigate the uses of metaverse in different healthcare systems and provide further details on how it may effectively enhance patient clinical management.

### 19.4.1 Metaverse Interfacing

a) **AR:** Modern technology, such as augmented reality (AR), has the power to change how we interact and perceive our surroundings. AR can improve our sensory experience by allowing us to interact with digital information in real-time with remarkably precise accuracy. It does this by seamlessly merging virtual items into our physical environment. The capacity of AR to create a harmonic merging of the digital and physical worlds by achieving precise and smooth 3D registration of virtual and real items is critical to its success. Among the benefits AR may provide are face recognition, object identification, plane detection, and movement monitoring [19].

b) **VR:** Virtual reality (VR) is characterized by its exceptional ability to create a state of profound immersion [20]. This experience stems from the sophisticated technological capabilities of the hardware and software, which enable a convincing replication of reality within the user's sensory environment [21]. Head-mounted displays (HMDs) are the foundation of modern VR, offering unprecedented degrees of presence and immersion. This makes it feasible for virtual environments to potentially affect users' cognitive, behavioral, and emotional states in ways that were not possible before [4]. The technology produces lifelike sounds and visuals, resulting in a completely immersive and potentially life-changing experience [22].

c) **MR:** By fusing the elements of AR and VR, mixed reality (MR) creates a novel perceptual space in which real-time interaction between digital and physical phenomena is possible. An MR environment combines virtual and real-world components onto one screen. In essence, MR technology allows the user to see both virtual and actual items at the same time [23]. A user may move between the actual and virtual worlds with ease thanks to this immersive experience, creating an unmatched sense of presence and interaction.

d) **AI:** This alludes to a machine's ability to mimic human intelligence, allowing it to display cognitive capacities like those of a human and carry out tasks with human-like proficiency [24]. AI is divided into several subcategories, including computer vision (CV), natural language processing (NLP), and machine learning (ML). The integration of AI into the metaverse is greatly aided by these particular technological advancements. ML technology is very beneficial to the metaverse because it enables it to learn from past interactions between participants and itself, which improves outcomes over time. Additionally, by making the metaverse more capable of acting like a human, this technology can lessen the need for human intervention and create new opportunities for growth and scalability. The metaverse provides a seamless user experience with NLP technology, which transforms natural language into computer-readable formats that are then processed and analyzed to provide the desired result. Combining several AI technologies, including deep learning, neural networks, and NLP, is necessary to get the best speech recognition accuracy. Natural language speech can be recognized and translated into an ML format using NLP technology. The ML format can then be further processed and translated back into natural language. This technology facilitates worldwide user engagement and allows avatars to speak in a natural language, both of which are beneficial to the metaverse.

The metaverse of medical technology and AI (MeTAI) has been presented as a metaverse that can support the development, evaluation, control, and improvement of AI-based medical practice, with raw data sharing, augmented regulatory science, virtual comparative scanning, and metaverse medical intervention as essential components [25].

e) **Digital Twins:** The concept of digital twins revolves around creating a full digital representation of physical objects and systems [26]. This enables the creation of digital copies of real-world physical objects, which in turn enables accurate predictions and optimization of their virtual equivalents. The utilization of cutting-edge artificial intelligence technology facilitates the creation of realistic simulations of complex physical processes, which offers substantial advantages for developing and exhibiting extensive metaverse environments.

Additionally, digital twins provide accident monitoring and preventative maintenance, which boosts real-world efficiency and lowers the danger of potential risks. The digital counterpart of the metaverse acts as a window into reality, allowing users to interact and explore virtual world offerings. Both micro and macro sizes could be used to build digital twins, with macroscopic DT being able to replicate the entire cosmos [27]. This replication is essential to the development of the metaverse and permits thorough investigation.

Microscopic DT, on the other hand, mimics molecules and offers a way to look into subatomic events. This developmental path demonstrates how DTs may be tailored to capture varying degrees of complexity, offering a flexible framework for comprehending and simulating phenomena at different scales. To better understand human well-being, a potential new field of study called "human digital twins" (DT) includes gathering actual data from people and using ML to derive health-related insights [28].

Getting these data without using uncomfortable and dangerous health-sensing gadgets is a major hurdle, though. One significant area of unmet research need is the application of DT technology to intricate applications in human health. Heart rate, breathing rate, blood oxygen saturation, blood pressure, and other bio-signals are vital for the diagnosis of both physical and mental health disorders, including mood, exhaustion, stress, and sleep patterns. These bio-signals are becoming more and more important for the telemedicine and virtual health services that have become more popular in the post-pandemic period.

### 19.4.2 Employment of Healthcare Technologies with Metaverse

a) **Virtual Clinics:** Patients' access to healthcare has been redefined by virtual clinics located within the metaverse. Thanks to this creative method, people may now contact medical professionals from the comfort of their own homes, regardless of where they are in the world. Patients can discuss their medical concerns with doctors and specialists in real time in these virtual clinics, where they can also get diagnoses and treatment recommendations. Virtual clinics have many advantages. They improve access to healthcare, especially for those who live in distant places or have restricted mobility. These virtual interactions lessen the demand for in-person visits to medical facilities, which relieves pressure on already overburdened healthcare systems. Virtual clinics provide help in the proper management and distribution of medicines.

b) **VR Therapy:** The use of VR treatment is revolutionizing how people manage their pain, anxiety, and other psychological issues. With the help of this leading-edge method, patients are fully submerged in therapeutic virtual environments where they can partake in activities intended to reduce their symptoms and enhance their general well-being. A comprehensive approach to patient care is provided via VR therapy. Creating environments that are immersive and distraction-free helps improve pain and anxiety management. Calm, virtual environments help patients feel better mentally and emotionally during treatments or recuperation. Whether during routine check-ups, surgeries, or even hospital stays, anxiety is often a part of the healthcare experience. A potent answer to this problem is provided by the metaverse. VR exposure therapy (VRET) [29] is one such technique that mimics frightening stimuli in a secure setting. This study examines the benefits and drawbacks of treating particular phobias with VRET. For soldiers suffering from post-traumatic stress disorder (PTSD), a VR exposure treatment is recommended by another study [30]. Veterans have found that the immersive treatment, which exposes patients to a variety of virtual environments, including one with a Middle Eastern theme, is a useful tool for assisting them in overcoming trauma.

By exposing patients to calming virtual settings, stress and anxiety are reduced, making the encounter more comfortable and less intimidating. Patients can select from a range of tranquil settings, such as placid woodlands or beaches. These virtual getaways offer a digital haven away from the frequently eerie clinical environments. The metaverse improves the whole patient experience by lowering anxiety related to medical procedures, which leads to improved health results.

c) **Virtual Labs:** Research and drug discovery are known for their expensive and prolonged processes. With the use of virtual laboratories that allow scientists to work together and more effectively test possible therapeutic molecules, the metaverse has the potential to completely transform this area of healthcare. Without the requirement for actual materials, researchers can mimic tests and assess drug interactions using virtual labs. As a result, research expenses and time are greatly reduced, hastening the creation of novel therapies and maybe saving lives. The metaverse encourages international cooperation. In virtual laboratories, researchers from all around the world can collaborate and exchange ideas. This cooperative setting fosters efficiency and creativity, which speeds up medical advancements. Regardless of where they are in the world, scientists can collaborate easily to address some of the most urgent problems in healthcare. Better patient care is the result of quicker medical discoveries and breakthroughs made possible by this integrated approach to research.

d) **Radiology:** An advanced imaging method called holography aids radiologists in locating fractures or other injuries in patients' hard or soft tissues. Patients receive improved care and safety as a result. A radiologist can quickly review a patient's medical history thanks to a fresh imaging approach that helps store all of the patient's prior medical records digitally. It can be used in a variety of radiological settings, including pediatric, head and neck, musculoskeletal, genitourinary, cardiovascular, and neuroradiology. Holography is a very good tool for radiology when it comes to using 3D images that are fully virtual. Compared to 2D photographs, it gives radiologists more information, and because of its electronic storage capacity, it can save a large amount of data. By directing invasive treatments, this technology aids in the planning of various surgical methods in radiology [31, 32]. It can store and retrieve three-dimensional data, which was previously very difficult for conventional imaging technologies to do.

e) **Immersive Learning Environment and Realistic Training:** The technological innovations of the metaverse present chances to enhance educational programs. Students can engage in unrestricted, genuine interactions with real-world learning circumstances in the metaverse. The emergence of the metaverse has presented new opportunities for medical education, leading academics to speculate about the new world of clinical enhancement. The potential transformation of metaverse into an online learning environment. In this virtual environment, medical educators would be able to skillfully teach pupils, concentrating on difficult subjects [33]. A paradigm for online learning has been actively developed by several academics for use in virtual classrooms. According to scholarly research published by Mesko [34] recently, there is a possibility that the metaverse may become a virtual learning environment where medical teachers could teach students. Metaverse is an encouraging resource for teaching emergency medicine since it gives students an unmatched experience that can support the growth of crucial decision-making, teamwork, and skills for resuscitation [35]. This technology plays a key role in educating medical professionals to manage large numbers of casualty situations, where the capacity to make prompt and knowledgeable orders to save lives, and decisions can make all the difference. The anatomy of the human body was traditionally understood through the dissection of living things. As a result, anatomy is a fundamental subject for medical professionals since without a comprehension of the body's normal and dysfunctional structures, medical professionals cannot cure or repair patients [36]. Therefore, understanding anatomy is essential to understanding both normal and dysfunctional bodily activities. However, the way we study and teach anatomy has changed dramatically because of technology, and we now have the convenience of metaverse applications to help us along the way. These innovative resources offer practitioners and students an engaging and participatory approach to learning about and enhancing their comprehension of human anatomy. Table 19.3 shows different technologies used for healthcare.

**Table 19.3** Immersive research in healthcare technologies.

| Institute/ company | Technology | Platform | Use case |
|---|---|---|---|
| University of Northampton | Virtual reality (VR) simulation suite | Large projection screen | Nursing students hone their skills and understand medical concepts through immersive VR simulations [37]. |
| University of Newcastle, Australia | Virtual reality (VR) and mixed reality (MR) | PC, Mac, Android, iOS, Microsoft HoloLens, and HTC Vive | Midwifery students learn about pregnancy complexities and childbirth stages through detailed 3D visualizations [38]. |
| MOOG Simodont | VR haptic dental simulator | Computer screen with 3D projection | Dental training with verisimilar haptic force feedback allows students to practice manual dexterity and dental procedures with realistic engagement [39]. |
| CVRSB Platform | VR CPR training system with HTC VIVE and Unity 3D | HTC VIVE | Medical trainees acquire CPR skills, including AED use, chest compression, and rescue breathing, with accurate haptic feedback and practical training [40, 41]. |

(*Continued*)

**Table 19.3** Immersive research in healthcare technologies. (*Continued*)

| Institute/ company | Technology | Platform | Use case |
|---|---|---|---|
| Gordon Center for Simulation and Innovation | AR, VR, and MR platforms for emergency management training | Various AR, VR, and MR platforms | Healthcare personnel prepare for emergency medical scenarios like stroke, heart attack, and arrhythmia using simulated environments [36]. |
| Inselspital, University Hospital Bern, Switzerland | VR simulations for COVID-19 clinical diagnostics | Oculus Rift headset and hand controllers | Medical students receive COVID-19–specific training, enhancing relevant skills through the CVRSB module [42]. |
| NU of Singapore's Yong Loo Lin School of Medicine | AR holographic system (Project Polaris) | Microsoft HoloLens 2 | Medical students gain a comprehensive understanding of anatomy and crucial procedures through augmented reality, enhancing their proficiency [43]. |

(*Continued*)

**Table 19.3** Immersive research in healthcare technologies. (*Continued*)

| Institute/ company | Technology | Platform | Use case |
|---|---|---|---|
| GigXR and Elsevier | Mixed-reality anatomy application (HoloHuman) | Microsoft HoloLens headgear and mobile devices | Learners engage with holographic learning environments to understand human anatomy in detail, with remote and in-class participation [44–47]. |

# References


1. Chen, Y., Zhang, T., Hua, M., IEEE Photon., J., Convolutional Neural Network for Phase-only Hologram Optimization based on the point source method with the Holographic Viewing-window. *IEEE Photon. J.*, 14, 4, Aug. 2022.
2. Chakravarthula, P., Peng, Y., Kollin, J., Fuchs, H., Heide, F., Wirtinger holography for near-eye display. *ACM Trans. Graph.*, 38, 6, 1–13, 2019.
3. Gerchberg, R.W. and Saxton, W.O., A partical algorithm for the determination of phase from image and diffraction plane pictures. *Optik*, 35, 2, 237–246, 1972.
4. Zhang, J., Pegard, N., Zhong, J., Adesnik, H., Waller, L., 3D computer generated holography by non-convex optimization. *Optica*, 4, 10, 1306–1313, 2017.
5. Tsang, P.W.M. and Poon, T.C., Novel method for converting digital Fresnel hologram to phase-only hologram based on bidirectional error diffusion. *Opt. Exp.*, 21, 20, 23680–23686, 2013.
6. Chen, J.S. and Chu, D.P., Improved layer-based method for rapid hologram generation and real-time interative holographic display applications. *Opt. Exp.*, 23, 14, 1404–1412, 2013.
7. Zhang, H., Collings, N., Chen, J., Crossland, B., Chu, D., Xie, J., Full parallax three-dimensional display with occlusion effect using computer generated hologram. *Opt. Eng.*, 50, 7, 074003, 2011.
8. Lee, W., Im, D., Hahn, J., Kim, H., Semi-analytic texturing algorithm for polygon computer generated holograms. *Opt. Exp.*, 22, 25, 31180–31191, 2014.

9. Jia, J., *et al.*, Reducing the memory usage for effective computer-generated hologram calculation using compressed look-up table in full-color holographic display. *Appl. Opt.*, 52, 7, 1404–1412, 2013.
10. Jia, J., Liu, J., Jin, G., Wang, Y., Fast and effective oclusion culling for 3D holographic displays by inverse orthographic projection with low angular sampling. *Appl. Opt.*, 53, 27, 6287–6293, 2014.
11. Gao, H., Li, X., He, Z., Su, Y., Poon, T.C., Multiplexed holographic display based on a fast response liquid crystal film. *Proc. Biomed. Opt. 3-d Imag.*, Vol. DM2C.4, 2012, DOI: 10.1364/DH.2012.DM2C.4.
12. Hahn, J., Kin, H., Lim, Y., Parket, G., Lee, B., Wide viewing angle dynamic holographic stereogram with a curved array of spatial light modulators. *Opt. Exp.*, 16, 16, 12372–12386, 2008.
13. Gao, H., Dai, Z., Liu, J., Li, S., Zhou, W., Xu, F., Fang, H., Cheng, X., Yu, Y., Zheng, H., Super-fast refresh holographic display based on liquid crystal films doped with silver nanoparticles. *Opt. Exp.*, 11, 3, 6901107, Jun, 2019.
14. Wu, Z., Zhou, X., Wu, S., Yan, Z., Li, Y., He, G., Dyanmic holographic display based on pervoskite nanocrystal doped liquid crystal film. *Opt. Exp.*, 13, 6, Dec, 2021.
15. Blanche, P.A., *et al.*, Holographic three-dimentional telepresence using large-area photorefractive polymer. *Nature*, 468, 7320, 80–83, 2010.
16. Tsutsumi, N., Kinashi, K., Anomura, A.N., Sakai, W., Quickly updatable hologram images using poly(N-vinyl carbazole) (PVCz) photorefractive polymer composite. *Materials*, 5, 8, 1477–1486, 2012.
17. Sasaki, T., Ikegami, M., Abe, T., Miyazaki, D., Kajikawa, S., Naka, Y., Realtime dynamic hologram in photorefractive ferroelectric liquid crystal. *Appl. Phys. Lett.*, 102, 2013, DOI:10.1117/12.930587.
18. Li, X. *et al.*, High-efficiency video-rate holographic display using quantum dot doped liquid crystal. *J. Disp. Technol.*, 12, 4, 362–367, 2016.
19. Musamih, A., Yaqoob, I., Salah, K., Jayaraman, R., Al-Hammadi, Y., Omar, M., Ellahham, S., Metaverse in healthcare: Applications, challenges, and future directions. *IEEE Consum. Electron. Mag.*, 12, 4, 33–46, Jul. 2023.
20. Steffen, J.H., Gaskin, J.E., Meservy, T.O., Jenkins, J.L., Wolman, I., Framework of affordances for virtual reality and augmented reality. *J. Manage. Inf. Syst.*, 36, 3, 683–729, Jul. 2019.
21. Parong, J., Pollard, K.A., Files, B.T., Oiknine, A.H., Sinatra, A.M., Moss, J.D., Passaro, A., Khooshabeh, P., The mediating role of presence differs across types of spatial learning in immersive technologies. *Comput. Hum. Behav.*, 107, Art. no. 106290, 106290, Jun. 2020.
22. Hershfield, H.E., Goldstein, D.G., Sharpe, W.F., Fox, J., Yeykelis, L., Carstensen, L.L., Bailenson, J.N., Increasing saving behavior through age-progressed renderings of the future self. *J. Marketing Res.*, 48, S23–S37, Feb. 2011.
23. Badruddoja, S., Dantu, R., He, Y., Thompson, M., Salau, A., Upadhyay, K., Trusted AI with blockchain to empower metaverse. *Proc. 4th Int.*

*Conf. Blockchain Comput. Appl. (BCCA)*, pp. 237–244, 2022, doi: 10.110 / BCCA55292.2022.9922027.

24. Russell, S.J., *Artificial Intelligence a Modern Approach*, Pearson, London, U.K, 2010.
25. Wang, G., Development of metaverse for intelligent healthcare. *Nature Mach. Intell.*, 9, 922–929, Nov. 2022.
26. Chu, N.H., Hoang, D.T., Nguyen, D.N., Phan, K.T., Dutkiewicz, E., Niyato, D., Shu, T., MetaSlicing: A novel resource allocation framework for metaverse, 2022. arXiv:2205.11087.
27. Lv, Z., Xie, S., Li, Y., Hossain, M.S., El Saddik, A., Building the metaverse by digital twins at all scales, state, relation. *Virtual Reality Intell. Hardw.*, 4, 6, 459–470, Dec. 2022.
28. Al-Zyoud, I., Laamarti, F., Ma, X., Tobón, D., El Saddik, A., Towards a machine learning-based digital twin for non-invasive human bio-signal fusion. *Sensors*, 22, 24, 9747, Dec. 2022.
29. Slater, M., Gonzalez-Liencres, C., Haggard, P., Vinkers, C., GregoryClarke, R., Jelley, S., Watson, Z., Breen, G., Schwarz, R., Steptoe, W., Szostak, D., Halan, S., Fox, D., Silver, J., The ethics of realism in virtual and augmented reality. *Frontiers Virtual Reality*, 1, 1, Mar. 2020.
30. Rizzo, A., Hartholt, A., Grimani, M., Leeds, A., Liewer, M., Virtual reality exposure therapy for combat-related posttraumatic stress disorder. *Computer*, 47, 7, 31–37, Jul. 2014.
31. Haleem, A., Javaid, M., Vaishya, R., Holography applications for orthopaedics. *Indian J. Radiol. Imaging*, 29, 477–9, 2019.
32. Bernhardt, M., Nicolas, J.D., Osterhoff, M., Mittelstädt, H., Reuss, M., Harke, B., *et al.*, Correlative microscopy approach for biology using X-ray holography, X-ray scanning diffraction and STED microscopy. *Nat. Commun.*, 9, 3641, 2018, doi: 10.1038/s41467-018-05885-z.
33. Suh, I., McKinney, T., Siu, K.-C., Current perspective of metaverse application in medical education, research and patient care. *Virtual Worlds*, 2, 2, 115–128, Apr. 2023.
34. Mesko, B., *The Promise of the Metaverse in Cardiovascular Health*, Oxford Univ. Press, London, U.K, 2022.
35. Wu, T.-C. and Ho, C.-T.-B., A scoping review of metaverse in emergency medicine. *Australas. Emergency Care*, 26, 1, 75–83, Mar. 2023.
36. Ullah, H., Manickam, S., Obaidat, M., Laghari, S.U.A., Uddin, M., *Exploring the Potential of Metaverse Technology in Healthcare: Applications, Challenges, and Future Directions*, vol. 11, June 2023, doi: 10.1109/ACCESS.2023.3286696.
37. Pottle, J., Virtual reality and the transformation of medical education. *Future Healthcare J.*, 6, 3, 181–185, Oct. 2019.
38. Jones, D., The road to birth: Using digital technology to visualise pregnancy anatomy, in: *Digital Anatomy: Applications of Virtual, Mixed and Augmented Reality*, pp. 325–342, Springer, Cham, Switzerland, 2021.

39. Al-Saud, L.M., Mushtaq, F., Allsop, M.J., Culmer, P.C., Mirghani, I., Yates, E., Keeling, A., Mon-Williams, M.A., Manogue, M., Feedback and motor skill acquisition using a haptic dental simulator. *Eur. J. Dental Educ.*, 21, 4, 240–247, Nov. 2017.
40. Almousa, O., Prates, J., Yeslam, N., Gregor, D.M., Zhang, J., Phan, V., Nielsen, M., Smith, R., Qayumi, K., Virtual reality simulation technology for cardiopulmonary resuscitation training: An innovative hybrid system with haptic feedback. *Simul. Gaming*, 50, 1, 6–22, Feb. 2019.
41. Zikas, P., Kamarianakis, M., Kartsonaki, I., Lydatakis, N., Kateros, S., Kentros, M., Geronikolakis, E., Evangelou, G., Apostolou, A., Catilo, P.A.A., Papagiannakis, G., COVID-19–VR strikes back: Innovative medical VR training. *Proc. ACM SIGGRAPH Immersive Pavilion*, 1–2, Aug. 2021, DOI: 10.1145/3450615.3464546.
42. Birrenbach, T., Zbinden, J., Papagiannakis, G., Exadaktylos, A.K., Müller, M., Hautz, W.E., Sauter, T.C., Effectiveness and utility of virtual reality simulation as an educational tool for safe performance of COVID-19 diagnostics: Prospective, randomized pilot trial. *JMIR Serious Games*, 9, 4 Art. no. e29586, Oct. 2021, DOI: 10.2196/29586.
43. Bansal, G., Rajgopal, K., Chamola, V., Xiong, Z., Niyato, D., Healthcare in metaverse: A survey on current metaverse applications in healthcare. *IEEE Access*, 10, 119914–119946, 2022.
44. Zammit, C., Calleja-Agius, J., Azzopardi, E., Augmented reality for teaching anatomy. *Clin. Anatomy*, 35, 6, 824–827, Jun. 2022.
45. Khazanchi, D., Kumar Vyas, A., Hiran, K., K., Padmanaban, S., De Gruyter, *Blockchain 3.0 for Sustainable Development*, De Gruyter, Berlin, Boston, 2021, https://doi.org/10.1515/9783110702507.
46. Kant Hiran, K., Khazanchi, D., Kumar Vyas, A., Padmanaban, S., *Machine Learning for Sustainable Development*, De Gruyter, Berlin, Boston, 2021, https://doi.org/10.1515/9783110702514.
47. Vyas, A.K., Balamurugan, S., Hiran, K.K., Dhiman, H.S. (Eds.), *Artificial Intelligence for Renewable Energy Systems*, John Wiley & Sons, 2022, ISBN: 9781119761693.

# 20

# XAI with Different Methods and Applications in Healthcare

**Mamta Motiramani[1], Nainsiben Patel[1] and Alok Kumar Singh[2*]**

[1]*Computer Science Engineering, Adani University, Ahmedabad, Gujarat, India*
[2]*Electrical Engineering Department, Adani University, Ahmedabad, Gujarat, India*

## *Abstract*

In recent times, artificial intelligence (AI) has been used in most of the domains. The algorithms used by generative AI only focus on the final decisions that lack transparency and make it a "black-box" model. This article discusses how explainable AI (XAI) can be used in the healthcare industry as it provides the reasoning behind the final decision that increases transparency and reliability. XAI can be integrated with open data, knowledge graphs, and metaverse applications. Open data provides several benefits such as identifying patterns and trends, whereas the knowledge graph can be re-traced providing information about each step taken for the final decision. Moreover, metaverse applications combine the real and virtual world with the help of technologies such as 5G or 6G Internet, augmented reality (AR), virtual reality (VR), mixed reality (MR), blockchain, Internet of Things (IoT), and AI. It will create many opportunities like remote patient care, antiaging healthcare, online medical education, training of surgeries, and medical research opportunities along with the use of XAI in deep learning approach for image analysis in medical, in applications such as to determine pancreatic cancer, and for dynamic pruning technique.

***Keywords*:** XAI, healthcare, metaverse, open data, knowledge graph, dynamic pruning, deep learning

**Corresponding author*: Alok.singh@adaniuni.ac.in

Ajay Kumar Vyas, Harleen Kaur, Sourabh Sharma and Bhavya Alankar (eds.) Metaverse Technologies, Security and Applications for Healthcare, (431–450) © 2025 Scrivener Publishing LLC

## 20.1 Introduction

Artificial intelligence (AI) has applications in the medical industry to automate diagnosis, make precise decisions in medicine, and increase the effectiveness and efficiency of resources [1]. The three major issues in AI to be implemented first are reliability, transparency, and data protection in models [2]. Generative AI uses the black-box method that creates uncertainty which leads to a lack of trust [1, 3, 4]. By providing the reasoning behind the choices, explainable AI (XAI) aims to make the decision process more transparent [1]. The main motive behind the development and research of XAI techniques is to facilitate the faster monitoring and maintenance of AI systems. These methods can help to minimize the risks that can occur while developing and using AI models, and they boost the trust and confidence of people in AI systems, making them more trustworthy and more reliable [2].

XAI provides the necessary explanation of how decisions are made in the healthcare industry. It uses different methods and algorithms such as LIME (local interpretable model agnostic explanations) and SHAP (SHapley Additive exPlanations) that provide reasoning and explanation behind the final decision. When patients are provided detailed information on how the AI systems are providing recommendations, they are more likely to trust the treatment procedure [1]. LIME provides a linear and local explanation that decides the outcome by figuring each instance at once not the whole model at a time [5]. LIME works either on SP-LIME (selective pick LIME) or RP-LIME (random pick LIME). SHAP operates on a payout methodology which means the greater the contribution of an input for the output, the greater its importance [6]. Apart from the above-given techniques, there are some other techniques like Counterfactuals, Counterfactuals mentored from Prototypes, Kernel SHAP, Anchors, Contrastive Explanation Method (CEM), Integrated Gradients, and Tree SHAP. All these techniques are already discussed by Devam Dave. By giving straightforward clarifications of AI algorithms, healthcare experts can way better understand and utilize these advances in their clinical practice, improving patient care and results [1].

The healthcare industry is one of the AI applications that is expected to undergo significant impacts due to AI development in the coming years. This increases ethical issues, especially about the guarantee of the quality of medical services like clinical trials and test findings. The challenge for using AI in healthcare is about clarifying the reasonings behind AI decisions since it is important for establishing physicians' trust and encouraging effective technology adoption. When explanations are given, patients and physicians may learn from AI algorithms and the healthcare industry can undergo a digital revolution, given that the adoption of AI techniques by medical professionals is a prerequisite for learning from AI algorithms. By analyzing model explanations and performance measurements, healthcare organizations can recognize regions for improvement and upgrade their AI frameworks to improve patient results and security. This issue has been addressed by several governmental, non-governmental, and international organizations as well as by large AI companies. The Cybersecurity Act and the General Data Protection Regulation (RODO) are two important examples of regulatory solutions [2]. The artificially intelligent tools need to be trusted and understandable by humans, for which explainable machine learning (ML) models have been developed with the help of XAI [7].

In this chapter, various methods that can be integrated with XAI are discussed, including open data and knowledge graphs (KGs). Additionally, this chapter explores how XAI can be used with metaverse applications as deep learning in medical image analysis, for the detection of pancreatic cancer, and dynamic pruning technique.

## 20.2 Leveraging Open Data and XAI

The data that can be freely accessed by everyone is known as open data. The combination of ODDS (open data and datasets) and XAI can develop healthcare by identifying patterns, trends, more accurate treatments, and diagnoses. Open data with XAI increases accuracy in decision-making, identifies risk factors, predicts outcomes, provides more efficient diagnoses and treatment, and automates routine patient care tasks. By analyzing this information, AI can distinguish where certain diseases are more common, where healthcare administrations are most required, and how environmental factors may influence well-being results in numerous regions. It automates data input and analysis and provides real-time patient health information to healthcare practitioners. ODDS will foster transparency and will build trust in AI models.

ODDS in Healthcare: It provides datasets that include medical records, imaging all data, and laboratory tests for training AI models. It improves patients' outcomes such as treatment response, disease diagnosis, and mortality rates but it challenges the accuracy, completeness, and privacy concerns.

### 20.2.1 Explainable Open Data

It refers to transparent, publicly available data that are accompanied by clear explanations. Visual analysis is the base of the explainable ML that allows in detailed understanding of model behavior and its outputs. Better visualization and interpretation can be achieved through the following:

**PCA (Principal Components Analysis):** It extracts important information from large datasets to a smaller set of variables. It is used to uncover patterns and correlations of medical records, images, and genetic data.

**ICA (Independent Component Analysis):** It is used to split multiverse signals into two different components, both of which are not dependent on each other and are non-Gaussian in nature. It is used for isolating noise factors.

**Isomap:** It reduces the high dimensions of datasets to datasets consisting of low dimensions and also preserves the geodesic distance between the data points.

**LDA (Linear Dissimilarity Analysis):** It identifies the linear sequences of attributes to differentiate between classes of objects or events. It extracts characteristics from medical images to classify patients.

**t-SNE (t-distributed Stochastic Neighbor Embedding):** It provides 2D or 3D visualization of high-dimensional data. It can be used for data exploration in domains such as tumor analysis and medication discovery, as it combines comparable data points.

**UMAP (Uniform Manifold Approximation and Projection):** It is similar to t-SNE. It is used in medical imaging and ERs.

**LDS (Linear Dissimilarity Scaling):** It creates low-dimensional representation from high-dimensional datasets using pairwise dissimilarity between data points. It is used in surgical gestures and to identify patterns.

**KDE (Kernel Density Estimation):** It is a statistical approach to approximate the probability density function of a random variable. It has been used in the visualization of data.

**Heatmap:** It represents data using colors to indicate the matrix values. It is used to visualize large datasets.

**Software Libraries:** These are sets of tools designed to support the explanation and visualization of open datasets for researchers and practitioners. Examples of some Python libraries:

***Pandas*:** Used to manipulate and analyze tabular data which are in the form of series and data frames.

***Matplotlib*:** Core Python library for creating various plots, charts, and data visualizations.

***Seaborn***: Built on Matplotlib, it offers advanced features for creating beautiful and informative visualizations.
***Sklearn***: A popular library for ML tasks like classification, regression, and clustering.
***Wordcloud***: Creates visualizations of text data, highlighting frequently used words with larger font sizes.
***NetworkX***: Specialized library for working with network data, allowing creation, analysis, and visualization of networks and graphs.
***NumPy***: Provides powerful tools for numerical computations, array manipulation, linear algebra, and more. Efficiently handles large multi-dimensional data.

### 20.2.2 XAI in Healthcare

The libraries used are the following:

***Keras***: It simplifies the experimentation of deep neural networks that allow researchers to explore architectures and hyper-parameters for application.
***TensorFlow***: It uses some tools for data manipulation, training, and development to accelerate the modeling of complex AI models.

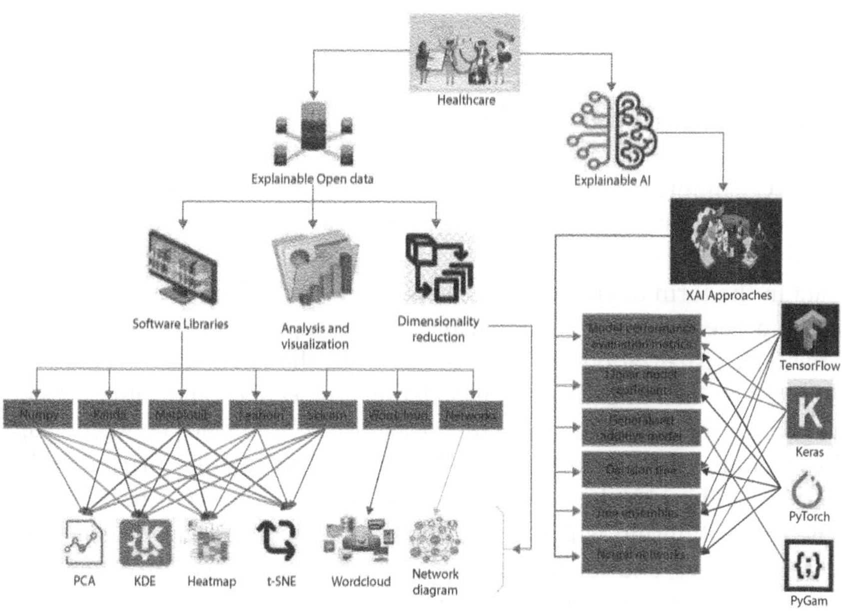


**Figure 20.1** Overview of XAI and the explainable open data.

***Pytorch*:** It provides a dynamic computation graph that can enable developers to train and make up the neural networks with ease of use and more flexibility.
***PyGam*:** It has specialization in (generalized additive models) GAM to capture intricate interactions with datasets especially when there is a lack of clear definition between the response variable and predictors.

An outline of how explainable open data and XAI can be integrated to improve the healthcare sector is shown in Figure 20.1.

**Approaches:** The linear model coefficient determines the relation between a particular feature and a target variable. Decision tree describes relationships between variables and decision-making processes. GAM does not assume the linear relationship between the predictor variable and response variable and allows for flexible or nonlinear relations. Neural networks can learn patterns but they lack explainability. Tree ensembles merge multiple decision trees to provide better and more accurate predictions, which will make it more complex. So, to handle this, STEL (simplified tree ensemble learner) and Tree Interpreter are used. Metrics of the model performance evaluation are responsible for the transparency of the XAI model.

Using ODDS in developing XAI will ensure data quality, provide in-depth explanations, maintain data privacy and security, continuously update ODDS for accuracy, and adhere to ethical standards for unbiased decisions [8].

## 20.3 Knowledge Graph

The KG can interconnect health data, diseases, drugs, and treatments and it is also traceable. This can help the healthcare professionals to diagnose the disease and to offer the best treatment possible. The KG represents the data in the form of employing triplets that consist of two entities (e1 and e2) and one relation (r). These triplets have a significant role as they provide data visualization and tend to maintain the relations. KGs are constructed by inferring missing links, defining objectives, and gathering and transforming data. It can be used to establish relationships between drugs by examining the symptoms. Hyper-relational KG (HKG) merges multiple KGs and avoids duplication. It provides a solution that is based on the disease relationship which is crucial for drug repurposing. KGs contain entities (nodes) and edges (relationships) which can be used to connect the information in such a way that the computer can understand. Electronic health records (EHR) contain patient's history, treatments, and outcomes which can further be used to diagnose the treatments. Inductive Logic Programming (ILP) and Markov Logic Networks (MLNs) are some symbolic logic models that can extract logical rules from KGs. These logical rules represent the relationships, and by combining these logical rules with embeddings, in which entities and relationships are present as numerical vectors, these models improve generalization in healthcare reasoning. To ensure accuracy and explainability, we use human-in-the-loop techniques that involve validation from the humans to help in the development which will solve the errors and will improve the overall quality. Each choice made by an AI framework can be followed back to basic information sources, clinical rules, and industry information utilizing information charts. This traceability guarantees transparency and accountability in decision-making processes, permitting clinicians to confirm and understand the method of reasoning behind AI-based recommendations.

The applications of KGs are drug development, drug-drug interaction, adverse drug reaction, drug target interactions, and bioinformatics research [4].

## 20.4 Metaverse Using Immersive Technology

The metaverse has made a computer-generated environment where people interact with each other virtually. Metaverse applications have huge potential to change healthcare by encouraging remote consultations through virtual clinics, remote patient monitoring through portable gadgets, and immersive medical knowledge for experts. It offers healthcare experience as per individual needs by using telepresence, blockchain, and AR/VR. The patient's computed tomography (CT) scan results, vital signs, and medical histories could be integrated and used to track his health condition. These results can be accessed through virtual dashboards and interact with professionals for personalized care and treatment with the help of XAI. With the help of technologies such as haptic interfaces and TI-driven 6G networks, we can create virtual hospitals and clinics. These stages also promote worldwide collaboration between researchers, increase patient engagement through gamified experiences, and empower progressed visualization of complex therapeutic information.

### 20.4.1 Technologies for Metaverse Healthcare

***AI with Explainability (XAI)***: Natural language processing (NLP) is used to provide text-and-speech–based interaction. AI-related technology such as ML, TL, and computer vision are used for model building and training and can be used for disease prediction and treatment.

***AR and VR*:** These innovations improve the capabilities of telemedicine by empowering immersive patient-doctor intelligent and virtual restorative instruction. Healthcare experts can visualize complex health-related information, perform inaccessible surgeries, and prepare in practical scenarios without physical limitations.

***Blockchain*:** Blockchain ensures the decentralization of the metaverse due to its decentralized ledger architecture. It ensures security, patient empowerment, privacy, cost-effectiveness, and efficiency.

***IoT*:** The Internet of Things (IoT) plays an important role due to its mobility restrictions, and because of this, the IoT is integrated into the metaverse. In a proposed framework, a data collection system based on the IoT is used to allow the synchronization between the physical and metaverse worlds from the side of virtual service providers (VSPs).

***Cloud and Edge Computing*:** Edge computing is responsible for making data storage and computing nearer to where data are used and generated. It enables the availability of on-demand access to information and training in VR and AR, and due to adjacency of the edge computing, it also ensures uninterrupted experience. It also allows real-time management of medical devices between the hospital and the other facilities while traveling.

***High-Speed Network*:** 5G or 6G provides rate, latency, range, and much more, which is important for healthcare. It will ensure online consultation, training of doctors, conducting metaverse telesurgery, and much more.

***Immersive Technology*:** Technology like AR, VR, and XR are improving the healthcare field by providing drug-free treatment and by enabling live collaboration of doctors worldwide. Digital twin, combining IoT, AI, XR, and cloud enhances decision-making and data analysis in healthcare.

***3D Reconstruction (3DR)*:** 3DR uses medical images to provide better treatment and it is also used for preoperative surgical planning and assessment to improve success rate and to reduce operative rate. VR provides visualization of the patient's health condition and can be used for teaching purposes.

Together, these innovations encourage a more open, effective, and engaging healthcare encounter within the metaverse. They bridge separations, improve symptomatic capabilities, and empower imaginative treatment models, eventually progressing in understanding results and getting to treatment.

Figure 20.2 describes the architecture that creates integrated environments for patients, physicians, and a metaverse by combining blockchain, AI, and immersive technology. Professionals and patients interact with one another in the metaverse using AR, VR, and MR, and data in different

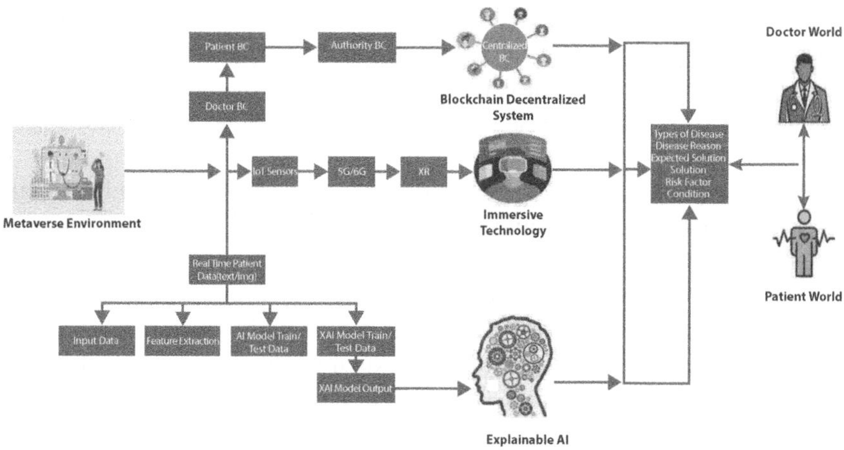


**Figure 20.2** Healthcare metaverse architecture.

formats is processed by NLP and convolutional neural network (CNN) and saved on the blockchain. Working with XR technologies in a virtual environment, physicians can better identify illness factors by using XAI techniques like Gradient-Weighted Class Activation Mapping (Grad-CAM) or LIME. All information is safely kept on the blockchain in the patient's world, allowing for prompt treatment if the patient's ID is already on file, or otherwise starting the process of recording new information [9–14].

## 20.5 Deep Learning–Based Medical Image Analysis

Nowadays, healthcare imaging modalities are rapidly growing due to advancements in technology; machines decrease in cost, XAI, etc. Deep learning (DL) methods have been started in healthcare applications by AI, a large collection of input data can be easily analyzed, and output can be found without getting the help of human brains. XAI, when coordinated with profound learning models, increments straightforwardness and believes in medical image analysis. Within the context of pancreatic cancer detection, XAI strategies can give knowledge into how a profound learning model makes its conclusions.

The major disadvantage of a "black-box" model is the transparency of the models. To overcome these issues, a model called "white box" is used. To be qualified as a "white box," the models' features need to be understood first and the ML processes must be transparent. These types of methods are called XAI or deep learning.

The XAI methods in the method of medical image analysis are divided into two subparts which are interpretability methods and explanation techniques. The method of explanation can be divided into five distinct categories: mixed-based, visual-based, textual-based, example-based, and rule-based.

Visual explanations have been frequently used for XAI in medical analysis. Class activation mapping (CAM) is a method that includes input in the form of an image given to the layers that are fully connected at the furthermost of the neural network via a GAP (global average pooling) on the last fully connected layer and the map is promoted in the convolution layer's final layer. The deep explainer is an explainability technique that can be applied by DEEP SHAP models with neural networks. The deep learning models need unique concept learning as input during the post hoc model along with the labels and the features.

Unappealing, un-scalability, prolixity, dependence, and complexity are some cons of the XAI techniques. Flexibility, schematic, intuitiveness, informational value, and completeness are pros of the XAI techniques [10].

## 20.6 Dynamic Pruning via XAI

Detecting tumors, drug development, and denoising medical images for the accuracy of diagnosis are the medical use cases in which AI plays a key role. Fitting AI computation is allowed on IoT models without compromising privacy and accuracy status. Talking about the real world, training of machines, fine-tuning, and healthcare systems, it becomes clear that precise AI models are very limited. Recently, research institutions and medical organizations have started using transfer learning, pre-trained models, or federated learning (FL) strategies for obtaining high performance without giving accurate and complete data. Therefore, data privacy constraints and access restrictions are now nonviable in the healthcare systems. Due to the problems that occurred because of not using fine-tuning, there is an efficient way to use a pruning strategy which can be based on the XAI with no fine-tuning. Dynamic pruning procedures optimize AI algorithms for medical image examination. By specifically removing repetitive connections during training or inference, these strategies decrease model complexity and computational necessities. In healthcare, particularly when analyzing medical images such as X-ray or magnetic resonance imaging (MRI) scans, dynamic pruning speeds up processing while maintaining precision. This effectiveness empowers real-time or near–real-time examination, which is basic for timely diagnostic and treatment decisions. A pruning criterion is designed for the CNN which is computed with the help of layer-wise relevance propagation (LRP). LRP is the method for explaining the decision-making in which slices of the data have contributed more. In expansion, dynamic pruning encourages the arrangement of resource-constrained gadgets, which improves healthcare access. Persistent optimization guarantees flexibility to change datasets and clinical needs, improving overall diagnostic precision and patient results [11].

## 20.7 Predictive Analytics of Pancreatic Cancer

Pancreatic cancer can be the most aggressive and deadly tumor of the digestive tract. Currently, MRI, positron emission tomography (PET), endoscopic ultrasound (EUS), and CT can be considered as the imaging modalities most commonly utilized in the treatment of pancreatic cancer. In the path of pancreatic cancers, AI-based diagnostic methods are utilized to check the risk of detecting the effectiveness as well as sharpness of post-treatment therapy and distinguish cancer cells' growths from some other reviewed pancreatic symptoms. Wei Xuan has suggested a hierarchical CNN (HCNN) for the detection of pancreatic tumors. It has been very tough for the users to think practically how all the predictions for any problem are generated so recent deep learning models are sometimes "Back boxes." The main goal of fast-growing XAI is to transform black-box AI models and system outputs into understandable models or representations that are reasonably explainable and simple. Now, human users can understand and trust the output as well as outcomes of the deep learning algorithm for which the credit goes to XAI. Whenever a company starts the production of any AI model, it must have confidence and trust in its development [12].

## 20.8 Approach to Interpretable Healthcare Model

This study uses XAI techniques with deep neural networks to differentiate between normal and pneumonia cases obtained from chest X-ray images. XAI techniques like LIME, SHAP, and Grad-CAM with deep neural networks—CNN, residual network with 50 layers (RESNET50), visual geometry group with 16 layers (VGG16), and MobileNetV3—are used to interpret the results.

Table 20.1 represents different algorithms, datasets, accuracy, and XAI techniques that have recently been used for research studies. Algorithms used are shallow artificial neural network (ANN), light gradient boosting (LGBM), support vector machine (SVM), ANN, random forest (RF), RESNET50, Inception V3, DenseNet, CNN, visual geometry group with 19 layers (VGG19), VGG16, and VDSNet. The datasets used are electroencephalogram (EEG), Wisconsin Diagnostic Breast Cancer database (WDBC), white blood cell (WBC) data, electrocardiogram (ECG), chest X-rays, a dataset related to COVID-19, lung X-rays, and the National Institutes of Health (NIH) chest X-ray dataset. The XAI techniques used are SHAP, LIME, and Grad-CAM.

**Table 20.1** Synopsis of XAI algorithms used in medical datasets.

| Reference | Algorithms | Dataset | Accuracy | Explainable AI techniques |
|---|---|---|---|---|
| Alshayeji *et al.* [23] | Shallow ANN | WBC dataset | 99.47% | |
| Mohi *et al.* [24] | LGBM, SVM, RF, and ANN | WDBC dataset | Not specified | SHAP |
| Hussain *et al.* [25] | Random forest | EEG dataset | 80.33% | LIME |
| Narin *et al.* [26] | RESNET50 and Inception V3 | Chest X-ray dataset | 96.1% | |
| Jahmunah *et al.* [27] | DenseNet and CNN | ECG dataset | >95% | Grad-CAM |
| Hemdan *et al.* [28] | VGG19 and DenseNet | Covid-19 dataset | Not specified | |
| Bharati *et al.* [29] | CNN and VDSNet | NIH chest X-ray image dataset | 73% | |
| Panwar *et al.* [30] | CNN and VGG16 | Lungs X-ray dataset | Not specified | |

Using these XAI techniques enhances the understanding of neural networks and makes the decision-making process easier to understand. Deep learning analyzes diverse data, particularly unstructured data, by guiding it through multiple layers of neural networks. CNN transforms computer vision tasks by using LeNet, AlexNet, VGGNet, and ResNet.

Deep learning is applicable in different fields such as robotics, recommendation systems, gaming, image analysis, NLP, healthcare, and finance. Transfer learning helps reduce computational expenses by addressing the problems of limited datasets through utilizing pre-trained models such as ResNet50, VGG16, and MobileNetV3. ResNet50 improves depth and performance in computer vision, VGG16 is used for its convenience use and effectiveness, and MobileNetV3 is designed for mobile devices to balance size, efficiency, and accuracy in edge computing. To provide better insights into DL methods, methods such as LIME, SHAP, and Grad-Cam are used.

**Methodology:**
To create a deep neural–based model for identifying pneumonia from chest X-ray, two methods are used: Firstly, four deep neural models were created using CNN and pre-trained models (ResNet50, VGG16, and MobileNetV3) and then the best model was evaluated for explanations.

Table 20.2 describes different methodologies used for detecting pneumonia from chest X-ray images. It focuses on some major concepts such as dataset description, experimental setup, evaluation metrics, and result discussion of various neural network models. The dataset description provides details about 5863 images obtained from Kaggle which are categorized as pneumonia and normal. The experimental setup describes experiments that are conducted on Google Colab with NVIDIA Tesla K80 GPU (graphic processing unit). It involves using Python with libraries such as TensorFlow and Keras. The images are resized into 250 x 250 pixels. Evaluation metrics provide information about metrics used to evaluate the models and it includes accuracy, F1-score, precision, and recall. The result discussion provides information on the performance accuracy of CNN, VGG16, MobileNetV3, and ResNet50 [15, 16].

**XAI results:**
As discussed above, it uses three methods: LIME, SHAP, and GRAD-CAM. The result concludes that LIME provides local linear explanations for decisions, SHAP differentiates the region by highlighting the important ones, and GRAD-CAM highlights the area from X-ray images where signs of pneumonia are observed, mostly in the lungs [6].

Table 20.2 Different methodologies and their performance metrics for pneumonia detection.

| Aspect | Details |
|---|---|
| **Dataset description** | Obtained from Kaggle, "Chest X-Ray Images (Pneumonia)"<br>- 5863 images in JPEG format<br>- Two categories: pneumonia and normal<br>- Divided into training and test sets |
| **Experimental setup** | Conducted on Google Colab with NVIDIA Tesla K80 GPU (12 GB RAM)<br>- Utilized Python (v3.12), Keras (v3.10), TensorFlow (v2.7.0)<br>- Images resized to 250 x 250 pixels<br>- Dataset partitioned into training and test sets |
| **Evaluation metrics** | Employed evaluation metrics: accuracy, F1-score, precision, recall |
| **Result discussion**<br>**CNN performance:**<br>**VGG16 performance:**<br>**MobileNetV3 performance:**<br>**ResNet50 performance:** | Set early stopping criteria for model training to 30 epochs<br>Average training accuracy: 93.40%<br>Validation accuracy: 93.75%<br>Testing accuracy: 82%<br>Training accuracy: 93.57%<br>Validation accuracy: 93%<br>Testing accuracy: 87%<br>Training accuracy: 91%<br>Validation accuracy: 93%<br>Testing accuracy: 82%<br>Training accuracy: 86%<br>Validation accuracy: 91%<br>Testing accuracy: 82% |

## 20.9 Challenges

Open-world assumptions mean building KGs without any strict guidelines. It offers good flexibility and also collects a broader range of information, but it does not ensure the quality of the graph which will be risky as there could be inaccurate information [17, 18].

Using techniques such as ontology matching and schema alignment helps the terminologies, but handling these data and ensuring integrity have been a challenge.

XAI should balance the transparency and explain the AI model's decision; for that, it should traverse large graphs that also require sophisticated algorithms which is quite challenging.

Further research is required to optimize visualizations and semantic representation as the explanation should be clear to a diverse group that includes non-experts. In healthcare, data privacy and security are also crucial [4].

***Privacy***: Cybercriminals usually target digital anti-aging healthcare. The voice and facial movement required for security could be replicated and misused by hackers.

***Integration***: The healthcare metaverse should be integrated seamlessly with EHRs (electronic health records) to maintain accuracy and updated data.

***Standardization***: In healthcare, different technologies should work smoothly which might create a problem when the metaverse is introduced [9].

Overcoming the abovementioned challenges of making proficient calculations for transparent and interpretable AI models requires efforts to combine logical AI methods into model architectures. At the same time, to make it understandable and accessible, it is necessary to contribute to research to optimize visual clarifications used by diverse groups of users. Moreover, securing the data of patients against cyber threats requires the execution of progressed security measures that require consistent upgrading and carefulness against evolving threats. Building interoperable rules for consistent integration of EHR systems is essential for streamlining healthcare processes and improving data exchange proficiency. Working with healthcare professionals to make and follow standardized rules for healthcare technology integration ensures consistency and compatibility of systems. In addition, the execution of quality control mechanisms within the development and approval processes of a KG ensures the accuracy and reliability of experiences based on data. Finally, improving information integrity by implementing strong methods to check all errors and mistakes makes the data more reliable and improves its accuracy [19–22]. To achieve better results, XAI may be combined with other approaches such as domain adaptation (DA) and FL [14].

## 20.10 Conclusion

The demand for AI in every sector is increasing, but because of its black-box nature, it is not trusted in the healthcare industry. If the reasoning behind the decisions made is provided, then it will increase transparency and trust can be built; that is why, in the healthcare industry, the demand for XAI is rising. When utilizing AI in healthcare, it is necessary to think about how we handle patient information. We must guarantee that patient data are secure and private. This implies that individual data are not shared unless patients assent. Patients should know how their information will be utilized and how this will be helpful for their health. It is moreover important to check AI frameworks for unfair biases and make sure they do not discriminate against anyone. XAI can be integrated with open data and KGs to increase the transparency and reliability of the model. ODDS is helpful for both patients as well as for the development of new treatments. It creates better research productivity and cooperation in the healthcare sector. KG, on the other hand, has the benefit of retracibility, providing more clear explanations. It can be used for bioinformatics research, drug interaction, drug development, and determining adverse reactions. The distributed DNNs combined with the online pruning system can be a feasible solution as it can reduce communication and the given data overhead. With the increase in technology development, metaverse can be integrated with the healthcare industry to create a virtual environment providing better visualization and simulation. Metaverse can provide a digital simulation of a patient's anatomy by providing vital signs, results of genetics tests, CT scans, and medical histories. XAI models using algorithms such as SHAP and LIME are used to detect chest X-rays in the datasets of pneumonia. These technologies have been used in diverse healthcare application areas which include medical image processing, expediting disease diagnoses, supporting triage assessments, automated patient monitoring, and supporting biopharmaceutical development. However, it still needs improvement to overcome all the challenges discussed above.

## References


1. Rao, H. and Khan, A., Explainable A.I. @ in Healthcare. *International Conference on Computational Science and Computational Intelligence (CSCI)*, pp. 1725–1729, 2022.

2. Raif, P., Suchanek-Raif, R., Tkacz, E., Explainable AI (XAI) in Healthcare - Tools and Regulations. *IEEE EMBS Special Topic Conference on Data Science and Engineering in Healthcare, Medicine and Biology*, pp. 151–152, 2023.
3. Costa, B. and Georgieva, P., Explainable Artificial Intelligence in Healthcare Applications: A Systematic Review. *International Scientific Conference on Computer Science (COMSCI)*, pp. 1–8, 2023.
4. Garg, S., Parikh, S., Garg, S., Navigating Healthcare Insights: A Bird's Eye View of Explainability with Knowledge Graphs. *IEEE Sixth International Conference on Artificial Intelligence and Knowledge Engineering (AIKE)*, pp. 54–61, 2023.
5. Pawar, U., O'Shea, D., Rea, S., O'Reilly, R., Explainable AI in Healthcare. *International Conference on Cyber Situational Awareness, Data Analytics and Assessment (CyberSA)*, pp. 1–2, 2020.
6. Zahoor, K., Bawany, N.Z., Ghani, U., Explainable AI for Healthcare: An Approach Towards Interpretable Healthcare Models. *24th International Arab Conference on Information Technology (ACIT)*, pp. 1–7, 2023.
7. Ali, S., Imran, A.S., Kastrati, Z., Daudpota, S.M., Visualizing Research on Explainable Artificial Intelligence for Medical and Healthcare. *4th International Conference on Computing, Mathematics and Engineering Technologies (iCoMET)*, pp. 1–6, 2023.
8. Alam, G., McChesney, I., Nicholl, P., Rafferty, J., Improving Prospective Healthcare Outcomes by Leveraging Open Data and Explainable AI. *3rd International Conference on Computing and Information Technology (ICCIT)*, pp. 486–492, 2023.
9. Mozumder, M.A., II, Sumon, T. P. T. A., R., IIR. I., Uddin, S.M., II, Athar, A., XXXH.-C., K., The Metaverse for Intelligent Healthcare using XAI, Blockchain, and Immersive Technology. *IEEE International Conference on Metaverse Computing, Networking and Applications (MetaCom)*, pp. 612–616, 2023.
10. Bhati, A., Kant Hiran, K., Kumar Vyas, A., Maad, M., M,.M.A., Ahmed Sayed, M., Metwally, M.F.A.-A., Awang, M.K., Ahmad, H., Low-cost Artificial Intelligence Internet of Things based water quality monitoring for rural areas. *Internet Things*, 27, 101255, 2024. DOI: 10.1016/j.iot.2023.101255.
11. Shah, H. and Ajay K., V,., A systematic review for 6G and beyond 6G enable IoT Network, in: *2024 2nd International Conference on Computer, Communication and Control (IC4)*, IEEE, pp. 1–5, 2024.
12. Pathmudi, V.R., Khatri, N., Kumar, S., Abdul-Qawy, A.S.H., Kumar Vyas, A., A systematic review of IoT technologies and their constituents for smart and sustainable agriculture applications. *Sci. Afr.*, 21, e01577, 2023, DOI: 10.1016/j.sciaf.2023.e01577.
13. Patel, S., Kumar Vyas, A., Kant Hiran, K., Infrastructure Health Monitoring Using Signal Processing Based on an Industry 4.0 System. *Cyber-Phys. Syst. Ind. 4.0 Pract. Appl. Secur. Manage.*, 1, 249–260, 2022.

14. Patidar, Y., Jain, M., Vyas, A.K., Optimal Stable Cluster Head Selection Method for Maximal Throughput and Lifetime of Homogeneous Wireless Sensor Network. *SN Comput. Sci., 5*, 218, 2024. DOI: 10.1007/s42979-023-02459-9.
15. Priya Dharshini, S., Ram Kumar, K., Venkatesh, S., Narasimhan, K., Adalarasu, K., An Overview Of Interpretability Techniques For Explainable Artificial Intelligence (XAI) In Deep Learning-Based Medical Image Analysis. *9th International Conference on Advanced Computing and Communication Systems (ICACCS)*, pp. 175–182, 2023.
16. Baccour, E., Erbad, A., Mohamed, A., Hamdi, M., Guizani, M., Dynamic Pruning for Distributed Inference via Explainable AI: A Healthcare Use Case. *ICC IEEE International Conference on Communications*, pp. 3394–3400, 2023.
17. Srinidhi, B. and Bhargavi, M.S., An XAI Approach to Predictive Analytics of Pancreatic Cancer. *International Conference on Information Technology (ICIT)*, pp. 343–348, 2023.
18. Yang, W., Wei, Y., Wei, H., *et al.*, Survey on Explainable AI: From Approaches, Limitations, and Applications Aspects. *Hum-Cent. Intell. Syst.*, 3, 161–188, 2023, https://doi.org/10.1007/s44230-023-00038-y.
19. Chaddad, A., Peng, J., Xu, J., Bouridane, A., Survey of Explainable AI Techniques in Healthcare. *Sens. (Basel)*, 23, 2, 634, 2023. doi: 10.3390/s23020634. PMID: 36679430; PMCID: PMC9862413.
20. Khazanchi, D., Kumar Vyas, A., Kant Hiran, K., Padmanaban, S., *Blockchain 3.0 for Sustainable Development*, De Gruyter, Berlin, Boston, 2021, https://doi.org/10.1515/9783110702507.
21. Kant Hiran, K., Khazanchi, D., Kumar Vyas, A., Padmanaban, S., *Machine Learning for Sustainable Development*, De Gruyter, Berlin, Boston, 2021, https://doi.org/10.1515/9783110702514.
22. Ajay Kumar, V.,., Balamurugan, S., Kant Hiran, K., Dhiman, H.S. (Eds.), *Artificial Intelligence for Renewable Energy Systems*, John Wiley & Sons, New Jersey, 2022, ISBN: 9781119761693.
23. Mohammad, R.G., Alshayeji, H., Ellethy, H., Abed, S., Computer-aided detection of breast cancer on the Wisconsin dataset: An artificial neural networks approach. *Biomed. Signal Process. Control*, 71, Part A, 2021, doi: https://doi.org/10.1016/j.bspc.2021.103141.
24. Mohi Uddin, K.M., Biswas, N., Rikta, S.T., Dey, S.K., Qazi, A., XML-LightGBMDroid: A self-driven interactive mobile application utilizing explainable machine learning for breast cancer diagnosis. *Eng. Rep.*, 5, 11, 1–23, 2023, doi: 10.1002/eng2.12666.
25. Hussain, I., Jany, R., Boyer, R., Azad, A.K.M., Alyami, S.A., Park S.J., Hasan, M.M., Hossain, A.M., An Explainable EEG-Based Human Activity Recognition Model Using Machine-Learning Approach and LIME, *Sensors,* 23, 17, 7452, 2023.

26. Narin, A., Kaya, C., Pamuk, Z., Automatic detection of coronavirus disease (COVID-19) using X-ray images and deep convolutional neural networks. *Pattern Anal. Appl.*, 24, 3, 1207–1220, 2021, doi: 10.1007/s10044-021-00984-y.
27. Jahmunah, V., Ng, E.Y.K., Tan, R.-S., Oh, S.L., Acharya, U.R., Explainable detection of myocardial infarction using deep learning models with Grad-CAM technique on ECG signals, 146, 105550, 1–46, 2022.
28. Hemdan, E. E.-D., Shouman, M.A., Karar, M.E., COVIDXNet: A Framework of Deep Learning Classifiers to Diagnose COVID-19 in X-Ray Images, 2020, [Online]. Available: http://arxiv.org/abs/2003.11055.
29. Bharati, S., Podder, P., Mondal, M.R.H., Hybrid deep learning for detecting lung diseases from X-ray images. *Informatics in Medicine Unlocked (IMU)*, 20, 100391, 2020, doi: 10.1016/j.imu.2020.100391.
30. Panwar, H., Gupta, P.K., Siddiqui, M.K., Morales-Menendez, R., Singh, V., Application of deep learning for fast detection of COVID-19 in X-Rays using nCOVnet. *Chaos Solit. Fract.*, 138, 109944, Sep. 2020, doi: 10.1016/j.chaos.2020.109944.

# Index

Printed and bound by CPI Group (UK) Ltd, Croydon, CR0 4YY

17/09/2026

14964263-0007